PORT CITIES

Ports have been and continue to be critical in not just the global movement of goods, but also the global movement of ideas, social change, and cultural phenomena, including architecture and urban form. The connected points of a multi-faceted network, ports profoundly affect both each other and the cities and regions to which they belong. Shipping and trade networks have created a legacy embodied in the street patterns, land use and buildings of interconnected port cities. Multiple forces are at play: technological requirements, elite preferences and working class needs, urban policy and globalization.

Port Cities brings together original scholarship by both well-published and younger scholars from multiple disciplines and builds upon long-standing research on the international exchange of architectural and planning ideas. A carefully selected series of essays examines comprehensively and globally the changing built and urban environment of selected port cities. They explore similarities, dissimilarities, and how sea-based networking has influenced urban landscapes and architecture and socio-economic and cultural development from the nineteenth to the twenty-first century.

The first section examines global networks linking ports and cities and explores the effect of inter-continental transfers on architecture and planning. The second part focuses on interconnected port cities in regional contexts, analyzing socio-economic structures and urban and built form. The third section examines the built environment of selected cities in view of their response to changing technology, transforming socio-economic networks and political contexts, as well as evolving design concepts. Overall, the book proposes a networked analysis of the built and urban environment, arguing that international maritime networks are paradigmatic for the creation of dynamic, multi-scaled, and interconnected "port cityscapes."

Carola Hein is Professor at Bryn Mawr College (Pennsylvania) in the Growth and Structure of Cities Department. Her current research interests include the transmission of architectural and urban ideas along international networks, focusing specifically on port cities and the global architecture of oil.

PORT CITIES

Dynamic landscapes and global networks

EDITED BY CAROLA HEIN

Routledge
Taylor & Francis Group

LONDON AND NEW YORK

First published 2011
by Routledge
2 Park Square, Milton Park, Abingdon, Oxon OX14 4RN

Simultaneously published in the USA and Canada
by Routledge
711 Third Avenue, New York, NY 10017

Routledge is an imprint of the Taylor & Francis Group, an informa business

British Library Cataloguing in Publication Data
A catalogue record for this book is available from the British Library

Library of Congress Cataloging-in-Publication Data

Hein, Carola.
Port cities: dynamic landscapes and global networks/Carola Hein.
  p. cm.
  Includes bibliographical references and index.
  1. Harbors. 2. Globalization–Social aspects. I. Title.
  HE551.H45 2011
  307.76–dc22

                                                          2010046665

ISBN: 978-0-415-78042-1 (hbk)
ISBN: 978-0-415-78043-8 (pbk)

Typeset in Sabon
by Wearset Ltd, Boldon, Tyne and Wear

MIX
Paper from
responsible sources
FSC® C004839
www.fsc.org

Printed and bound in Great Britain by
TJ International Ltd, Padstow, Cornwall

"Wir bewohnen keine Landschaften und Gärten, keine Häuser am sanften Hang oder auf der leichten Dünung, wir bewohnen ein Netz von sichtbaren und nicht sichtbaren Funktionen und Relationen, Strukturen und Aggregaten aus Metallen und künstlichen Gesteinen, die sie Dörfer, Städte, Staaten und Kontinenten genannt haben."

"We do not inhabit landscapes and gardens, not houses on a gentle slope or on an easy groundswell, we inhabit a network of visible and invisible functions and relations, structures and aggregates of metals and artificial stones, which they have called villages, cities, states, and continents."

(Bense, 1949: 191; translation by the author)

CONTENTS

CONTRIBUTORS

Lars Amenda is Research Fellow at the Institute for Migration Research and Intercultural Studies (IMIS) at the University of Osnabruck and postdoctoral Fellow of the Research College. His research interests include migration history, urban history, maritime history, and global/local history. Publications include his revised doctoral thesis *Fremde – Hafen – Stadt: Chinesische Migration und ihre Wahrnehmung in Hamburg 1897–1972* (2006), (ed. with Malte Fuhrmann) "Hafenstädte – Mobilität, Migration, Globalisierung," in *Comparativ* 2 (2007); *"Tor zur Welt"* (with Sonja Grünen, 2008); "Food and Otherness: Chinese Restaurants in West European Cities in the 20th Century," in *Food & History* 7 (2009).

Johnathan A. Farris is an architectural historian with a Ph.D. from Cornell University. His research interests include the architectural history of Asia, and of modern China in particular. He has worked in depth on the issue of architecture and urban fabric as a reflection of cross-cultural relations in the city of Guangzhou (Canton). Farris has taught art and architectural history at numerous institutions, and is currently professor of art history at SCAD – Hong Kong. He has worked in the field of historic preservation, and has authored several individual and district nominations to the U.S. National Register of Historic Places.

Céline Frémaux, an architectural historian with a Ph.D. on church building in France during the second half of the twentieth century, is currently a cultural heritage officer in French Guyana. Her research interests include religious architecture as a way in which migrant communities make themselves visible in a colonial urban context. She has worked as a researcher at the CNRS (French National Centre of Scientific Research) on a project funded by the French National Research Agency: "Inventing Space in the Age of Empire: Planning Experiments and Achievements along Suez Canal in Egypt (1859–1869)."

Malte Fuhrmann is a research fellow at the Orient Institute Istanbul. He earned his Ph.D. in Modern History from the Free University Berlin in 2004, was a research fellow at the Centre for Modern Oriental Studies (ZMO) in Berlin, and taught at Fatih University Istanbul. His publications include *Der Traum vom deutschen Orient* (2006); (ed. with Lars Amenda) "Hafenstädte – Mobilität, Migration, Globalisierung," in *Comparativ* 2

(2007); (ed. with Vangelis Kechriotis) "The Late Ottoman Port Cities," in *Mediterranean Historical Review* 2 (2009); and (ed. with Ulrike Freitag, Nora Lafi, and Florian Riedler) *The City in the Ottoman Empire* (2010).

Sakis Gekas is an assistant professor of Modern Greek and Mediterranean History in the Department of History at York University, Toronto. He is currently completing a history of the Ionian State, and has published articles on the economic and social history of the Ionian Islands under British rule. Recent publications include "Class and Cosmopolitanism: The Historiographical Fortunes of Merchants in Eastern Mediterranean Ports," in *Mediterranean Historical Review*, and he is co-editor of a special issue in the *European Review of History* (2011), *A Colonial Sea: The Mediterranean, 1798–1956*.

Mathieu Grenet is a postdoctoral fellow of the Italian Academy for Advanced Studies in America, at Columbia University. He is currently engaged in a research project, "Foreigners, Languages, and Interpreters in 18th-century Italian Port-cities." A former junior lecturer at the University of Lyon 2, France, he recently completed a Ph.D. at the European University Institute in Florence, Italy. His dissertation compared three communities of the Greek diaspora between the 1770s and the 1830s, and he has published several articles on this issue.

Carola Hein is Professor at Bryn Mawr College (Pennsylvania) in the Growth and Structure of Cities Department. Her current research interests include the transmission of architectural and urban ideas along international networks, focusing specifically on port cities and the global architecture of oil. With an Alexander von Humboldt fellowship she investigated large-scale urban transformation in Hamburg in the international context between 1842 and 2008. Her books include: *The Capital of Europe* (2004), *European Brussels: Whose Capital? Whose City?* (2006), *Brussels: Perspectives on a European Capital* (2007), *Rebuilding Urban Japan after 1945* (2003), and *Cities, Autonomy and Decentralisation in Japan* (2006).

Carol Herselle Krinsky, Professor of Art History in the College of Arts & Science at New York University, is the author of five books on architectural history and many articles on art, architecture, and urbanism. She developed the Urban Design/Architecture undergraduate major at her university, and served in the past as President of the Society of Architectural Historians and of Cooperative Preservation of Architectural Records. She held the Frederic Lindley Morgan chair at the University of Louisville (2001), is a Senior Fulbright Specialist, and has received teaching awards from the College Art Association and New York University.

Patrick O'Flanagan is Professor and Head of the Department of Geography at University College, Cork, Ireland, and he maintains close links with the Atlantic universities on the Iberian Peninsula and elsewhere in Europe. His current research interests include merchant communities and their networks, the form and fabric of port cities, and occupational change in port cities. He has published widely on the historical and cultural geography of the Iberian Peninsula, Ireland, and Atlantic Europe, and he has lectured widely on these themes on both sides of the Atlantic. He has edited and contributed to many books and journals.

Stephen J. Ramos is a founding editor of the journal *New Geographies*, which focuses on contemporary issues of urbanism and architecture. He received his doctorate from the Harvard University Graduate School of Design. His book *Dubai Amplified: The Engineering of a Port Geography* is published by Ashgate Press. He has published in various journals, including *Volume*, *Harvard Design Magazine*, and *Neutra*.

Huibert Schijf is a sociologist in the Department of Sociology/Anthropology at Universiteit van Amsterdam, where he also earned his Ph.D. His research interests include modern and historical elites and the application of network analysis to historical topics. His publications include: "Jewish Bankers 1850–1914: Internationalisation along Ethnic Lines," in I.B. McCabe, G. Harlaftis, and I.P. Minoglou (eds.), *Diaspora Entrepreneurial Networks* (2005); and with M. Kuitenbrouwer he published "The Dutch colonial business elite at the turn of the century" in *Itinerario* (1998).

Dirk Schubert is Professor of Urban Planning, Comparative Planning History, Housing and Urban Renewal, HafenCity University Hamburg, and Dean of the Master Programme in Urban Planning. His research interests include urban history, planning history, and housing and urban renewal, particularly in harbour and waterfront areas in seaport regions and city/port interfaces. His latest books are *Changes in Port and Waterfront Areas Worldwide* (3rd edn, 2008), *Growing Cities* (with Uwe Altrock, 2004), and *Residential Areas in Hamburg* (2005). He is co-editor of the journals *Planning Perspectives* and *Portus*, and a founding member of the International Urban Waterfront Research Network.

Stephen V. Ward is Professor of Planning History at Oxford Brookes University, UK. His current research interests include the global circulation of urban planning ideas and practices. He is a former president of the International Planning History Society (1996–2002) and editor of both *Planning Perspectives* (2002–2007) and *Planning History* (1990–1994). Among his books on urban planning history are *Planning and Urban Change* (2nd edn, 2004), *Planning the Twentieth-Century City* (2002), *Selling Places* (1998), and *The Garden City* (ed., 1992).

Marisa Yiu is Assistant Professor at the School of Architecture of the Chinese University of Hong Kong, a founding partner of ESKYIU, and an architect. Previously she taught at the University of Hong Kong (HKU), Columbia University, and the Architectural Association. Her current research examines how design and social networks shape dense city ecologies. She has published in *Architectural Design* (AD), *LOG*, *Domus China*, *Architectural Record*, and *Journal of Architectural Education*; and was awarded "40 under 40" by Perspective for outstanding contribution to the field of architecture in greater China. Recently she served as the Chief Curator of the 2009 Hong Kong & Shenzhen Bi-City Biennale of Urbanism/Architecture, located in the future West Kowloon Cultural District.

ACKNOWLEDGMENTS

This book is the result of a complex process of several years. Many people helped shape it and several institutions provided support. I am most grateful to the Alexander von Humboldt Foundation for a fellowship (2008–2011) that gave me the opportunity to start and finish this project as part of my research at the HafenCity University (HCU) Hamburg. I wish to extend particular thanks to my main advisors in Hamburg: Hartmut Frank, my mentor of many years, and Michael Koch, my official host at the HCU. This volume would not have been possible without two conferences that brought together a range of scholars interested in port cities and global networks. Together with Lars Amenda I convened a session, "Port Cities: Social, Cultural, and Built Repositories of Globalization and Networking in the 19th and 20th Century," at the conference of the European Association of Urban Historians (EAUH) in Lyon in August 2008; and with the help of faculty colleagues from Bryn Mawr and Haverford Colleges – Jeffrey Cohen, Linda Gerstein, Laurie Kain Hart, Peter Magee, Steve McGovern, Kalala Ngalamulume, Jim Wright – I organized a conference and workshop at Bryn Mawr College, "Global Port Cities and Networking from the 20th to the 21st Century," in November 2008. The Bryn Mawr conference was made possible by a Mellon Tri-Co Seed Grant that also provided funding for preparatory meetings. The conference received further support from various entities at Bryn Mawr College, notably the Center for Social Sciences, the Center for Visual Culture, the Middle Eastern Studies Program, the Center for International Studies, the Provost's Office, the Dean's Office, and the Growth and Structure of Cities Department.

Presentations and discussion at the two conferences, the thoughts and ideas of speakers have helped shape this book, and I wish to thank all participants not yet mentioned for accepting the challenge for interdisciplinary collaboration. Some came to Lyon but could not attend the Bryn Mawr event: Laurent Fourchard, Malte Fuhrmann, Sakis Gekas, Mathieu Grenet, and Marisa Yiu. Those who came to Bryn Mawr: Brenda Chalfin, Gene Desfor, Myron Echenberg, Johnathan Farris, Céline Frémaux, Hans Harms, Stephanie Kane, Carol Krinsky, Louis Nelson, Patrick O'Flanagan, Stephen Ramos, Huibert Schijf, Dirk Schubert, Sandra Schürmann, Stephen Ward, our discussants Jeffrey Cody, Lynn Hollen Lees, and Rosemary Wakeman, as well as Denise Scott Brown, who came with Robert Venturi to provide final reflections. I am also grateful to the students, staff, and attendees who helped make the Bryn Mawr conference a success.

The current manuscript would not have been possible without the splendid editorial help of Laura Helper-Ferris, as well as several reviewers, including David Gordon, Carol Krinsky, Nona Smith, and Rosemary Wakeman, whose detailed comments helped smooth out the last kinks. I would also like to thank Louise Fox, editorial assistant at Routledge, who was very supportive in finalizing the manuscript.

As always: For Wuppi and Walter[†], Patrick, Caya, Aliya, Jolan, and Joris, with love.

1 PORT CITYSCAPES

A networked analysis of the built environment

CAROLA HEIN

Thomas Holme, surveyor general for William Penn, the proprietor and governor of the province of Pennsylvania, arrived in America in June 1682 to lay out a "large town or new city" (Penn, 1774b: 9). Describing the overall layout of the new settlement, Holme emphasized the importance of rivers in the selection of the site and the city plan, writing: "The city of Philadelphia ... is now placed and *modelled* between two navigable rivers, upon a neck of land. And that ships may ride in a good anchorage, in both rivers, in six or eight fathom water close to the city." (Holme, 1774: 10) Maritime trade – access to ocean-going ships on the Delaware River and inland ships on the smaller Schuylkill River – and port functions were thus a key aspect of the design of Philadelphia, influencing its overall layout as well as the plans for each lot.

In the city charter, Penn himself emphasized the waterfront as public space and the port function as part of the city's structure: "And I do, for me, my heirs and assigns, grant and ordain, that ... the end of each street, extending into the river, shall be and continue free for the use and service of the said city and inhabitants thereof; ... and build wharfs so far out into the river there, as the mayor, aldermen, and common-council, herein after mentioned shall see meet" (Penn, 1774a: 13). Holme, taking into account the financial means and functional needs of the future proprietors, specified the details of the plan: "The city is now so ordered,... that it hath a front *to each river*; one half at Delaware [River], the other half at Schuylkill [River]. And though all this cannot make way for small purchasers to be in the fronts, yet they are placed in the next streets contiguous to each front, *viz.* All purchases of a thousand acres and upwards, have the Fronts and High Streets; and to every five thousand acres purchase, about an acre in the front; and the smaller purchasers, about half an acre in the backward streets" (Holme, 1774: 10). This ordering created a landscape of warehouses, wharves, shops, factories and homes mediating between the sea and the city center (Cohen, 2008) (see Figure 1.1). The city's design thus incorporated the needs of maritime trade and larger exchange networks between Europe and America, to which Philadelphia was a key entrance point.

The city was also already part of a larger circulation of ideas. Its layout referenced notably the great port city of London, Penn's birthplace. The large lots and detached houses expressed Penn's desire to avoid the dangers of London's overcrowding and dense construction with flammable materials that had resulted, respectively, in the great plague (1665/1666) and the Great Fire of 1666 (Reps, 1969). Holme specified that Philadelphia squares were "to be for the like uses as *Moorfields* in London" (Holme, 1774: 10), one of the last pieces of open land in London and the chief refuge for displaced citizens after the Great Fire. The first plan was published in 1683 and sold in London, and a slightly revised map was available in Amsterdam in the following year (Penn, 1983; Phillips, 1926).

Port activity on the Delaware River was also a core concern for Philadelphia's new inhabitants, who clustered in a half-moon-shaped dense settlement pattern on the eastern shore. But despite Penn and Holmes' careful design, as people settled in the newly laid-out city, they followed their own needs and interests, not necessarily respecting the original plan. Individual actions and investments created a concentration of commercial, industrial, wholesale, and financial activities on several blocks. There, ship-related commerce and craftsmen formed a district that was heavily influenced by the port, while the western side of Penn's projected city remained largely undeveloped until the later nineteenth century, as documented in the map by A. P. Folie and R. Scot of 1794 (see Figure 1.2).

Over the centuries, global political, economic, and technological developments – particularly migration and changes in shipbuilding, cargo, and fuel – reshaped the port and city of Philadelphia (Reps, 1969). Even though the port was essential to the design of Philadelphia, the city's shipping industry started to decline in the late nineteenth century and the business community moved away from the riverfront; by the mid-1950s the shipping industry largely abandoned the city (McGovern, 2008). In response, planners and policymakers introduced a north–south urban highway, interstate I-95, separating the river from the city center. On landfill along the Delaware River, they also created Penn's Landing that has since been the focus of multiple visions for waterfront revitalization, only small parts of which have been completed (see Figure 1.3). Despite interventions by internationally successful developers such as Rouse & Associates (headed by the Philadelphia-based Willard Rouse III, nephew of James Rouse, Baltimore's waterfront developer), world-famous architects, including Robert Venturi and Denise Scott Brown (Venturi, Scott Brown and Associates Inc. 2003), and most recently a civic initiative led by Penn Praxis, Philadelphia has not joined the global movement for waterfront revitalization. Penn's Landing still awaits development (see Figure 1.4).

This brief examination of the urban design and development of Philadelphia in relation to its port raises many larger issues that are at the core of this book. As the example of Philadelphia shows, urban and architectural ideas can travel along shipping lines and connect distant places. Without the example of London, Penn and Holme might have designed Philadelphia very differently. The citizens used and reshaped Penn's idealized plan into an urban form that better suited their needs and practices. They showed that while global practices and networks affect the reach of people, goods, and ideas, local conditions and people shape their implementation. Moreover, as the political, economic, social, and cultural context, ship design and technology, and the trading realms and networks of a city evolve, local residents adapt and transform the built environment accordingly, even turning their backs to the water. In the last four decades, while port cities around the world have

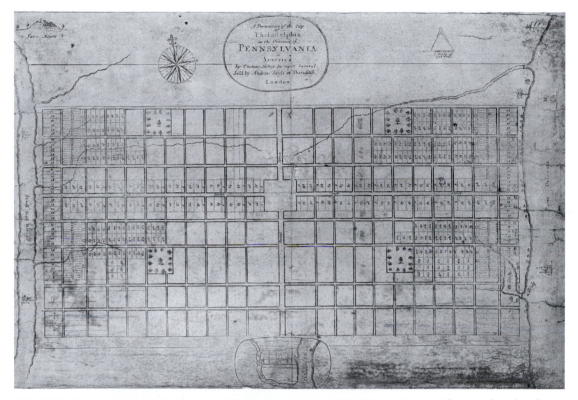

Figure 1.1 Thomas Holme, plan of Philadelphia, 1683 (source: The Library Company of Philadelphia).

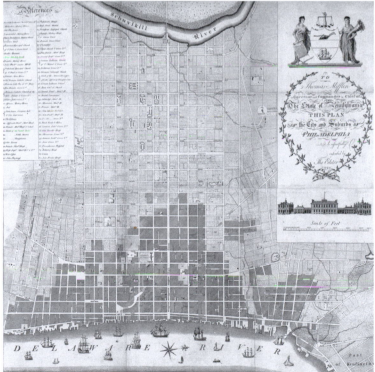

Figure 1.2 A. P. Folie and R. Scot, plan of the city and suburbs of Philadelphia, 1794 (source: The Library Company of Philadelphia).

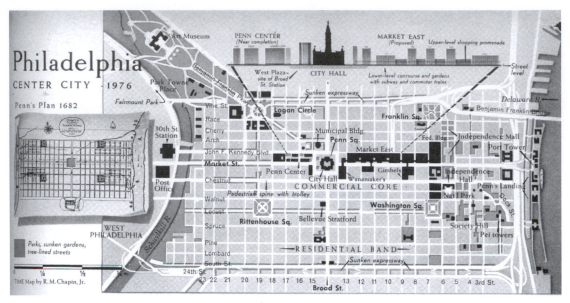

Figure 1.3 Philadelphia city center in 1976 based on a proposal by Edmund Bacon published in *Time Magazine*, November 1964 (source: *Time Magazine*, November 6, 1964 (84, 20). Urban Renewal: Remaking the American City. Philadelphia's Ed Bacon. "The City: Under the Knife, or All for Their Own Good").

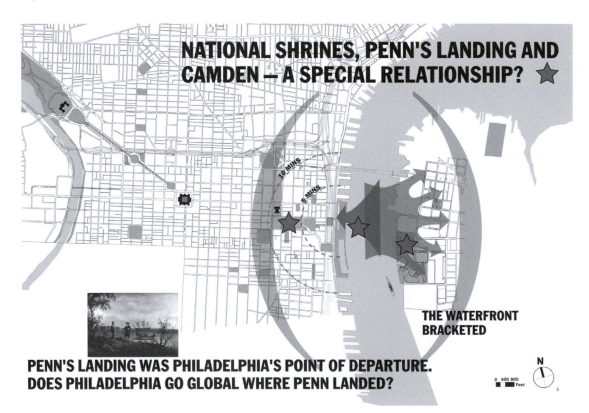

Figure 1.4 Venturi, Scott Brown and Associates, Inc., *Penn's Landing Planning Study*, 2003 (source: Courtesy, Venturi, Scott Brown and Associates, Inc).

adopted waterfront revitalization projects and while Baltimore's transformation has inspired projects abroad, Philadelphia has been unable to develop a comprehensive policy.

Finally, as Philadelphia illustrates, part of the definition of a port city is that shipping links it with other port cities and that the form and needs of ships have long designed the port; for example, the great East India ships forced the expansion of the Docklands and the whole East End of London long before containerization provoked the more recent transformation of ports. This book argues that maritime and associated networks create dynamic, multi-scaled, and interconnected cityscapes. I call them *port cityscapes*, and they exist around the world. Port cities are literally connected through shipping, trade, or traders, but also other networks – of diasporas, trade groups, religious congregations, ethnic groups, elites, family, migration, artisans, slaves, shipworkers, etc. – that relate people symbolically through kinship and other social ties. As a result of the various flows between port cities, specific elements of their respective urban environment are related through a range of factors such as funding, technology, style, concept, or building material. This book concentrates on the network of port cities and how the diffusion of people and cargo, of new technology and new planning ideas changed the built form of the port area, the waterfront, and the city as a whole. A *networked analysis* of the urban environment thus helps us tell more complex stories about these connections as well as about highlighted and hidden elements of built form in specific locations. Again, in order to make that argument, we cannot solely look at material culture but must take into account a wide range of invisible networks.

These studies are inherently interdisciplinary, bringing researchers in the history of architecture and urban form into conversation with geographers, planners, economists, and sociologists. This creates an interdisciplinary and global approach to focused studies by urban morphologists or architectural historians, without assuming a direct correlation between architecture and culture. Such research also requires a certain reimagining of key terms such as *architecture* or *built form*, taking them to include engineering works such as cranes, bulkheads, piers, bridges, etc., as well as urban structures, land lots, streets, places, and tying these to socio-economic structures or urban cultures. The analysis of port cities therewith provides us with a focus to contribute to the advancement of social scientific debates around network analysis, and theories of network analysis.

This book thus proposes a specific methodological and historiographical approach: a multidimensional, interdisciplinary, and networked analysis of built and urban form in port cities understood as embodiments of the interaction between larger global forces and local interests and nodes in larger networks. It even takes this investigation one step further, by considering the changes in these networks over time in spatial extent, intensity, or formality and consequently the changes in the participating port cities and their built environment. The extent to which these various globally determined or inspired elements appear in the built and urban environment of a specific port city depends upon numerous variables that need to be investigated in detailed case studies.

NETWORKED ANALYSIS OF PORT CITYSCAPES

Ships were for hundreds of years the most reliable and fastest (as well as most ecological) means of long-distance transportation of goods and people, and they continue to be the most important means of transport for long-distance trade of bulky and imperishable products. Geographical and natural features, and physical and technical conditions are important. They helped many early port cities to emerge, when technology had yet to develop, but human activity and foresight, political, economic, and social factors have been the main drivers in the rise and fall of all ports and port cities. The intimate connection between social structures and physical urban form in port cities has been recognized by numerous researchers, including the geographer Guido G. Weigend. His research and methodological approach to port cities are still relevant to understanding the basic elements of port geography and port transformation, and he has carefully outlined the various factors influencing port development (Weigend, 1958).

Many of the leading port cities have shaped and reshaped their coastlines and harbors, overcoming astounding obstacles. Development can occur even on "a barren rock," as the British foreign minister Lord Palmerston famously described Hong Kong in 1841. Over the centuries, port cities have overcome environmental changes – the retreat of the sea, the silting up of a harbor – by building new harbors disconnected from the city itself – Piraeus, developed as the port city of classical Athens; Bremerhaven, the nineteenth-century outport for Bremen (Buse, 2008), Yangshan deep water port, under construction on an island some 30 km (19 miles) off the Shanghai coast – or through technological interventions, notably land reclamation in Singapore, New York, and Tokyo (Glaser *et al.*, 1991). Even major urban destruction through natural or man-made disasters such as fires, earthquakes, and warfare have served some local elites as a basis for port improvement. Examples include Hamburg and Osaka, which used post-war rebuilding to overcome structural and operational problems due to the sinking of the harbor area and the growth of the city away from the center (Hasegawa, 2003). Political and economic transformation, such as the fall of the Iron Curtain, has led to extensive network transformation. The repositioning of ports that were under Soviet control after the Second World War, such as Riga and Tallinn, necessitates vision and design as they try to catch up with or even overtake their Western neighbors, Helsinki and Stockholm.

To test this approach of analyzing changing trade networks and their influence on evolving architectural and urban form in port cities, and thus to tie the global into the local, and to investigate urban transformation in relation to larger network change through the examples of port cities, this book concentrates on the period from the nineteenth to the twenty-first centuries. Starting with industrialization and increased globalization and the accompanying efficient technologies and growth of exchange, this period saw an affirmation of global networks linking ports and port cities, further promoting port cities as major nodes. It encompasses the emergence of the modern industrialized port as well as its post-industrial redevelopment.

Trading networks, and associated social and business networks, have spanned different regions of the globe for hundreds of years, connecting port cities and places in distant locations through maritime traffic. Port cities, key nodes within trading networks, render visible the multiple flows of people, goods and finances as they cross from and to their forelands – the seaward side of a city (Weigend, 1952, 1958) – as well as their hinterlands, and shape the built environment in all the interconnected locations. Trading networks and travel patterns can change quickly in response to shifting economic or political global or local conditions. Institutions and citizens in the different cities of a network take more time to respond to new or changed networks by establishing or adapting institutions and social structures, as well as buildings and infrastructure. Setting up new authorities for waterfront regeneration, for example, takes time. They often retain elements of preceding periods, which may later provide the foundation for the establishment of other, for example recreational, networks, such as global efforts at waterfront revitalization and the reuse of abandoned structures.

As places of passage for people from faraway destinations, port cities were also places prone to diseases transmitted through rats and their fleas (plague), or through contaminated water (cholera). The rapid spread of these illnesses illustrates the connectivity of maritime networks. Policies to control disease have unified port aspects of otherwise very different cities. Maps show how the diseases travel faster by sea than by land and specifically through ports; they spread more slowly along roads and rivers to landbound cities and the countryside (Park, 2003). Thus, Genoese ships brought plague to Sicily from the Black Sea in the autumn of 1347, at about the same time it appeared in Alexandria; the third wave spread globally from Hong Kong (1894), Bombay, and Calcutta (1896) thanks to increasingly rapid maritime transportation in the mid-eighteenth century (Carmichael, 2003; Park, 2003). As diseases traveled, port authorities took action: they insisted, for example, on circular disks on hawsers to prevent rats from making their way ashore. Building codes for warehouses began to require that foundations, high walls, and roofs be constructed, not of brickwork, but of rat-proof material such as smooth cement, which rats could not climb (Echenberg, 2007, 2008). Colonial powers used growing knowledge about diseases to identify local populations as carriers of disease and to impose the residential segregation they wanted on racial grounds; historian Kalala Ngalamulume's examination of the example of Saint-Louis du Senegal, founded in 1659 by the French *Compagnie Normande*, shows this clearly (Ngalamulume, 2008).

The very multiplicity of connections raises questions about the stability and governance of networks and their built form. Administrations, institutions, and traders have kept records on export/import and logistics, and thus on their trade networks, as long as shipping has existed. These books were essential to urban elites and document the changing scale and density of trade networks. Business people, engineers, and port specialists have dominated maritime connectivity for a long time; understanding these documents as a basis for a networked analysis would allow researchers to explore the built environment from a new perspective, one that would complement network approaches pursued by other disciplines and notably by geographers, but that also necessitates an investigation into the meaning and usefulness of diverse approaches to network theory. The German economic geographer Gernot

Grabher's overview of network theory in economic and social geography provides an example of the multiple types of multiscalar networks (informal, project, strategic). They sometimes overlap, and show different levels of formality and stability that can be relevant for this study (Grabher, 2006). Central place theory, formulated by Walter Christaller and developed by other scholars, including Paul Hohenberg and Lynn Hollen Lees, built on this research to examine the impact of urban networks on cities and the hierarchical relationships between cities, or, as did G. William Skinner for China, by discerning macro-regions in China (regional urban cores and their accompanying secondary centers and hinterlands) (Christaller, 1969 (1933); Hohenberg and Lees, 1996; Skinner, 1977). The number of studies on world city networks is growing, providing information about individual cities and comparisons among them. Research rarely focused on the links between them. Researchers around Peter J. Taylor have since performed quantitative analyses of world city networks, collecting extensive data on locational policies of major service firms, but without examining the concrete influence of these networks on the form of the built environment (Beaverstock, 2002; Jacobs *et al.*, 2010; Taylor, 2003). As the Belgian economic geographers Ann Verhetsel and Steve Sel have pointed out, researchers have yet to closely examine port cities as global cities. Verhetsel's examination of shipping companies and container terminal operators explores the world maritime city network, showing that Hong Kong, Hamburg, Singapore, Shanghai, Tokyo, New Jersey/New York, Bangkok/Laem Chabang, and London are the world's leading maritime cities, with Hong Kong, Hamburg, and New York as the main nodes of decision-making for container shipping companies (Verhetsel and Sel, 2009). Verhetsel and Sel's (2009) map of World Maritime Cities Network (Alpha level) provides a great starting point for a networked analysis of architecture and urban form such as I am suggesting and would allow art historians or historians to tie together, for example, the study of aesthetic influences and the investigation of social networks.

In his conclusion to *Brides of the Sea*, the Australian maritime historian Frank Broeze noted the possibility of examining morphology to understand the importance of port functions for the rise and development of a city (Broeze, 1989). This book takes up his challenge, using it to analyze urban form from a network perspective. This combination is a relatively new approach. Though geographers, historians, economists, sociologists, and political scientists have examined port cities and their networks, only a handful have specifically considered the urban form of port cities, or the development of particular port-related areas, from sailor towns to waterfronts and container terminals. The intimate connection between physical urban form and social structures in port cities has been recognized and pointed to by numerous geographers, including Weigend, who carefully outlined the various factors influencing port development (Weigend, 1958). From the 1970s to the early 2000s, another geographer wrote extensively on port cities: The British transport geographer Brian S. Hoyle focused on port cities, proposing an overview of internal port–city relationships and their changes over time that has proven relevant for the study of urban and built form (Hoyle, 1989). It is, however, the extensive works on port cities by Broeze that stand out both for their theoretical innovations and for the inclusion of new, well-researched case studies (including work by Rhoads Murphey, another eminent port city researcher) as a basis for networked analysis of built form (Broeze, 1989, 1997; Murphey, 1970). Meanwhile American historian Josef W. Konvitz analyzed how and why Europeans have planned and built port cities since the Renaissance (Konvitz, 1993).

The interaction between the local and the global, between shifting social and economic flows and changing physical structures plays out in multiple ways in port cities. Building on Hoyle's investigation of the relationships among port, port sector (waterfront), and city, I propose a closer reading of urban and built form in those three areas as related to a city's port function and its role as a node within international networks (Hoyle, 1989). The port function is manifest to varying degrees in the built environment in these areas; the location of particular functions in one area or another informs us about the changing identities of a city and its parts. The location and design of specific urban areas and buildings speak of relationships spanning the seas, and of local needs and opportunities both at a certain time and in response to global changes and transformation.

For functional reasons, the port itself depends heavily on global premises and on the handling of cargo and passengers. Ports are literally shaped by the necessary commonalities of measurement. Containers, weights and measures have long been standardized, in fact weights and measures were "interchangeable among Mesopotamian, Levantine, Egyptian, and Aegean systems" (Wright, 2008). Not only did the goods that were shipped have to be standardized, but also the harbor facilities had to offer similar wharves, docks, and tools for loading and discharging to accommodate the same vessels across the world. The form of the cargo and its particular needs, from spices to coffee or carpets, shaped the buildings that accommodated them. They created, for example, the warehouses of the Hanseatic cities in the North and Baltic seas that resemble each other closely and similar docklands in the nineteenth century (see Figure 1.5). The type of cargo, the focus of shipping companies, and the available technology further shape networks and the participating cities. Unloading and storage of cheap bulk goods will require other facilities and have a different impact on urban form than the transport of luxury goods, of migrants, or of leisure travelers. Probably the most striking example of global standardization and the expanse of maritime networks are container terminals around the world, which are distinguishable only when we see recognizable elements in the background (see Figure 1.6).

All port cities have to fulfill the same functions to be part of the network. As a result of technology transfers, of sharing of professionals, of migration, etc., and as goods and people (both elite administrators and lower-class workers) travel along those trade connections, they create a network not only of goods but also of cultural capital. The socio-economic, political, and cultural conditions in a specific city, region, or nation inflect the ways in which a port location responds to global demands. Multiple actors, public and private institutions, elites and workmen, and others who make the port work, administer trade, and direct money flows have to adjust to the requirements of trade, leading to the development of specific maritime economic cultures.

Figure 1.5 Traditional houses in former Hanseatic towns of Northern Europe.
Top left: Lübeck (source: Carola Hein).
Top right: Hamburg (source: Carola Hein).
Bottom left: Amsterdam (source: ©Hartemink | Dreamstime.com Title: Canal Houses in Amsterdam, the Netherlands, August 1, 2010).
Bottom right: Tallinn (source Carola Hein).

Many of those requirements are expressed in similar buildings. The way that cities respond to port functions determines their competitive advantage or disadvantage and their viability within their trade networks. Cities that don't adjust will drop out as networks shift over time.

How any of these requirements are filled in a particular city depends on local conditions, including climatic, geological, political, economic, social, cultural, or religious necessities as well as the energy, foresight, and connectedness of human actors and institutions. As global and local factors add up differently and distinctively, they make each port city a particular place. There is no single urban form, pattern, or dynamic that characterizes them. Yet port cities show common traits, making them faraway mirrors of each other. The combination of difference and similarity makes port cities uniquely valuable for thinking about global city networks and their reflection in built form, and for thinking about changes in these networks and their influence on the urban environment.

The port city caters primarily to local needs, but also hosts activities and people that are related in some way to the port. Traders and other globally connected locals acted in each of these cities, maintaining networks of trade, influence, and knowledge beyond regional and national boundaries. Trade itself, and trading and shipping companies have connected distant places for several centuries regardless of the support of political institutions. Business trips have been an important part of maritime networks (Akveld and Bruijn, 1989; Blussé, 1981; Goor, 1986; Jones, 2000; Miller, 2003). Traders intervened

Figure 1.6 Almost indistinguishable container terminals in major port cities.
Top left: New York/New Jersey (source: Port Authority of New York and New Jersey and affiliates).
Top right: Dubai (source: Halcrow Group).
Bottom left: Bremerhaven (source: bremenports GmbH & Co. KG).
Bottom right: Hong Kong (1978 Kwai Chung Port Terminal) (source: courtesy of the HKSAR Government).

in the form of their host cities on numerous levels, injecting their knowledge into the construction of shipping facilities and infrastructures, designing company headquarters and private homes, religious and leisure institutions, introducing new approaches to recreation, law and politics to the cities in which they were active. A historic example of religious presence related to trade is the mosque in Guangzhou (Canton), built by merchants who entered the city via the Maritime Silk Route. Merchants have needed a range of spaces on land, beyond the edge of the water: shipbuilding and maintenance facilities, workshops for shipping equipment, as well as provisioning shops for sailors, economic facilities such as customs offices, exchanges, insurance agents, maritime education, and recreation, including coffee shops and restaurants. Not only elite networks of traders have transformed port cities. Passenger traffic has demanded facilities, from hotels and boarding houses to ticket offices and waiting rooms. Passengers of all classes, from the elite traveling for pleasure to immigrants, as well as the men who work on the ships, transformed cities of departure and arrival, leaving similar traces of their religious or ethnic affiliations, sites of prayer, restaurants, or leisure facilities.

The city's maritime façade, its port sector and waterfront, embodies the relationship between the city and its global foreland, including buildings hosting foreign institutions and featuring non-local styles. It offers an opportunity for establishing façades that can function as maritime business cards showcasing the presence of global institutions and worldwide trade, as well as numerous buildings dedicated to arriving and departing passengers and to the storage, treatment, or transformation of goods. A façade on the water's edge showcases a city's international character. It is also the place that visitors first view when arriving by sea. Views of the waterfront become trademarks and help construct the global urban mindscape of port cities. The maritime façades of New York, Dubai, Bremerhaven, and Hong Kong are diverse in their appearance and influenced by specific historic, local political, technical, socio-economic, and other factors (see Figure 1.7). Some of these maritime façades, such as the New York skyline or the Shanghai Bund, are world famous, while others reflect the diversity of cities that are among the leading ports. At waterfronts, global interests meet local needs and desires; foreign forces inscribe their values into the cityscape. They are places where the urban mindscape of a city and its brand or trademark are constructed (Weiss-Sussex and Bianchini, 2006). Given their location on the edge of the water, the difficulty and expense of land reclamation, and its need for public control, these places are practically safe from unwanted and cluttered construction.

Not all port-related businesses and activities are located on or near the port. Some institutions and buildings do not need to be near the port; they may not be able to afford a waterfront location, or have been relegated to other parts of the city. Some may prefer proximity to the civic core or the edge of the city for various reasons. These institutions include maritime academies, trading spaces such as stock exchanges, town halls, political representations such as consulates, religious institutions, or residences. Some of these

Figure 1.7 Diverse waterfronts of major port cities.
Top left: Manhattan (source: © Minh Tang | Dreamstime.com. Title: Manhattan Skyline by day, August 24, 2009).
Top right: Dubai (source: Copyright C Motivate Publishing 2002).
Bottom left: Bremerhaven (source: bremenports GmbH & Co. KG).
Bottom right: Hong Kong (source: © Guodingping | Dreamstime.com).

institutions are part of the public spaces of the city, while others, less prominent, are nodes in the hidden networks of the port. Ethnic districts, most prominently Chinatowns, are often located close to the port; the Chinatown gate and Chinese characters on billboards are iconic images that identify them as part of a global network among port cities. The location of businesses – in relation to the waterfront, the public and commercial core of the city, its upper-class or lower-class districts – provide us with information on the relevance and position of specific functions and social groups within a city. Port workers often live in crowded working-class districts, while many traders and shipowners live in elite residential areas (from Philadelphia's Main Line to Hamburg's Elbchaussee), creating through their patterns a broad range of port cityscapes.

Given the networked character of port cities, we may posit yet another (fourth) zone of influence of the port beyond the port itself, the port city, and the waterfront: buildings and urban structures that are tied to the workings and finances of a specific city but that are located in different cities and which we can call port city support structures. A good example of a port city within an urban network of global exchange that is expressed in built form is sixteenth-century Seville. Despite having been the entrance point of huge amounts of gold and silver from South America, the city's wealth was tied to Genoa, Antwerp, and Augsburg, where the financial markets were located (Kennedy, 2011). Stock exchanges and town halls, elite residences, and other types of housing, religious, or leisure facilities in other cities need to be taken into account for a networked analysis of urban form as I am proposing it.

As we observe the different layers in which port-related networks express themselves in built form, we see that Hoyle was correct in observing that these relationships change over time. As political, economic, and social conditions change, as trade networks are transformed, as ships, channels, and containers evolve, cities change too, and these functions move within and beyond the city. While a networked analysis of architecture could include numerous themes and examples, the chapters selected for this book reflect specific disciplinary approaches (geography, history, planning, art history, architectural history, urban history) structured according to different scales of approach (global, regional, local). Their authors have been encouraged to cross disciplinary and spatial boundaries, to converse with each other. No single book can address all the questions (or review all the relevant literature), but for this book I have selected a range of articles that both highlight possible interdisciplinary approaches and address selected questions within the topic of networking and the creation of a port city landscape, standing in for broader themes.

The three parts of this book elaborate three different scales of investigation, crossing disciplinary and international boundaries from a qualitative perspective. Part I examines a range of global networks mediated through ports in view of their impact on urban and built form. It looks back briefly at the colonial and trading realms of the Imperial Age (fourteenth to seventeenth centuries). It then establishes and describes other types of global networks (financial, migration, professional, etc.), their main actors, and engines of network transformation (such as new technology), and their impact on the built environment. Part II, on regional dynamics, compares transformations of built and urban form in a specific spatial context and in response to a variety of changes that relate to ports. Each chapter proceeds comparatively, investigating how selected groups of cities have responded differently to similar outside opportunities and how diverse groups of traders and planners can shape buildings and cities connected through port city networks. Examples here include the competition between Amsterdam and Rotterdam, city space and waterfront transformation in Mediterranean and Ottoman ports, as well as the emergence of Chinese treaty ports and the creation of the cities of the Suez Canal. Part III, considering dynamic landscapes, examines urban cases in regard to the impact of global networks and port activity on a specific city or urban section. Each chapter in this final part presents a specific port cityscape to focus on its development. Rather than trying to provide a complete reading of a city in view of its port functions, these contributions examine specific aspects of the many possible ways in which port activity can shape a single city, using examples from around the world. The conclusion suggests further opportunities for an application of this networked approach to architectural and urban analysis.

The remainder of this introduction maps the three parts of the book in more detail, tying together a brief overview of key literature with core points from the articles featured here.

PART I: PORT CITIES: GLOBAL NETWORKS AND URBAN FORM

Port cities are often key components of larger political or economic realms, and these realms are well studied from a variety of perspectives. French historian Fernand Braudel has investigated the Mediterranean and the Mediterranean world, referring also to the major cities in these economic networks (Braudel, 1979, 2001). Other scholars have studied seaborne empires such as the Portuguese and the transmission of arts and culture, with reference to cities and architecture (Bethencourt and Curto, 2007; Boxer, 1969; Brockey, 2008; Pearson, 1998; Russell-Wood, 1998). Similar studies exist for other realms, including the Spanish or the British Empire, the Indian realm, Africa, or the West Indies, as well as for religious or ethnic, notably Jewish, networks (Armytage, 1953; Cesarani and Romain, 2006; Floor, 2006; Hall, 2008; Hoyle and Hilling, 1970; Parry, 1966; Subramanian, 2008; Wiese, 1981).

The development of the port and city of London, the paradigm of a great port city and a model for many of the cities discussed here, necessarily runs through the chapters of the book. As the capital of an empire that "ruled the waves," the construction of wharves and docks was essential to the city's economy. As the location of the first world's fair in 1851, it set the standard for celebrating a city's global connections. The design and revitalization of the various docks on the Isle of Dogs have attracted global attention (Brownill, 1993; Edwards, 1992; Harms, 2008; Hoyle et al., 1988). Gilbert and Driver in their study of London showcase the official and popular promotion of the city as the centerpiece of empire (Gilbert and Driver, 2000). Indeed, strong hierarchies, primary cities, and a capital city, where the various links of the network come together, characterize port city networks within empires or other political entities. The buildings and materials used in capital city ports make trade patterns visible; the use of rare materials in capital buildings and art, and often in the creation of impressive port cityscapes, points to trade in luxury goods.

Many capitals originated as port cities (Constantinople/Istanbul, Amsterdam, London, Lisbon, Tokyo), as did many current global cities (Sassen, 1991). Control over trade and faraway goods is often considered a sign of a government's power. In turn, the presence of a national, imperial, or colonial government has helped many a port city consolidate its role as a leader in the urban hierarchy and promote itself globally. Already in the Akkadian Empire 2300–2100 BCE, Sargon of Agade proudly commented that ships from faraway places such as Dilmun, Magan, and Meluhha were docked in his capital. As the archaeologist Peter Magee has pointed out,

> the *control* of these ports was an important component of the process of political and social legitimization in newly emerging states. Controlling ports not only meant monitoring the importation and export of goods but also acted as a symbolic proxy for the geo-political reach of early states.
>
> (Magee, 2008: 1)

Capital status has also brought a constant or temporary military presence to the harbor (notably during wartime), and involved direct control of shipping lines and commercial activities. Colonial regimes helped merchant communities sculpt port city hierarchies. Nevertheless, capital functions have also impeded port functions, as central control can interfere with infrastructural decisions, transportation policies, economic policies, and urban hierarchies, as well as with the importance of national boundaries. For example, a land-bound political entity may find it easier to secure and control trade on land than on water. Finally, capital cities are often chosen to be centrally located, whereas port cities are mostly peripheral (on peripheral cities, see Connolly, 2008). It is precisely the absence of centrality, however, that allows port cities to flourish within international frameworks; Shanghai, Osaka/Kobe, Buenos Aires, and Hamburg are examples.

Part I of this book, entitled "Port cities: global networks and urban form," offers four approaches to the theme of global networking, anchored respectively in geography, history, planning, and planning history. This part starts with a premodern contribution by Patrick O'Flanagan (Chapter 2), who gives the reader a vivid sense of the pivotal position of port cities in global large-scale networks – in historical change, in the distribution of goods, as military features, and as receivers and movers of people. The fortifications of Cadiz or Havana testify to the riches that crossed these spaces and that needed protection. Examining examples of the various Atlantic systems carved out of their interests by the main colonial powers, he acknowledges their urban planning preferences and cultural backgrounds. His work thus complements the research by historians Franklin Knight, Peggy Liss, and other scholars, who provide extensive information on individual cities of the American Atlantic façade, by including examples from both sides of the Atlantic and by tying his findings closely to those of the built environment (Davis, 1973; Knight and Liss, 1991; Liss, 1983; Price, 1974). Port cities on both sides of the Atlantic functioned as hubs, and administered and distributed the goods and people and ideas that moved along these lines. Built and urban form, exemplified by the earlier Law of the Indies (1573) decreed by King Philip II of Spain, embodied these flows.

The malleability of the shipping networks, their growth and disappearance, contribute to the rise and decay of port cities. The network control that European cities exercised before the nineteenth century led to the emergence of cities on other continents that later became leaders of newly independent entities. New York, the North American hub, and Hong Kong, the gateway from China before the First World War, are examples. In response to the end of former networks, notably of colonialism, and former colonies' formation of independent new nations, governments moved capitals inland, away from the seaport, such as from Rio de Janeiro to Brasilia, or from Lagos to Abuja. Similarly, Portuguese *feitorias*, usually heavily fortified trading posts built by Portuguese traders along the African coast to facilitate trade and protect inhabitants of these coastal entrepots, remain as stony expressions of a colonial power's far-reaching administration and of premodern ports, such as Mozambique Island that failed to develop after the departure of the colonial forces (Newitt, 2008).

Technological transformation (and foresight) have been major drivers of networked transformation in port cities. Some are only mentioned in passing here, including new shipping vessels, new fuels, new cargo, and the railway and the telegraph. Lars Amenda (Chapter 3) examines, from the perspective of a historian of migration, two major changes in technology that have reshaped maritime networks and port cities over the last two centuries. He presents these two changes as they have led to similarly complete overhauls of practices and financing in the shipping industry, of trade and migration patterns and their increased scale, of labor conditions, of port and port sectors of cities. The first major change was the switch from sailing ships to the more economical steamships in the mid-nineteenth century. As Amenda points out, knowledge (including political convictions) traveled from Chinatown to Chinatown. Cuban towns, little Italys, Korean, Vietnamese, or other ethnic urban areas in port cities would provide material for further research into networked port cityscapes.

The second major transformation at the heart of Amenda's chapter (and discussed in many other chapters) is containerization. The change from bulk cargo to the container provides another, even clearer, example of the ways in which a transformation in transportation has reshaped shipping lanes and harbor facilities, creating new functions for the port and promoting the arrival of new groups of people. These changes drained many waterfronts of life, but also inspired planners and investors to invent new uses for port areas, including office work and leisure activity, notably tourism and the provision of cruise terminals. The emergence of the container as the main package format was thus at the core of harbor transformation and expansion around the globe as well as of the waterfront revitalization projects in Baltimore, London,

Hamburg, Shanghai, or Sydney – as Dirk Schubert and Stephen Ward's contributions highlight.

Technological innovation influences port areas, waterfronts, and the city as a whole in different intensities. The role of the waterfront through history is at the heart of Schubert's chapter (Chapter 4), which provides a link between the history of networks and the consideration of networks' influence on urban and built form. From the geographical and historical approach to networking and from the concentration on social networks, Schubert takes us to the physical space of the city and provides a networked approach to the relationship between port and city. Using Hoyle's scheme of the port–city interface and his own addition locating waterfront renewal in the historic development of the city, he sets up the commonalities and common forces shaping port cities without denying that each city has distinctive complexities and history. His acknowledgment of specificities and his call for nuanced studies lead us to the case studies that make up the rest of the book. As Schubert outlines the waterfront's critical position at the interface between global and local powers, he sets up the analytical framework for Stephen Ward's chapter investigating waterfront revitalization in Baltimore and its subsequent copies (Chapter 5).

Waterfront regeneration is one aspect of the network puzzle that this book attempts to investigate and perhaps the most currently visible. Ward considers port cities as "knowledge hubs," and points to the multiple actors who are interested in knowledge exchange, as he discusses how they transmit and repackage information. He emphasizes the importance of the linkage between port and city, addressing both specific city dynamics (particularly Baltimore's) and the international spread of one city's model via extensive yet specific networks. This essay builds on his earlier study of the exchange of planning ideas (Ward, 2000, 2002). While scholars and lay people have celebrated Baltimore as an example of waterfront revitalization, they ignored the decay of large parts of the city and the displacement of the black and Chinese populations (as Ward points out) who had used these areas because of their affordability and proximity to the working port.

PART II: REGIONAL DYNAMICS OF PORT CITIES: POLITICS, PEOPLE, AND THE BUILT ENVIRONMENT

Building upon the initial examination of global networks, the five chapters of Part II examine regional networks. The term "cosmopolitan," already mentioned in earlier chapters, comes to the fore here, as authors examine the impact of cosmopolitan and local elites and, in turn, their impact on the built environment. Their work is comparative: groups of cities exposed to identical changes allow them to highlight the particularities of global–local interactions. We can also consider these cities that are connected through trade as coming together to constitute evolving "world systems," as the American sociologist Immanuel Wallerstein calls them (Wallerstein, 1976). These world systems can be regions that have interdependent economies (in regard to necessities such as food, fuel, and protection), but do not possess a clear political center or overarching political structure.

Given the multitude of local conditions (geographic, physical, technical, as well as political, economic, or social), responses to similar requirements take on a variety of forms. Numerous scholars have discussed the social production of urban space, including Henri Lefèbvre (1974), Mark Gottdiener (1994), Anthony King (1997, 2007), and David Harvey (2001). The geographer Jon Goss has carefully examined the study of architecture within geography (architectural geography), discussing various approaches by geographers – of building as a cultural artifact, as object of value, or architecture as sign, or as a spatial system – and calls for a comprehensive discussion of architecture. His approach supports the current undertaking (Goss, 1988) without, however, focusing on port cities.

The first two chapters here further the discussion of human networks and of people who control and shape, use, or serve these networks and influence the appearance of harbors, waterfronts, and port cities. The essays demonstrate the power of local vision, action, and foresight. As a result, we see new built forms, sometimes hidden and hesitant, sometimes highlighted. These chapters identify the trading elites (emigrants, diasporic travelers, or families) and how they have shaped global infrastructures, urban form, and architecture. The chapter by Sakis Gekas and Mathieu Grenet (Chapter 6) builds on O'Flanagan's broad sketch of geographical networks, drawing attention to the *social* networks of cosmopolitanism (and stateless actors) that make possible the exchange of ideas. They show how various actors, even from different national, ethnic backgrounds (Greek and Jewish diasporas in Trieste, Livorno, Corfu), have intervened in a city and left traces, such as church buildings. The chapter also highlights the ways in which politicians included and used the traders, giving them a free hand if that benefited the city in some way, but reining them in, even sometimes expelling them counter to a city's long-term benefit (with the result that they would take their trade with them; this is particularly visible in regard to Jewish traders).

The next chapter, by Huibert Schijf (Chapter 7), takes this examination to a different level, investigating the different trajectories of Rotterdam and Amsterdam as port cities. The chapter also illustrates how capital status can help and hinder port city development. Schijf compares how different local elites have altered their city's fate by taking advantage of transformed foreland and hinterland relationships that resulted from shifting colonial relationships as well as from local innovative action. Thus, Amsterdam, a long-standing global port and financial center, declined, because its elites neglected to adapt to the changing needs of shipping and to shifting networks and opted to develop their city into a modern staple port, whereas the leading families of Rotterdam, a small port that lacked direct access to the North Sea just like Amsterdam, notably built new waterways and brought their city into global networks as a transit port. This chapter stands as exemplary for other rivalries of neighboring cities such as Hamburg and Bremen or Philadelphia and New York (Aggarwala, 2002; Broeze, 1991).

The following three chapters highlight varied local responses to larger impulses – political, economic, technological. When Western port technology and port city imagery challenged cities around the world, local responses, even in geographically related areas, often differed. Here, three chapters address a range of transformations, the impact of the presence of Western powers on various cities in China, the changing urban form of Ottoman cities faced with modernization, and the impact of the construction of the Suez Canal on urban and built form.

Treaty ports in Asia – ports opened to foreign trade and residence under pressure from foreign powers – allow for a comparative investigation of groups of cities confronted with the presence of Western powers. The foreigners left numerous markers of contact and exchange, from architecture to food. In his essay (Chapter 8), Johnathan Farris examines the built environment in Chinese treaty ports as a field of tension between the global and the local. The new settlements had to compete with imperial capitals, brought a new foreign way of seeing, demonstrated the reach of Western capitalism, and transformed local practices of everyday life. Imported classically inspired façades signaled a taste of home, stated superiority, and revealed the existence of new technologies. Beyond Western-controlled selected spaces that served as business cards of the foreign presence, urban plans were dependent on local situations. Even the foreign elites had to depend on Chinese labor and materials.

In contrast to Farris' study of the Western-controlled design that characterized Chinese cities, Malte Fuhrmann (Chapter 9) inquires specifically into waterfront quays of Ottoman cities, their maritime façades. He shows how locals responded to the modernizing and innovating foreland. Fuhrmann carefully reads the built environment and its transformation in particular places as a thermometer of the integration of people by examining two gazes crossing the waterfront – to and from the sea. He also emphasizes the importance of imaginaries in shaping real places – a theme that recurs throughout the volume – and the turn to debate and conflict over those changes.

The construction of the Suez Canal and adjoining cities represents the transformation provoked in cities around the world through the opening of new maritime connections from the Panama Canal to the North Sea–Baltic Sea Canal. These new corridors reshaped shipping patterns, and led to the death and rise of new cities. In fact, the creation of the Suez Canal revived Mediterranean cities that had lost their importance after the discovery of the Americas, and gave rise to new centers. Céline Frémaux (Chapter 10) shows specifically how the creation of a new shipping connection reshaped cosmopolitan and other networks to create new cities and formed a new built environment that reflected all these forces. This chapter adds a further level of specificity to the volume, illustrating the dynamic negotiations between global and local, public and private forces that shaped urban form in these port cities down to the level of building materials.

PART III: DYNAMIC LANDSCAPES: GLOBAL CHANGE AND LOCAL TRANSFORMATION

Global networks link each port with other ports, transmitting cultural practices, ideas, and architectural and urban form. These global outside influences interact with local institutions, governance systems, metropolitan structures, and actors, and respond to local particularities and needs. Depending on the extent and transformation of political, economic, and technical realms, the role of the port city will shift and, in turn, the built environment will emerge and change. Specific areas of a city will respond differently to the global port network, depending on physical and functional proximity to and integration with the port. These networks carry more than ideas, products, and people. Another way to highlight and illustrate their concrete existence is through port cities' responses at the level of the built environment to the spread of steamships, the rise of containerization, or waterfront revitalization.

Containerization in particular has reshaped cities extensively, leading to the abandonment of waterfronts and a more recent period of waterfront reclamation and revitalization. Literature on current waterfront transformation in specific port cities is abundant, as several chapters in this volume illustrate. Existing studies mostly focus on individual projects – flashy successes and high-profile failures – and the various redevelopment agencies that led them (Brown, 2009; Bruttomesso, 1993; Doig, 2001). The focus of each of these studies is varied. Dirk Schubert (2008a and b, 2009) and Hans Harms (2003), for example, have concentrated on planning aspects in waterfront development. Among compilations of port city and waterfront studies beyond the ones mentioned above are works by urban planners Han Meyer (1999), Rinio Bruttomesso (1983), Richard Marshall (2001), and Ann Breen, with journalist Dick Rigby (1994, 1996) (co-founders of the Waterfront Center), and a study by the Urban Land Institute. More theoretical approaches are featured in Hoyle's (1988) geographic approach and in professor of urban planning Susan Fainstein's (2001, 2008) investigation of political economy and planning aspects of the waterfronts in New York and London. Only the chapter on London by planning historian Peter Hall in his book *Cities and Civilization* (1998) considers the diffusion of ideas. An entire biannual journal, *Portus*, published by RETE – Asociación para la Colaboración entre Puertos y Ciudades – an association for the collaboration between harbors and cities (edited by Joan Alemany and Rinio Bruttomesso), is dedicated to the port–city relationship, with a focus on waterfronts in post-industrial cities (notably in Southern Europe, the Mediterranean, and Latin America). Recent contributions in *Portus* on waterfront issues – the environment, historic preservation, recreation and tourism, identity, or security – illustrate the broad range of contemporary research related to port cities and themes in contemporary waterfront planning. This work links analytical investigation to contemporary planning questions pursued by groups such as the Association Internationale Villes et Ports (AIVP). Recent literature on port cities reflects this broad spread of port activities and needs, ranging from port systems to seascapes and pirates (Bentley *et al.*, 2007; Wang *et al.*, 2007).

Having established the existence of global networks and examined their impact on a regional scale, the volume turns in Part III to showing how global networks and their changes have transformed the built environment of selected cities around the world. The four chapters analyze relationships between individual cities, their ports, and their hinterland, in view of their urban transformation and their response to global shipping and transportation patterns, imported building materials, changing design concepts, architecture, and urban planning ideas.

Each author has selected a specific perspective, highlighting large-scale urban redevelopment or street patterns, examining marketing or the construction of the new port. The present chapters contribute a specific reading of urban development through the lens of changing port functions to the extensive literature on these cities. The first two chapters in this part explore urban form and architectural design. My own chapter (Chapter 11) concentrates on large-scale redevelopment in Hamburg and the multiple ways in which these transformations are inscribed by international networks, ranging from the participation of foreign professionals in urban planning and design to the naming of buildings as a reflection of global trade. Carol Krinsky (Chapter 12) highlights the emergence of the global city New York as a port, evoking port dynamics in regard to their effect on the shape of the city.

The section shifts with Marisa Yiu's contribution, which links back to the discussion of elites and the importance of local action in the promotion of port cities. Using the example of Hong Kong, she demonstrates how a city can establish its global position through aggressive and innovative marketing, despite political, economic, and geographic adversities. The quasi-governmental Trade Development Council's (TDC) swift responses to shifting political, economic, and cultural conditions and networks exemplifies the power of port authorities and local institutions. Hong Kong thus stands as a representative of other cities and port authorities that have used port areas for promotional purposes in world's fairs, trade fairs, and model building. It illustrates the importance of the port to the mental landscape of the city (harbor models are one way of promoting port cities throughout the world (Schürmann, 2008)) and the power of imaginaries in shaping the real urban fabric.

Stephen Ramos (Chapter 14) closes the discussion with the examination of the construction of a new port, Jebel Ali port in Dubai, in response to new political, economic, and technological changes worldwide. He describes the impact of economic imperatives on urban form and the dynamics of ports here, as Dubai opted to construct a new port to compete with a neighboring emirate and to secure its economic future. The chapter holds a mirror to many of the themes discussed in earlier chapters – such as changes in cargo, shipping, technology, evolving political, economic, and professional global networks, the importance of local vision and leadership – and illustrates through the example of planning and architecture how these global structures make their imprint on territorial decisions. As Ramos points out, the result is not a hodgepodge of different ideas, but rather a very carefully composed development and a core example, of how the sheikh has used foreign ideas to reinvent and reimagine the port city on an unprecedented new scale.

Networks of trade and transport not only shaped port cities at certain times; they also comprised personal, physical, and other relationships that persist beyond the reason for which they were initially created. They allow cities to address new themes of common interest such as the transformation of former harbor areas or the redefinition of identity after port functions move. Similar built heritages and challenges lead port cities to adopt comparable responses to contemporary challenges. Leisure and port geography have become closely related issues, as the examples of Baltic Sail (Baltic Sail, 2010), a maritime festival around the Baltic Sea, Titanic Quarter (Titanic Quarter, n.d.), a waterfront redevelopment project in Belfast, or BallinStadt (BallinStadt, n.d.), the Hamburg-based emigration museum, illustrate.

In the future, networks will continue to inform architecture and urban form as port cities face similar challenges and opportunities – as they have done for a long time. For example, ports are part of various types of warfare. Attacks on the military in ports, from Pearl Harbor to the attack in the Port of Aden in Yemen, as well as the recent activity of Somali pirates, highlight the importance of these places. Drug activity through ports is another example of hidden and illegal activity that can link these ports. Global port cities face a range of environmental risks, such as rising water levels and flooding due to climate change. Asian developing countries are especially vulnerable, as a 2007 OECD (Organization for Economic Cooperation and Development) report details, raising questions about global trade and requiring a transformation of existing port facilities (Nicholls *et al.*, 2007). Port cities are already collaborating and competing, for example, to exploit the opening of new shipping lanes which has resulted from melting sea ice. Port cities continue to be at the forefront of cultural, social, and technological, developments.

Building on the long-standing tradition of business records, a look at economic statistics on leading global ports published by the American Association of Port Authorities (AAPA) in 2008 shows Singapore and Shanghai as ranking respectively number 1 and 2 in terms of total cargo volume and TEU (Twenty-foot Equivalent Units, the measurement of standard containers, and a standard for the capacity of containerships and transhipment). They are followed by several other Asian, mostly Chinese, cities (as well as Dubai Ports for containers), while the ports that are at the core of this volume – with the exception of Rotterdam (respectively ranked number 3 and 9) – Hamburg, New York/New Jersey, and Antwerp, are ranked between numbers 10 and 20 (American Association of Port Authorities, 2008). It would thus be interesting to apply this networked approach to the leading Asian ports and emerging new port cities. We could read the new port of Shanghai, for example, in terms of rewriting global networks, as a part of regional competitive networks that respond according to their specific local identities to outside challenges, or as an example of various types of maritime functions within a single port city landscape. In the case of Shanghai, we see the creation of a new (possibly the biggest) container terminal on a man-made area between two islands, connected to the land by the new Donghai Bridge, more than 30 km (18.6 miles) long. The Shanghai Municipal Government selected a Hamburg-based design firm, Von Gerkan, Marg und Partner Architects, for the design of the new city associated with the Yangshan deep water port.

Initially called Luchao Harbor City, Lingang New City is designed to accommodate 800,000 people as one of eleven new satellite towns in the port of Shanghai's latest urban planning concept. It is situated 55 km (34.2 miles) from downtown. A circular city around a lake, it engages a multitude of themes. The architect suggested a falling drop and the concentric waves it creates as a reference for the design. The geometric form can be seen as a reference to the historic Chinese square city that functioned as the symbol of the emperor and imperial city for several thousand years, and its counterpart the circle, which the Chinese historically incorporated into architecture as a reflection of heaven (as in the Temple of Heaven in Beijing). We can further discuss

discuss the design as a descendant of Ebenezer Howard's garden city, with its various functional rings surrounding a public core. While water has always been an important feature of Chinese cities, the inclusion of a lake in the center of the city also points to Hamburg, the home town of the designers, and presents yet another example of the integration of port functions into urban utopias.

The further growth of ships and the acceleration of transhipment continue to revolutionize port activity, reshape networks, and create new cities. In those cities, we once again find the same range of different types of built environment, the port, the port district, the city, and a broader support area. New ports currently under construction often include entire city plans. One new global port hub is emerging in Saudi Arabia; King Abdullah Economic City (KAEC) is designed to be "the greatest enabler of socioeconomic development," with its seaport as one of its major economic wheels (King Abdullah Economic City, n.d.). Companies from across the globe are participating, including the New York-based architectural office SOM (Skidmore, Owings & Merrill) and Singapore-based rsp (Raglan Squire and Partners), an architecture planning and engineering firm. When finished in 2025, the new city is projected to have a population of 1.4 million. Ports thus once again function as creators of cities. The KAEC website shows a map of world ports, featuring cities simultaneously that seem to have little in common, major world cities – New York/New Jersey, Tokyo – as well as smaller cities with major harbors – Bremerhaven, Southampton – inviting a networked analysis that allows us to understand what exchange takes place beyond the transmission of goods.

Following the ship or container through a network across time, or considering a particular building at the intersection of multiple networks – might allow us to go beyond Europe, America, and some glimpses of the rest of the world to include those places that are foci of development at any given time. We could write a truly global history of architectural and urban form.

Part I

PORT CITIES

Global networks and urban form

2 PORT CITIES

Engines of growth in an emerging Atlantic system

PATRICK O'FLANAGAN

The 'First Imperial Age', between 1400 and 1715, witnessed the dynamic expansion of minor ports along Europe's Atlantic façade into major international centres of banking, business, commerce and trade and, sometimes, into proto-industrial centres (Scammell, 1992). Nation-states, wittingly or unwittingly, sculptured their ports through distinctive political economies. Each of the major imperial powers carved out an Atlantic system to suit its commercial requirements and objectives. Each of these Atlantics – the Dutch, the English, the French, the Portuguese and the Spanish – was an exclusive imperial domain and only overlapped at its edges with neighbouring domains. A port city is essentially a node in a network, and a network is a construct redolent with spatial meaning. Lines interconnected nodes and were animated by flows of different kinds, whether of bullion, merchandise or people. The construction of trading networks by different actors and agents, particularly merchants' networks, promoted the growth and functional diversification of multiple port cities. It also laid the basis for future flows of migrants and exchanges.

Port cities were fortified entrepots, and this chapter considers their role as hubs in an emerging Atlantic system. This piece illustrates how political economies influenced port formation and consolidation; it details how merchants functioned within regulated and non-regulated contexts. Often through massive defensive investments, individual states contributed to their consolidation. More permissive inheritances were endowed by merchants and migrants on urban fabric and form.

THE ATLANTIC SYSTEM IN THE FIRST IMPERIAL AGE

Europe's leading states used the inner Atlantic, the zone extending from Tromsø to Cadiz, as a platform to launch these maritime endeavours. Before the discoveries of new lands in the New World, the ports here had been trading items coming from central Europe with Atlantic Europe. There were also exchanges between different Atlantic ports and, finally, between them and those on both sides of the Mediterranean. Most of these interchanges involved primary products with little added value, such as cattle and meat products, fish, metals and wood. The foundations of this Atlantic system were, in turn, assembled on a more ancient and venerable inner Atlantic network of ports. Southern Atlantic and Mediterranean products such as wine, fruits and salt had long moved northwards; northern goods, for instance butter, leather, provisions and fabricated items, had moved southwards. Merchandise and other goods from Russia and the North Sea had come down from the Baltic and the Rhine, respectively, and continued onwards to the Mediterranean.

But much of the South Atlantic had to wait until the late eighteenth century to witness the emergence of major ports. Exceptions were a string of Brazilian ports, as they were vital hubs in the Portuguese *Carreira da India*. This term originally stood for the maritime network which linked Lisbon to the Indian ports of Cochin and Goa. It subsequently meant the maritime network of forts, ports and seaways that connected Portugal with the East Indies, China and Japan. Many of these ports were enlivened by commodity trades such as sugar, gold, precious stones and slaves, and later coffee and cotton. The ports of Portuguese Africa only expanded significantly after the independence of Brazil, when Portugal sought to exploit other vast potential resources.

The Caribbean may be regarded as another antechamber of the Atlantic. In this 'First Imperial Age', it was at the forefront of developments, only to slip back into obscurity later. Its ports played pivotal roles in the distribution of products from its cash crop economies; distinctive societies emerged in its ports and countrysides. The emergence of sugar plantations facilitated the evolution of rich land and slave owning societies. Havana was unique, operating as an early sixteenth century New World metropole as well as the capital of the richest Caribbean island. It was a marshalling centre for goods and fleets moving to Europe and a hub for transactions between Veracruz, Cartagena de Indias, Seville and Cadiz. It was also a pivotal military, shipbuilding and outfitting centre; remaining in Spanish hands until 1898, it swallowed massive investments in its defensive infrastructure.

The Indian Ocean was another Atlantic annex. It was a platform of enterprise and home to India's impressive collection of port cities (Arvind Palat, 1991). These ports played the role of entrepots across this great expanse of water, and their commerce sustained the rise of opulent merchant classes. Indian merchants imported gold and slaves from East Africa, horses from Persia, and porcelain and silk from China. The vast lands surrounding the Indian Ocean fell under no single authority. The East Indies and parts of South East Asia hosted a dense network of settlements and many pivotal ports involved in intensive long distance trade. Here the Portuguese seaborne empire grafted itself on to several port cities through superior naval firepower (Boxer, 1969). To support these maritime enterprises, a land based infrastructure had to be created. In Portugal's case, the firepower of its navy equalled or exceeded investment in land based defences.

PORTS AS ENTREPOTS AND FORTS

The coincidence of a capital city and a port city usually acted as a powerful stimulus to generate additional expansion and growth. Amsterdam, Constantinople, Lisbon and London for centuries combined these important attributes, consolidating their positions as leaders of their national urban hierarchies and cultural melting pots.

Historically, port cities maintained robust military and naval installations to defend themselves and their realms, like the substantial and diverse military and naval complexes around the Bay of Cadiz and Southampton. Such installations comprised many customised buildings and docks: barracks, arsenals, graving docks and shipbuilding and repair facilities. To build these expensive features, platoons of skilled personnel had to be contracted to provide requisite expertise; this involved the hiring of cartographers, engineers, architects and skilled craftspeople. Carpenters, caulkers, turners, architects, engineers, sail makers, cartographers, coopers and joiners were some of the diverse range of professions listed by chroniclers as working at Lisbon during the sixteenth century (Feist Hirst, 1967). Cadiz, like its mirror port city Havana, was a metropole and *plaza fuerte* (stronghold). Its defences were gargantuan, complicated, and extremely expensive (see Figure 2.1). In 1727, military and secular civic interests combined to establish an agency, known as *La Real*

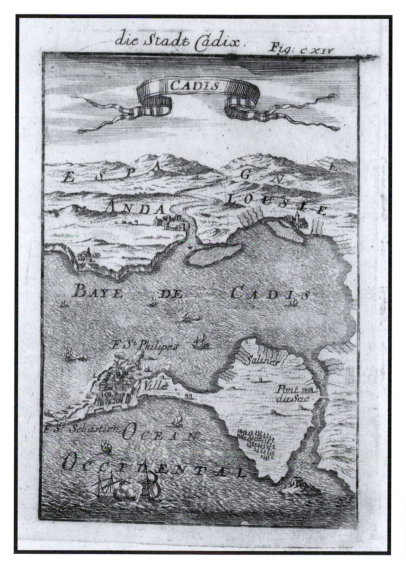

Figure 2.1 The city of Cadis (Cadiz) by Alain Manesson Mallet, 1686 (source: image courtesy of www. RareMaps.com, Barry Lawrence Ruderman Antique Maps).

Junta de Fortificaciones, to physically develop the city (Ruiz Nieto-Guerrero, 1999). For more than a century, it coordinated urban expansion. It did so without ever devising a city-wide plan; instead it melded defensive requirements with urban growth by setting up a series of *cordones*, or lines of expansion. So block by block (*manzanas*), like a chequerboard, the city grew within its ever imposing military cocoon of defences.

At a much larger scale, the building of the Spanish *Carrera de Indias* required enormously expensive fortification of an entire series of metropoles on both sides of the Atlantic and ports such as Cadiz, Cartagena de Indias and Havana. Arsenals, naval dockyards, barracks, and biscuit making, gunpowder and sail manufactories were all features of these newly important port cities (Ruiz Nieto-Guerrero, 1999). In sum the Spanish *Carrera* denoted both a hierarchy and network of ports, a surface of seaways and a convoy system that connected the Spanish metropole to a series of American hubs at Havana, Veracruz and Cartagena de Indias. Throughput of raw materials, in today's jargon, for these and other facilities entailed a national supply-chain effort (Goodman, 1997). It also involved the recruitment and movement of thousands of seamen, sailors, specialised naval craftspeople such as caulkers from other ports to Cadiz, for instance, and on from there to overseas duties. The net outcome, as far as home ports were concerned, was to deplete local and regional maritime manpower for inter-port tramping trades and fishing expeditions (Goodman, 1997). Many of these movements were voluntary; in times of crises, seamen were cashiered or conscripted into service by the military authorities.

But port cities during the 'First Imperial Age' were far more than national capitals or military bases. Perhaps most importantly, they coordinated the throughput of goods and merchandise and all of the trade and exchange associated with such activities. In short, 'entrepot' is a key descriptor of a major port whose lifeblood is marine commerce, and a key dynamic in the shaping of ports' urban form. As in the wool trade out of Basque Bilbao during the sixteenth century, for example, goods had to be assembled, stored, packed, housed, processed and exported (Phillips and Phillips, 1997). Some states erected a complex edifice of institutions to regulate all of these activities, including exchanges, consulates and consuls, customs, licensing procedures for merchants, merchant 'factories', maritime education facilities, missionary schools and seminaries (Jesuits at Cadiz). They also promoted added value facilities like sugar milling or tobacco drying, all of which have led to different built forms, many of which resemble each other around the world in form and function, if not in style, especially within European imperial domains, as between Cadiz and Havana. Trading companies further expanded these connections.

REGULATING TRADE: FREE MARKETS, MONOPOLIES, AND THE PORTUGUESE *FEITORIA*

Monopoly was commonplace in the organisation of European commerce and was for centuries to remain a widely accepted way of handling valuable long distance trades (Scammell, 1992: 97). In Spain a number of key institutions were founded at different times during the sixteenth century to deliver the monopoly, most located at the metropole and providing employment for many people: *La Casa de Contratación* (crudely, House of Trade), *El Consulado* (the consulate) and *La Aduana* (the customs). The functions discharged by these institutions waxed and waned over the centuries. *La Casa de Contratación*, for example, managed mapmaking, seafarer education, postal services and the convoy, as well as victualling. The role of the customs is self-explanatory and the consulate was an early state–private partnership designed to be a forum where merchants could settle their disputes. These institutions were replicated at several New World exclusive hubs, such as at Havana, Cartagena de Indias and Veracruz, and they served Spain well during the period of the monopoly.

In Portugal, an institution named *A Casa da India* managed a monopoly on all eastern commerce, its model based, to a large degree, on the Venetian control, distribution and sale of Asian spices in Europe. The Portuguese achieved a monopoly on spices for a short time, even without capturing the principal sources of supply. Spices were brought to Lisbon on licensed ships; there, much of their cargo was then redirected to Antwerp, where in turn it was redistributed throughout Europe. Even though this monopoly was in shreds in the latter half of the seventeenth century, it made some Portuguese merchants wealthy enough to build themselves elaborate houses or engage in philanthropic grants to the convents and monasteries of Goa.

The Dutch and English developed similar trading control instruments for the Indian Ocean. Joint stock companies held the monopolies, making the investments and taking on all the risk. Founded in 1602, the Dutch *Vereenigede Oost-Indische Compagnie* (VOC) found early success. The range of its activities was indeed considerable: it built its own ships and could declare war, occupy territories and make commercial treaties. Headquartered at Amsterdam, it helped this port city retain its rank as northern Europe's largest port city. It was conceived by its founders – the States General – as a vehicle for enriching the Low Countries, breaking the commercial power of Portugal, dividing the commercial interest of the then united Iberian crowns and drawing off Iberia's land armies from this fledging state. In its early form, it achieved most of these objectives. Meanwhile, it found a serious rival and constant threat in the British East India Company, whose emergence and consolidation coincided with England's materialisation as a leading global sea power.

Spain itself founded a series of state or royal trading companies (Shakespeare, 1989) as part of its monopoly policy. Some promoted overseas trading and ensured that bullion, goods and merchandise coming in from the New World came in Spanish built and registered vessels. Most were formed during the eighteenth century, including the *Compañía de Honduras* (1714), *de Galicia* (1734), *de La Habana, de Barcelona* (1755) and *de Filipinas* (1785). Beside goods, their ships carried many migrants on their transatlantic crossings. Other companies, established on the peninsula, offered much-needed employment and ensured that Spain's overseas possessions were exclusively supplied with goods from Spain. Among the most famous of these were *La Real Compañía de Comercio y Fábricas de Zaragoza*, founded in 1746, bankrupt in 1774, and *La Real Compañía de San Fernando de Sevilla* (1747), bankrupt in the early 1770s. Their mission was to invigorate Spanish textile production for the peninsula and abroad. Monopolies were also promoted by the Spanish crown on salt, tobacco, shipbuilding, joint stock companies and manufacture of goods for colonists abroad.

So arose the Portuguese *feitorias* in the Old and the New World, walled settlements attached to existing ports in the East Indies, where small communities of Portuguese merchants, administrators, military personnel and priests resided. Portuguese merchants met and discussed trading opportunities under the eyes of the *feitor*, a delegate appointed by the crown to oversee and arbitrate merchant activities. Here the crown set prices as the holder of the monopoly and also confirmed those who could or could not trade. The Portuguese constructed nearly fifty of these forts in strategic locations around the Indian Ocean, including at Goa, Macau, Hormuz and Ternate. These Indian Ocean *feitorias* also traded in circuits, as between Goa and Macau and on to Nagasaki. Of these, Goa was the principal hub; from here, companies dispatched merchandise, especially porcelain and spices, to Lisbon's *Casa da India*. Portugal's monopoly was permissive, relying more on free enterprise as its population was too small and its national economy remained grossly underdeveloped. Spain's was more prescribed; it depended on actors and agencies usually paid and funded by the state.

Demonstrating the increasing propinquity of commercial and political ties with the Portuguese, the English established at least three 'factories' in late sixteenth/early seventeenth century Portugal, sited, respectively, at Viana do Castelo, Oporto and Lisbon. The 'factory' at Oporto emerged as the largest and the most lavish and opulent, and it remains active to this day (see Figure 2.2). The degree of English involvement in the affairs of these facilities was substantial, although each 'factory' maintained a considerable degree of autonomy (Delaforce, 1990). The consul was elected by the members of each 'factory'; the crown then ratified their choice.

In turn, the Portuguese later maintained a network of consulates throughout Europe. These kinds of Consulates were different to 'factories' or *feitorias* and also different to the *Consulados* (which were a kind of expatriate merchant club) of Spain. Often headed by one locally elected individual but sanctioned by a government and known as a consul, they were often sited at the offices of a leading merchant. In a sense, consuls were commercial spies constantly reporting about trade, trading and political conditions to the government which appointed them, as was the case with the Portuguese consul at Cork, who was a successful English merchant (Gonçalves Horta, 2008). They were a feature of European and American nineteenth century port cities.

The Americans (Kennedy, 1990), English and Dutch (Tamse, 1981) all established so-called consulates in key foreland hubs. 'English factories' appeared at many Iberian ports during the sixteenth through to the seventeenth century such as Oporto or Cadiz. Merchants often founded and financed a facility called an 'Exchange' in England and Ireland (see Figure 2.3). The 'Factory' or 'Exchange' was a dealers' domain where all of the leading movers and shakers of the city could meet and transact their business (O'Flanagan, 2005). Commercial 'intelligence' was sometimes shared, sometimes kept secret (Müller, 2004). Ideas about built form spread along these lines.

Figure 2.2 English factory at Oporto (Portugal), 1790 (source: Professor João Sarmento, Guimaraes).

Nations which traded with Spain also maintained a series of 'factories'/consulates on Spanish territory, the largest of which was located at Cadiz. Here paradox ruled, probably as a result of the constantly strained relations between Spain and England (who continued to engage in trade even during periods of hostilities). Merchants forged many trading alliances here, and so-called trading houses (*casas*) were established between different merchant families. Insurance agents, brokers, lawyers and *notarios* (solicitors) must have been among the many actors who frequented these facilities. Resident English and Scottish merchants never made up more than 5 per cent of the total membership, yet it was always from their ranks that a consul was elected. Irish merchants made up the vast body of this fraternity (O'Flanagan, 2008). In addition, local authorities encouraged Irish merchants to apply for licences (*matrículas del mar*) to trade with the New World. But in order to do so, these merchants were advised to apply for Spanish citizenship. This was a convoluted process whereby applicants had to provide detailed bone fides

Figure 2.3 Exchange at Cork (Ireland), 1708–1709 (source: Cork University Press).

concerning their character and religious background, no easy task for Irish migrants at such a distance from home, and who because of cultural, political and religious persecution in Ireland were not allowed to trade directly out of their own country.

SPECIFIC ORDINANCES/POLICIES OF EXCLUSION: MONOPOLIES AND THE CREATION OF PREFERRED HUBS

Factories and consulates were but one element in the relatively new and still emergent Spanish political economy. This political economy was to have immense economic and spatial implications for the 'First Imperial Age' of globalisation. Undoubtedly, some of its leading ingredients, like the *feitorias*, were borrowed from existing Portuguese templates. At its core were concepts of exclusion, including monopolies. The imposition of the monopoly quickly reordered Spain's urban network and port network so that only one port, Seville, was allowed to trade with New World ports; transport of goods and flows of people on the peninsula were deflected accordingly. We can categorise this port as a metropole which enjoyed exclusive and sole commercial trading rights with New World ports. Seville's foreland embraced the so-called *Carrera de Indias* and its New World hierarchy of ports and regions, simultaneously acting as a port network, transport system and surface of contacts. The *Carrera* was by no means an amorphous expanse of ocean, but was an oceanic thoroughfare for shipping traffic in fleets (after 1556) across the Atlantic to the New World. It constituted a set of clearly recognisable navigation routes, protected by Spanish naval escorts and harried and threatened by the navies and privateers of other states.

Spain designated other hubs on the other side of the Atlantic as exclusive ports, including Havana, Veracruz and Cartagena de Indias. New World ports belonging to Spain were forbidden to trade directly with each other, obliging them to trade only with these metropoles. These ordinances skewed urban and port evolution in both the New World and the Old. One part of this legacy was the long delayed emergence of trading ports on the River Plate at Buenos Aires and its ports (O'Flanagan, 2008). It then signalled the ascendancy of the Atlantic over the Mediterranean, which was to endure for at least three centuries, and ushered in a phase of commercial and physical stagnation at such places as Barcelona, Malaga and Valencia. Only when they were lifted in the late eighteenth century did Mediterranean ports challenge the primacy of their Atlantic counterparts.

MERCHANT FAMILY NETWORK: EXAMPLES FROM AMSTERDAM AND CADIZ

One migratory group had a vital role in the widening and strengthening of Amsterdam's commercial networks: families of Sephardic Jews, involuntary migrants who arrived during the sixteenth century after they had been expelled from Portugal (Boswell *et al.*, 1991). The Portuguese had originally chosen Antwerp as their northern export redistribution centre, and Antwerp's decline from the middle of the sixteenth century became Amsterdam's opportunity. The Sephardic Jews opened up new routes in and out of Amsterdam, and their efforts, expertise and pre-existing networks allowed this port to broaden merchandise throughput range. They helped grease the wheels of trade by introducing new financial products and developed a range of new social networks (Antunes, 2005).

Similarly, networks of Irish merchants strengthened commerce in Cadiz, Spain (O'Flanagan and Walton, 2004). Cadiz acted as Spain's exclusive metropole for most of the eighteenth century and it was to this city that a significant number of Irish people voluntarily migrated to take advantage of its breathtaking commercial opportunities. Most came from the extreme south of Ireland, many more from Irish communities in France, and smaller numbers from the Low Countries and England. Settling in Cadiz, many made commercial and marriage ties with resident Spanish merchant families. They extended their networks to the New World by sending their children on business missions, several of whom settled at ports such as Santa Cruz de Tenerife, Havana and Veracruz (Guimerá Ravina, 1985). They also amplified Cadiz's trading networks by linking them to their existing networks, especially in France, and opened up new ones in Ireland and possibly in Anglo-America.

The Irish were, of course, one of several highly successful national groups who availed themselves of this port's metropole designation; others included French, Flemish and Italian residents. Each of these national groups carried in its wake considerable retinues of business assistants, translators and servants. Social gradations amongst the merchants, whether native or newcomer, were configured in terms of the number of employees, their ethnic origins and the offices of their servants. The Italians came first, during the sixteenth century, the French followed later, in the seventeenth century and the Irish came in the first quarter of the eighteenth century.

WEALTHY MERCHANTS AND URBAN FORM: PRIVATE CHOICES AND PUBLIC POLICY IN CADIZ

Migration to, and through, port cities was often triggered by the extra-ordinary wealth of many of their merchants and some of their civic institutions (Checkland and Checkland, 1984). Merchant houses were often sumptuously decorated and highly skilled artisans were often imported to deliver complex plasterwork, marble-work or detailed work in wood. At Cadiz, Spain, for instance, it was commonplace to import Italians to accomplish such tasks, and because of the amount of work available at that metropole many artisans settled there permanently. Plentiful wealth prompted many merchants to engage in all sorts of acts of philanthropy, such as the building and decorating of churches, convents and hospitals, all of which often necessitated the involvement of skilled artisans. The magnificent *Hospital de Mujeres*, erected in 1749 at Cadiz, is such an example. At the port of Waterford in Ireland, philanthropy emanating from an Irish merchant family at Cadiz was invested in the erection of a church (O'Flanagan and Walton, 2004).

Generous philanthropists allowed many religious orders to erect seminaries, churches and schools as well. Indeed, prominent among voluntary migrants were Catholic missionaries from Spain and Portugal during the sixteenth and seventeenth centuries, who established themselves throughout Ibero-America, especially in port cities associated with Iberian colonial endeavours. Highly educated Jesuits described, often in minute detail, exotic and unimagined worlds for readers back in Europe, and some, like Bento de Göes, even crossed into western China (Bernard, 1934). Faith-based institutions promoted the construction of missionary schools and seminaries, establishing worldwide networks such as those of the Presentation Sisters (see Figure 2.4).

The construction of new, often upmarket, merchant districts within, or close to, the core areas of port cities is characteristic of many Atlantic European port cities, for example at Cadiz, La Plaza de San Antonio, and at Santander, La Puebla Nueva, on the Iberian peninsula, at Nantes in France and at Cork in Ireland. Many of these new districts were deliberately planned for wealthy resident foreign and native merchants, for their families and businesses. The *Cantones* at Corunna and the Baixa at Oporto were outstanding and emblematic merchant quarters. Planned much earlier were the Barrio de San Vicente at Seville and the Barrio Alto at Lisbon (O'Flanagan, 2008).

VOLUNTARY MIGRATION: PERSPECTIVES FROM CADIZ AND CORK

A raft of expertises and a consummate variety of craftspeople were drawn in to design and erect a vast array of philanthropically supported religious and secular buildings representing the immense wealth of some of these leading movers and shakers. Thus prosperity during the latter part of the eighteenth century was attended by waves of new migrants arriving to seek their fortunes at many centres. Their arrivals were etched in local urban censuses. At least 60 per cent of the 1773 population of Cadiz were born outside this metropole; the vast majority of these in-migrants were unskilled (O'Flanagan, 2008).

Temporary migration also shaped many ports. Particular crafts and the guilds associated with migrants occupied specific streets or districts in centres such as Seville or Lisbon. Triana at Seville, for example, was a district occupied almost exclusively by 'sea-people'. But demand swiftly overtook supply, radically inflating rentals and triggering a trend towards multi-family residence. In 1753, figures from a national census for the prosperous Spanish port city of Santander confirm that almost two-thirds of the housing stock comprised single-family residences (Autoridad Portuaria, 1998) and one-third were rentals. These merchant houses were known as *Casas-Tiendas* or 'house-stores', with the bottom floor of three storeys being a dedicated work-place and warehouse (Maruri Villanueva, 1985), and residences on the upper floors. The corresponding figures for 1829 were precisely the reverse; two-thirds were multi-family units known as *cuartos*. Many of the more affluent merchants had, by then, moved out of La Puebla Vieja and settled in La Nueva Población. These transformations also heralded the emergence of a robust *rentier* fraction.

At Cadiz, where space was even more at a premium, a privately and solely occupied family residence was a critical emblem of social distinction. Here,

Figure 2.4 Foundation dates and global distribution of Presentation Sisters, a religious order, 1775 (source: Cork University Press).

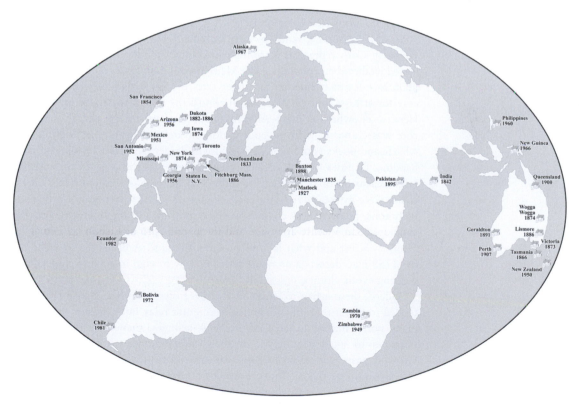

some of the leading foreign merchants lived in elaborate residences called *Casas Palacios*; many of these have survived down to our day, such as *Casa de las Cuatro Torres*, built by a Syrian resident merchant between 1736 and 1745. At the other end of the social scale, migrant workers lived in buildings that contained households of up to twenty males (females were seldom recorded in official census documents). This was the case at No. 49 on *Calle Nueva*, where some twenty-three recently arrived Maltese immigrants resided. Even today, some of these packed households are in evidence at Cadiz's old core. Merchants at Santander, as in most other Atlantic European port cities, had relatively free rein to develop new districts. They invested themselves and convinced local civic bodies on which they also sat to embark on schemes of reclamation and development. Conditions at Spain's metropole Cadiz were different. Here strategic defensive considerations were supreme and more complex coalitions were formed to deliver change.

Other Atlantic port cities, like Nantes, experienced impressive makeovers, as did smaller but no less cosmopolitan port cities such as Cork in Ireland (O'Flanagan, 2005). Here, merchant enterprise rather than civic initiative was responsible for the remaking of this critical provisions-exporting port city. This was a period when enormous numbers of new residents made Cork their home. Over 20,000 people were reported to migrate there temporarily to participate in all the trades involved with the provisions preparation, their packing, warehousing and export overseas. Data from contemporary sources confirm that new central residential opportunities were initially sought by many of the city's Protestant elite trading and artisan fractions (see Figure 2.5).

In a 1759 survey, made by cartographer John Rocque (see Figure 2.6), Georgian Cork represents a triumph of commerce over a cluttered and congested medieval morphology. 'The Main Street' running north to south – built upon a series of islands on an upper river estuary – had formed the urban core for at least four centuries, until almost the end of the sixteenth century. Here, as elsewhere in many Atlantic European port settlements, its medieval core was cramped, often in poor condition and unhygienic. In addition, its wharfs and docks could no longer deal with larger merchant vessels and new handling facilities were developed. Hence, there was the urgency of reclamation, expansion or rebuilding. As individual merchants reclaimed this urban centre piece by piece during the early eighteenth century, Georgian Cork gradually took shape. It was characterised by neat lines of three and four storey solid residences and warehouses along its principal thoroughfares, such as George's Street and what is now the Grand Parade. A brilliant cartouche on the 1759 map depicts a quayside populated by foreign merchants and sailors wearing exotic clothes.

Indeed, these urban reclamation projects fostered further change. We have tended to forget that, besides acting as migrant relay hubs, seismic growth at many port cities made them act like vast sponges, sucking in thousands of migrants to avail themselves of their lifestyle and work opportunities. Growing passenger traffic later on also demanded a discrete range of onshore facilities such as ticket offices, hotels and boarding houses, translators and accountants.

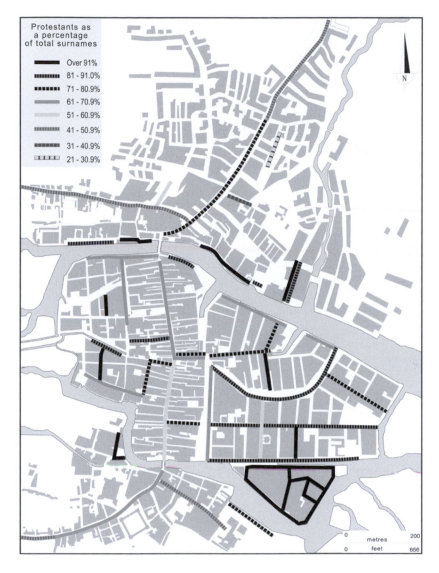

Figure 2.5 Protestants as a percentage of total surnames, Cork (Ireland), 1787 (source: Cork University Press).

INVOLUNTARY MIGRATION

But much migration through ports prior to the early nineteenth century was involuntary. Huge numbers of slaves were moved from Africa to the Caribbean and Ibero-America. In the sixteenth century and beyond, the Portuguese held what was known as the *Asiento*. This was a Spanish crown contract awarded to Portugal in 1538 to transport slaves to the Caribbean and Brazil from West Africa. On their Atlantic journey, few slaves moved through the ports of Europe but were transferred from a complex of holding areas and *feitorias* on the coast of Senegambia, such as those of São Tomé, Axim (1515) and Elmina (1482) in modern Ghana, directly to the mines and sugar plantations of Ibero-America and the Caribbean (Kamen, 2003). Nonetheless, contemporary descriptions of some major cities, such as Seville and Lisbon, note

Figure 2.6 John Rocque, a survey of the city and suburbs of Cork, 1759 (source: Cork University Press).

that at least one-fifth of their population were of slave origins during the late sixteenth century (Thomas, 2004). Slaves worked largely as domestics and over time gained their place as free members of society, often travelling as servants to the New World with their former masters. They might well have performed jobs left empty by the many urban residents who had already left for the New World.

Old World famine migrants were another involuntary group on the move to and through port cities; for instance, during the nineteenth century, enormous numbers of people fled famine in Ireland for North America and Australia. Many small ports around the coast of Ireland developed rudimentary infrastructures to accommodate this apparently ceaseless flow of humanity. The arrival of the railway in 1862 made Queenstown (now Cobh) in County Cork, Ireland, a leading port for famine migrants heading overseas. This once-small anteport developed an impressive portfolio of facilities to cater for this mass migration (see Figure 2.7). Hotels, boarding houses, public houses, ticket offices and tea houses all sprang up along and behind the waterfront. At the same time, Dublin and Kingstown (now Dún Laoghaire), acted as Ireland's leading ports of departure for migrants to the United Kingdom.

Older currents of involuntary migrants had left Ireland for the Caribbean. Many refugees had departed as indentured labourers (to their English sugar masters), such as the *Redlegs* of Barbados, fleeing from the turmoil around

Cromwell's landing and intervention during the mid-seventeenth century. Many of these people were transported from the port town of Cork in Ireland. They settled on some of England's main Caribbean sugar islands, such as Barbados, Jamaica and Montserrat.

Figure 2.7 Waterfront at Cobh (Ireland) (source: J. Pollock, used through Creative Commons License).

PORTS AND DISEASES

If these ceaseless waves of migrants, both voluntary and involuntary, made prominent port cities into cultural melting pots, they also made them hubs for the diffusion of diseases. Mass movements of people accelerated the spread of plagues and other diseases during the first era of globalisation. Portugal and Spain, for instance, were afflicted during the last decade of the sixteenth century by plagues. The 'Atlantic' plague (1596–1602), so called because of its perceived origin at Santander, spread to Seville, where popular belief ascribes to it a harvest of almost 10 per cent of contemporary Castile's population and the label of a contributory factor towards the decline of that immense region. Soon afterwards, the 'Great Plague of Seville' (1646–1652) was the final chapter in a series of economic and public health reverses recorded there during the first half of the seventeenth century.

Later, as sailors and poor migrants came to be feared as public health hazards, some states erected a new infrastructure of surveillance (including police, fever hospitals and quarantine stations) on the peripheries of many major ports. Port cities such as Pennsylvania and Seville were constantly the targets of infectious diseases such as typhoid and yellow fever. It is reported that one-tenth of Pennsylvania's population died during a severe epidemic in 1793. This jolted the city's elites to found a Board of Health some few years afterwards.

CONCLUSION

Port cities represent a very early form of urbanism and have been a constant feature on nearly all continents. Some have been national capitals or military bases, while many more have served as entrepots, or relay centres for merchandise, voluntary and involuntary migrants, and ideas of all kinds. The technologies to move all of these, plus diseases and fears of disease, ideas and migrants themselves, have in turn helped to define the morphology of many port settlements. More broadly, specific political economies and financial instruments for controlling trade, particularly the monopoly, have shaped both port networks and urban form, setting the stage for other actors to make a mark.

Despite the variety in the histories, connectedness and morphologies of particular sites, many functions of port cities have remained constant over the centuries, and since the 'First Imperial Age' they have remained vital actors in globalised transportation networks that cover the planet (Broeze, 1995).

ACKNOWLEDGEMENTS

I am happy to acknowledge the work of Helen Bradley, GIS Officer, and Michael Murphy, Cartographer, Department of Geography, University College, Cork. Their contributions to illustration preparation have been sterling.
Thanks are due to my colleague, Professor João Sarmento for figure 2.2.

3 CHINA-TOWNS AND CONTAINER TERMINALS

Shipping networks and urban patterns in port cities in global and local perspective, 1880–1980

LARS AMENDA

In the age of sail, ports represented human control of nature and naval power in general. The sites and sights of the waterfront attracted many tourists, who included them on their itineraries from the advent of modernity (Corbin, 1994). Both vessels and sailors were literal links with regions and countries abroad and fired the imagination of many visitors (as well as locals). The waterfront represented a 'contact zone' (Pratt, 1991) where the flows of trade and the networks of migrants concentrated in urban space. In fact, 'otherness', in people and urban form alike, became the very essence of the docklands of major port cities in popular views and later representations in mass culture. The history of port cities was a very visual history; or, in other words, the many foreign seafarers and seagoing vessels entering the ports embodied global connections and made them comprehensible.

The history of port cities, both in the 'western' world and in the global South, demonstrates that the process of globalisation was not limited to only one direction. While colonial power heavily relied on naval power to maintain control in faraway places, ships also brought many colonised people to the maritime hearts of European empires in the age of imperialism. The metaphor of the 'gateway' – which port cities such as Southampton or Hamburg in the early twentieth century used to describe themselves – perfectly symbolised the place of port cities in the process of globalisation. It was certainly no accident that gates of migration and mobility control were erected in these 'gateways to the world', demarcating social and 'racial' inclusion and exclusion.

THE ADVENT OF STEAM AND THE RISE OF CHINESE WORKERS

In the course of the nineteenth century, the conversion from sailing to steam vessels significantly changed the maritime world. Steamships became increasingly competitive with sailing vessels between the 1840s and 1880s, and the 'steamer' changed the structure of shipping companies, maritime labour and seaports. These changes accelerated globalisation: regular shipping lines were now possible that were both faster and cheaper (see in general Bayly, 2004; Hopkins, 2002; Osterhammel and Petersson, 2003).

Steamships enhanced global entanglements and migrations from the end of the nineteenth century by rendering passages cheaper, faster and more reliable. Tickets were cheaper than on sailing vessels, so more people travelled to new destinations. Hence, steamships simplified international migration, as we can see in the large numbers of Europeans who emigrated to the New World, particularly in the three decades prior to the First World War (Nugent, 1992). For European powers, regular shipping was essential to keeping up contact with overseas colonies and supplying them with goods and people. Despite the concentration of maritime traffic in western Europe – most of the greatest ports around 1900 were situated in Europe, like London, Liverpool and Hamburg – a number of global hubs formed elsewhere in the course of the nineteenth century.

Privately run shipping companies thus gained major importance and high status in the age of imperialism; they represented the civil aspect of colonialism and 'world policy'. British companies like Alfred Holt's Blue Funnel Line from Liverpool (Hyde, 1957), the Cunard Line from Southampton, the North German Lloyd from Bremen and the Hamburg-Amerikanische Packetfahrt-Actien-Gesellschaft (Hapag) or, for short, Hamburg-America Line, for example, elevated themselves into big business and global players as well as major local actors.

Trade and migration were two major economic fields that benefited shipping companies and ports around the world alike. A ranking list of world ports would indicate the economic and industrial rise of non-European regions and countries. For example, the port of New York City served as the United States' central gateway for incoming immigrants on the East Coast; the migration control station on Ellis Island, just next to the Statue of Liberty, opened in 1892 to select welcome newcomers from the unwanted using criteria of health and hygienics. The city became one of the most frequented prior to the First World War (Broodbank, 1921; Wiedenfeld, 1903); its dynamic growth fuelled the ascent of the United States and several of its cities that are today metropolises.

Shipping not only fuelled industrialisation and globalisation but was itself industrialised and globalised at the same time. The steamships themselves turned some maritime labour into industrial work: stokers and trimmers, dubbed the 'black gang', had to feed ships' boilers with huge amounts of coal (see Figure 3.1). So the new technology of steam vessels opened up job opportunities for 'coloured seamen'; major European shipping lines sought to hire Chinese seamen in the 1890s as stokers and trimmers because they could pay them less, undercutting the labour movement. Their numbers reached several thousand in western European countries (Küttner, 2000; Tabili, 1994). The Blue Funnel Line and the North German Lloyd, for example, started to sign on Chinese stokers in the 1890s in order to reduce their personnel costs.

For their part, the Chinese seamen mostly originated from Siyi, the surrounding districts of Guangzhou (Canton) in the Pearl River Delta, where the majority of Chinese migrants in the United States came from too. The mostly very young men gathered in Hong Kong, looking for temporary jobs on European vessels, and they constituted a considerable pool of around 120,000 to 150,000 seamen in the early twentieth century (Chan, 1991; Chesnaux, 1968).

Figure 3.1 The global network of the shipping lines of the Hapag/Hamburg-America Line, 1914 (source: Himer, 1927: 154).

A massive rise in commercial traffic to and from Hong Kong had transformed that port into a global hub under British rule. As the central emigration port for the Chinese, it saw nearly 5 million people pass through in the period from the middle of the nineteenth century to the First World War (Skeldon, 1994). But although they meant to leave China, they did not necessarily seek employment or residence in Europe. Most Chinese immigrants came to Europe by accident, stranded like other sailors in the dock areas of one of the major port cities. Indeed, the vast majority of Chinese migrants aimed to go from China to the United States or Australia. Given the exclusion of Chinese migrants in both of those countries, the Chinese had to find their ways illegally (Ngai, 2005). Steamships offered Chinese crews in European shipping manifold possibilities to smuggle people, with numerous places to hide stowaways.

The patterns of illegal migration elucidate how maritime and migration networks overlapped and remind us of the major importance of shipping for migration in general.

CHINATOWN AT THE WATERFRONT

Because of their employment on European steamships, Chinese seamen frequented the dock areas of the major west European port cities in significant numbers from the late nineteenth century. 'Sailortown', the docklands of major ports, constituted a very particular urban space. Here at the waterfront, many foreign seamen and passengers gathered and created a markedly international atmosphere.

Even in the age of steam, it could take several weeks to stevedore ships with piece goods that might have already been stored for many weeks in waterfront warehouses since the exact dates of ship arrivals were often simply not known. Many workers were needed to load and unload big vessels, and the demand for labour could shift substantially from day to day. So seamen from all over the world lived at the docklands for anything from several days up to one or two weeks until they sailed to another destination. People with different ethnic backgrounds and native languages turned the waterfront into a local representation of the whole world (Hugill, 1967; Rudolph, 1979; Burton, 2001; Mitchell, 1917), and they made the area cosmopolitan.

Chinese workers now settled in these areas. In London, for example, a small 'Chinatown' (or 'Chinaport', as the Chinese called it) emerged in the East End in the Limehouse district next to the West India Docks (Seed, 2006). Cantonese seamen opened boarding houses, shops and restaurants, and made a livelihood out of serving their fellow countrymen temporarily staying there (Benton and Gomez, 2008). Their numbers were quite limited: only a few hundred migrants and Chinese seamen on shore leave set up this Chinese community.

The First World War significantly changed the role of Chinese seamen in European shipping, and Chinatowns became more visible features of various ports. Many Chinese seamen replaced British sailors who were called up (Halpern, 1994). In the 1920s, Chinese migrants expanded their global networks in Europe, visible in 'Chinese quarters' in continental European port cities such as Rotterdam, Amsterdam and Hamburg (Amenda, 2006) (see Figure 3.2). Former Chinese seamen opened boarding houses, restaurants and shops in Rotterdam's Katendrecht, a traditional dock area located at the very waterfront, and were the pioneers of the miniature Chinatowns there. A string of Chinese seamen left English ports for Germany, and purchased shops and restaurants in Hamburg's St Pauli district, also right on the waterfront. Just like many visitors from abroad, they had heard of the very low prices for foreigners due to inflation and decided to come to Germany to benefit from them economically (Feldman, 1993). The Chinese communities concentrated in a few streets located at the very waterfront (as in Rotterdam) or its vicinity. Former Chinese seamen stuck to the port because they realised the economic opportunities in running their own little businesses, and the small 'Chinatowns' also served as a shelter against discrimination.

These 'Chinese quarters' indicated the global scope of both shipping and Chinese migration. Along regular shipping lines, seamen established networks between many different ports, including many translocal contacts from docklands to docklands. Chinese seamen and migrants were entrepreneurs who communicated and shared their knowledge about economic opportunities. Both communication and personal networks thus helped Chinese migrants to explore new niches that were still attached to the maritime world. Chinese communities in European port cities in turn became social networks of Chinese migrants, and they played a role in keeping those networks up.

Seafarers also played a crucial role in forging another global network during the 1920s, one of Communists. In China, both the labour movement and the Communist Party were gaining importance in this period. Chinese

Figure 3.2 Press coverage on the Chinese community in Rotterdam's Katendrecht district, 1922 (source: *In de Rotterdamsche China-Town*, 1922).

seamen were certainly politicised by the exploitation they suffered in European shipping. Many were influenced by national and anticolonialist thought, and some were strong followers of Sun Yat-sen, the first president of the Chinese Republic in 1912 and himself 'a pure product of maritime China' (Bergère, 1998: 3). The Comintern took on the sailors' cause in the 1920s, sending Chinese communists to Europe to organise them (Thornton, 1969). One of them was Liao Chengzi, who lived between 1928 and 1932 in several west European port cities, including Rotterdam, Antwerp and Hamburg (Zhuwei, 1998; Radtke, 1990). The communist-run International of Seamen and Harbour Workers (ISH) established a worldwide system of International Seamen's Clubs, or Interclubs, in the major port cities of New York, San Francisco, London, Liverpool, Rotterdam, Amsterdam, Hamburg, Bremen, Copenhagen, Marseilles, Wladiwostok, Leningrad and still others. Chinese seamen could gather in the clubs, read books, newspapers and communist leaflets in Chinese, and learn how radical politics analysed their situation. Only a minority of Chinese seamen adopted communist ideas, but the global dispersion of the Interclubs is one aspect of the maritime networks of Chinese seamen and illustrates their truly global scope (see Figure 3.3).

Figure 3.3 Communist pamphlet in Chinese, produced in Hamburg, 1932 (source: Political Archives of the Foreign Ministry, Berlin, PA/AA, R 85736).

Like the First World War, the Second World War had a great impact on shipping and the situation of Chinese seamen. In Britain, roughly 20,000 Chinese seamen worked in shipping in the early years of the war, sailing on the so-called Liberty Ships on the Atlantic and maintaining war supplies. The Ministry of Wartime Transport faced severe problems with the Chinese, who reacted to discriminatory, unequal pay by leaving (Lane, 1990; Whittingham-Jones, 1944). About 20 per cent of all Chinese crews on these ships deserted in New York City, most of them disappearing without a trace in Manhattan's Chinatown. It was only a walk from the piers in Manhattan or Brooklyn to Chinatown and its ethnic infrastructure (Wong, 1982). Even during wartime, the Chinese maintained their networks. However, between the ravages of aerial warfare and the horrors of Nazi persecution, the war had a deep impact on Chinese communities in Europe.

Then, in the early post-war period, the small Chinatowns mostly vanished. A new technological change, this time the conversion from steamships to container vessels, closed the chapter of the maritime Chinese communities at the European waterfront.

CONTAINERISATION AND ITS IMPACT ON PORT CITIES

With the advent of containerisation in the 1960s, shipping suddenly required fewer workers. Vibrant dockland areas, including Chinatowns, became obsolete almost overnight. Just as the reliability and speed of steamships had made sailing vessels irrelevant, the standardisation of containers and their vessels speeded up work: loading and unloading, and the once unwieldy move between sea and land, were tasks now smoothly performed by machines.

Since time immemorial people have transported goods in boxes and crates to protect them on the way and to simplify the loading process. Forerunners of the idea of transporting goods in special and more spacious containers date to the mid-nineteenth century. Nevertheless, it remained time-consuming and expensive to move boxes between sea and land transport until the mid-twentieth century, particularly in the bottlenecks of seaports, with their considerable congestion and frequent delays. In the 1950s, a new innovative technology was introduced that would change shipping and transportation dramatically during the following decades: the shipping container revolutionised trans-shipment and had a deep impact on the urban pattern of port cities (Broeze, 2002; Woods, 1972).

The standardised container was primarily the invention of the American trucker Malcom McLean (1913–2001) (Levinson, 2006), who envisioned that making the containers a uniform size would make it easier to move them between ports and ships. In the mid-1950s, to carry his containers, he acquired two old oil tankers, demobilised by the US Navy after the Second World War, and converted them into container ships. One of them, which he named the 'Ideal-X', was the first container vessel ever. It made its maiden voyage, from Newark to Houston, on 26 April 1956. McLean then established container shipping on several American routes, for example between New York City and the Gulf of Mexico. He expanded his business by buying other companies, such as the Pan-Atlantic Steamship Company, which he renamed Sea-Land-Corporation in 1960, highlighting his aim to overcome the gap between land and sea transportation.

A lively debate arose about a container's ideal size, and the best way to link different systems such as shipping and rail. One idea, for example, was 'piggybacking' – loading truck trailers directly on trains and ships – and was meant to simplify trans-shipment (Shott, 1961). The major boost for containerisation, however, came during the Vietnam War, a serious logistical challenge for the US Army (Wilbanks, 2006). Again, it was Malcom McLean and his containers who made the movement of supplies for US troops more efficient, driven by both patriotism and his search for profits (Levinson, 2006). European maritime professionals at that time closely observed his use of container vessels, since it demonstrated the practicality of the whole idea on a large scale. The first decade of container shipping was nevertheless limited to US American companies and ports, and despite European attention to America's wartime containerised shipping, most European shipping companies regarded containers as a typical (and somehow peculiar) American idea that would never prevail on the global scale.

It is no coincidence that containerisation suddenly became very dynamic in the late 1960s and early 1970s: the *Containerisation International Yearbook* called the speedy development 'breathtaking' in its first number in 1971 (*Containerisation International Yearbook*, 1971: 21). By the mid-1960s, European nautical circles were experiencing 'container hysteria' (Witthöft, 1977: 15). In April 1966, for example, Sea-Land introduced a weekly service between New York City and Rotterdam, Bremen and Grangemouth (in Eastern Scotland) (Church, 1968).

Many European shipping experts travelled to the United States to inspect the new container terminals and personally get an impression of the controversial subject of containerisation. When Helmuth Kern, the senator for economic affairs of the state of Hamburg, visited the abandoned piers of Manhattan and, in sharp contrast, the new container port at Port Elizabeth, New Jersey, he was suddenly convinced that the future lay with the shipping container (Eilers, 2009). The European debate on the prospects of containerisation in that period is very intriguing because it reflects the perception of both the image of Americans and global connections. At a certain point, many observers realised that the container would change global traffic dramatically.

Indeed, the notably increasing numbers of container ships (counted in container units of 20 feet) indicate the massive expansion of container shipping around 1970. While in 1968 a worldwide capacity of only 47,221 containers existed, the number climbed to just under 132,000 in 1970, over 277,000 in 1972 and almost 100,000 more in 1974. In 1973 a 'wave of enthusiasm for buying new container ships' was noticed, but when soon afterwards the world oil crisis overtook the shipping companies it changed everyone's strategies; now ship owners were determined to reduce the oil consumption of their container vessels (*Containerisation International Yearbook,* 1975: 5). Many independent companies amalgamated with former rivals to strengthen their market position and to be able to accumulate enough capital for the very expensive acquisition of up-to-date container ships. For example, the shipping companies Hapag and North German Lloyd, major enterprises from Hamburg and Bremen, Germany's principal ports, joined in 1970 due to such economic challenges under the name of Hapag-Lloyd, despite a more than century-long history of fierce competition (Wiborg and Wiborg, 1997). In other European countries, shippers established consortia, such as the Royal Nedlloyd in 1971, which integrated the four major Dutch lines (Broeze, 2002).

In Europe, many ports were containerised very quickly at the end of the 1960s and again the numbers of containers handled illustrate the dynamic growth. In Hamburg, for example, the numbers of the TEU (Twenty-foot Equivalent Units), the measure used to express container capacity, almost tripled in the early 1970s, and amounted to 137,596 (1972), 294,332 (1974) and reached 411,240 (1976) (Mävers, 1968). A state-run container terminal, the Buchardkai, opened in 1968 and one year later a private-run terminal (Eurokai) followed. In general, competition played a pivotal role in the age of containerisation and in particular in its early period. Rivalry between ports had been crucial for a very long time and this was especially true for regions with several ports within a small range, like the so-called 'Antwerp range' with its several ports at the North Sea (Rotterdam, Antwerp, Bremen, Hamburg). Competition enhanced containerisation: many city governments were afraid of coming too late and hence made considerable investments in container terminals. Competition between ports was just the other side of the coin of global networks (see Figure 3.4).

The way the container advanced was, nevertheless, no linear path. The history of containerisation is instead a history of national and global standardisation and normalisation (Levinson, 2006). In the early stage, when pioneers like Malcolm McLean operated the first container ships, containers came in various sizes. McLean and the Sea-Land-Corporation, for example, used specially built 35-foot containers because American trucks simply could not handle larger sizes. Other companies, such as the American Matson Line,

Figure 3.4 Port Elizabeth near New York City, 1974 (source: *Containerisation International Yearbook 1974*, 9).

preferred other sizes, in this case 24 feet. So in the 1960s there was no container system. But different stakeholders throughout the transportation industry, in particular the European newcomers, clamoured for common standards. The International Organisation for Standardisation established an extra commission (ISO/TC 104) to assess the best standards for containers in the early 1960s (Levinson, 2006). It finally opted for a system that reflected the pioneering role of entrepreneurs in the USA, with their 10-, 20-, 30- and 40-foot sizes. The ISO established a virtual unit, the 'Twenty-foot Equivalent Unit' (TEU), which is still in use.

The standardised shipping container was nothing short of revolutionary. It considerably accelerated and cheapened transportation; moreover, the high reliability of container ship schedules and the closed chain between sea and land transport changed both producing industries and consumer societies. Many factories closed their large warehouses, ordering components on demand and produced *just in time*, following a tight schedule, so that they no longer needed huge depots (Levinson, 2006).

Containerisation had a deep impact on ports as well, rendering many old ports obsolete: cities found it was worth investing in entirely new infrastructure to accommodate the larger container ships. New York City's harbour served as a role model in the early stages of the invention of the container (see Chapter 12). Less than two decades after the container terminals in Port Arthur and Port Elizabeth opened in 1964, New York City completely lost its maritime functions in the city centre. The Brooklyn and Manhattan waterfronts had been characterised by vivid maritime traffic, with many longshoremen loading and unloading countless vessels; now the Manhattan piers were orphaned. In fact, the decline of New York City's old port and the rise of the new container port on the other side of the Hudson River constituted a sharp contrast that made it very clear that the shipping container would prevail in the near future.

Similarly, the English ports of London and Liverpool, which were two of the most important maritime hubs in the world, declined dramatically in the wake of containerisation. The Port Authority of London opened a container terminal in Tilbury at the mouth of the Thames River in 1968, to come geographically towards the container vessels because they could not navigate the shallower Thames; this heralded the coming decline of the port of London. Over the course of the 1970s, maritime London almost completely disappeared as, like New York's old port, the port of London became history within several years. Containerisation dramatically changed the urban patterns and the character of port cities because the harbour became a separate and isolated area no longer connected with the city (see Chapter 4). While a group of traditional ports were losers from containerisation, others highly benefited from it. Rotterdam, for example, strengthened its position and became the second busiest container port (939,469 TEU) in 1974, after New York City (1,836,000 TEU) (see Chapter 7) (see Figure 3.5).

As labour costs declined in shipping, many manufacturers outsourced manufacturing to Asian factories, where labour was significantly cheaper, particularly in Japan and later increasingly in China. The same factors that had made Chinese seamen attractive to shipping companies now made Chinese factory workers attractive to manufacturers who shipped products:

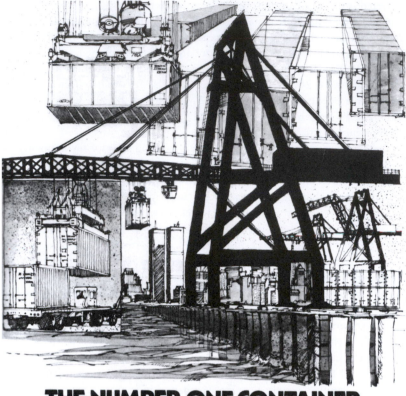

Figure 3.5 Advertisement for New York's and New Jersey's container port, 1978 (source: *Containerisation International Yearbook 1978*, 21).

low wages and a way to attack unions. Western consumers could buy Chinese-made products and clothes in the 1970s at lower prices. At the same time, industrialised western countries like England experienced a fundamental decline in manufacturing that pushed many workers into unemployment, a huge challenge for politics and societies. Since the 1970s, the 'workshop of the world' – a synonym for industrialised Britain in the nineteenth century and at the turn of the century a popular slogan for Philadelphia's industrial centre – has been East Asia.

The containerisation of the 1970s was so dynamic and enormous that it finally set in motion a contrary movement. As the container seemed mechanical, passionless and beyond the human scale, people began to romanticise sailing vessels and steamships. Parades of 'windjammers' and maritime festivals aimed at recalling the 'glorious' past of shipping when seafarers struggled with the forces of nature (Amenda, 2008). Similarly, containerisation had so deeply changed urban patterns in port cities that the citizens rendered the previous age as nearly mythic. New networks of people appeared in the port cities searching for the global 'around the corner' (Hugill, 1967: 74). While the old 'Chinese quarters' at the waterfront had almost disappeared, remaining Chinatowns now gained a new meaning and were even regarded by city governments (as in London since the 1960s) as a positive emblem of globalisation that would attract and mesmerise western tourists.

CONCLUSION

Port cities served as important relay stations in the history of globalisation, constituting essential hubs of traffic and trade. The 'Chinese quarters' that emerged in late nineteenth century port cities in western Europe were directly connected to the technological shift in shipping from sail to steam power, and to new requirements of maritime labour. They significantly contributed to the international atmosphere at the waterfront and provoked local authorities that aimed at banning the immigration of 'coloured' people. The waterfronts of major port cities were populated by many foreign visitors, migrants and seamen, who embodied global connections in local urban spaces. In the popular imagination, port cities were conceived of as gateways and foreign countries *en miniature* within the very homeland. Ports represented nodal points in the global flows both of commerce and of migration. Chinese seamen and migrants, for example, established persistent social networks within and between cities that helped them to explore new economic niches beyond maritime labour. But containerisation, a new technological development in shipping, made Chinese labour and working waterfronts alike old-fashioned and cumbersome.

In the heyday of the old ports, Chinese seamen had gone all over the world to help move goods and people; with containerisation, the factories themselves went to China, and the goods alone continued to move through global networks. The maritime networks might have changed in the course of history; shipping and port cities, however, still keep up global connections and the flow of goods.

4   SEAPORT CITIES
Phases of spatial restructuring and types and dimensions of redevelopment

DIRK SCHUBERT

For several decades now, port cities have been restructuring derelict docks and waterfronts in their inner cities, from Antwerp to Zeebrügge, from Brisbane to Yokohama (Schubert, 2008a). For much of the history of port cities, waterfronts were vibrant, cosmopolitan places. Then, after World War II, the technological requirements of transport changed with the advent of containerisation, and the interfaces between land and sea – the docks and the port – had to be reorganised (Löbe, 1979). Port cities transformed and even relocated port functions, abandoning their historic waterfronts. The dereliction of historic waterfronts in turn presented a challenge to cities. Their abandonment and then reclamation of the waterfront can only be understood in the context of worldwide economic restructuring, changes in dock labour, and the urban spatial framework of city and port. This chapter first examines the historic transformation and interrelation between cities and ports in five development phases, considering in particular the rise and fall of the waterfront. It proposes a sixth phase, one of redevelopment.

Seaport cities hold a special position as transport hubs; they are traditionally crystallisation places where new developments occur and converge. They share structural similarities, developed in response to common dynamics, yet in a way no two seaport cities are alike, and no seaport in the world is like another. Each has its own face, special character and individual history. Their geographical conditions, technical possibilities, historical development, constellation of stakeholders and transport connections to the hinterland are different. How, then, do we construct a comparative analysis? The predicament of the waterfront in the era of containerisation offers a site for exploring this question.

HISTORICAL PHASES OF URBAN AND PORT SPATIAL RESTRUCTURING

Across the history of port cities, we can discern six development phases in the relationship between city and port, the first three creating a vibrant waterfront area (Hoyle, 1989). Considering both historical change and processes of economic growth and expansion of trade, we can read how, in each phase, urban land uses connected with port functions across a contact zone (Schubert, 2009). The port-city system has been subject to the influence and control of primary factors, such as technological changes, environment, economic development, politics and legislation. It is important to stress that these phases, like historical changes in general, are not gradual changes and continuities but inconsistencies and disruptions (see Figure 4.1).

The *first phase* was the primitive city harbour (Hoyle, 1989). The sea was considered dangerous, unwelcoming, unpredictable, while the harbour provided safe shelter. Merchants aspired to make the force of the sea controllable and set up shipping connections (Corbin, 1999). Access to ocean routes soon enabled traders to establish a worldwide economic and political network. Access to whole continents was via ports and coastal cities. Up to the end of the eighteenth century, large seaports were primarily staple markets and trading centres for international high-grade goods. Numerous town plans confirm that moorings and harbours were an integral part of the city that was closely integrated into the urban fabric. This is why harbours were generally located within the town fortifications. Buildings for living accommodation, commercial uses, storage and offices were built immediately on the water's edge, facilitating direct unloading of goods (or unloading by barge) from the ships into the warehouses. The handling of perishable goods, especially, called for the construction of warehouses from the eighteenth century. A close spatial interdependency of the city, handling of goods, storage, trade and port-related services prevailed into the nineteenth century. Ports were busy public places.

Figure 4.1 Phases of port city development according to Hoyle (1989), with a sixth stage added combined with 'long waves' by Kondratieff (1926) by author (source: Dirk Schubert).

Phase	Period	Symbol ○City ● Port	Spatial Characteristics *Economic characteristics*
I Phase	Ancient/medieval to 19th century		Primitive port/city *Preindustrial stage*
II Phase	19th – early 20th century		Expanding port/city *Rapid industrial/commercial growth*
III Phase	mid – 20th century	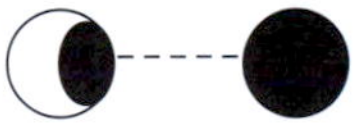	Modern industrial port/city *Fordism/Economies of scale*
IV Phase	since 1960s – 1980s		Retreat from the waterfront *Post-Fordistical stage*
V Phase	since 1970s – 1990s		Redeveloping of waterfront *Flexible accumulation*
VI Phase	since 1990s – 2010+		Renewal of port/city links *Globalisation*

Industrialisation and the expansion of world trade disrupted these patterns and a change in scale transformed port–city relations. In the *second phase*, starting in the nineteenth century, cities and their ports expanded; more space was needed for their rapid growth. The decisions taken in seaport cities at this time – on the organisation of harbour operations, the type of harbour development or redevelopment and on housing associated with the docks – had a great impact, and were often found later to be irreversible and are still effective today in city and port development. Technical innovations facilitated new and improved means of transportation over short and long distances. The discovery of telegraphy, the optimisation of sailing vessels, and the introduction of ocean-going steamships and steam trains on land shortened the time for travelling distances, and economic transactions became more plannable. Industrialisation provided the connection between production, transportation and distribution.

Sailing ships had mostly disappeared from the ports, replaced by iron ships. The sizes of ships increased and increased again. More largely, notes one scholar, 'dominant trade functions of the port were replaced and extended by functions of transport and conveyance' (Läpple, 1994: 2). The port facilities of pre-industrial times no longer met the requirements of modern transhipment. To cope with these structural changes, port cities had to build new and larger docks, install modern transhipment technology and deepen shipping lanes. They mechanised the handling of goods with cranes.

In turn, the construction of new docks necessitated the expansion and reorganisation of urban areas. The close connection of port, work and living started to dissolve. The economic activities of the port changed and ports readjusted the allocation of land uses accordingly. Quayside warehouses and storehouses replaced the sheds, and offices were relocated from the harbour to the town centre, where a dense network of banks, stock exchange, insurance and shipping companies, etc. developed.

Yet at the same time a dockworkers' (sub-)culture emerged, remnants of which have continued into the present. The specific type of labour, the diversity and danger of the work, the irregular workload (casual labour), the contact with foreign seamen and the life close to the docks fostered the emergence of a solidary community of dockworkers (Miller, 1969). Attempts to locally stabilise the irregular working hours by introducing special guild or trade union regulations further brought out the particularity of casual labour on the docks and its militant repute (Phillips and Whiteside, 1985).

The inter-war period can be roughly outlined as the *third phase*, with modern industrial seaports. Fordist industrial production and its guiding themes of precision, efficiency, economy, reliability and speed are mirrored in seaports in monostructural spaces and highly specialised zones. The rhythm of work and life dramatically accelerated (Osterhammel, 2009). The growth of the economy and trade went hand in hand with plans for new port extensions and industrial development. The enhancement of crane technology – from steam crane to electric full gantry crane – facilitated the mechanisation of increasingly large sectors of transhipment. Construction methods in shipbuilding changed from riveting to welding, which sped up considerably the construction of vessels. These (seaport) industries became established alongside existing commercial activities and transformed the harbour landscape with silos, cold storage houses and tank farms.

Ever larger vessels after World War II necessitated further dredging of the shipping lanes and required special cargo handling facilities, or, as the maritime scholar Hans J. Witthöft (2000) has said, 'ships design the port'. Increasing oil consumption caused by mass motorisation and the switch from coal to oil demanded additional land and transhipment facilities. The dependency on overseas imports of raw materials and fuels led to a jump in the amount of bulk transport by sea. Seaport regions thus became privileged locations for seaport industrialisation. A few seaport cities tried to exploit this development by planning and constructing outer ports, as in Bremerhaven for Bremen, Le Havre for Rouen and Warnemünde for Rostock.

COSMOPOLITISM AND DIASPORAS IN SEAPORT CITIES

Meanwhile, the waterfront in older, still vibrant port cities was a distinctive and cosmopolitan urban space. 'Special' harbour-related districts, the 'sailortowns' (Rudolph, 1979), had been integral parts of the fabric of ports throughout this history. Their international orientation turned them into conglomerates that had a multitude of functions and services, including shops for clothing, beverages, tobacco and souvenirs, sailors' churches, lodgings, pubs, tattoo studios, dance halls and brothels.

And common dynamics had long characterised these districts and their place in the urban fabric. Jewish, Chinese (Amenda, 2006) and people of colour, among others – people from other cultures, with different ways of living, eating, working and sleeping – had long been present in seaports. Braudel described in his renowned study of the Mediterranean world the colourful and cosmopolitan population in ports: 'Eine Rasse, in der alle Rassen in eine zusammenfließen' ('A race in which all races merge into one') (Braudel, 1998: 560). Such places represented the first 'stepping stone' for newcomers, opening up opportunities for processes of informal adoption and development of ethnic economies. In Spanish speaking countries these port districts and hideouts of otherness are called 'Barrio Chino', a term that makes reference to internationality – in this instance China ('Chinatown') (Amenda, 2006). Such Chinatowns are and were found in many seaport cities: Rotterdam (Katendrecht), Amsterdam, New York, Singapore, Bangkok, Havana, Panama City (Christiansen, 2003).

The multi-ethnic port cites were not only 'open' melting pots in which different population groups coalesced, but also places of conflict and argument. Cosmopolitanism and openness towards modernisation in port cities were frequently opposed by the narrow-mindedness and backwardness of inland towns and populations (Fuhrmann, 2007). Harbour districts were considered 'dangerous' and often reputed to be unsafe and 'amoral' (El Raval) (Christiansen, 2003). The seamen's shore leave and visits to the entertainment districts in port cities were exceptions to their everyday life on the ships and at sea, a difference which fostered a distorted picture and provided 'ample material for picturesque descriptions and romanticising makeovers'

(Heimerdinger, 2005: 77). Cross-linked to the social networks, the niches and (sub-)cultures of dockworkers and seamen also had a special, exotic flair and appeal for the local petty bourgeoisie.

The perception of 'strangers' was ambivalent, often with negative connotations and associated with terms such as 'freedom', 'unsettled', 'fathomless', 'out of place' and 'uprooting'. The trend of relocating the functions of capital cities from the sea into the hinterland can be taken as proof of the 'dangerous' multi-ethnic open-mindedness in port cities. This was due to other important reasons such as the relocation to the country's geographical centre or the strengthening of the national identity and military aspects, but the trend 'away from the coast' cannot be ignored. So the capital of Australia is not Melbourne or Sydney but Canberra, in Turkey Ankara followed Istanbul, in Brazil Brasilia followed Rio de Janeiro and in India Delhi followed Calcutta.

Because of their diversity, however, seaports were the culmination of innovations in the economy, society and culture. They have been places in which the local and the exotic, the foreign and familiar, poverty and riches, tradition and modernisation, and phenomena of globalisation have been anticipated before they became common later and were distributed globally (Osterhammel and Petersson, 2003).

MODERN PHASES OF URBAN AND PORT SPATIAL RESTRUCTURING

Just as technology, industrialisation and shipping networks had shaped urban waterfronts, new technologies killed these distinctive urban spaces, the changes begun by the requirements of larger vessels now appearing decisive. In sharp contrast to the long history of port cities, then, the *fourth phase* (since the 1960s) was defined by the retreat of land uses from the traditional harbour areas near the city centre.

The decline in importance of many port cities was concurrent with the de-industrialisation of areas around the harbour (Davis, 2003). Many ports lost their significance not only as places of transhipment and trade, but also as locations for seaport industries. Increasing international competition in shipbuilding and the decline of shipbuilding in Europe had a devastating effect on many ports. Many companies relocated production to Southeast Asia, which led to massive unemployment in almost all European shipbuilding locations and to dereliction of shipyards in Europe and North America. The oil crisis, the decline in oil-tanker building, followed by an increase in the use of nuclear power – all of this led to structural changes in the economies of significant seaport cities. The trend towards the coast for allocation of industries looking for deepwater access had only brought a short-lived location advantage; a new stage in the international division of labour began to favour the relocation of industries to countries rich in raw materials, such as Brazil, Morocco, Saudi Arabia, etc.

This *fourth phase* was chiefly characterised by changes in transport technologies (Witthöft, 2000). The invention of the container by Malcolm McLean heralded a new era of maritime traffic and for its ports: in 1966, the first container ship, the *Fairland*, docked in Bremen. Initially dismissed as 'containeritis' and rated as a fad, it brought in its wake the lasting transformation of seaport cities. Containerisation revolutionised dock labour and again required new transhipment sites and port facilities. The period of time a ship was berthed was no longer measured in days or weeks, but in hours. The rationalisation of dock labour became possible with homogenised and standardised loading units; the container turned into a symbol of global trade. The container revolution increased productivity exponentially and brought with it dramatic job losses in the core operative sector of the port economy. Entire occupation fields were no longer needed in ports, such as stevedores, porters, packers, tallymen, etc. 'A good docker handled 5.4 tons of goods in one shift in 1948, his present-day colleague now manages 294 tons' (Karstedt and Worm, 1999: 61).

The *fifth phase*, starting in the 1980s, was characterised by both highly modern terminals away from the city and neglected and/or sub-optimally used inner city harbours and waterfront sites. The post-Fordist city disintegrated into a polycentric fragmented structure with aggravated social conflict. The waterfronts were often degraded by highways. The cranes of the shipbuilders' yards, which used to be a characteristic feature of the city silhouette and a symbol for dynamic port economies, were dismantled, the land left derelict and contaminated.

Seaport cities now saw the increase of differentiation processes. Large container ships only called at a few main ports, while smaller harbours were supplied by feeder services. Improved access by rail and motorways to the hinterland and sufficient depths for seafaring ships offered location advantages, and accelerated transhipment has gained even greater importance as a location factor. In contrast, ports where ships were delayed by having to pass locks or enter or exit docks suffer disadvantages. In all ports of the world there are evident trends for the isolation/decoupling of transhipment on the one hand and added value by grafting, enhancing worth and gaining local employment on the other.

The transhipment of containers from ships to other means of transportation required much larger areas of land. Good railway and road connections with motorway junctions made possible the rapid delivery and removal of containers in overland transport. The water side of container transhipment required other types of quays than earlier forms of shipping because ships didn't have to berth as long and quays have to be always available and of sufficient depth for the very large seafaring ships (Bonz, 2006). The increase in containerisation meant declining employment in transhipment, i.e. fewer dockworkers, but ever larger land areas, more costly infrastructure and the ever deeper – and ecologically questionable – dredging of rivers and ports.

The type of work in ports changed from casual to permanent positions combined with a reduction of jobs (de-casualisation), and often spatially the port moved seawards to a location away from the city centre. Containerisation and computerisation continued to accelerate the rationalisation of transhipment, while functions that used to be bound to the port moved to new spaces. Seen in this context, the areas where port and city meet underwent severe changes in land use, economic activity and the built environment. The traditional port, with its narrow finger-piers, multipurpose terminals and quayside warehouses, had been rendered obsolete, and quayside storage and warehouses, sheds used for temporary storage and protection from the weather, were no longer necessary.

The stormy and far-reaching structural change of sea trade and its related port economy brought about the complete reorganisation of working docks. The formerly close functional and spatial relationship of port and city was dissolved. Changing economic circumstances and trends of dissociation of transhipment, and profitability and employment, have reshaped all world ports; all first abandoned historic waterfronts and then faced the challenge of derelict urban areas.

CYCLE OF WATERFRONT (RE)DEVELOPMENT

Globalisation entered a more intensive phase in the last decade of the twentieth century and dominated the world economy at the beginning of the twenty-first century. Now the seas no longer separated, but connected countries and continents. Shipping provided the fastest, simplest and most ecological means of transport. Just-in-time production, vertical disintegration and slim-line organisations became characteristic of global structural changes. These new forms of post-Fordist spatialisation were defined by far-reaching shifts, rejections and spatial–temporal inconsistencies and often made obsolete the traditional understanding of the term 'city'. While at the beginning of the twentieth century ocean-going vessels were synonymous with modernity and celebrated as the fastest means of transport, they are now synonymous with leisureliness and superfluousness, transport for old age pensioners who are not pressed for time (Borscheid, 2004).

In this context we can identify a *sixth phase* of waterfront transformation and regeneration on a regional scale. Generally, revitalisation began in the oldest parts of the port and the city, slowly moving to more peripheral areas, which were developed later. Often this was done with a step-by-step approach, beginning with the most attractive sites, but without integrating these projects into a sustainable urban or regional development strategy. In order to define this process as a new phase, it must be looked at in comparative studies, while complex practical problems need to be considered by city planners, and analytical and theoretical questions arise for scholars at the macro, meso and micro levels in this field.

Generally, the process of transformation at this interface has followed a similar cycle:

- dereliction of old port areas near the city, relocation of modern, containerised trading facilities to areas suitable for expansion outside the city centre;
- disuse, temporary and sub-optimal usage of areas and buildings in the old ports;
- visions and plans for the reallocation of uses for buildings and land in derelict areas, architectural competitions;

- implementation of plans, establishment of new land uses (offices, recreation, housing) in these areas;
- redevelopment, new land uses, acquisition, enhancement of the desirability of these areas;
- occasional transformation of already redeveloped zones for other more suitable and more profitable uses.

Discussion on suitable and sustainable strategies to deal with the potential of former port areas has led to controversial debates concerned with practical planning as well as theoretical issues, about aims and priorities. Despite the unique potential of these areas, considerable delays between dilapidation and renewal were common.

HOW TO EVALUATE WATERFRONT (RE)DEVELOPMENT: A FRAMEWORK FOR COMPARATIVE ANALYSIS

But port reclamation projects vary as much as port cities themselves, and can help us think about how to construct a comparative analysis of port cities. Many existing case studies (Breen and Rigby, 1996; Bruttomesso, 1983) look at 'successful' waterfront redevelopment projects from different viewpoints and provide uncritical analysis, lacking objective and comparable criteria. Problematic approaches include:

- Listing the projects according to their size and dimensions. This might seem to be a reasonable approach, establishing their relation to the urban context and their urban-regional significance. However, different studies and planners delimit projects differently. While some projects are the result of the redevelopment of former harbour areas (Hamburg Hafen-City), mostly starting with a clean slate and sometimes including single historic buildings, other projects incorporate surrounding residential neighbourhoods (Dublin Docklands) or existing projects into the redevelopment (Bremen Überseestadt). Often the site boundaries are altered too, generally to enlarge the site, so that the evaluations must also incorporate different sites.
- Comparing projects according to their duration. When comparing the structure of the project at the onset and at completion, conclusions may be drawn regarding the (local) political context, the relevant initiators and stakeholders as well as the reason for development. However, putting an exact date on the start of a project is often difficult. Even more difficult is determining its end or the date of completion. This is either because the site area was altered or because other projects were incorporated and 'older' projects renewed. Thus, transformations are never 'final', but should be understood as a continuous process.
- Categorising waterfront reclamation projects according to their intended dominant uses or planning targets. Incorporating dominant focal points in renewal projects on derelict sites is a common reaction to deficient and/or absent urban regional structures. They are generally not one-sided or finally defined, even though the focus is often placed on clusters of

uses: housing (Amsterdam Eastern Docklands); offices (London Dock-lands); culture (Bilbao Abandoibarra); mixed use (Gothenburg); events (Barcelona). But often the uses that planners envisage at the onset of a project are later augmented, optimised and 'improved' with other structures. Relaxed or tense conditions in the urban regional housing and office sector are often the cause for corrections of the land use designations.

• Comparing the geographic location of seaports, allowing consideration of a redevelopment project in the global network of economic relations. Such an approach might compare socio-economic and political structures found in the respective nations and regions, including their history, culture and tradition. Yet comparison based on just 'facts' and dates cannot mirror the complexity of contextual integration, specifics and stakeholders on different levels, as shown in many studies.

For a systematic comparative study, it is relevant to identify similar and dissimilar structural characteristics. Here a framework for analysis and for a comparative perspective is suggested, taking into account both qualitative and quantitative dimensions in regard to leadership of the plan, location, size, start of the project, planning cultures and planning targets (see Figure 4.2). With a brief comparison between European, Asian and American projects, it can be shown how the great variety of projects integrate into the dimensions deduced previously for the sixth phase.

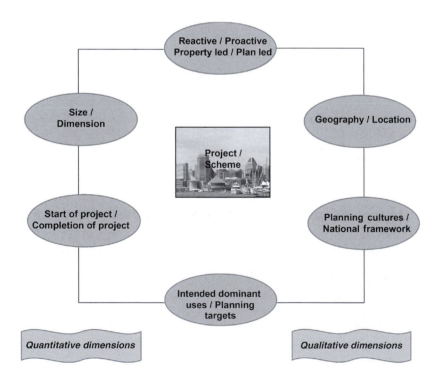

Figure 4.2 Dimensions of waterfront (re-)development for comparative perspectives (source: Dirk Schubert).

The first generation of waterfront revitalisation projects started in the mid-1960s in North American cities such as Baltimore, Boston and San Francisco, where problems of derelict and underused port areas first became an issue (Brown, 2009) (see Figure 4.3). As these projects represented a new planning task, a 'learning by doing' approach was often adopted. New uses frequently included tourist facilities, hotels and offices. This happened in the political era of privatisation, market-led approaches and deregulation, resulting in the 'sameness' of many projects in seaport cities. Like-minded architects, planners and developers dominated the scene, and there was much criticism of the new 'concrete curtains' along the waterfronts.

Baltimore's Inner Harbor became the most copied American effort of urban renewal and waterfront revitalisation. In Baltimore, the combination of a convention centre, hotel, sports facilities, aquarium and festival marketplace made up the specific ingredients. City marketing was another important issue, which exploited the success of waterfront revitalisation in the competition between cities. The strategy of 'returning the shoreline to the people' was quite a successful part of the improvements to the downtown district. The project was based on a 'shared risk' approach, splitting the responsibilities between the private and the public sectors. The thriving enhancement and commercialisation of the public space on Harborplace (Harvey, 1990) took place concurrently with the further decline of the adjacent city centre. The myth of the Baltimore model and the improvements around Harborplace is juxtaposed with a remarkably crisis-ridden urban reality (Ward, n.d.).

The 'festival market' approach (nicknamed 'Rousification') was often adopted, offering tourist-orientated shopping. It was named after the developer James Rouse, who was involved in similar festival markets in Sydney, Boston, New York, Norfolk, Santa Monica and Osaka (Olsen, 2003) (see

Figure 4.3 San Francisco, Fishermans Wharf, one of the first successful examples of waterfront revitalisation in North America, 2009 (source: Dirk Schubert).

Figure 4.4). This type of leisure-led revitalisation combined hotels, small shops, boutiques, restaurants and bars with public access to the waterfront (Breen and Rigby, 1996). As these areas were frequently located next to the city centre, they successfully combined inner city and waterfront revitalisation. It is remarkable how the US American model successfully copies European port cities and idyllic marketplaces, to then transfer these to Europe and Asia – modified into commercial US concepts.

At the beginning of the 1990s, cities and planners forged different approaches. In European seaport cities like Oslo, Rotterdam and Gothenburg, participatory planning became popular, as planners involved the local community in planning processes. Often a step-by-step approach involving design competitions and master plans was introduced to lead the way in restructuring former port areas. Events such as the Olympics (Barcelona) or culture and leisure facilities such as aquariums and museums were frequently used to push redevelopment (Meyer, 1999). At the beginning of the new millennium, a new generation of projects emerged. Private–public partnerships and professional planning management dominated the global competition between waterfront revitalisation projects. These projects were used in new city marketing strategies that were based on unique seaport heritage. At that time (luxury) housing and mixed-use developments became more widespread. The disuse of port areas and waterfronts, often dramatised in Europe because of delays in many areas, is the 'normal' process that will, at best, lead to rapid reutilisation. Here the revitalisation of ports and waterfronts often takes years, if not decades, from the time of disuse to the start of reorganisation.

In contrast, in Asia the continuous and rapid rebuilding of the waterfront seems to be the norm, often linked to land reclamation projects. History is

Figure 4.4 Boston, Rowes Wharf and downtown, a completely transformed waterfront without any remaining port uses, 2009 (source: Dirk Schubert).

systematically eradicated: everything is on the move, permanently. Shanghai, the Bund and Pudong deliver spectacular examples of rapid and permanent transformations. All port cities share the determination to rapidly adjust to the challenges of globalisation and to push the unparalleled reorganisation from former, insignificant colonial places into knowledge- and service-based centres, to subsequently emerge as important hubs in the worldwide network of seaports.

As this brief comparison between Europe and Asia signals, understanding planning history and planning cultures is crucial for understanding urban redevelopment projects on the waterfront, although often there is a diffusion of planning ideas (Ward, 2000). The reasons for and problems of revitalising land formerly occupied by the port and port-related industries are similar in many seaports, but aims, planning cultures, financing and scale are very different in seaports all over the world. National planning cultures mirror different national legal systems, political and cultural contexts and traditions, and vary a great deal throughout the world. In this context it is important to reflect the great variety of existing planning cultures and different understandings of planning tasks and governance structures when analysing waterfront redevelopment projects.

Within Europe, there are a variety of planning systems and cultures, against the backdrop of particular historic conditions, embedded in different national constitutions and legal systems that differ markedly, resulting in a great variety of urban planning projects. At the same time, a growing number of regulations are initiated at the EU level and take effect in revisions of national building and planning systems. This convergence towards similar procedures and solutions – towards harmonisation – has increased with European standardisation. Newman and Thornley (1996) have identified different national 'families' of planning systems: British, Napoleonic, Germanic, Scandinavian and Eastern European (see Figure 4.5).

This categorisation is based on a mix and overlap of geographical, historical and political dimensions. It can be supplemented through the development of centrality and decentrality, theory of the welfare state, legal effectiveness, forms of cooperation, as well as high or low flexibility at the local implementation of projects.

The abovementioned American projects in Baltimore and Boston, for example, provided general inspiration for the London Docklands, although in a different context and at a larger scale (22 sq. km or 8.5 sq. miles). It was in later periods mostly office-led redevelopment, although some luxury housing and vast areas of low-rise middle-class housing were also built in Beckton and Surrey Quays in the 1990s. But the tower of Canary Wharf dominates the image and was the flagship of the Thatcherite approach to planning (Edwards, 1992). The centre at Canary Wharf was built to challenge the financial hub in the City of London, several miles upstream. The project was implemented in the period of a new enterprise culture based on privatisation, deregulation and marketisation of activities. The London Docklands was the first project of this type of 'planning culture' in Great Britain, and Margaret Thatcher herself called it the 'flagship project' (see Figure 5.4).

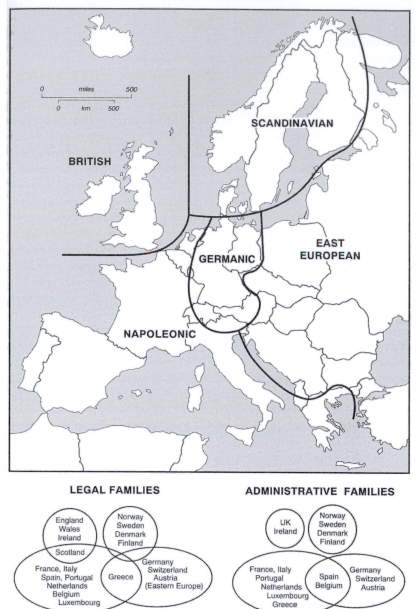

Figure 4.5 The legal and administrative 'families' of Europe (source: Newman and Thornley, 1996: 29).

The port was relocated to the mouth of the Thames, leaving empty derelict spaces in the Docklands. The deregulation policies of London Docklands Development Corporation caused an office space building boom in the former port area (Foster, 1999). What had started with the transformation of empty and derelict warehouses along the Thames by students and artists later became a mega-structure competing with the City of London and consisting of fragmented urban structures.

As in Europe, there are many different planning cultures in Asia as well. In contrast to the deregulation in Britain, long-term planning, rigid political control and resolute administration are the key political elements that have earned some cities exemplary status for urban planning (Kraas, 2004). In Singapore, the need for spatial planning arose due to the limited amount of available land. Land reclamation schemes have increased the area of Singapore by more than 60 sq. km; almost 10 per cent of the country's land is man-made (Glaser *et al.*, 1991: 367). Singapore has a unique planning system and a special planning tradition. Since approximately 80 per cent of land is in public ownership, planning and implementation can be done 'top down'. Largely modelled on the British planning tradition, the Singapore plan introduced zoning and master planning. The 'Ring Concept Plan', passed in 1991, subdivided the island into five regions and defined a spatial development concept for the entire island (Schubert, 2009). This is based on a system of motorways and rapid train transportation. The objective was to accelerate decentralisation and the formation of centres (decentral concentration). The model of the sustainable city, the vision of an 'environmental city', is to become a reality with the 'Singapore Green Plan – Towards a Model Green City'. The government praises rationality, pragmatism and efficiency. Singapore is alleged to be one of the cleanest and safest cites in Asia, and this reputation is used to attract streams of tourists onto the island (Kieserling, 2000). But excessive redevelopment has resulted in travellers perceiving modern Singapore as dull and sterile. Meanwhile citizens are consulted more often, and at least it appears as if their interests are recognised.

In China (see figure 4.6) and Japan authorities often combine waterfront revitalisation with land reclamation. The most important examples of this strategy can be found in Osaka, Kobe, Tokyo and Yokohama. In all these cases the ports moved seawards to provide deepwater access for the largest ships. As not enough land was available for the required new terminals, land reclamation measures were employed to produce as many zones for deepwater access as possible. Artificial new islands were constructed in the sea, with clearly defined zones which often comprised a mix of housing (especially for dockworkers) and new container terminals. The sites also accommodate airports, power stations and sport stadiums, although port uses are most relevant. The infrastructure that connects these artificial islands with bridges and tunnels is, of course, costly. As reclamation strategies are formulated for the long-term perspective, much vacant land is available on the new port islands (Hohn, 2008). Older, underused areas, derelict land and empty old sheds and warehouses close to the city centre were converted into shopping malls or festival markets, often combined with new hotels, museums and aquariums. These projects are somewhat similar to the North American festival market approach and seem to be extremely popular in Japan, as people love shopping in these places.

Redundant and derelict port areas and waterfronts remain one of the greatest challenges for town planners and offer great opportunities on a medium- to long-term basis for new uses such as tourism, housing and offices, and for the reintegration of these areas into the urban fabric (Priebs, 1998; Breen and Rigby, 1996). Generalisations are difficult to make and easy recipes do not

Figure 4.6 Hong Kong Victoria Island, central waterfront, 2004 (source: Dirk Schubert).

exist. Differences in cause, procedure, results and planning tradition need to be taken into account. Reclamation is not just a matter of architectural design, but of a complex set of planning, institutional, political, client-related, economic, ecological, legal and financial questions (Bruttomesso, 1983).

CONCLUSION

Cities seem to be growing more alike as shipping has become more special-ised. Ports have turned into secluded worlds, separated from the urban context, spatially and mentally severed from the city, with their own employ-ment, operators and administration structures. While older port areas near the city centre have been (re)integrated into the urban fabric, new port infra-structure is severed from the urban structure and located in areas where deep-water ports and large areas of land are available. Seaport cities and local port authorities will be less and less able to determine the course for their ports, and instead internationally operating logistics firms will be setting the agenda.

The local economy in seaport cities is no longer just focussed on tranship-ment, but has now diversified and has a much broader base. Nonetheless, port functions resulted in a dependency on routes and special development options compared to other (river) port cities. This complicates the diversification of economic activities (Jacobs *et al.*, 2010). Often seaport cities are not only transport hubs but also finance centres, the seats of large companies (trans-national corporations (TNCs) and Advanced Producer Service Firms (APSFs)), interfaces in the communication network and places for important events (Short *et al.*, 1996).

They are the locus of global trends in urban development reflecting the transition from Fordist production distribution and regulation to post-Fordist and neo-Fordist flexible structures, the worldwide increase and differentiation in the division of labour, the growing importance of knowledge-based economies, and the social split of the rich and poor.

Flexibilisation is the key term of the post-Fordist discourse, and it is expressed in economic, social and spatial terms (Schubert, 2001). New spatialisation is defined by far-reaching spatial–temporal inequalities and disruptions, and often makes the traditional understanding of the term 'city' obsolete. The post-Fordist city of flexible accumulation turns into a polycentric configuration that disintegrates into fragmented sections. The differentiation of the global city system and new disparities between cities corresponds with growing inequality within cities themselves. One example is the revitalisation of (old) harbour sites on the water's edge that are favoured (again) by the creative classes in a knowledge-based society. As popular urban researcher Charles Landry notes, 'Often these (creative) milieus were centred on redundant warehouses that had been the incubators for new companies' (Landry, 2008: xxix). They can be considered places where phenomena of subsequent globalisation are pre-empted. If globalisation is a multi-layered and ambivalent historical macro process, whose beginnings go back to the age of discovery, it is helpful to remember that seaport cities have always been culmination points for innovation in economy, society and culture.

5 PORT CITIES AND THE GLOBAL EXCHANGE OF PLANNING IDEAS

STEPHEN V. WARD

All cities are information hubs, geographical points where all kinds of knowledge are concentrated, accumulated, synthesised, circulated and exchanged. The nature of seaports as points where the 'national' encounters the 'exotic' has given them special significance in this respect. Major seaports have often been the places where foreign innovations first appeared in a country. Liverpool, for example, was a bridgehead for the introduction of American innovations into Britain in technology, business and culture; Hamburg for Germany's British and other westerly connections; New York for the introduction of European ideas and practices into the United States. This was even more apparent outside the West, where access to international information in the great port cities of the various colonial empires was immeasurably greater than in the often inaccessible interiors.

The role of seaports as knowledge hubs was greatest in the pre-industrial and early industrial eras, before successive new media of transportation and communication reduced the dependence on the sea. Canals, railways, the postal service, telecommunications and air travel eroded what was once the special prerogative of seaports. However, many cities that were first prominent as seaports have maintained dominant positions as these new media for the movement of knowledge have appeared, most strikingly New York and London. Even in those ports that were less successful in making this transition, such as Liverpool or Baltimore, there has remained a strong propensity to look beyond the country, showing a less insular outlook than many inland cities. In recent decades, this has been apparent in the planning concerns within all older port cities to regenerate the port areas themselves, as changing maritime operations have necessitated major physical and economic restructuring.

The interplay between these various trends forms the central theme of this chapter. It examines the global circulation of knowledge and expertise in connection with the regeneration of older port districts. These flows of knowledge were animated in part by learning through study visits and research. Yet the impacts of these more rational aspects were heightened, especially in the early years of port regeneration, by more impressionist imaginings. As we will show, a few cities came to be widely imagined across the world as 'models' where fabulous transformations were being realised with immensely positive impacts for the destinies of the host cities. These became the places that city leaders elsewhere sought to emulate or, to varying extents, imitate. For a variety of reasons, the optimistic imaginings were also actively promoted by more specific agents, particularly developers, politicians, planners and architects. In many cases this was simply done for business reasons, as developers and professionals capitalised on their association with 'model' regeneration schemes. But there were other motives, including bilateral technical assistance and more recent desires to promote international networks for mutual knowledge exchange. Gradually, as will be shown, the limitations of the erstwhile 'models' have also come to be recognised, leading to a more nuanced process of learning, from which negative as well as positive lessons are drawn.

THE OLDER PORT DISTRICTS AND TECHNOLOGICAL CHANGE

This chapter's physical setting lies in the older, more centrally located dock areas of major seaport cities (Du-Plat-Taylor, 1949). From around 1960 the cumulative effects of technological and other changes in shipping operations made these areas increasingly redundant for port purposes. The changes included the growing scale and specialisation in bulk commodity traffic; the decline of scheduled and rise of cruise passenger liners; the adoption of 'roll-on, roll-off' ferries for road traffic; and containerisation. Together these changes allowed a massive reduction in the time ships spent in port, loading and unloading in hours rather than days. To cope with this, ports had to reduce physical obstacles (e.g. lock gates) or the need for complex manoeuvring that would slow the movement of vessels to and from their berths. On docksides, there needed to be new types of highly specialised handling equipment and large areas free of buildings and with better links to landward transport routes (especially roads) than in older port areas.

It was virtually impossible to restructure the oldest docks to meet these new demands. These areas were typified by enclosed docks, often accessible only through narrow channels with lock gates, or slender finger-piers projecting into sheltered bodies of natural water. The immediate docksides were typically cluttered with a once functional but now largely obsolete apparatus of cargo cranes, railway tracks and warehouses. Beyond the port areas proper lay the tightly built-up central cores of major cities, generally with insufficient road capacity to service the newer kind of port. The result was that contemporary port functions were shifted to more peripheral and spacious settings within the metropolitan regions of the historic port cities.

Yet, for all their disadvantages, the underused and increasingly derelict locations which remained had immense real estate potential if only they could be reintegrated into the city to extend and diversify central area activities. Beneath the grime, many warehouse and other port buildings and structures also had historic interest and heritage value. Suitably revalorised by appropriate investment and re-imaging, these older ports could become the key element in a new phase of city development by strengthening and diversifying central area functions. Like many such transitions, however, the shift from being a working port to a new post-industrial space based on retail, finance and tourism was rarely smooth, often socially painful and frequently contested.

LEARNING AND IMAGINING IN THE GLOBAL CIRCULATION OF PLANNING KNOWLEDGE

The conceptual setting of this chapter reflects the two distinct intellectual processes by which planning ideas and practices are spread from one country to another. On the one hand, this flow can be understood as a relatively rational process of cross-national learning and pursuit of 'good practice' by professional and technical actors. On the other, it is a more culturally and ideologically conditioned process of imagining, reflecting the images and stereotypes of the 'source' country or city prevailing more widely within the 'receiving' country or city. This latter process is especially significant as exogenous information is converted into relevant lessons and then actual policies, as purely technical knowledge is politically and socially repackaged for application within its new host. However, both learning and imagining play their part in creating external 'models' that are introduced, alongside purely local and national considerations, into policy formation by cities about future change.

The conceptualisation of the former process draws on a distinct body of work, undertaken mainly by political scientists. It is often referred to, a little misleadingly, as the policy transfer literature (Dolowitz and Marsh, 1996, 2000; Rose, 2005). Actually it is concerned with the closely related processes of cross-national learning, lesson-drawing and policy transfer. These represent different stages in the international spread of planning ideas and practices. The first is concerned with knowledge acquisition, the second with adapting the learning into transferable lessons and the last with the introduction of actual policies that reflect the exotic knowledge. Rarely, however, is this literally transfer in the true sense; usually some degree of adaptation, hybridisation or synthesis is apparent.

Yet this way of understanding international knowledge flows is less effective for those aspects which lie beyond the professional and technical sphere. Larger cultural or political circumstances will frequently predispose governments to prefer policy knowledge from one source rather than another. This might well differ from, even contradict, the more strictly technical perceptions of relevance and value. A more useful way of thinking about this second dimension is through the idea of imaginative geography. This was pioneered in Edward Saïd's concept of 'Orientalism', which characterised Western perceptions of the Orient, more specifically the Middle East (Saïd, 1978). Instead of seeing the realities, Westerners saw a culturally constructed biased and negative image of barbarity, deviousness and inferiority that became self-reinforcing, inhibiting other ways of seeing the region.

A far more positive imaginary with more direct relevance here was the concept of 'Americanism', proposed by Cohen and Damisch (1993; Cohen, 1995). They argue that European architects and planners came in the twentieth century to look on the biggest cities of the United States as offering a modern, dynamic, innovative and progressive vision of an almost inevitable future. In turn, this way of thinking encouraged them to introduce this vision into their proposals for European cities, successively adopting each American innovation in a relatively uncritical fashion.

This chapter builds directly on and extends this way of thinking, taking it to specific cities – the first, significantly, an American city – which came to be imagined as models of 'successful' port regeneration. We also show how the making of these imaginaries did not depend entirely on externally constructed perceptions. Such models were consciously promoted and exported by a variety of agents directly associated with the city in question. Yet we also recognise that there were also more rational processes of learning and lesson-drawing, these becoming more significant as more ports embarked on regeneration.

BALTIMORE INNER HARBOR AS A GLOBAL MODEL

For many years, no city occupied a more important position in the imaginative geography of seaport regeneration than Baltimore (Ward, 2006) (see Figure 5.1). During the 1980s, it seemed to point a way from the grimy dereliction of the industrial era to a future built on tourism, leisure, retailing and office-based services. The basic story is well known: the Inner Harbor effectively closed in the 1950s and there was some limited city investment to maintain it sufficiently for an undetermined reuse (Lyall, 1982). At that time, however, the city's efforts were focused on the Charles Center, a complex urban renewal of retailing, offices, hotels and high value apartments in Baltimore's downtown, adjoining the Inner Harbor. 'Urban renewal' was an earlier policy label applied to what was, in many ways, an even more painful transformation than that which was set to occur in port areas. It had typically brought large-scale social displacement, frequently of poor black or Chinese populations, replacing them with upscale housing, retailing and business quarters aimed at creating a new class of wealthy urbanites. In Baltimore, this earlier urban renewal became the springboard for the transformation of the Inner Harbor itself and an important plan was prepared in 1964 (Wallace, 2004). Little then happened until 1972, when a historic warship was introduced as a tourist attraction. Public access to the waterfront was also created and the city began a programme of largely free entertainment.

This interest persuaded investors that new developments in the area would be worthwhile. From the mid-1970s, several major public projects were completed in quick succession (Wrenn with Casazza and Smart, 1983; Breen and Rigby, 1994). The Maryland Science Center opened in 1976, the World Trade Center the following year and the Marina in 1978, all broadly as envisaged in the 1964 plan. Then followed several additional developments: the Convention Center in 1979; the privately funded Harborplace festival marketplace (a tourist-oriented shopping mall that incorporated some of the atmosphere of a traditional urban market) in 1980 and a new Hyatt hotel and the National Aquarium in 1981. Further development continued in the eastern Inner Harbor from the mid-1980s with a concert hall, museums and other cultural facilities.

By then Baltimore's reputation as a national and global model of urban regeneration was well established. Policy makers, developers and planning experts from many other cities visited, looked, listened and then copied, adapted or were in a more general sense inspired by the Inner Harbor. In

STEPHEN V. WARD

Figure 5.1 Baltimore Inner Harbor (source: Baltimore Visitors and Convention Bureau).

Note
Baltimore Inner Harbor became the principal model of port regeneration in the early 1980s. This reflected its early concentration of key attractions and the very successful promotion of the model by its originators, particularly Martin Millspaugh and James Rouse, in the USA and increasingly internationally. It was heralded as a way of reversing the decline of cities that appeared to have no hope, though, in Baltimore's case, this proved very short-lived.

1983 alone the city received an estimated 4,000 visiting representatives from 87 cities around the world, eager to learn from its apparent renaissance (Olsen, 2003). But, very importantly, there were also more direct and active connections with other cities by those involved in its development, planning and design. These undoubtedly played a central part in making Baltimore, more than any other city, *the* first international model for the post-industrial waterfront.

The key figures were James Rouse and Martin Millspaugh. Rouse developed the most significant private development and premier visitor destination at the Inner Harbor, Harborplace. A pioneer of suburban shopping malls and planned residential communities, especially the new town of Columbia, Maryland, Rouse was the principal promoter of Baltimore as a global model (Bloom, 2004). In part this was because he was a charismatic and widely known figure, but it also reflected his direct role as a developer and development consultant who actively took the Baltimore model to other cities. Earlier, Rouse also helped bring the prior experiences of Boston back to his home city. In 1972, he had teamed up with the Boston architect Ben Thompson over the latter's plans to revive the historic but derelict Faneuil Hall and Quincy Market close to that city's waterfront, which opened as Rouse's first festival marketplace in 1976–1978. On the strength of this Rouse was invited by Millspaugh, a former journalist who led the Inner Harbor redevelopment project, to undertake a similar development in Baltimore, which became Harborplace (Olsen, 2003). Initially very controversial because it replaced what had become a popular waterfront open space, Rouse's Harborplace went ahead only after a narrow victory in a citizen poll (Rusk, 1996). Yet in its first full year of operation it attracted 18 million visitors.

Its opening coincided with Rouse's retirement from the development company which bore his name. However, the company's involvement in port and waterfront regeneration projects continued, with developments during the 1980s at South Street Seaport in New York; Bayside, Miami; Riverwalk, New Orleans; and elsewhere (Metzger, 2001). Rouse, however, did not retire in the literal sense and became even more significant in the global spread of the model. In 1981, with Millspaugh, he established a well-known not-for-profit venture, the Enterprise Foundation, and, more significant for this story, a for-profit Enterprise Development Company (EDC) (Olsen, 2003). It soon became a powerful vehicle promoting the Baltimore approach (Global Harbors, n.d.).

Over the next few years, EDC co-operated with several smaller US cities, promoting festival marketplace developments, some in waterfront locations. With the exception of the first, Waterside in Norfolk, which opened in 1983, these all failed because they lacked the critical mass of attractions that under-pinned Baltimore's and Boston's successes (Enterprise Real Estate Services, n.d.; Olsen, 2003). They were also victims of the dramatic economic changes and erosion of governmental spending during the Reagan era. It was the increasing difficulties with these smaller US projects which encouraged EDC to look to the wider world. Rouse himself had no great inclination to become a globetrotting evangelist for the Baltimore model. Before EDC's first and most important international project, in Sydney, came up in 1983, Rouse had apparently already refused 120 invitations to visit non-US cities to give development advice (Perkins, 2001).

He was persuaded to break this habit by an Australian developer, Thomas Hayson, who was impressed by the parallels between the Inner Harbor and the Darling Harbour that adjoined Sydney's downtown (Perkins, 2001; Mills-paugh, n.d.) (see Figure 5.2). The New South Wales Government had decided to initiate its reuse and Hayson had agreed to participate (Young, 1988). Having read about Baltimore in a newspaper article, Hayson visited the city and contacted Millspaugh and a reluctant Rouse. Both immediately grasped the potential of the Darling Harbour. They were soon giving detailed and highly influential planning, development and management advice both to Hayson and to the Darling Harbour Authority. EDC also had a financial stake in Hayson's Harbourside festival marketplace – which ended up being remarkably similar to Rouse's Baltimore development.

EDC was also very actively involved in the planning and development of Port Vell in Barcelona (Meyer, 1999; Enterprise Real Estate Services, n.d.). In 1985 it undertook master planning for the port authority on the reuse of the area. Later, it served as a partner to the Spanish developer of the Maremagnum leisure and retailing complex in the port. Another well-known port regeneration in which EDC was involved was the Kop Van Zuid in Rotterdam (Rotterdam: the Kop van Zuid, n.d.). Here the Company joined a consortium with the Rotterdam city estates and planning departments, and Dutch investment and construction companies to produce a strategic vision in 1988. EDC proposed the public–private partnership delivery structure, following the Baltimore template (Hajer, 1993). The particular mix of development included some Baltimore features, notably a festival marketplace in the old Custom House, though there were also some very important differences in the mix of activities.

Figure 5.2 James Rouse with the detailed proposal for the Darling Harbour in Sydney, 1988 (source: Golden Wattle publishers, Sydney).

Note
Rouse's Enterprise Development Company worked closely with the Sydney developer Thomas Hayson in developing the festival marketplace, Harbourside, shown in the right foreground. It also had an important role in shaping the Darling Harbour Authority's plan for the whole area.

A further important example, in Japan, was much more directly based on the Baltimore model: the Tempozan Harbour Village which opened in 1991 (Olsen, 2003; Enterprise Real Estate Services, n.d.; Model for the world…, n.d.) (see Figure 5.3). It was developed by a consortium headed by the Osaka Port Authority, with EDC providing Baltimore expertise as consulting developer. It included a festival marketplace, an aquarium, a cruise ship terminal and several other attractions. Also in 1991, the Laganside Development Corporation, the public development authority for the Belfast waterfront, selected a development consortium which included EDC and two Northern Irish developers.

EDC also worked with developers in Melbourne, Izmir, Cairo, Shanghai, Freeport and Port Columbus (Bahamas), Kobe, Sakai (Japan), Malaga, Rio de Janeiro, Warsaw, Puerto La Cruz and Porlamar (Venezuela), Zagreb, Kuwait City, Cancun (Mexico), Guanica (Puerto Rico) and Bridgetown (Barbados) (Enterprise Real Estate Services, n.d.). Many of these contacts took the form of advisory consultations, not necessarily with any direct development outcome but important in reinforcing a common way of thinking about cities, especially waterfront areas.

For all the extraordinary role of Rouse's EDC in spreading elements of the Baltimore approach, the company was not the only agent of its diffusion. Some professionals who had been associated with Rouse and Millspaugh played an independent role in spreading elements of the model. Perhaps the most important was the architecture and planning firm led by Benjamin Thompson. Thompson himself had evolved the design concept of the festival marketplace before Rouse. His firm designed Rouse's most successful marketplaces. Independently of Rouse, they designed variants of the concept in Guatemala City and Buenos Aires for different clients during the 1990s (BTA Architects Inc., n.d.). At the wider planning level, they also master planned the reuse of the Custom House Dock in Dublin in 1987, followed by more specific design commissions. Waterfront areas in several other cities, including Auckland and Cardiff, were similarly master planned by them.

Figure 5.3 Tempozan Harbour Village, Osaka, Japan, 1991 (source: Osaka Waterfront Development Company).

Note
This was another example of an international involvement by the Baltimore-based Enterprise Development Company. Though the architecture differs from Baltimore, the development concept is strikingly similar. The aquarium (left background) and festival marketplace (main subject) were designed by the Cambridge Seven architectural practice, also architects of the Boston and Baltimore aquaria.

Another important agent in the international spread of the Baltimore (and Boston) approach to waterfront development was Cambridge Seven Associates (Cambridge Seven Associates Inc., n.d.). They had designed the pioneering Boston aquarium as well as the more ambitious later one at Baltimore. The Tempozan aquarium and marketplace in Osaka, in which EDC was involved, were also designed by Cambridge Seven and they subsequently worked in Lisbon and Kuwait on similar projects. Another firm which had worked with Rouse over a long period and had designed several buildings in downtown and harbourfront Baltimore were RTKL Architecture and Urban Design (RTKL Associates Inc., n.d.). Their global practice has undertaken several master plans of waterfront development, for example in Shanghai and at Leith Docks (Edinburgh) and Salford Quays (Manchester) in the UK.

Around Rouse, therefore, were many other actors who in various ways spread aspects of the approach adopted at Baltimore. But even without such Baltimore figures being directly involved, there was also much learning and borrowing, variously adaptive, selective or uncritical, of ideas from Baltimore by other cities and their planners and developers. Knowledge of the city (also Boston) was particularly influential on the activities of several British urban development corporations during the 1980s and 1990s. This was particularly so for London and other British cities undertaking dock regeneration schemes (Imrie and Thomas, 1999; Syme, 2000). Among other links, collaborative research projects between universities increased UK awareness of key American developments and helped to reinforce many similarities in urban policy between the two countries during the Reagan–Thatcher era (Barnekov *et al.*, 1989).

While many aspects of the 'how' and 'where' of the story of the diffusion of the Baltimore model are clear, the most fundamental question has only been partially answered. Though individual and institutional actions were important, they cannot fully explain why the Inner Harbor so completely captured the imaginations of city leaders, planners and developers across the world. It helped, of course, that it was an American city since this echoed the persistence of 'Americanist' sentiments across the world, especially in Anglo-phone countries. Yet this was a very different vision of the American city to the functionally zoned, dispersed, motorised modernity which had dominated previous imaginings. Paradoxically, this new post-industrial American city-scape was inspired by an older, more European, idea of the city, with a dense, vibrant and car-free street life.

In relation to the realisation of this historic-romantic vision of the American city, the most important point was that Baltimore by 1980 had secured a critical mass of new attractions. This was very important, but much of what was apparently being achieved was (or soon turned out to be) illusory. Thus, despite many claims, the Inner Harbor did not in any lasting sense transform the city's destiny. By the 1990s, Baltimore's decline, which briefly seemed to have been stemmed in the 1980s, had resumed. The Inner Harbor was also an imagined showpiece for the new 1980s-style public–private partnership. Here old-style and inflexible government planning was supposedly replaced by a new form of regime politics that was more dynamic and responsive to market realities. Yet Baltimore was by no means the first city to adopt partnership. It had actually been pioneered in Pittsburgh during the 1940s. Moreover, apart from Rouse's Harborplace, the Inner Harbor contained surprisingly little that was truly private investment. The city and other public sector agencies had created most of the developments that visitors saw.

Nor were the individual developments that were present in Baltimore even genuinely innovative. Boston was more significant in this respect but its stronger economy and established status as a tourist destination made it a less convincing example of the narrative of a city rising from the dead. Paradoxically, it was the very improbability of changing Baltimore's image of decline into that of a successful 'comeback' city that made it an altogether more compelling narrative.

LONDON DOCKLANDS: A CONTESTED MODEL

If Baltimore was the first truly global exemplar of port reuse, the massive scale of the London Docklands regeneration and its location in a major world city ensured that it too could not be ignored. Covering some 8.3 square miles (21.5 sq. km), the activities of the London Docklands Development Corporation (LDDC) dwarfed the Inner Harbor. In contrast to Baltimore, however, the attention was certainly not all admiring and the narrative of Docklands was a contested one (Brownill, 1993).

Regeneration actually began before the LDDC was formed in 1981. From the late 1960s the St Katherine Docks, near Tower Bridge, began to be renewed with a mix of public and private development, in new and reused buildings. By the early 1980s tangible results remained modest but attracted limited but positive international interest (Editorial, 1982). Within a few years, however, the formation of the LDDC transformed ideology, as well as the mode of operation, pace and scale of change associated with it, and prompted much more varied international perceptions.

A mix of culture, tourism and leisure activities dominated Baltimore; the LDDC offered this but also much more. It was especially notable for pioneering major private sector housing developments and very large-scale office, largely finance-related, development in waterside settings. Even more than Baltimore, the London Docklands became a demonstration project for the more capitalist-led form of Anglo-American political economy that was dominant in the 1980s and 1990s. Docklands was also the most tangible symbol of the Thatcher government's vision of a Britain transformed (Brownill, 1994). Here capitalist enterprise would be (and to a large extent was) freed from state regulation and the 'dead hand of socialism' would be lifted from urban planning (Heseltine, 1987). Key battles in Thatcher's emasculation of trades union power occurred in Docklands, and the government sidelined older working class communities associated with the port. In their place came a new, more affluent and acquisitive population embracing a newly identified 'yuppie' lifestyle. Here too, at Canary Wharf, the showpiece of the Docklands, could be glimpsed the first European signs of the coming world of globalised finance (see Figure 5.4).

Quite independently of Baltimore, this particular development also drew very directly on transatlantic precedents. The original concept for a major financial district in the Docklands enterprise zone was launched in 1985 by a consortium of American banks, led initially by the Texan G. Ware Travelstead (Brownill, 1993). In 1987 the Canadian developers Olympia and York, led by the Reichmann brothers, took over the development. Since 1980, they had been developing the major financial district at Battery Park City on a large land-filled former port site on New York's Hudson River (Gordon, 1997; Meyer, 1999). The Reichmanns adapted many facets of their earlier New York development at Canary Wharf. Its master plan, prepared by the American practice of Skidmore, Owings and Merrill, followed many precepts of the 1979 Battery Park City plan by Alexander Cooper and Stanton Eckstut.

Figure 5.4 Canary Wharf, London Docklands, UK, c. 2007 (source: © Godrick | Dreamstime.com).

Note
This came to be the most powerful example of how redundant port spaces could be used for major office and financial development. It became a symbol of London's reinvigoration as a world centre of finance in the late twentieth century. Though it was a highly contested vision, it ensured that the London Docklands could not be ignored by other port cities.

The visual similarities were also underlined by the commissioning of the architect responsible for all four of the Battery Park towers, Cesar Pelli, to design the centrepiece tower at Canary Wharf.

A key difference was, however, the greater distance of Canary Wharf from London's established financial district compared to Battery Park's location in New York. Rather like Baltimore, therefore, the very improbability of such a development happening and attracting prestige tenants confirmed the notion of London Docklands as a success. As in the story of Baltimore, many details of this narrative were only partially true and, much more so than in Baltimore, their value was doubted by many observers. Yet the imaginative geography of Docklands formed a very powerful vision of success.

Paradoxically, however, compared to Baltimore and several other cities later undergoing waterfront regeneration, surprisingly little was done to promote this imaginary as a positive model of regeneration. A major strand of the LDDC's activities was place marketing, but it was directed primarily at international business, real estate developers and potential new residents rather than city leaders or planners. The projected message was overwhelmingly one of success, first anticipated, then imminent and then inexorable. Combined with wider Thatcherite reforms to the UK business climate in the 1980s, Docklands was physical testimony that a relatively unregulated London was open to the world for business. In these circumstances it was natural that city leaders and planners elsewhere would be curious. As in Baltimore, many began to visit and learn what they could about the massive transformation that was underway.

But London's Docklands soon became the subject of strong negative as well as positive understandings. Many British planners, architects, commentators and politicians were almost immediately critical of Docklands (Thornley, 1991). To many of them, the project appeared ideologically driven, undemocratic, socially insensitive and aesthetically crude, concerned more with profits for private developers than wider planning or design considerations. Specific aspects of the Inner Harbor (particularly Rouse's Harborplace) had also, initially, been viewed negatively by many of Baltimore's citizens. Yet in that city the positive impressions soon dominated and were, as shown, actively propagated by EDC and others.

By contrast, the more vocal criticisms of Docklands immediately resonated with wider international suspicions of Anglo-American political economy in the Thatcher–Reagan era. In particular, some of Britain's European neighbours equated Docklands with Thatcher's unconcealed hatred of the stronger traditions of state intervention and market regulation that prevailed within most other European Community nations. The consequences of such thinking were especially marked in France. Here the balance of professional comment about Docklands was very negative and it was criticised as a model based on illusion (Hollamby and Da Luz, 1988; Villeneuve, 1988; Ducher, 1989). There was certainly no desire to replicate the London Docklands experience within French cities.

Elsewhere in Europe, however, more mixed lessons were drawn. In Amsterdam, for example, the LDDC's success in creating major new areas of housing in waterfront settings was emulated in the Dutch city's Eastern

Docks. The first parts of the regeneration of the Gothenburg port area also closely followed London (McCauley, 2009; Hall, 1991). Interestingly, however, there was a later revision of this approach. By 2001 the city planners of the new Norra Älvstranden district of the Gothenburg port were stressing that it should be a 'vibrant quarter that would *not* be similar to the London Docklands' (Ander and Ekman, 2001; cited in Cadell, Falk and King, 2008: 32, my emphasis).

A more positive Docklands narrative was also carried by those who had worked as LDDC employees or as consultants to the LDDC or Docklands developers. The subsequent career paths of these people took the Docklands experience to new places. A key figure in actively internationalising the experience of the London Docklands was Reg Ward, the first Chief Executive of the LDDC (see Figure 5.5). He was in charge when its style was most dynamically pro-developer and least planning or community friendly. Most of the dramatic changes were initiated under his leadership (Brownill, 1993). In late 1987 he left the LDDC and the following year travelled to New Zealand and Australia as an advisory consultant to several cities. He subsequently worked in other parts of the world, including St Petersburg, St Kitts and Barcelona (London Docklands Development Corporation, n.d.; Warrender, 2007).

Australia, with its historic connections with the UK, was particularly receptive to ideas and practice from that source. Already, independently of Ward's specific involvements, the organisational model of the urban development corporation, based directly on the LDDC, had begun to be used in similar Australian waterfront regeneration settings. The first was the Darling Harbour Authority in Sydney, created in 1984 (Searle, 2005). It was, however, in the rival Australian city of Melbourne that links with Ward and the London Docklands were closest.

In 1988, a business booster organisation, the Committee for Melbourne (CFM) commissioned Ward to make proposals for the moribund port area (Pappas, 2005; Warrender, 2007, 2009). CFM had been formed in 1985 to

Docklands inspirator Reg Ward moving on

LDDC CHIEF executive Reg Ward, one of the chief architects of the regeneration of Docklands, is leaving the Corporation at the end of the year.

Mr Ward, aged 60, who was appointed seven years ago to help mastermind the area's revitalisation, is to pursue other urban development interests.

He said he had decided two years ago to move on when the future of Docklands had been secured.

"With more than £5 billion of private investment now committed, we can clearly see an

"Emerging City"—a far cry from the dereliction and despair which existed in 1980. The future holds unparalleled opportunities for local residents and East London as a whole," he said.

"My seven years at the head of such an exceptionally capable, committed and successful team has been a totally exciting and fulfilling experience."

It was now time for him to take up opportunities in urban redevelopment elsewhere in the UK and overseas, drawing on "the unique Docklands Experience".

This year had been a dramatic one with the opening of the

Docklands Light Railway and the signing of the Canary Wharf master building agreement which represented "a pinnacle" in both Docklands regeneration and his own career, he added.

Mr Ward, who is married with two children, was formerly chief executive of Hereford and Worcester County Council. He has also been chief executive of Hammersmith Council and was secretary of Irvine Development Corporation.

A glowing tribute was paid to him by Corporation chairman Christopher Benson who said: "Reg Ward was the inspiration for

much that has happened in Docklands.

"His imagination and energy would be hard to match—and it is particularly fitting that his decision to leave is announced shortly following the signing of the Canary Wharf agreement—a project with which he identified from its conception. The Docklands Light Railway and the STOL airport were also conceived by Reg Ward.

"He leaves with the gratitude and good wishes of his colleagues and friends throughout Docklands."

Figure 5.5 Reg Ward was the dynamic first chief executive of the London Docklands Development Corporation (source: courtesy of Sue Brownhill).

Note

Ward set the LDDC's early style as very pro-developer, anti-planning and unsympathetic to the existing dock community. For many it epitomised the Thatcher government's vision for London. After he left the LDDC, he played an important role in spreading knowledge about this particular brand of Docklands regeneration, exerting particular influence in Melbourne.

move Melbourne out of the economic doldrums (see Figure 5.6). A dynamic initiative to transform the docks was thus a way of signalling a wider desire for change in the city (Wood, 2009, and personal communication, 15 June 2009). Like London, therefore, the perceived imperative, at least by the business lobby, was to make something big happen that would attract attention to the city. Ward's report was delivered in 1989 and, based on this, CFM published two further reports about the docks area in the following year. These contributed to the formation of the Melbourne Docklands Authority (MDA) in 1992, which undertook a major transformation of the area.

Though his specific proposals were not taken up by the MDA, there is no doubting Ward's role as a catalyst and inspirational figure. Melbourne is also generally seen as the Australian city where port renewal has corresponded most closely to the London approach. Especially telling is that Melbourne was one of very few port regenerations outside London which adopted the actual name 'Docklands' in its title. However, the CFM and the city's planners also referred to other international cities undergoing regeneration, including Baltimore, Boston, Glasgow and Liverpool. There have subsequently been disavowals of parallels with the London Docklands (e.g. Procter, 1997).

Space does not permit extensive discussion of other carriers of the Docklands message but another, rather different, example can be mentioned. He was Angus Gavin, who worked as Principal Urban Designer and Development Manager for the Royal Docks area in the eastern Docklands. In 1992 he became the leader of the team preparing the master plan for the reconstruction of central Beirut after the Lebanon Civil War. The public–private Solidere company, which has undertaken the planning and managed the development, drew extensively but selectively from international experience.

Figure 5.6 Simulation of regeneration of Melbourne Docklands, date unknown (source: Melbourne Docklands Authority).

Note
Although the results differed markedly from what he originally proposed, Reg Ward (and the London Docklands) was a major inspiration for the transformation of the redundant port. It was one of only a few examples around the world to borrow the 'Docklands' name (Dublin and Cork were others).

London Docklands was one of the leading examples (Gavin, 1996: 75). Yet London was certainly not the only referent here. With Gavin's assistance, the plan also showed explicit learning from cities across the world, including Baltimore, Sydney and Barcelona.

OTHER MODELS AND THE EMERGENCE OF MUTUAL LEARNING NETWORKS

As this last point suggests, the proliferation of examples of port regeneration provided an ever wider selection of referents, some of which became new models that other cities sought to emulate. In some cases, as in Baltimore, developers actively promoted these new models and took them to new settings. The closest rival to EDC in this has been the international development consultancy arm of the Victoria and Alfred Waterfront Company in Cape Town (Anon., 2005). This waterfront regeneration began in 1988 and was itself influenced in a general sense by Baltimore and Boston. However, it soon became South Africa's biggest tourist attraction and won widespread international admiration that fuelled the demand for the expertise which had created it. During the 1990s the international development consultancy subsidiary of the Victoria and Alfred Waterfront Company began to undertake commissions in a variety of places (Van Zyl, 2005). These included Libreville (Gabon), St Louis (Mauritius), Lagos (Nigeria), the Black Sea resort of Gelendzhik (Russia), as well as Gunwharf Quays in the British naval port of Portsmouth (The Portsmouth Society, 1998; Cook, 2004: 24–25) and aspects of the Maremagnum complex at Port Vell in Barcelona.

Meanwhile, in the wake of its exposure to world attention in the 1992 Summer Olympics, Barcelona itself became one of the most beguiling cities in the imaginations of city leaders, planners, architects and developers throughout the world (Monclús, 2003). Like Baltimore and Cape Town, its emergent imaginative geography was assiduously fostered by actors from the city. In Barcelona's case, however, they were more directly associated with the city's government, especially the mayor, Pasqual Maragall. From the mid-1990s, the city was actively promoting itself as a model, especially in Latin America. It did, of course, have much to offer the repertoire of waterfront planning that went beyond Baltimore, especially the new beach waterfronts created during the 1990s. Yet it was Port Vell, the most Baltimore-like part of Barcelona, which became a partial model for Puerto Madero in Buenos Aires (Keeling, 2005; Puerto Madero, n.d.). Under a formal co-operation agreement between the two cities, architects from the Catalonian capital undertook much of the early planning of this area during the late 1980s.

Network organisations promoting the regeneration of port areas also began to be formed during the 1980s, with the US-based Waterfront Center, founded in 1981, being one of the first (The Waterfront Center, n.d.). The Le Havre-based Association Internationale Villes et Ports (AIVP) was formed in 1988, its membership mainly comprising port organisations in countries speaking French or other Latin-based languages (Association Internationale Villes et Ports, n.d.). Within the European Union, port networking tendencies have been strengthened by funded support for regeneration projects that link several cities in mutual learning networks. The Waterfront Communities Project, which operated from 2004 to 2007, involved Hamburg, Gothenburg, Schiedam, Aalborg, Odense, Oslo, Edinburgh, Gateshead and Hull (Waterfront Communities Project, n.d.). Port cities are also a project theme in the current URBACT II programme, which covers many aspects of sustainable urban development. The particular port focus in this programme is the CTUR project, on cruise liner traffic, urban regeneration and heritage (URBACT II, n.d.). It is led by Naples and the other partners are Alicante, Helsinki, Leixoes (Portugal), Dublin, Valencia, Rhodes and Rostock.

CONCLUSIONS

The relatively short history of the global circulation of knowledge about port regeneration since the 1980s has therefore shown characteristics familiar to many other aspects of urban development and planning (or indeed any other kind of innovation that is being diffused). An initial example (in this case Baltimore Inner Harbor) was perceived as being the main innovator and garnered a disproportionate amount of attention. There were earlier examples that were more truly inventive (notably Boston). However, the example that came to be imagined as *the* model for others did so because it successfully synthesised earlier initiatives, produced impressive physical results at an earlier stage than anywhere else and was more extensively promoted by its protagonists. Despite some clear disparities between the perceived and actual nature and results of the Inner Harbor, it exerted a disproportionate impact on early thinking in the field. Though other partial models appeared, such as the London Docklands, they proved too controversial (flawed in many perceptions) to have such a big impact as and were less effectively promoted than Baltimore.

As the numbers of port regenerations proliferated, others later came to be admired for various real and imagined reasons. Some of these too began to become new exemplars, especially if, like Baltimore, they had active promoters. Often, though, it was the design and organisational know-how that was being utilised, rather than a tightly defined physical and organisational template as it had often been in Baltimore's case. Further actual innovations to the original model were now relatively minor refinements. Increasingly by the 1990s, and especially since 2000, the notion of one or a few models had diminished, with a greater shift towards mutual learning networks. These tend to encourage multi-directional flows of knowledge and a stronger emphasis on actual learning based on real knowledge and understanding rather than simply imagining. Even within these mutual networks, however, the experience of some partners, often larger cities, will tend to dominate. In general, though, when city leaders, planners and developers can refer to many different experiences, they are likely to become more discerning.

All this partly insures against the rather uncritical acceptance of a few external models, particularly Baltimore, which characterised the earliest phases of port regeneration. Over time it has been noticeable that there has been a professional and political reaction against both the 'fun city' and the 'financial yuppie city' models that Baltimore and London pioneered. In recent years port cities have also been less ready to surrender the maritime functions of their historic docks. It is now more common to see more nuanced port regenerations which involve working port functions and combinations of other activities.

In many respects, therefore, the international diffusion of ideas and practices about port regeneration has echoed the pattern of dispersal of many other innovations. What is most striking, however, at least in the planning field, is how rapidly it has occurred, how far it has spread and with what great impacts. We began by noting the traditional role of (functioning) major ports as international knowledge hubs and points of entry of exotic knowledge into national territories. Ultimately, though, the speed and extent of this were constrained by the stately pace of ocean travel. In the late twentieth and early twenty-first centuries, the diffusion of thinking and action about the regeneration of redundant dockside spaces has been accelerated by all the globalising forces of the contemporary age.

Part II

REGIONAL DYNAMICS OF PORT CITIES

Politics, people, and the built environment

6 TRADE, POLITICS AND CITY SPACE(S) IN MEDITERRANEAN PORTS

SAKIS GEKAS AND MATHIEU GRENET

In his famous account of a visit to the London Stock Exchange at the beginning of the eighteenth century, Voltaire noted that 'you will see there the representatives of all nations gathered for the utility of mankind. There the Jew, the Mahometan and the Christian deal with one another as if they were from the same religion, and only call infidels those who go bankrupted.'[1] This sort of coexistence between people of different ethnic and religious backgrounds has been celebrated since the Enlightenment as one of the ways to enhance political peace and social harmony, a view best exemplified by Immanuel Kant, who argued that the spread of republicanism and commerce would make possible the 'universal cosmopolitan existence' (Reiss, 1984). In this respect at least, Voltaire's account of the London Stock Exchange strikingly resembles recent historical studies of some Mediterranean port cities in the eighteenth and nineteenth centuries. The elites of these port cities are described as 'cosmopolitan', successful and polyglot traders and businessmen, with strong commercial and cultural connections to both Western and Eastern metropolises. Situating these traders in their host urban societies, we have chosen to compare merchants in the port cities of Livorno/Leghorn, Trieste and Corfu from the 1770s to the 1870s. These cities, and to some extent Marseilles, were similar in their socio-economic development, size and particularly in their immigrant merchant population and the resulting diversity.

Since the turn of the century, the notion of 'cosmopolitanism' has raised increasing interest among social scientists working in the fields of sociology, anthropology, political sciences, history and, more recently, geography. As a result of its prominence in such a variety of intellectual fields and research agendas, the notion has developed into what the anthropologist Henk Driessen recently called 'a Protean commonsense term referring to a rather elusive set of historical, social and cultural phenomena' (Driessen, 2005: 136; Dogo, 1996–1997; Vassilikou, 2002). Within historical research, a lingering confusion exists between what is defined as 'cosmopolitan' and what is trans- or international, multicultural and diverse, while a similar confusion between the notions of 'cosmopolitanism' and 'multiculturalism' persists, the latter being often considered as evidence for the former. But rather than an attempt to review the many (mis)uses of the notion of 'cosmopolitanism' from the Enlightenment to today, this chapter is an attempt to approach in a concrete and comparative way and to historicise the cosmopolitanism of cities and individuals. In this perspective, we have decided to take as a working definition the four-fold typology recently drawn by German historian Malte Fuhrmann. These four criteria are: (1) a publicly visible diversity; (2) an ability of individual or collective agents to navigate between different coded spheres; (3) an active practice of sociabilities that cross community borders; and (4) a belief and a policy of enhancing cohesion without a monolithic base (Dogo, 1996–1997; Vassilikou, 2002).

We aim to test the pertinence of the notion in a dynamic way, by considering in particular the relations of Greek and Jewish merchants with civic and state authorities. There is no doubt that these three ports were connected with each other, just as local Greek and Jewish communities, although they are rarely studied together (Dogo, 1996–1997; Vassilikou, 2002), belonged to wider diasporas that expanded all across the Mediterranean and beyond. Indeed, we shall also recall that one understanding of these two diasporas is that the 'cosmopolitanism' of merchants stood in contrast to nationalism (Dogo, 1996–1997; Vassilikou, 2002). Yet we prefer to situate the Greek and Jewish merchants in their local contexts: without arguing that there is only elite cosmopolitanism, the 'cosmopolitanism' we look at accompanied the merchants' commercial prosperity, the leadership they demonstrated in their communities and their social standing in their host societies.

In these cities, 'foreign' traders, Jewish and Greek, were not autonomous from the political sphere of their host societies but integrated residents. One group in particular, Greek merchants, is exemplary of 'cosmopolitan' trading groups resident in port cities. In Trieste, at least, there is little doubt that it was Jews and Greeks who flourished and became the heart of the city's merchant class (Dubin, 2004). In Livorno, the Greek and Jewish elite enjoyed a vigorous presence, entrepreneurial success and social status (Chatziioannou, 2005; Trivellato, 2009; Vlami, 1996/2000). In Corfu, Christian and Jewish merchants comprised the city's merchant class in almost equal numbers (Gekas, 2004). Of course, we shall also keep in mind that Greeks and Jews are important cosmopolitans in other Mediterranean cities as well, notably Odessa and Alexandria. Last, this cosmpolitanism also accompanied the increasing conception that minorities lived in an interconnected world (therefore rendering the transnational, or, rather, translocal, nature of diaspora more than a mere rhetorical figure), while being rooted into common local social practices and both shared and distinct uses of urban space.

THE GREEK PRESENCE IN TRIESTE, LIVORNO AND CORFU: A BRIEF OVERVIEW

In the course of the seventeenth and especially the eighteenth century, the ports of Livorno, Trieste and Marseilles attracted large numbers of foreigners, a direct consequence of trade activities. The number of Greeks in Trieste rose from 54 in 1752 to 752 in 1792, 1,500 in 1821, and dropped only due to the Greek war of independence to a figure of around 1,000 by 1890 (Katsiardi-Hering, 2001). In Marseilles the number of recorded Greeks also rose from the end of the eighteenth century onwards, though in smaller proportions: from 51 in 1799 to 156 in 1821, and 345 in 1825, then fell slightly (again due to the war of independence), to 303 in 1861 (Mandilara, 1998). As for Livorno, a mere 156 Greeks were settled in 1810, while two decades later we find in Greek governmental sources that 'one finds in Livorno more Greek traders than in any other city in Europe',[2] a statement clearly exaggerated given the number of Greek merchants in Trieste just listed, not to mention Odessa, with probably the fastest rising Greek population outside Greece. As these numbers testify, Greeks were no longer an 'invisible minority' in urban space, and as many of them planned to settle in their host cities, they petitioned the state and city authorities to have their presence officially recognised. As one might expect, their two requests were the building of an Orthodox church and the foundation of legal bodies (confraternities or brotherhoods) in charge of representing them. In most of their host cities, the 'tandem' formed by the church and the brotherhood quickly became the physical and symbolical centre of Greek communal life and activities.

In Livorno, a Greek church (*Santissima Annunziata*) was built as early as 1606, and was shared by the Orthodox and Uniate members of the 'Greek nation' (*nazione greca*). As the control over the church led to many conflicts between the two groups, the 'nation' eventually split in 1757, as the Orthodox were expelled from the *Santissima Annunziata* and granted the authorisation to build their own church (*Santissima Trinità*), inaugurated in 1760 at a certain distance from the main square and public core of the city (see Figure 6.1). Fifteen years later, the foundation of the *Santissima Trinità* brotherhood would come to finalise the legal existence of Orthodox Greeks in Livornese society (Panessa, 1991). In Trieste, a similar scenario led to the division of the original 'Greek nation', but this time as the result of the conflicts between Greek and Serb (*Illirici*) elements. Sharing an Orthodox church (*Annunciazione e Santo Spiridione*) as early as 1751, the two groups gradually diverged, until reconciliation became impossible, and in 1782 the Greeks were granted permission to build their own Orthodox church (*Santissima Trinità e San Nicolò* or *San Nicolò dei Greci*), as well as to found their own brotherhood (De Antonellis Martini, 1968).

In Corfu, the majority of merchants and other residents belonged to the Orthodox rite, while we know practically nothing about the Roman Catholic merchants. There were also a few Protestants, several thousand Jews but apparently very few, if any, Muslims.[3] Under British rule merchants from Epirus and other areas of the Ottoman Empire, from the Italian states, Malta, Britain, Holland and even Switzerland enriched the trading class of Corfu (Mousson, 1995). Significant numbers of Maltese and Italians serving previously under the British Navy settled in Corfu town, adding to the diversity of the town's population. Even in a city like Corfu with an overwhelming Orthodox majority, however, immigrants from Epirus, the mainland opposite Corfu, built the *Panagia ton Xenon*, or Madonna of the Foreigners Church, at the heart of the city, distinguishing themselves in their new place of residence.

The plurality of the cities notwithstanding, the diversity of the ports cannot automatically qualify these cities as cosmopolitan.

Legend

∙∙∙∙∙∙∙ Via Ferdinanda

□

1. Grand Duke's Palace
2. Governor's Palace
3. Duomo (Cathedral Church)
4. Muslims' housing (Bagno)
5. Synagogue
6. Armenian Church

▬

7. Greek-Catholic Church
   (*Santissima Annunziata*)
8. Greek-Orthodox Church
   (*Santissima Trinita*,
   inaugurated in 1760)

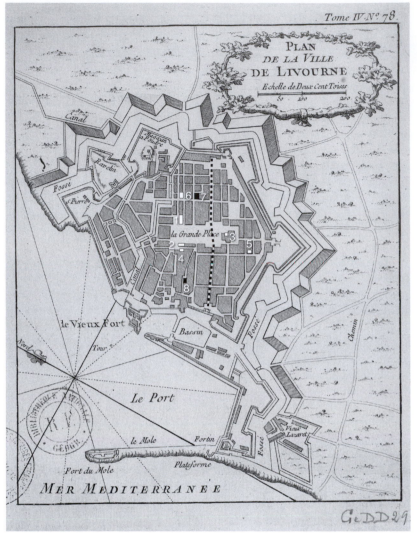

Figure 6.1 Livorno in the 18th century: abridged map of the main public buildings and non-Catholic places of worship plotted on a map by Jacques-Nicolas Bellin, 1764 in *Petit Atlas Maritime* (source: Eighteenth-century map of Livorno by Jacques-Nicolas Bellin (*Petit Atlas Maritime*, [S.l.]: [s.n.], 1764), with additions by the authors).

STATE POLICIES AND THEIR IMPACT: FREE PORTS

The opening of 'free ports' (i.e. ports in which imported goods could be held or processed free of customs duties before re-export) was at the heart of the economic policy of several early modern states, a development that determined the economic and social trajectory of some major Mediterranean ports. Livorno was declared a free port in 1593, when Ferdinando I of the Medici granted freedom of trade in Livorno 'a tutti uoi mercanti di qualsiuoglia natione, leuantini, e' ponentini spagnioli, portoghesi, Greci, todeschi, & Italiani, hebrei, turchi e' Mori, Armenij, Persiani, & altri' (Frattarelli-Fischer and Villani, 2007). This was more than just a sign of the openness of the Tuscan state vis-à-vis foreigners; it was the expression of Ferdinando's will to find a commercial niche for his port city, orienting its activities towards the

Levantine trade. Trieste was declared a *porto franco* following the treaty of Passarowitz in 1717 and in the course of the eighteenth century a number of other treaties confirmed the intention of the Habsburg authorities to create a more beneficial commercial environment by allowing duty exemptions and privileging Levantine trade (De Antonellis Martini, 1968). The links between the opening of the free port of Trieste and cosmopolitanism have not eluded historians' attention (Christopoulos, 2007). Similarly, in 1669 Marseilles was declared a free port, a status that would quickly change under the pressure of the Marseillese mercantile elite into a port that offered foreigners the chance to settle and thus enabled French trade to compete with the Dutch and English traders in the Eastern Mediterranean (Forbonnais, 1755).

In all three ports under scrutiny, the opening of free ports was therefore no magnanimous act of cosmopolitanism and tolerance, but rather part and parcel of the political economy of the Habsburg and French empires and – in the sixteenth century – of the at the time still powerful Tuscan state. Corfu, when declared a free port in 1825, belonged to a plan of imperial expansion given that the Ionian Islands had been a British colony in everything but name since 1815. Thus, and in contrast to the ports of Livorno, Marseilles and Trieste, which were used by the Tuscan, French and Habsburg states, respectively, for maintaining a competitive advantage in trade with the Eastern Mediterranean, the port of Corfu – essentially a port under colonial rule – was granted free port status in order to cater to British economic interests that were expanding in the Eastern Mediterranean and would continue to do so later in the nineteenth century.

ACCOMMODATING A FOREIGN PRESENCE IN THE CITY: INCENTIVES, TOLERATION, REGULATIONS

A striking feature of most early Greek settlements is, once more, the role played by state authorities in the 'management' of the foreigners' presence. It is essential to recall that cosmopolitan toleration and coexistence among diverse groups, or *convivance* (Georgeon and Dumont, 1997), was originally made possible by the efforts of articulated policies to attract foreigners and protect them. Just as the grand-dukes of Tuscany Cosimo I and Francis II personally authorised the Greeks to settle in Livorno and to celebrate the Orthodox mass, Empress Maria-Theresa invited them to reside in Trieste and granted them special protection.

In Marseilles, though Greek presence was not significant before the very end of the eighteenth century, this strong bond between state authorities and foreign minorities is particularly visible in the establishment of an Orthodox cult. Orthodox masses were privately performed around 1818 in the house of a Greek merchant. Greek traders played a major role in the city's trade and provisioning by the 1820s, but Orthodox celebrations remained *tolerated* rather than *authorised* for most of the nineteenth century. Rather than merely ignoring the Greek presence, French authorities kept looking for agreements that would not lead to the official recognition of the Orthodox cult. In 1821, the Ottoman consul in Marseilles (who was then a Greek) obtained approval from both the mayor of the city and the prefect of the Bouches-du-Rhône for the establishment of an Orthodox church in a small chapel he henceforth rented.[4] But when, to everyone's surprise, the French Home Secretary finally refused to give his authorisation for the opening of the chapel, the consul simply cut a deal with the mayor and the prefect: the two of them would tolerate the existence of the chapel and keep the Home Secretary out of the secret, and the Greeks would in exchange pledge to celebrate their rites in the most discreet way possible. When he eventually learned about the affair after some years, the Home Secretary had no choice but to 'maintain this toleration, as long as no problem occurrs'.[5] In spite of its tacit nature, the terms and conditions of this agreement were very clear: on the one hand, the Greeks obtained freedom of worship and, on the other hand, they committed themselves to give up any attempt to make their religion a 'public' one (Grenet, 2010). In Marseilles as elsewhere, such calls to keep their religion 'discreet' and 'private' blatantly contradicted the increasing economic and social achievements of Greek or Jewish traders.

Local and national authorities in most Western European port cities strictly regulated minorities' visibility in the urban fabric, from the early modern period up until late in the nineteenth century. This is even more striking in the case of Livorno, which is often celebrated as the cradle of a state-driven cosmopolitanism. Despite all their tolerance, Tuscan authorities often set strict limitations to the visibility of foreigners in the city. For instance, as late as 1757 and 1760, two personal orders (*motuproprii*) of Grand-Duke Francis II contained drastic measures limiting the construction of the Orthodox church of the *Santissima Trinità*: the building was to remain hidden from public sight, with neither façade nor sign on the street, and no use of bells. All kinds of Orthodox processions were banned from the city space, and funerals were to take place without any religious symbols (crosses, lamps, dresses, etc.), preferably late at night or early in the morning (Panessa, 1991). Such measures recall the ones taken during the same time in other cities, such as Vienna, where non-Catholic churches could not have their main entrance on the city streets (Porfyriou, 2007). Likewise, Empress Maria-Theresa would order in 1751 that the Greeks' presence in Trieste be confined 'within the walls of their own church' ('dentro il circuito o chiusura del proprio Tempio') (Porfyriou, 2007). Although their demographic and economic importance made them 'visible' on the streets or in the ports of Livorno, Trieste and Marseilles, Greeks were kept in a religious 'invisibility' by the authorities of these cities. There is little doubt that, over time, such ambiguity provoked many misunderstandings, resentments and conflicts between the foreigners and their 'hosts'. But while the Livornese and Marseillese measures would remain vigorous far into the nineteenth century, the Greeks in Trieste obtained a ruling in 1782 that ensured that the new Orthodox church of *Santissima Trinità e San Nicolò*, adorned with a neo-classicistic façade, could be built in everyone's sight on the waterfront (Katsiardi-Hering, 2001) (see Figure 6.2).

Differences between local situations should not make us forget that the Greek diaspora remained an interconnected space of its own during the whole period under scrutiny. The leaders of the different communities were in regular contact, constantly looking to benefit from each other's negotiations with the authorities of their host city. For instance, the Livornese Greeks would consult with the community of Trieste regarding the privileges granted

Figure 6.2 The façade of the Greek-Orthodox church of *San Nicolò e Santissima Trinità* in Trieste (view from the seafront), 2006.

to them by Maria-Theresa, in order to negotiate on similar terms with the Tuscan authorities (Porfyriou, 2007). The communities were communicating at a time of changes in the status of religious and ethnic minorities, and they displayed a strong consciousness of their shared conditions and identities. Yet this consciousness seems to have followed a strict and exclusive understanding of 'Greek-ness', as we find little, if any, sign of such cooperation among the different minorities of a same city.

STATE POLICIES AND THEIR IMPACT: CITIZENSHIP AND INTEGRATION

The policies of different states towards merchants from the Eastern Mediterranean involved not only welcoming them as foreigners and granting them rights to build their temples and organise in corporate bodies, but also giving them citizenship status. From very early on, foreign merchants petitioned state and local authorities for citizenship in their host societies. But policies that explicitly included granting citizenship to traders were directly linked to the rise of commercial exchanges between the ports of Livorno and Trieste and the Levant.

The case of the Jewish elite in these two cities constitutes the most prominent example of this process of civic emancipation and inclusion as a direct result of commercial success (Dubin, 1999; Ferrara degli Uberti, 2004). In Trieste, naturalisations of Greeks became more frequent after the 1780s, when merchants from the Ottoman Empire and the Ionian Islands increasingly moved to the port to live permanently, trading on equal terms with other nationals, raising the Austrian flag on their ships and enjoying the security afforded by the Austrian authorities. Once these merchants became Austrian subjects, they lost the rights they enjoyed as foreign (mostly Ottoman) subjects trading in the Habsburg Empire; apparently, the benefits of Austrian citizenship were significant enough to offset the loss of another citizenship (Porfyriou, 2007). In Trieste, the majority of naturalised Ottoman Greeks came from Smyrna, Chios and the Morea, as well as from the Venetian-ruled Ionian Islands, all areas from which most trade with the Habsburg *emporium* originated. Naturalisation in Trieste advanced integration of Greeks in their local society, not least through public offices, since it allowed several of them to participate in the *Borsa* and the *Tribunale Mercantile* and to work as public brokers (Katsiardi-Hering, 1986). In Livorno, by the end of the eighteenth century the Jewish 'nation' was so populous and important for the city's commercial prosperity that the authorities granted to Jews the right of citizenship, known as *ballotazione*. The citizenship right integrated the Livornese Jews into the Tuscan nation and distinguished them from members of other nations. The right was soon followed by the privilege of being allowed to become magistrates (Ferrara degli Uberti, 2004).

The British-protected Ionian State passed its naturalisation law in 1820 in order to deal with the issue of refugees from Parga, located in the Ottoman mainland opposite Corfu, when the British sold that town to Ali-Pasha, the regional ruler.[6] Between the 1830s and 1860s, the entries of naturalised subjects in the official newspaper of the Ionian State show that the status of the Islands as a British protectorate and the position of the port of Corfu induced foreigners to ask and obtain Ionian nationality. The proximity of the island with Epirus and southern Italy explains the origin of most of the foreigners asking for Ionian citizenship. Approximately 75 per cent of those petitioning for Ionian citizenship asked for Corfu to be their political domicile, and 33 per cent of those recorded were merchants. One observes a steady increase in the number of naturalisations throughout the 1850s and a sharp decline in the early 1860s, reflecting the foreseeable unification of the Islands with Greece, which made naturalisation redundant, or at least less attractive.[7] In all ports the granting of citizenship status was an important first step to the further integration, and in some cases assimilation, of foreign merchants in their host societies.

COMMERCIAL INSTITUTIONS

In all cases, from seventeenth-century Marseilles to nineteenth-century Corfu, the state and municipal authorities, whether Tuscan, Habsburg or Anglo-Ionian, were keen to create the best possible conditions for the merchants under their supervision, devise the best possible commercial policy and reap the optimal commercial and fiscal benefits. In devising the rules and regulations for commercial operations, the authorities recognised and catered for the linguistic diversity of their subjects: when the law for the Corfu brokers was devised in 1831, for example, the qualifications required were working knowledge of both Greek and Italian, reflecting the linguistic and ethnic diversity of the Corfu business world and their trading partners, even though Greek was set to become the official language of the Ionian State.[8] Commercial institutions such as Chambers of Commerce were instrumental in the 'management of cosmopolitanism' in all the ports in question.

Commercial associations were a common feature of many Mediterranean and non-Mediterranean ports; new conditions of trade required the formation and 'institutionalisation' of a merchant group that was recorded in lists, became stratified, elected representatives and acquired a meeting place for business as well as entertainment. The founding of commercial 'intermediate' institutions – that is, between market and government – was perhaps the most important associational activity and space of negotiation between merchants and authorities in all the ports we examine (Ridings, 2001). These associations were part and parcel of the flourishing associational activity noted by many historians (Anastassiadou, 1997b); in contrast to the communal associations, however, such as the community of Greeks in Venice, Livorno and Trieste, commercial associations were multiethnic, operated under different rules, and negotiated individual and collective interests with state and municipal authorities. For some Greek merchants residing in the ports in question, commercial associations were as important as their communal ones, and the two were not in conflict (Selekou, 2004). These were sites of sociability and business, where convergence of interests and negotiation with central authorities took place.

Through commercial institutions, merchants acquired further control of their economic environment and improved their negotiating position in relation to state authorities. At the same time, they emerged as a more coherent occupational group, despite the different ethnic groups that participated. Merchants formed commercial associations, societies or clubs and Chambers of Commerce that advanced their cohesion as a group and, we argue, their cosmopolitanism as well. This is where merchants met, socialised, conducted business, read both local and international newspapers, and addressed municipal and national issues. Above all, this is where merchants crossed communal boundaries set by the religious and ethnic associations. This is where cosmopolitan attitudes developed. This diversity of the merchant group enriched the ports' commercial and social life since it provided new opportunities and expanded trade with the Levant.

While foreigners' inclusion in these associations came in recognition of their increasing economic importance, this process was not as peaceful as it is sometimes described. This is, for instance, the case with the Chamber of Commerce of Marseilles, founded as early as 1599 in order to represent the interests of the economic and social aristocracy of the local trade. While Greek traders began settling in the port in the eighteenth century, the Chamber strongly opposed their business activities, claiming that the Levantine trade had to remain in Marseillese hands (Echinard, 1973). However, the economic success met by Greek firms in Marseilles gradually made it impossible for the local trading elites simply to ignore this presence (see Figure 6.3). This integration process, nevertheless, was long and at times chaotic – as when most of the Marseillese merchants took a clear stand against the movement for Greek independence, which they considered a threat to the Levantine trade. Not until 1861 do we witness the admission of the first Greek member, Paul Rodocanachis, to the Chamber of Commerce of Marseilles, so far the exclusive stronghold of the local business elite (Marseillese Chamber of Commerce, 1862).

In Livorno, the *Deputazione di Commercio* was founded in 1642, and in 1717 its records mentioned that it consisted of eight *negozianti*, four from

Tuscany and four from foreign communities. It is important to note the financial dependence of the Tuscan governments on the Chamber, due to several loans that bankers and merchants of the Chamber (three Greeks among them) had granted to governments. This development gave the Chamber considerable negotiating power. The administration of the Chamber in Livorno was regulated by an edict, according to which 4 of the 12 governing members had to be Tuscan, 2 were Greeks, 2 French, 1 was English, 1 Swiss, and 2 represented the Jewish community. Between 1802 and 1819, Greek merchants were elected president of the Chamber of Commerce no less than twenty-eight times. This period of Greek dominance in the Chamber coincides with their interests in public affairs, on the one hand, and with their important role as leading members of the Greek Orthodox brotherhood, on the other (Vlami, 1996/2000).

When the Habsburg authorities in 1754 took the initiative to organise the commercial activities of the port of Trieste by establishing a *Borsa*, most of the merchants were not very sympathetic to the idea. The Greek trader Pietro Coniali was an exception, since he envisaged a very 'democratic' institution in which all merchants would participate, which in the end was not approved.

Figure 6.3 The Greek trading elite in Marseilles: spatial distribution of the main commercial houses in the second quarter of the nineteenth century (source: Marseilles in the 1840s, located by the author (Mathieu Grenet) on a map published by the London-based Society for the Diffusion of Useful Knowledge. David Rumsey Historical Map Collection).

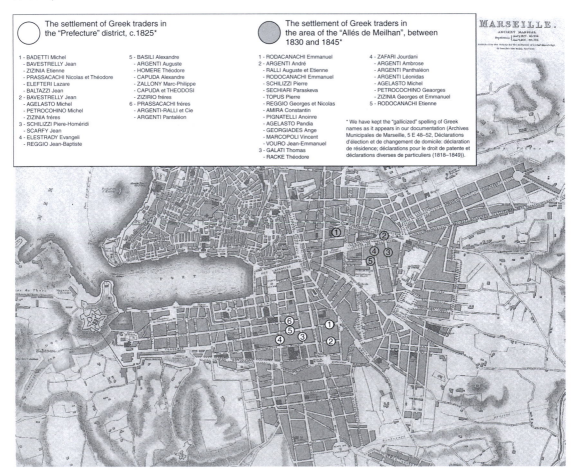

The settlement of Greek traders in the "Prefecture" district, c.1825*

1 - BADETTI Michel
  - BAVESTRELLY Jean
  - ZIZINIA Etienne
  - PRASSACACHI Nicolas et Théodore
  - ELEFTERI Lazare
  - BALTAZZI Jean
2 - BAVESTRELLY Jean
  - AGELASTO Michel
  - PETROCOHINO Michel
  - ZIZINIA frères
3 - SCHILIZZI Piere-Homéridi
  - SCARFY Jean
4 - ELESTRADY Evangeli
  - REGGIO Jean-Baptiste

5 - BASILI Alexandre
  - ARGENTI Auguste
  - HOMERE Théodore
  - CAPUDA Alexandre
  - ZALLONY Marc-Philippe
  - CAPUDA et THEODOSI
  - ZIZIRIO frères
6 - PRASSACACHI frères
  - ARGENTI-RALLI et Cie
  - ARGENTI Pantaléon

The settlement of Greek traders in the area of the "Allés de Meilhan", between 1830 and 1845*

1 - RODACANACHI Emmanuel
2 - ARGENTI André
  - RALLI Auguste et Etienne
  - RODOCANACHI Emmanuel
  - SCHILIZZI Pierre
  - SECHIARI Paraskeva
  - TOPUS Pierre
  - REGGIO Georges et Nicolas
  - PIGNATELLI Anoinre
  - AGELASTO Pandia
  - GEORGIADES Ange
  - MARCOPOLI Vincent
  - VOURO Jean-Emmanuel
3 - GALATI Thomas
  - RACKE Théodore

4 - ZAFARI Jourdani
  - ARGENTI Ambrose
  - ARGENTI Panthaléon
  - ARGENTI Léonidas
  - AGELASTO Michel
  - PETROCOCHINO Geaorges
  - ZIZINIA Georges et Emmanuel
5 - RODOCANACHI Etienne

* We have kept the "gallicized" spelling of Greek names as it appears in our documentation (Archives Municipales de Marseille, 5 E 48–52, Déclarations d'élection et de changement de domicile: déclaration de résidence; déclarations pour le droit de patente et déclarations diverses de particuliers (1818–1849)).

MARSEILLE.

Initially the *Borsa* became the representative body of the *Ceto Mercantile* or 'Commercial Body' of the *negozianti* of Trieste, the company owners, directors and merchants involved in international trade and approved by the Commercial Tribunal, and a year later the *Borsa* operated also as a Chamber of Commerce. It functioned as a consulting body to the central authorities and became exclusive when a membership fee of 20,000 florins was set (Katsiardi-Hering, 1986). Although initially Greek merchants residing in Trieste were not included in the *Borsa*, after the 1780s their participation in it increased significantly, to the extent that in 1807 one in five members was Greek. Greeks often presided in the administration of the *Borsa*, reflecting the increased importance of Greek merchants in Triestine society. In all the ports occupied by the Imperial French in the first years of the nineteenth century, merchants were forced to lend the authorities extraordinary sums, being, as they were, (among) the richest inhabitants; sums that on many occasions were never recovered.

The right of Jewish merchants in Trieste to serve as *Borsa* deputies came as a confirmation of their economic power and status among the Christian merchants of the city; this was 'qualitatively different from any of their previous rights' (Dubin, 1999). The legislation of the 1780s gave to Triestine Jews the right to serve in the *Borsa* together with Greek Orthodox and Protestant merchants, thus distinguishing them from other Habsburg Jews and equating them with other merchants. Trieste was a commercial society and its most distinguished members were rewarded for their services, regardless of ethnic origin and religious affiliation, whether they were Greek Orthodox or Jewish merchants. In Corfu, English and local merchants founded the Corfu Exchange in 1841, 'following the example of the most eminent metropoles of Europe', and quickly became one of the 'establishments that sign the advanced pace of civilisation'.[9] The Exchange functioned primarily as a place for conducting business.[10] Douglas, High Commissioner of the Ionian Islands at the time, supported the merchants' initiative, as he saw in the establishment of new commercial institutions the incorporation of the Islands into a larger imperial modernising project; merchants in Corfu were instrumental in the success of the project.[11] The records of the Chamber of Commerce show that by the 1860s Greek merchants dominated the administration of the Chamber.

The participation and role of minority merchants (Greek and Jewish in our case) in institutions of urban governance and urban politics demonstrate emancipation, integration and cosmopolitanism on their part. The case has been made before. Historians have argued that in Trieste the merchant class (many Greeks among them) became more cosmopolitan through the participation in the Masonic lodges (Katsiardi-Hering, 1986). Similarly, the activities that took place in Marseilles lodges can be considered a cosmopolitics that was at play outside the commercial elite and other associations of the port (Grenet, 2006). The activities of Greek merchants extended to literary and philanthropic as well as Masonic and commercial associations, and their cosmopolitan attitudes can be found there too. The merchants of Corfu, for example, participated in literary and philosophical societies, as well as in philanthropic initiatives that aimed at preventing social problems – such as unemployment and vagrancy – escalating to social crises. Such activity indicates the spread of worldviews that were influenced by the principal ideas of an urban modernity, or rather a modern urbanism. The local elite of local and foreign merchants of different religions and denominations was linked through international trade and political liberalism to Mediterranean ports further north and west. This was a cosmopolitan attitude that entailed the development of personal and group intellect, aesthetics and worldview, certainly an elite cosmopolitanism.

In Livorno, from the early nineteenth century onwards, Greek merchants belonged to dense networks of social and professional relationships and were members of a rising professional 'elite' that included the big merchants of Tuscany; in fact, some of the most prominent Greek merchants converted to Catholicism (Funaro, 2006). These networks advanced socialisation and ideological identification and solidarity among their members, and fostered relations through participation in urban politics and social life, as well as through the management of free time (LoRomer, 1987). The most important fields of agency were spaces of interpersonal relations, such as the Livorno Chamber of Commerce, the ad hoc committees that were appointed by the government with specific duties on political, social and economic issues, philanthropic associations and clubs of public good, entertainment clubs, literary and cultural, theatrical and sport clubs and competitions (Vlami, 1996/2000). A very similar pattern of sociability and interaction with the rest of the urban elite can be found in Marseilles at a later period, when in the mid-nineteenth century prominent Greek traders started entering en masse the philanthropic and other voluntary associations (Paris, 2001).

THE LIMITS OF COSMOPOLITANISM

State authorities, however, were not always sensitive to ethnic and religious diversity. Though in the 1850s Jewish merchants in Corfu constituted one-third of those registered in the Chamber of Commerce, no Jewish merchants were considered eligible for election as assessors to the Commercial Tribunal for cases of bankruptcy and insolvency.[12] The Jewish merchants of Trieste were facing exactly the same problem and in order to redress their exclusion from the town's *Borsa* put forward a claim for equal representation on the Chamber of Commerce. Eight Jewish merchants of Corfu did the same, using in fact the same arguments about the essential contribution of Jewish merchants to the town's commercial life and the benefits the city would derive from the participation of Jews in the regulation of commerce through its institutions (Dubin, 1999). The case of the exclusion of Jews from commercial associations shows that initially the cosmopolitanism developed in Chambers of Commerce such as that of Corfu was first and foremost a Christian cosmopolitanism.

Moreover, a closer look at the functioning of the Greek communities and Corfu society shows that their own cosmopolitanism was to be found mostly in the public sphere. Whether responding to official and social exclusion or interested in preserving their distinct culture, Greek merchants kept marrying Greek Orthodox women, were being buried apart from other Christians or were doing business overwhelmingly with their co-nationals and co-religionists during the nineteenth and early twentieth century. The case of Livorno demonstrates the ethnic and religious segregation after death. A quick survey of Livorno's cemeteries in 1832 shows that the city's inhabitants were buried in no less than 10 different locations, according to their faith or their 'ethno-national' identity – besides the old and new Catholic cemeteries, one would find a new and an old Jewish cemetery, an English one, a Dutch, an Armenian, a Greek Catholic, a Greek Orthodox and a Muslim one (Bortolotti, 1970). Likewise, an analysis of the parish registers of the Greek Orthodox Church in Marseilles shows that the choice of both spouses and witnesses obeyed basic (yet unwritten) principles aiming to preserve the exclusively Greek and Orthodox profile of the group. As late as 1906, the community ostracised one Cleopatra Christophides-Petrokokkino for having married the French Catholic Paul-Adhémar Clairefond (Paris, 2001). Similar cases are to be found in Livorno and reveal that the Orthodox Church, as well as many conservative scholars and writers, was very sceptical about, if not outright hostile to, marriages with non-Orthodox, or even socialisation with them. Mixed marriages became a public concern for the Greeks of Livorno, to the point that, as early as 1775, the statutes of the Greek Orthodox confraternity would ban from its administration any member married to a non-Orthodox woman.[13] Some of them protested against their exclusion since their spouses and children had been baptised into the Orthodox rite; the measure would only be abolished in 1873, on the occasion of the first rewriting of the confraternity statutes (Cini, 2007). Such exclusion measures proved efficient: between 1760 and 1807 in Livorno, only three out of 30 marriages of Greeks were mixed. At the same period in Trieste there were no mixed marriages out of 158 among Greek Orthodox, and only after 1815 do we have mixed marriages in the Austrian port (Katsiardi-Hering, 1986; Vlami, 1996/2000). As late as 1874, Ambrosios Rallis, the most prominent Greek trader in Trieste, advised his children to marry not only Greek Orthodox women but women who would have a 'greater homogeneity of morals and education', namely women from a similar class. In Rallis' mind, tolerance did not mean acceptance, and in any case concerned the public sphere and not marriage and family (Katsiardi-Hering, 1986; Vlami, 1996/2000).

These testimonies show that cosmopolitanism cannot be defined as merely a way to transcend the boundaries of the group one belongs to. The much celebrated cosmopolitan mentality was part of the formation of cosmopolitan identities; and identities are always multiple: local and regional, national and transnational, ethnic and racial. In other words, it is not easy to find a Mediterranean subject that was *always* or exclusively cosmopolitan. We therefore think that the expression 'communitarian cosmopolitanism' is particularly apt to capture the dichotomy and duality of minorities' identity (Trivellato, 2009).

CONCLUSION

Cosmopolitanism was managed by authorities, and by collective and individual actors, and it followed a particular pattern of state policy that included opening free ports, granting citizenship rights, allowing and facilitating – not simply tolerating – the observance of religious practices and encouraging the formation of commercial associations.

The management of cosmopolitanism was not the consequence of commercial and educational capital employed by a few merchants (Yerasismos, 1999), but the result of a constant negotiation between individuals, groups and state authorities. The three ports, different as they certainly were, faced similar increasing pressures because of their diverse populations; on the other hand, commercial growth and the settlement of foreign merchant groups of various ethnoreligious communities created opportunities. As state authorities and merchants leading the various communities – certainly the Greek ones – recognised that coexistence was in the interest of everyone, they promoted the settlement of foreigners as a political tool and managed the diverse social milieu that was conducive to the cosmopolitan public identity of some merchants. Yet a closer look at the 'social engineering' in action in all three cities shows that this cosmopolitanism did not constitute a 'social equaliser', just as it did not remain immune from religious, ethnic and social prejudices. In many respects, the issue of urban form and city space aptly illustrates this feature: while the planning of both Livornese, Triestine and Corfiote (and, for that matter, Marseillese) public spaces during the period of study appears increasingly homogeneous and coherent, one cannot fail to notice the persistence of minor forms of spatial discrimination or 'withdrawal', which also supported the preservation of distinct communal identities among foreign groups. In this perspective, and unlike the much celebrated figure of the 'citizen of the world', we would argue that a cosmopolitan person in an early nineteenth-century Central Mediterranean port city was more likely to be both a member of his own community and a denizen of his host city.

ACKNOWLEDGEMENT

We would like to thank Henk Driessen for his helpful comments on an earlier draft of the chapter.

NOTES

1 Voltaire, 1734. Lettre VI. Sur les Presbytériens. In *Lettres philosophiques*, Amsterdam, 'Chez E. Lucas, au Livre d'or': 'Entrez dans la bourse de Londres, cette place plus respectable que bien des cours, vous y voyez rassemblés les députés de toutes les nations pour l'utilité des hommes. Là le juif, le mahométan, et le chrétien, traitent l'un avec l'autre comme s'ils étaient de la même religion, et ne donnent le nom d'infidèles qu'à ceux qui font banqueroute; là le presbytérien se fie à l'anabaptiste, et l'anglican reçoit la promesse du quaker. Au sortir de ces pacifiques et libres assemblées, les uns vont à la synagogue, les autres vont boire: celui-ci va se faire baptiser dans une grande cuve au nom du Père, par le Fils, au Saint-Esprit; celui-là fait couper le prépuce de son fils, et fait marmotter sur l'enfant des paroles hébraïques qu'il n'entend point; ces autres vont dans leur église attendre l'inspiration de Dieu leur chapeau sur la tête: et tous sont contents. S'il n'y avait en Angleterre qu'une religion, son despotisme serait à craindre; s'il n'y en avait que deux, elles se couperaient la gorge; mais il y en a trente, et elles vivent en paix et heureuses.'
2 Historical Archives of the Greek Ministry of Foreign Affairs, 1833, 37/6, Minister Trikoupis to King Otho, 12/10/1833: '*Livourne compte plus de négociants Grecs que toute autre ville d'Europe*'.

3 The records of the Catholic Church of Corfu were destroyed in the 1943 bombardment of the city by Nazi Germany.

4 Marseilles, Archives Départementales des Bouches-du-Rhône [A.D.], 128 V 1, *Grecs schismatiques et cultes christophiles*, Letter from the Ottoman Consul in Marseilles to the Prefect of Bouches-du-Rhône (24 March 1821); A.D., 128 V 1, Letters from the Prefect of Bouches-du-Rhône to the Mayor of Marseilles (29 March 1821), from the Mayor to the Prefect (4 April 1821) and from the Prefect to the General Director of Police (9 April 1821).

5 A.D., 128 V 1, Letter from the General Director of Police to the Prefect of Bouches-du-Rhône (29 November 1825).

6 The Ionian State Naturalisation Law was passed in 1820, although the first regulation came a year earlier when the citizens of Parga, on the mainland opposite, which was sold to Ali Pasha, found refuge in Corfu and were given citizenship rights (*diritto di cittadinanza*). Atto di Parlamento, No. XIV, Seconda Sessione, Primo Parlamento, 22/05/1819 (Korgialeneios Library), Argostoli, Kefalonia.

7 49 or 55 per cent of the 89 merchants naturalised asked for their political domicile in Corfu, while 38 or 42 per cent asked for domicile in Zante. Ionian Islands Government Gazette [hereafter: IIGG], 1840–1963, The National Archives, London, and Reading Society Library, Corfu.

8 Istoriko Arheio Kerkyras [Corfu Records Office], Ektelestiki Astynomia [Executive Police], 22.

9 IIGG, No. 411, 29 October/10 November 1838.

10 IIGG, No. 377, 7/19 March 1825.

11 IIGG, No. 539, 12/24 April 1841.

12 National Archives, London, CO 136/857, Petition 400, 8 December 1857.

13 *Costituzioni e capitoli della nostra chiesa eretta in Livorno sotto l'invocazione della Santissima Trinita*, Livorno: Thomas Mazi and Co, 1775: 'Quei Confratelli però che avessero sposata, o sposassero Donna di Comunione diversa, saranno privi del Voto negli affari che riguardano il Regolamento della Chiesa, e l'esercizio della Religione Greca Orientale, e saranno incapaci della Cariche addette al regolamento della stessa Chiesa, ed alla Religione.'

7 MERCANTILE ELITES IN THE PORTS OF AMSTERDAM AND ROTTERDAM, 1850–1940

HUIBERT SCHIJF

In the 1860s, a period sometimes called 'the second Golden Age', bankers in Amsterdam and Rotterdam founded new financial institutions, and ship owners started modern shipping lines with steamships providing fast and reliable routes to other ports, above all to the Dutch Indies. These innovations generated industrial activity and opportunities for merchants in the Netherlands. Changes in the economic regime and the lifting of the state monopoly on agricultural products (among them opium) opened new opportunities for private entrepreneurs in the Indonesian Archipelago after 1870. At the same time, ship owners built the necessary infrastructure of wharves and factories for steam engines, although overall industrialisation remained limited. Much of the early industrialisation in Amsterdam had to do with the position of the port as a staple market, for instance processing commodities (Van Zanden, 1987).

Both Amsterdam and Rotterdam became, in short, global ports. Elite families were key to these transformations. A small group of bourgeois families in Rotterdam, connected through frequent intermarriages, play a central role in the innovations of its port in the second half of the nineteenth century. Similarly, in Amsterdam, a relatively small group of families were involved in the City Council and the Chamber of Commerce, the so-called patrician families. But this elite consisted of several distinct groups, and animosity towards each other was a long-standing phenomenon. This created an opportunity for Mennonite merchants and Jewish bankers, religious minorities excluded from administrative functions, to play a substantial role in transforming the ports.

THE RISE AND FALL OF DUTCH PORTS BEFORE 1860

In fact, Amsterdam had already been a global port for centuries – a hub of colonial trade, a staple port and a financial centre – though Rotterdam had not. Home to the great Dutch East-India Company (VOC), founded in 1602, and other important trade companies, it was also 'a great Staple of News', as there worked excellent mapmakers – the famous father and son Blaeu were employed as mapmakers by the VOC – and many book printers, who also printed foreign books. A constant influx of immigrants created networks of trade and information all over Europe (Lesger, 2006). Without doubt these factors contributed to the success of Amsterdam as a trading centre and its position as the most prominent staple port of Northern Europe. But the key factor was the sacking of the port of Antwerp by the Spanish army in 1585. Thereafter the Westerschelde came under control of the Northern Netherlands and Amsterdam's most important competitor was eliminated as a global port. With the arrival of Flemish and Sephardic merchants who fled Antwerp, Amsterdam also evolved as an important financial centre, certainly after the opening of the earliest stock market in the world in 1609.

But by the end of the eighteenth century and the first decades of the nineteenth century, the prominence of the port of Amsterdam had diminished and its economy went into a deep decline. By the time the Netherlands regained independence after the end of the French Period in 1813, the English blockade and the temporary loss of the Dutch Indies had made earnings based on international trade almost impossible, and Amsterdam ended this period as a poor city.

Over these same centuries, Rotterdam was just one of several small ports along the rivers of the western part of the Netherlands. The laborious voyage through the Waal and Rhine estuary to the North Sea offered few prospects for expansion. The port of Dordrecht was of equal size and easier to reach. Rotterdam counted only 15,000 inhabitants, when Amsterdam was a city of roughly 100,000 inhabitants. Nonetheless, around 1650, Rotterdam started to become a transit port for goods transported along the river Rhine to German cities and states.

It would have been impossible to predict at the turn of the nineteenth century that either port would develop rapidly during the following decades. The economy of neither Amsterdam nor Rotterdam could be called dynamic. Amsterdam's connection with the North Sea remained time-consuming, as cargo had to be transferred to lighters in order to reach the merchant warehouses along the city canals. Rotterdam too lacked a good and direct waterway to the North Sea, preventing further developments. The infrastructure of both ports urgently required modernisation. In the early decades of the nineteenth century, the port of Amsterdam had little to offer to owners of increasingly bigger ships. The accessibility of the IJ estuary declined because it silted very quickly. That kind of misfortune happened to many smaller ports around the Zuiderzee (the present IJsselmeer). The available warehouses in the city were insufficient and outdated. Delivering cargo became an expensive and time-consuming process, even more so than in the past. Plans were in the making to give Amsterdam a short connection with the North Sea through the North Sea Canal with an opening to that sea near the town of IJmuiden (see Figure 7.1). Authorities in Rotterdam debated their own plans for a direct connection to the North Sea. Merchants and port authorities in Amsterdam observed these debates with apprehension as they realised that Rotterdam's port would become a fierce competitor to their own. Meanwhile, from the 1830s, Rotterdam faced increasing competition from other European harbours such as Antwerp and Hamburg.

Change started slowly. In 1817, the Dutch regained the colonies in the Far East. As Amsterdam's merchants were able to pursue their traditional trade in colonial commodities once more, Amsterdam started little by little to function again as a staple market, and slowly regained some of its former prominence

Figure 7.1 The Netherlands in 1890 (source: Huibert Schijf).

as a financial centre. At the same time 'the commercial staple markets ports ... became more and more involved in the transhipment of raw materials and the efficient handling of industrial commodity flows' (Van de Laar, 2003: 63). In Rotterdam, new industrial developments in the western part of the German hinterland, starting in the early 1830s, inaugurated it as a transit port: its ships started to carry bulk cargos of coal, grain, ore and oil.

INTERNATIONAL AND NATIONAL FACTORS IN THE RISE OF DUTCH GLOBAL PORTS

By the 1860s, Amsterdam, a large city with a proud past, started to regain some of its former economic and cultural glory. The commercial elite focused their discussions on recapturing elements of that colonial past. As Amsterdam hardly experienced external pressure to transform itself into a transit port, they preferred to develop the city into a modern staple market. At the same time Rotterdam's elites had consolidated their city's role as a transit port. Technical and infrastructural breakthroughs nationally and internationally – the opening of the Suez Canal, the telegraph, the steamship and, perhaps most importantly, new waterways – were of great importance to the development of Rotterdam and Amsterdam as global ports.

At the international level, the opening of the Suez Canal in 1869 provided Dutch merchants and entrepreneurs with a much faster route to the Dutch Indies and as a result there was a steep rise in the number of joint-stock companies in the Netherlands oriented to the Dutch colonies (Kuitenbrouwer and Schijf, 1998). The use of the new telegraph substantially improved communication with the colony in the Far East (cf. Lew and Cater, 2006) and innovative entrepreneurs founded new steamship lines in this period. Because of their initiatives, a new industry came into existence in support of the port and its users, and also for processing imported and exported cargo. The external method of financing the new joint-stock companies gave financial institutions an important, although sometimes reluctant, role in this new industry. This happened in both cities, but primarily entrepreneurs from Amsterdam founded new shipping lines to and from the Dutch colonies, while Rotterdam's merchant elites developed a more global orientation. That orientation was first towards Germany, but also to America and Africa.

For the mercantile elites in both ports, transport to and from the Dutch Indies and investments in the Dutch Indies itself became more attractive when the national government decided to abolish the monopoly of the Nederlandse Handel-Maatschappij (Dutch Trading Company) in 1870, creating incentives for innovation. The foundation of the Dutch Trading Company in 1824, an initiative of King Willem I, had been decisive for the development of colonial trade. However, because of its almost complete monopoly of this trade, merchants became complacent about new economic and industrial developments elsewhere, satisfied as they were with the protection and being subsidised by the Company (Wijtvliet, 1989).

Perhaps the most crucial new infrastructure for the growth of Dutch ports was the digging of new waterways. In Rotterdam, it took a long time to start digging the much-needed direct waterway to the North Sea. Even as late as 1857, the president of the Chamber of Commerce argued strongly to realise the plan, as he feared that ships would sail to Antwerp, Bremen or Hamburg instead. A further threat was the opening of the Antwerp–Cologne railway line in 1843. The Belgian government decided to dispense with transit duties on goods transported by rail, while the German government greatly moderated its duties (Callahan, 1981). In 1862, the waterway was ready at last and the first steamship sailed down it to the port of Rotterdam. However, it soon became clear that the new channel was not deep or wide enough, as the engineers who built it quite mistakenly saw no need for a waterway that 'monstrous floating castles' could navigate. The engineers also underestimated how quickly the channel would silt, and the need for constant dredging to keep it open. It took another ten years before the authorities finally agreed upon the financial resources for these deepening works (Van de Laar, 2000).

By then, relations between Rotterdam and the German hinterland had changed profoundly. In the 1840s, the Prussian government became more and more reluctant to abide by Dutch trading rules and to pay high duties, as it desired economic independence from Dutch trade policy. Because of the threat of new railways bypassing the port of Rotterdam (Antwerp was the obvious alternative), the Dutch government was forced to negotiate. The dispute, settled in 1851, offered the Dutch economy the opportunity to follow Germany's dynamic economy (Bläsing, 1973). Rotterdam, as a transit port on the rise, would profit most. The harbour soon started to expand in the Feijenoord area south of the river Maas. Feijenoord would become a household name for shipbuilding and new working class neighbourhoods. A strong indication of these developments was the enormous growth in Rotterdam's population. In 1822, the city counted 63,187 inhabitants, a number that doubled by 1875. In 1895, Rotterdam's population counted 268,970 inhabitants (De Nijs, 2001: 393), and in 1940 the population had reached 619,686 (De Klerk *et al.*, 2008: 14). That the number of inhabitants doubled between 1875 and 1895 had much do to with the huge influx of manual labourers from rural areas in the southern provinces of the Netherlands. Rotterdam, once a provincial town, became the second city in the Netherlands.

The importance of port-related industry and the provision of services increased as well. In 1859, the two sectors contributed 44 per cent to the economy, while in 1909 this had increased to 55 per cent, although port-related industry remained at 9 per cent (De Klerk *et al.*, 2008). New infrastructure, housing projects and new neighbourhoods, offices and banks, and the development of new harbours were urgently needed. At the end of the nineteenth century, local political and commercial elites had laid the foundations for a future Rotterdam as one of the largest transit ports in the world.

Meanwhile, after several false starts, Amsterdam builders finally finished the Noordzeekanaal in 1872, giving the port a direct connection with the North Sea at last. The opening initiated the rise of a new class of commercial entrepreneurs, as steamships replaced smaller sailing ships. As in Rotterdam, the old commercial elite, with its protective and cosy relations with the Nederlandse Handel-Maatschappij, had preferred sail to steam for a long time, but it became clear that they had lost. However, as Amsterdam still lacked a modern canal to the river Rhine, the most important waterway to the German hinterland, the new connection to the North Sea did not generate the immediate success that local policy-makers and the commercial elites had hoped for (Aerts and De Rooij, 2006). As a staple market the port of Amsterdam and its merchants also experienced new uncertainties caused by new means of communication as it became easier – and cheaper – to reroute ships to other ports when they were still on the open sea (Wagenaar, 1990).

Amsterdam did not see the same growth as Rotterdam in such a short period. In 1830, Amsterdam had a population of slightly more than 200,000 inhabitants, a number that steadily grew to about 500,000 in 1899, mainly due to immigration (Aerts and De Rooij, 2006). However, it can be argued that the social and cultural capital of many immigrants to Amsterdam, German Jews among them, was relatively higher than of that of the men and women who migrated to Rotterdam.

As in Rotterdam, the new developments required new offices for merchants, shipping lines and banks. As legacies from the past, the largest and most splendid canal houses in Amsterdam offered enough space to turn these houses into offices. It was only after the 1870s that purpose-made buildings were designed: for example, the Scheepvaarthuis (1916, nowadays a hotel), with its magnificent exterior and interior decorations, was designed to house six shipping companies (see Figure 7.2).

LOCAL MERCHANT FAMILIES

Commercial elites are always embedded in local economic life and vulnerable to changing economic circumstances. Merchant families, whose businesses were directly related to the running of the port, were incorporated in a variety of economic, social and political networks. Apart from political institutions and commercial institutions, various agents operated at the local level, such as families in kinship networks and firms embedded in a network of interlocking directorates, lobbying groups and, of course, individual entrepreneurs. Merchants apprenticed their sons abroad and travelled themselves on business trips, creating global contacts that were elements in the success of their family firms (cf. Miller, 2003; for Hamburg: Evans, 1987). These kinds of networks started to develop in Antwerp after the reopening of the Westerschelde in

Arch.J.M.van der

Figure 7.2 Scheepvaarthuis. The Shipping House, built as an office block housing six shipping lines in Amsterdam in 1916 (source: Stadsarchief Amsterdam).

Note
It is widely regarded as a masterpiece of the so-called Amsterdam School of Architecture. Nowadays it is in use as a hotel.

1795 as well (Greefs 2008). The rising mercantile elite participated in cultural institutions and social clubs, while creating a common mercantile culture, and enterprising new German immigrants (some immigrants came even from Amsterdam) established new international links.

For centuries, the patrician families of Amsterdam and Rotterdam formed the core of local political and commercial elites. The religion of the dominant families was either Reformed Protestant or a dissident Protestant denomination. Mennonites, Lutherans or Remonstrants held prominent positions within the commercial elites of Amsterdam. They looked down on some entrepreneurial newcomers who had obtained their wealth more recently in the Dutch Indies, seeing the so-called 'Indische capitalists' as parvenus. Although some wealthy Catholic bourgeois families lived in the city, they rarely belonged to the inner circles of Amsterdam's high society as they were more or less socially excluded. So were successful Jews.

Jewish bankers and stockbrokers formed a small but prominent group of their own. As financial operators they supplied a substantial contribution to the (international) financial operations of Amsterdam. Amsterdam had a long experience with Jewish bankers and merchants. In the past, internationally oriented Sephardic Jews had contacts in the Iberian Peninsula, Morocco, the Ottoman Empire, Brazil and New Amsterdam (Israel, 1989). This experience hardly existed in Rotterdam and in the nineteenth century the important exception was Jewish Lodewijk Pincoffs, who as city councillor played an important role in the development of Rotterdam's harbours. In collaboration with his Reformed Protestant friend, the banker Marten Mees, he advanced important financial plans, but Pincoffs' plans ended in a scandalous fraud and he fled to the US (Oosterwijk, 1979). Apart from their prominent position in banking, the garment industry and the diamond-processing industry in the late nineteenth century, Jews rarely participated in port activities as such. No one like the prominent Jewish director of the Hamburg-America Line, Albert Ballin, in Hamburg operated in either Amsterdam or Rotterdam.

In Rotterdam, bourgeois families formed a much smaller and more homogenous group than in Amsterdam, as the town was still a provincial backwater in the first decades of the nineteenth century. The old patrician families dominated the City Council and the Chamber of Commerce. The merchant members of the Chamber of Commerce believed that their old commercial methods of doing business in the Dutch Indies, dating back to the time of the local Chamber of the VOC, were still adequate, as they enjoyed the protective hand of the Nederlandse Handel-Maatschappij (Callahan, 1981). The City Council showed little concern for improving the port and expanding the port facilities, such as building larger warehouses and using mechanical methods to unload the cargo. 'Transit trade – the new economic reality which would underlie and, in some ways, force Rotterdam's development – was scorned by most of the commercial elite' (Callahan, 1981: 65). The conservative and more progressive members of the City Council followed predictable patterns of political decision-making, as the two groups wanted either to constrain or to initiate the process of modernisation. Without doubt, their short-term strategy provided high earnings, but even contemporaries were aware that this short-sighted attitude would lead to stagnation. The competition between the old merchants, who were much favoured by the monopoly of Nederlandse Handel-Maatschappij, and a new, rising commercial elite intensified after a new Municipal Law came into force in 1851. The law expanded the group of male voters and the number of men who were allowed to stand as candidates for the City Council. The newcomers initiated plans to improve the infrastructure of the harbour with a new waterway and connections between Rotterdam and the burgeoning national railway network.

In both cities, mercantile elites and political elites overlapped to a large extent for a long period. In 1814, 50 per cent of the members of the Amsterdam City council were merchants, bankers and entrepreneurs. Until 1869 this percentage remained almost stable; but after 1884 the percentage started to drop, falling to 26 per cent in 1899 and to only 9 per cent in 1929 (Hofland, 1998). In Rotterdam we see something comparable happening. For the period 1851–1887 there were 118 city councillors, of whom about 50 per cent had a profession as merchant, banker, ship owner, or were entrepreneurs for port-related industries. Again, that percentage started to drop around 1900 (Baggerman, 1994). At least at the local level, this indicated a growing divide between the political and commercial elites.

Mennonites had formed a small but prominent part of the population of Amsterdam since the seventeenth century. The dominant Reformed Protestant municipal authorities had excluded these religious dissenters from political councils and public office. Therefore, many chose trade as a profession and a good many amassed great personal wealth, although their lifestyle was far from conspicuous. Around 1890, the Mennonites formed only 2 per cent of the population of Amsterdam. However, this small religious group had a large impact on the local economy of the city, as did the Quakers in the City of London (Cassis, 1994). Such an influential group of Mennonites hardly existed in Rotterdam.

Through the many marriages within the Mennonite church, the bonds between families remained strong. Around 1890, merchants still formed the majority among the Mennonite citizens in Amsterdam, but there were also a few bankers and insurance brokers. Moreover, they held positions in the Nederlandsche Bank, the Dutch central bank. In the second half of the nineteenth century, Mennonites created a central network of interlocking directorates between companies in trade, finance and shipping, the three main economic activities in Amsterdam at that time (Schijf, 1993: 97–99).

Central positions within the network were held by members of the Van Eeghen family, who had been active as merchants in Amsterdam for eight generations. The family owned its own trading house, Van Eeghen & Co. Around 1900, Samuel Pieter van Eeghen, as its leading partner, succeeded in changing the focus from trade to finance and the trading house was transformed partly into a private banking house. Samuel Pieter was then one of the most influential businessmen in Amsterdam. He was married to a sister of William van Loon, who had a top position in the financial world of Amsterdam. It had rarely happened in the history of Amsterdam that two brothers-in-law had as strong an influence in Amsterdam's business world. One derived his prominence from his position at the stock market, while the other gained influence through his seats on many boards of directors (Van Lennep, 1962). The prominence of the Van Eeghen family firm lasted until the 1930s and then steadily declined. The merchant family De Monchy can be seen as the Rotterdam Mennonite counterpart of the Van Eeghen family in Amsterdam. E.P. de Monchy even became president of the Nederlandse Handel-Maatschappij, which had its head office in Amsterdam.

BANKERS AND SHIP OWNERS

A key factor in the success of the new shipping lines was the involvement of bankers, because the founding of the new shipping joint-stock companies required huge external financial resources, as the earlier small family firms had not. Bankers in Amsterdam and Rotterdam were both reluctant to invest in these companies. One reason was that bankers were unwilling to provide loans over twenty years, instead of the usual ten years. A rare positive example is Marten Mees, who was a partner in the banking house R. Mees & Zoonen in Rotterdam. He participated in the foundation of both the Rotterdamsche Bank and the Amsterdamsche Bank, and also in two shipping companies with offices in Rotterdam. Nevertheless, he saw himself more as an initiator of plans and a financial broker than as a financier of the shipping lines (De Goey and Van de Laar,1995).

Other bankers were interlocked with shipping companies by holding seats on their boards of directors. The network of interlocking directorships suggests at least the existence of integrated business elites. My research on the meaning of interlocking directorates in the Dutch economy at the end of the nineteenth century (Schijf, 1993) showed that some shipping lines were well connected through such interlocking with other shipping companies, and also with wharves and factories for steam engines. These links show strong cooperation between shipping lines at that time, at least at the personal level of the managers: people knew each other, met in other places or belonged to the same families.

The foundation of the first shipping line with steamships was a daring revolution within Amsterdam's circle of conservative ship owners. The founder of Stoomvaart Maatschappij Nederland, Jan Boissevain, even went to Hamburg to study the modern steamships of that city's shipping lines, and he inspected the harbour works and quays as well. Both a Rotterdam banker and an Amsterdam banker held seats on the board of directors of the new company; and in Rotterdam, the Rotterdamsche Bank traditionally occupied seats on the boards of directors of several shipping companies. However, their participation did not indicate the financial participation of the banks they represented. Moreover, the interest of bankers became less over time. Between 1910 and 1940 the number of seats occupied by bankers in the transport sector declined, while their number increased in the growing industrial and financial sectors. Buyers of stock of several shipping lines also acted cautiously, and with every misfortune sold their bonds immediately. As ports depend on the number of ships that visit, this constant uncertainty destabilised shipping as a whole, and many other linked trades and industries.

GLOBAL ORIENTATION 1914–1940

After 1900, the expansion and modernisation of the two ports continued. Their different global orientation, already visible in the nineteenth century, became more pronounced. A telling example is the handling of grain in both cities. At the end of the nineteenth century, a large and modern grain silo was built in Amsterdam, symbolising the city's position as a staple market (see Figure 7.3). The initiator was Jan Philip Korthals Altes, who belonged to a family of several generations of grain merchants. He was also a member of the City Council (Korthals Altes and Galesloot, 2008). In Rotterdam the development went in the opposite direction, with German grain merchants demanding a quicker transit of cargo to Germany. That was not in the interest of local grain merchants, who preferred a slower pace. The introduction of pneumatic unloading by floating elevators was another step for Rotterdam in the direction of a transit port, and a loss for local merchants; only one of the many middlemen in Rotterdam's grain business perceived a future for the new technology (Van Driel and Schot, 2005: 52).

Meanwhile, Rotterdam's port not only functioned as a transit port for cargo to the German hinterland, it also (with Hamburg) developed as a transit port for German emigrants heading to America. This led merchants to found shipping lines especially for that purpose. Although the port of Rotterdam certainly participated in the trade with the Dutch Indies, compared to Amsterdam its proportion of that trade was small. Because of the neutrality of the Netherlands in the First World War, Rotterdam kept its position as a transit port to some degree, although the total tonnage of cargo arriving declined substantially.

Arjen Taselaar (1998) studied the impact of lobbying groups of colonial entrepreneurs in the Netherlands on the national government in The Hague between 1914 and 1940. His sample consists of the largest limited-stock companies oriented on the Dutch Indies during the period. It shows how

Figure 7.3 The large grain silo built in Amsterdam in 1898 and intended to look like a medieval castle (source: Stadsarchief Amsterdam).

Note
Nowadays it houses apartments and small offices.

strong the orientation toward colonial Indonesia remained in Amsterdam compared to Rotterdam in the first half of the twentieth century. Table 7.1 shows
a summary of the long list of limited-stock companies. The majority (54 per
cent) were based in Amsterdam, 32 per cent of the companies were based in
The Hague and 8 per cent were located in Rotterdam. Many oil and mining
companies had their main office in The Hague because they preferred close
personal contacts with the Ministry of Colonies, as they had to apply regularly
for new permits to expand their operations. It is particularly interesting to
evaluate the global orientation of the two ports: four shipping lines and two
airlines operated from Amsterdam to colonial Indonesia; in contrast, Rotterdam was home to only two shipping lines to and from the Indonesian archipelago. Table 7.1 clearly shows that the colonial orientation of the port of
Amsterdam, which had started with the foundation of the VOC in Amsterdam
in 1602, still dominated. Even almost a decade after Indonesia's independence,
some corporations kept large business interests in Indonesia, benefiting the
port of Amsterdam. That came to an abrupt end in 1957, when Indonesia's
President Sukarno nationalised all remaining Dutch companies operating in
the Indonesian archipelago and ordered all Dutch citizens to leave.

During the German occupation and the Japanese occupation of the Dutch
Indies, Amsterdam was closed off from its most important commodities and
customers, and its port experienced economic disaster. It never completely
recovered. Although today it is still the fourth port in Europe, economic activities have shifted from the seaport to the airport. The national airport
Schiphol and its supporting companies are the largest employers in the region.
The most important waterfront developments are in housing. For instance,
the old warehouses, dating from 1830, have been transformed into housing
projects (see Figure 7.4).

Very few of Rotterdam's new office buildings and banks survived the
bombing of the city centre in 1940. By the early 1950s, however, reconstruction and repair of war damage had started and Rotterdam became a modern
and well-equipped port again. Each new harbour was built further away from
the centre of Rotterdam. The city is now one of the largest transit ports in the

Table 7.1 Corporations oriented to the Dutch Indies in the period 1914–1939,
by economic sector and location.*

Sector	Amsterdam	Rotterdam	The Hague	Other places	Total
Financial	10	–	–	–	10
Agriculture (Colonial Indonesia)	55	8	27	9	99
Transport	9	2	8	–	19
Trade	10	4	3	–	17
Oil/Mining	6	–	16	–	22
Industrial	10	1	4	3	18
Total	100	15	58	12	185

Note
*Calculations based on Taselaar (1998: 522–528).

114

Figure 7.4 New housing in old warehouses from the 1830s in the eastern part of Amsterdam (source: Huibert Schijf).

world – after Singapore and Shanghai – with a port size of 10,000 hectares (24.711 acres) and a length of about 40 km (24.9 miles) in 2008 along the Nieuwe Waterweg, ranging from the centre of the city to Hook of Holland at the North Sea. Its most important commodities are now oil, containers carrying other commodities, and ore. Oil is stored and processed in refineries at the opening of the Nieuwe Waterweg, on a man-made extension into the North Sea, the so-called Maasvlakte. The container harbours are also located close to the North Sea and connected by railway to the hinterland. Many of the arriving containers are loaded again onto ships destined for other European ports. The number of containers processed is huge. In 2008, the number was 6,487,464 (or 10,783,823 measured in Twenty Feet Equivalent Units).

Commercial elites still exist in both Amsterdam and Rotterdam, of course, but their links with the city have almost disappeared, especially in Amsterdam. Their heydays declined soon after the Second World War and their close connections to the port cities have gone. In Rotterdam, some traditional Harbour Barons still participate in local cultural institutions, but they do not play a political role in the City Council any longer. As a powerful lobbying group they try to influence policy-making concerning their port and business at the local and national level without direct participation in political institutions, leaving politics to professional politicians with little affinity with port activities. Moreover, economic globalisation replaced many elements of the Dutch 'old boys' network' that had been active for such a long period (Fennema and Heemskerk, 2008). The Amsterdam and Rotterdam port elites therefore followed the same pattern as all elites in the Netherlands. From the beginning of the twentieth century, local elites became national elites, and more recently some individuals have even become members of global elites. At the same time, the gaps between economic, political and cultural elites increased. The time of mercantile port elites who also dominated local politics and cultural institutions has gone.

8   TREATY PORTS OF CHINA
Dynamics of global and local in the West's architectural presence

JOHNATHAN A. FARRIS

China's treaty ports were trading cities opened for foreign trade by negotiations between foreign powers and the Chinese government. They reigned ascendant in China's commerce with the outside world from the end of the Sino-British Opium War in 1842 to the Japanese occupation in 1937. The imprint that they made on Chinese society during this era should not be underestimated, and it is not a coincidence that many of these cities were in the vanguard of re-emergent capitalism in the post-Mao era. By the early twentieth century, Shanghai was the port with the largest Western presence, in terms of both foreign population and architectural impact. There were, however, thousands of other Westerners scattered up and down the China coast and along the inland ports of the Yangzi River, with a not insignificant impact on the built environment. Here, then, a comparative approach is attempted. Are there architectural trends across these cities, with their diverse climates, constituencies, and histories? What aspects of treaty ports are truly imported, and what trends are truly local?

Before the eighteenth century, Western trade with China was sporadic, and with the exception of the Portuguese colony of Macao, established in the 1550s, no truly permanent Western presence had been established. The arrival of British and Dutch ships on the Chinese coast in the seventeenth century began to threaten Portugal's dominance in the Far East, however, and by the eighteenth century the Portuguese colony was declining in economic significance. The Qing government, uncomfortable with the prospect of Westerners spread throughout the empire, confined trade to Canton (Guangzhou) in the early eighteenth century, placing interaction with foreign merchants primarily in the hands of commodity-trading monopolists. This style of trade (the "Canton system") dominated Sino-Western interaction for more than a century (Downs, 1997; Van Dyke, 2005).

The eruption of the Sino-British Opium War (1839–1842), based on conflicts over trade concessions, would ultimately lead to the death of the "Canton system." The "Treaty of Nanjing," which ended the British assault on China in 1842, stipulated a range of Chinese concessions, including the abolition of monopolies in favor of open trading, and, importantly for this discussion, the opening of five Chinese cities to British subjects, "for the purpose of carrying on their mercantile pursuits, without molestation or restraint" (Hertslet, 1908: 7–12; Spence, 1990: 158–161). These treaty ports were Canton, Amoy (Xiamen), Fuzhou, Ningbo, and Shanghai.

British thirst for greater trade access was not satisfied with these gains, however, and the British military recommended hostilities, in what came to be known as the Second Opium War, or Arrow War (1856–1858) (Spence, 1990). They ended this war by negotiating the Treaty of Tianjin, which imposed very strict terms and concessions on the Chinese, and stipulated that all British gains would be shared by other foreign powers. The Treaty of Tianjin would open ten further ports to foreign residence. The most important of these treaty ports were Tianjin itself, Chefoo (Yantai), Swatow (Shantou), and the Yangzi ports of Hankou (now part of Wuhan) and to a lesser extent Jiujiang. Subsequent treaties dating from the late nineteenth century and the first decade of the twentieth would open up a total of around forty-eight ports of entry to Western residents, although not all of these would become sites of significant settlement.[1]

Nearly all of the treaty ports were attached to pre-existing towns and cities of some note, with the possible exception of the late addition of the German port of Qingdao. Additionally, they would all host an overwhelming Chinese majority in their populations. To follow the contours of the global and the local as they are applied to the built environment will require an examination of the plans of the ports themselves, the emergence of Western architectural language within the ports, the dawn of the architect and the accompanying importation of foreign building technologies, and the spread of building types.

CITIES AND PLANS

It is daunting to try to make generalizations about the plans of China's treaty ports. Topography, the size and status of the original Chinese city, and the predilections of the foreign inhabitants all had highly localized effects on urban form. In fact, the ocean-going nature of the first treaty ports, the riverine nature of the second phase of cities, and the increasing involvement of the railroad in the final phase of port construction insured that at least three different topographies shaped these cities. An examination of both the earlier and the more successful later treaty ports here will serve to introduce the local dynamics and foreign interventions that shaped these cities. The first shared aspect of plans of Western-controlled areas in the ports was how they were produced. Surveyors and engineers were largely in charge of generating a functional city, and were less concerned with the niceties of architectural design. The first European university programs in civil engineering were initiated on the eve of the Opium War and were churning out graduates harnessed to the engine of empire to design both full-fledged colonies as well as China's treaty ports; architectural designers with more aesthetic goals were late on the scene in China (Home, 1997).[2] With what elements, if any, were these men able to standardize treaty port urban fabric? What contextual issues informed individual city plans?

Canton (Guangzhou), the hub of Sino-Western trade before the treaty port era, remained an important center of trade throughout the later nineteenth and early twentieth centuries, though its foreign population was proportionally smaller than Shanghai's. The decline of Canton's premier status among ports was due at least in part to the rise of the colony of Hong Kong as the preferred foreign residence in southern China, as well as the rapid foreign development of Yangzi River commerce. Canton maintained its status as a Chinese city of first rank, however, and with its early twentieth century Chinese population estimated around 3 million (second in size among treaty ports only to Shanghai), it was not a market to be abandoned (Crow, 1933, reprinted 1984; Cartwright and Wright, 1908). The provincial capitol of the "two Guangs," Guangdong and Guangxi, Canton was the largest ancient city to which a foreign settlement was appended. This said, through most of the treaty port era, there were probably never many more than a thousand full-time foreign residents (most likely an average of 500–700 officials and merchants, with a substantial number of missionaries and educators scattered about the city by the 1920s).

Traders dubbed Canton's sector for the prolific China trade of the eighteenth and early nineteenth century the Thirteen Factories (i.e. residences of factors, not manufactories) (Farris, 2007). This was a densely urban neighborhood in a trading and manufacturing suburb on the banks of the Zhujiang (Pearl River) that housed all of the Western resident traders, supercargoes, diplomats, and missionaries within China. The Thirteen Factories lay southwest of the great walled city of Guangzhou, the long-time joint capital of Guangdong and Guangxi provinces. The buildings here were initially closely modeled on the urban premises of the great Chinese merchants, who in fact owned them and rented them to the foreign merchants. During the eighteenth century, the buildings acquired Western classical façades, but on the interior they were still definitely Chinese spaces adapted to Western purposes. More radical was the partition of exterior spaces by Western traders during increasing cross-cultural tensions in the second quarter of the nineteenth century, particularly with a walled garden serving both recreational and exclusionary purposes. The original pre-Opium War settlement of the Thirteen Factories remained the foreign district until the area was destroyed during the Arrow War. Its rebuilding in the 1860s witnessed (with the exception of a brief-lived "American Concession" on the urban former site of the Thirteen Factories) a retreat of the foreign community to a newly constructed island suburb (Farris, 2004).

Shamian (literally "sand-face") started its existence as a long, low sand bar in the bend of the front reach of the Pearl River, and supported small anti-quated Chinese forts laid to ruins during the Sino-British wars. In April of 1859, principals of British firms suggested the site for new factories to HMB Consul Sir Rutherford Alcock, who then pursued estimates for the construction of a granite sea wall around it and other site preparation. The site importantly offered protection from dangers to foreign property posed by riots and fire, threats that made deep impressions on the British during their conflicts with the Chinese in the previous decades. The decision to build was finalized in late May 1859. The Chinese government leased the site on a quit-rent, and the construction was financed by $280,000 from war indemnities paid by China and $325,000 from the British and French governments (Staples-Smith, 1938). Reflecting the proportion of the finances the European governments provided, the British would possess four-fifths of the island and the French one-fifth. Two main avenues were laid out running east to west, with a third lane (which would only later be turned into a wider street) running the length of the northern end of the island. Five north/south roads then divided the island up into blocks. A "bund" (see Shanghai discussion on pp. *120–122*) walk ran along the top of the retaining wall along the riverfront. The area between the bund and Front Avenue (in the earliest era called Consular Road) was retained for public recreation. The British government sold lots on its concession (here meaning territory whose administration has been ceded from the Chinese) commencing in 1861. The 1860s saw the regular grid of streets on the irregular island lined with allées of banyan trees, resulting in a suburban atmosphere rarely found in other treaty ports (see Figure 8.1). Shamian, tucked in to its neat grid, remained a hub of Western presence, but by the later 1910s through the 1930s, many foreigners located their residences and businesses throughout a rapidly modernizing Chinese city. The Republican era Canton municipal government sponsored the wholesale renovation of the city's old urban fabric by widening roads and constructing (often out of reinforced concrete) a modernized version of the southern Chinese shop-house, which would be a model for other southern treaty ports. New development to the east of the city, in the Dongshan district, followed either an orderly grid, or more innovatively curvilinear garden suburbs. These suburbs were occupied by foreigners to some extent, but had a majority population of economically ascendant Chinese. Western architects working in China and the first generation of Western-trained Chinese architects directly transplanted these design ideas from the West (and indeed America) into Guangzhou's city fabric (Cody, 2001, 2003; Lu *et al.*, 2001; Tsin, 1999), securing its place as one of China's architectural seats of modernity in the early twentieth century.

The foreign residents of Amoy (Xiamen) shared with their counterparts in Guangzhou an "insular" mindset in the choice of their primary neighborhood. Although there was a small British concession within the Chinese city, the foreign residences overwhelmingly occupied the natural island of Gulangyu in the great ocean-going harbor. In the hierarchy of Chinese cities, Amoy was of regional importance as a suitable ocean-going port in the

Figure 8.1 Shamian, the foreign settlement (source: Newspaper engraving from *The Graphic*, September 22, 1883, plate 293, from author's collection; reproduced here by kind permission of the Illustrated London News Picture Library).

Note

In Canton and other early treaty ports, the first planning instinct was to remove the Western communities from the Chinese city, often using water as a barrier as seen in this "constructed" island.

southeast, but it was not an administrative center. Population estimates for Amoy were highly variable – the Chinese population in the treaty port era was over 100,000 and less than 500,000 (Crow, 1933; Rea, 1919). The Western population may have hovered around the six hundreds (Rea, 1919). Here, much of the business of the port was conducted in Amoy proper, while foreigners and increasingly very wealthy Chinese who had amassed fortunes overseas resided in ample dwellings on Gulangyu. The concession island, however, had little in the way of formal planning: winding roads led over the variable terrain in an informally picturesque manner. This contrasts with the Republican Chinese wholesale renovation of the traditional city of Amoy following the Canton model in the 1920s and 1930s (Lu *et al.*, 2001).

The remaining three treaty ports south of Shanghai were Swatow (Shantou), Fuzhou, and Ningbo. What these ports have in common is their comparatively small Western population, and the settlement patterns of the foreigners. The foreigners in these three southern treaty ports never instituted formal community planning, and the forms of all three foreign neighborhoods were nearly entirely determined by their respective topographies. In each of these examples, foreigners erected concessions on the opposite bank of their respective rivers to the Chinese city proper. Fuzhou, in part because of its importance as a major shipping point for tea, had the largest foreign population: about 400, including many missionaries (Rea, 1919). This walled provincial capital was situated about two miles (3.22 km) from the north bank of the Min River; a substantial Chinese suburb occupied the north side of the river bank; the foreign residences tended to cluster along the south side of the river (in an area dubbed Nantai) and on a nearby tiny island in the river that served as an anchorage. The old walled city of Ningbo sat at the meeting of two branches of the Yung River. Its permanent foreign population (probably always measured in the tens rather than the hundreds) situated itself across the eastern branch of the river from the Chinese city, in the "V" formed by the confluence. Here foreign institutions lined the riverfront and a small suburban Chinese "village," presumably housing Chinese associated with foreign business, occupied the ground behind them. Swatow proper, situated on the north bank of the Han River, initially supported a foreign community on the rocky south bank of the river, but foreign residences did also spring up in the eastern suburb locally called "Kai-lat" and in the Chinese city (Dennys *et al.*, 1867). The municipality of Swatow would modernize its urban fabric on the model of Canton's road widening and modernized shop-house construction during the 1920s, as would Fuzhou.

The last and most northerly of the original five treaty ports, and one which would soon overwhelm all of the others in terms of prosperity, foreign population, and Western dominance, is Shanghai. Shanghai occupied an easily developed expanse of low flat land. Its situation near the mouth of the Yangzi drew Western traders immediately upon its opening as a treaty port. Civil disturbances and bad feelings generated by the British wars allowed Shanghai to drain from Canton both Western and Chinese commercial talent. Additionally, the Tai Ping Rebellion (1850–1864) drove a great many wealthy and talented Chinese into the city for foreign protection from the rebels, something that the Qing Dynasty was not providing. This pull of talent and trade in the mid-nineteenth century arguably gave

Shanghai the impetus it needed to continue developing into China's greatest commercial city. By the early 1930s, the city had accrued a population of over 3 million, over 30,000 of whom were Westerners (Crow, 1933).

The foreign settlement in Shanghai was divided into three major sections on the west bank of the Huangpu River, north of the Chinese city (see Figure 8.2). The oldest and most developed section was the British concession (Denison and Ren, 2006: ch. 3). In 1849, the French officially acquired for their concession a narrow strip between the southern edge of the British concession (Yang Jin Bang creek) and the Chinese city (Denison and Ren, 2006). The Americans started to settle north of Suzhou Creek in the 1840s and 1850s, and were granted a concession there in 1861 (Denison and Ren, 2006). The definite boundaries of this part of the foreign city were not settled with the Chinese authorities until 1893; despite this the American concession was combined with the British in 1862 to become the "International Settlement" (Denison and Ren, 2006). Within and among these early boundaries of the Western-controlled city, the guiding idea of urban development was the grid, but one that for whatever reason was very approximate – apparently following minor topographic undulations rather than a surveyed line. This is perhaps the result of the fact that Shanghai's British (and, later, International) Settlement was governed by a municipal council which then delegated issues like planning to a Committee of Roads and Jetties, whose decisions seem routinely to have been based on immediate rather than long-term concerns (Denison and Ren, 2006). At any rate, the council's naming of Shanghai's roads at least would impose an idea of orderliness, with the initial east–west roads of the British Settlement being named for China's important cities, and the north–south roads being named for Chinese provinces.

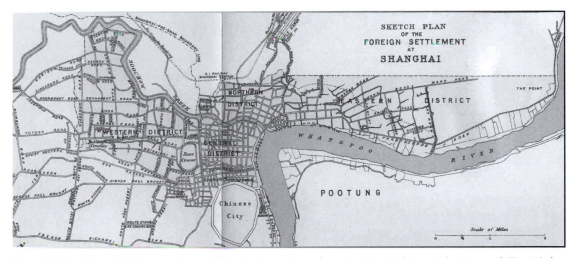

Figure 8.2 Sketch plan of the foreign settlement of Shanghai (source: insert from Hong Kong Daily Press's *The Directory & Chronicle for China, Japan, Korea...*, 1914 edition).

Note
Shanghai, free from natural boundaries, ideally situated near the mouth of the Yangzi, and unhampered by the small Chinese city to the south, was able to expand freely throughout its history. The "Central District" labeled here had been the British Concession initially, but early in the history of the foreign settlements combined with the American Concession to the north of Suzhou Creek to form the "International Settlement." The French, however, continued to maintain their independent sliver of a neighborhood between the Chinese City and the Central District.

The grandest and most influential of Shanghai's roads, however, was simply named the Bund, a colonial importation of a South Asian term for embankment. The broad avenue following the Huangpu embankment had its origins in the specification of a local Chinese official (the *daotai*) that a corridor within the foreign settlement of 2.5 *zhang* (8 metres or 26.2 feet) be maintained for common access to the river (Kuan, 2004). Because of its easy access to the river, the Bund was immediately lined with the premises of the most prominent Western firms. The subsequent development of the road into a riverside promenade as well as a major transportation artery kept it the most desirable address in the city, and in the early twentieth century it accrued a grand collection of many of the most monumental Western-style buildings in China. The Chinese always used the term, despite its foreign origins, to refer to the very specific model of Shanghai.

The notion of the bund is perhaps the only pervasive planning idea to tie many of the treaty ports together, even though it was applied to environments at quite a bit of variance from the Shanghai ideal. For example, an article in the January 1908 edition of the *Far Eastern Review* labels two illustrations the "Bund at Amoy," a waterfront strip of land here bristling with jetties and godowns (i.e. long low warehouses) – clearly a very work-oriented environment that contrasts with the emblem of civic pride of contemporary Shanghai (Rea, 1908). It was certainly the grander notion of a public space with monumental architecture that municipal planners of Guangzhou adopted when in the 1910s their first campaign of modernization constructed much-needed flood control measures in conjunction with a broad road following the Pearl River. In both of these examples, the focus is on a renovation of the older city. The influence of Shanghai's bund would be more literally imitated in the construction of new foreign concessions of many of the later-emerging treaty ports.

The inland Yangzi ports of Hankou and Jiujiang were very much the children of Shanghai. Both were important shipping points for tea, whose rise led to a decline in trade among the southern coastal treaty ports. Hankou was part of the tri-city complex now known as Wuhan, and with its adjacent sister cities boasted a population of about 1.5 million, of which around 2,000 were foreigners (Crow, 1933; Rea: 1919). Jiujiang perhaps had a population of 100,000 by the 1930s and a rather small foreign population (which, however, served some of the most important trading firms) (Crow, 1933). Despite their very different size, both from their early establishment sported long bunds, with floodwalls and an orderly march of foreign firms along the Yangzi shore (see Figure 8.3). Hankou's critical mass of foreigners engendered a sort of nationalist territorialism, with the grids of the British, Russian, French, German, and Japanese concessions, in that order, proceeding downriver from the Chinese city.

The three most notable northern treaty ports were Tianjin, Qingdao, and Chefoo (Yantai). They do not fit particularly well into the insular or the bund-and-grid patterns noted above. Tianjin was an important prefectural city at the confluence of the Grand Canal and the river Beihe (about 35 miles (56.33 km) inland from the sea) well before the arrival of the West. Upon the opening of the city to foreigners, settlement took the form of multiple

Figure 8.3 The Bund, Hankow (source: Feldwick, 1917).

Note
Following Shanghai's lead, most treaty ports developed some type of waterfront thoroughfare, often with space reserved for leisurely walks, which inevitably acquired the appellation "bund." Few followed Shanghai's example more exactly than the up-river entrepots, Hankow and Jiujiang.

independent foreign concessions along the banks of the river. Although Tianjin's total population by the 1930s may have been as much as 1.5 million, and its foreign population may have been 10,000 (a figure which, however, includes thousands of Japanese), the impression of the foreign settlements would have been one of low density (Crow, 1933). Each foreign concession encompassed no less than 100 acres (40.5 hectares) and the British and Russian settlements contained over 900 acres (364.2 hectares). The first settlements were south of the river and east of the Chinese city, including a French, British, and German concession (Cartwright and Wright, 1908). To this the Japanese added another concession on the south side of the river, and after 1901 the second-tier imperialist powers of Russia, Belgium, Italy, and Austria-Hungary appropriated concessions on the north side of the river. A bund along the Beihe tied the southern concessions together, but this was the only unifying gesture in the urban form of the foreign settlements. Each concession obeyed its own grid irrespective of the others, and some concessions (the British, for example) had a riverside grid and an inland grid on two different angles. The competing grids were echoed by a very diverse and independently developed set of nationalist expressions of architectural style. Indeed, Tianjin was a hothouse of nationalist architectural assertions. The unique impact of ideology and national rivalry here probably resulted from Tianjin's unique position as the closest treaty port to Beijing: competing powers felt compelled to display their identity to each other and to the Chinese imperial court.

The two major treaty ports in Shandong province, Qingdao and Chefoo, both overlook the sea from peninsular promontories.[3] Qingdao is exceptional among treaty ports for initially being the product of a single foreign presence, Germany, and for not having a relationship to a large, extant Chinese population center. Though there was a small walled Chinese settlement dubbed a "fishing village" in most contemporary sources, it seems that almost all pre-existing Chinese architecture, excepting a few official or religious buildings, was demolished by the port's new owners (Warner, 1994). German planners gave Qingdao most of its historic urban form in a rapid construction campaign between the Chinese ceding of the peninsula in 1897 and the Japanese military occupation of the city in 1914; the city was subsequently ceded back to the Chinese in 1922 (Haupt, 1934). In 1913, Qingdao possessed a European and American population of nearly 4,500, over half of which was military and which was also overwhelmingly German (Rea, 1914). The estimate for the Chinese population from the same year was 55,672.

The influence of the rising discipline of city planning was visible throughout Qingdao (see Figure 8.4). Planners intended from the outset that neighborhoods be distinctly segregated: a European Quarter, a villa quarter, a Chinese trade and commerce quarter, and two districts for workers (Warner, 1994). They constructed an equivalent to a bund in Qingdao, Kaiser Wilhelm Ufer (later Pacific Road), continuing it out of town to the Strand Beach, a very popular summer retreat for Westerners residing in the treaty ports in the 1900s and early 1910s and between Japanese occupations in the 1920s and early 1930s. Here, however, the bund and Strand Beach (on the south side of the city) had the luxury, thanks to the city's peninsular location, of not abutting the industrial and commercial "Kleiner and Grosser" harbors to the north. This separation of leisure and work functions certainly would have given the Qingdao "bund" a different character from the waterfront embankments of all of the other treaty ports.

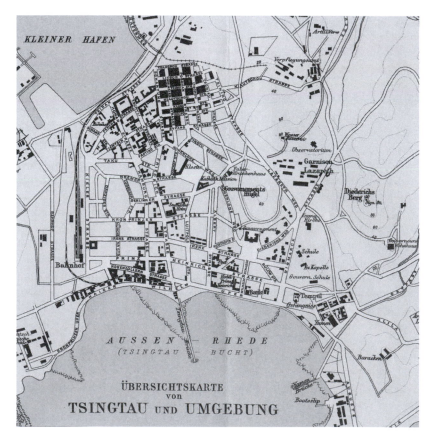

Figure 8.4 German Qingdao at its height (source: detail from insert in Hong Kong Daily Press's *The Directory & Chronicle for China, Japan, Korea...*, 1914 edition).

Note
Only in places like Qingdao, where a single European power held sway (and ultimately did away with the comparatively little pre-existing Chinese architecture on the site), did city planning ideals truly reach fruition. Although topography precluded an overly rational overall plan, episodes of symmetrical grandeur such as the government square, with its radiating avenues shown in the lower right, made this treaty port distinctive. Also, neighborhoods segregated by function and ethnicity, as well as separate functional harbors and leisure harbors, allowed Qingdao to approach a planner's ideal.

While Qingdao sported perhaps the most designed urban plans, its older competitor as a favored summer resort of the foreign resident of China, Chefoo, had perhaps one of the least considered urban plans. Never a great trading hub, it developed from a small walled Chinese city to a seaside resort town of about 150,000, with around 1,100 being full-time foreign residents by the 1930s (Crow, 1933). From the very beginning of its establishment as a treaty port, its government made no effort to divide the foreign-allotted territory into concessions, or even to define the very boundaries of the foreign settlement (Dennys *et al.*, 1867). Westerners simply built their houses and businesses between the small Chinese walled town and the bay to the north, and subsequent Chinese attracted by foreign business then built their residences nearby and among them. There was a sea wall constructed above Chefoo's beach that could be read as a reference to the notion of the bund. Otherwise the informality of the city's plan must be considered the result of a lack of tension between Chinese and Westerners, and among the Western residents themselves, that is unique to this particular city.

In summary, while Westerners brought ideas of city planning into the urban fabric of Chinese treaty ports, they did so sporadically and with high contingency on local topography, social relations, and brands of commerce. Apprehensiveness on the part of the foreign residents of the southern coastal ports due to their smaller numbers in relationship to the large Chinese cities to which they were attached initially led to a desire for separation, as shown in island settlements in Canton and Amoy, and in cross-river suburbs in Swatow, Fuzhou, and Ningbo. Shanghai's position as the most densely populated treaty port sets it apart from almost every other treaty port. The notion of the bund, which found its fullest manifestation in Shanghai, proved to be a concept common across ports. The actual manifestation of the bund notion, however, could vary widely – from a street interrupted by many jetties in the Chinese city of Amoy, to the orderly march of foreign concessions in the Yangzi ports, to the more fully recreational feel to the bays fronting Qingdao and Chefoo. Western and Chinese builders' creations within these divergent armatures bear witness to rather more shared phenomena.

BUILDING TRENDS AND TYPES

While the planning of cities and neighborhoods in China's treaty ports was largely contingent on local situations, resources, topography, and constituencies, the institutions of these cities and the buildings that housed them followed more similar trajectories of development. Both building practices and stylistic and typological phases, particularly in the architecture of transnational businesses, could be found in dialogue with worldwide trends. By the early twentieth century, global capitalism transformed these cities into accumulations of vertically conceived structures that both stood in stark contrast to the low-lying traditional city and permitted residents a new conception of their surroundings. Foreign building types, the institutions they housed, and the cultural cachet that they represented emerged as the larger treaty ports' shared legacy of "the modern" in Republican-era China.

Beginning in the eighteenth century, foreigners chose to build in a way that, at least superficially, stood out from their Chinese surroundings. The foreign patrons of building in the treaty ports had to rely on Chinese expertise and labor throughout the construction process, however. Chinese builders gradually acquired Western design techniques and knowledge, while still relying on local materials at least until the end of the nineteenth century. It was not until after 1900 that imported Western technologies and tastes had great currency among the Chinese inhabitants of the treaty ports.

Three phases of building define the Western architectural presence in China from the eighteenth century to the Second World War. In the first of these phases, the Thirteen Factories of Canton, Westerners' buildings grew wholly out of a regional Chinese courtyard house tradition. On the interior, these buildings were essentially houses interspersed with narrow courtyards, and in this way very similar to the premises of nearby Chinese merchants. The way space was occupied was somewhat different, as a matter of economy: in all of the factories except that of the British East India Company, different traders and firms occupied the different blocks or halls within the individual factory. Foreign firms otherwise adjusted these buildings to suit their tastes, chiefly by introducing classically inspired façades. In most of the factory buildings, Western classicism took the form of arcaded verandahs on the second stories, surmounted by keystones and interspersed by some version of Corinthian pilasters. Both the British East India Company factory and the Dutch factory sported projecting "terraces" fronted with pediments. After a catastrophic fire in 1822, the rebuilt factories sported a more restrained Doric order, but the essential spatial arrangements were unchanged.

While some of the factories were rebuilt after the fire, with American merchants acting as contractors, most were rebuilt under the direction of Cantonese compradors (Chinese business managers). In all cases, the models of the previous factories were closely followed. East India Company records illustrate the types and origins of materials used (India Office Records, G/12/229). The Chinese contractor was responsible for locally acquired bricks, tile, stonework, most of the wood, *chunam* (a term borrowed from India for lime for paving, stucco, and perhaps mortar), iron nails, lead tin, marble chimney pieces, and bamboo. All that the Company was supposed to supply was the teakwood for windows and stairs, iron door locks and stoves, and glass windowpanes. The construction of the Thirteen Factories was a mostly local affair, and influenced the surrounding Chinese city little, with the possible exceptions of the Western-designed classical balustrades (made of local earthenware) and louvered shutters that did start to appear in traditional Chinese urban housing in the mercantile western suburbs.

After the Opium War, the British introduced a new mode of building to the China coast in response to the need to create Western settlements in the other four treaty ports and in the colony of Hong Kong. In this phase of the treaty ports' architectural history, detached buildings of two or three stories, with hipped roofs and verandahs on at least one and sometimes on all four sides, pervaded the new Western settlements. This is one of the least studied phases of Chinese architectural history. Early twentieth century critics of this architecture called it "compradoric," and this label seems to have persisted

(Denison and Ren, 2006). It presumes the Chinese business manager of the foreign firms (again, the "comprador," who was often Cantonese in the first generation of treaty port development) played a central role in coordinating construction with a Chinese contractor. The basic form of these buildings likely originated in the British presidencies in India (Calcutta, Bombay, and Madras) as early as the third quarter of the eighteenth century. The hipped roofs were probably more prominent in Chinese examples, given the fairly wet climate of the southeastern China coast, but by and large the dwellings of Western merchants in China during this period very much resembled their counterparts' premises in India and the Straits Settlements. The mechanisms of British colonial bureaucracy newly ascendant in Hong Kong were likely the primary conduits of design in this phase of building, though this has yet to be fully documented. The designers who built several of the first generation of buildings on the new Shamian concession in Canton in the 1860s were a Carl Brumstedt "of Canton" and Thomas Kingsmill "of Hong Kong" (China Correspondence, FO 17/373, No. 101). Not much is known of the former, who may have been a merchant and amateur designer, while the latter was a British civil engineer turned architect who was involved in the first generation of Hong Kong building and later became prominent as a designer in Shanghai. Both men worked on the British consular complex in close contact with, and possibly even to the designs of, Charles St. George Cleverly, the Surveyor General of Hong Kong (Boyce, WORKS 10–56/6: 77). Later nineteenth century design of so-called "compradoric"-style building became universal in the earlier treaty ports, and representative of the spread of a particular imperialist language of architecture imported via the British Empire and adopted by other nationalities. Essentially stylistically conservative, the arcaded verandahs of this era usually had few stylistic references to contemporary European fashion. Apart from a few technological improvements, Western patrons still sponsored this exact type of building on the China coast into the first decade of the twentieth century.

The construction of these "compradoric" buildings was largely a local affair. It also relied on Chinese contractors, who rapidly were learning a new mode of architectural thinking. Chinese builders before this era had generally operated on a centuries-old modular method of construction that could readily be adapted to individual patrons and local circumstances mediated through oral exchange. In the mid-nineteenth century, however, the imported building forms desired by Westerners prompted a new mode of interacting with patrons. The Cantonese contractor styled "Aling," for example, made watercolor-tinted plans and elevations for semi-detached houses for both the London Missionary Society (see Figure 8.5) and the American firms of Smith Archer and Russell & Company.[4] This new conception of architectural information was also accompanied by legal documentation in the form of building contracts. Such contracts from the Russell & Company and Smith Archer & Company shared house took the forms of very exactingly translated documents drawn up in both Chinese and English.[5] They notably indicate that nearly all materials were local and the responsibility of the Chinese builder, the exceptions being the iron grates and door to the "treasure room" or vault.

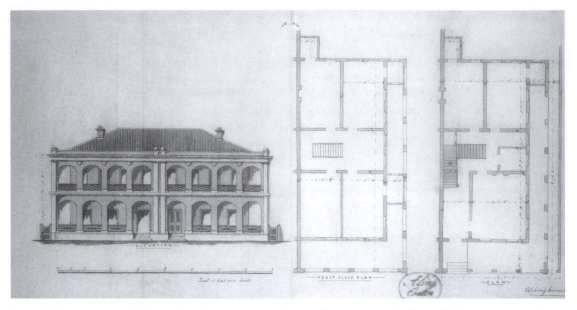

Figure 8.5 Drawing for a double house for the London Missionary Society's Canton premises, by Aling, 1871 (source: reproduced by kind permission of the Council for World Mission who own all rights to the Plan for London Missionary Society residence, Shamian, 1871 (by Aling) SOAS, LMS Archives, CWM, Incoming correspondence, box 7, Folder 1, Jacket B).

Note
Though portraying a fairly standard work of so-called "compradoric" architecture, the boxy verandah-clad hipped roof type of building that pervaded all treaty ports in the mid- to late nineteenth century, this is a highly significant artifact of changing building practice. The Chinese contractor, whose "chop" in Western lettering can be seen in the lower right portion, is producing a plan and elevation drawing for his bid on a contract (which in this instance he did not actually receive). Chinese builders had traditionally conceived of their projects in modular terms, negotiated verbally and by tradition. The introduction of this sort of rendering significantly shows design adaptability well before the first generation of professionally trained Chinese architects.

The "compradoric" mode of architecture was successful enough in its accommodation of foreign needs that low hipped-roof buildings characterized several treaty ports, either with a less numerous foreign population (like Fuzhou), or with a less dense layout and perhaps status as a resort (like Chefoo), into the mid-twentieth century. At first, engineer/architects like Kingsmill continued very much in the older mode, simply adding eclectic ornament (in Victorian Gothic or Queen Anne modes, for example) to suit the taste of the client. In the colony of Hong Kong, a more correctly classical language was applied to verandah-clad masonry buildings reaching five and six stories in height. Beginning in the 1890s, designers and builders would infuse new architectural practices in the third phase of architecture in the ports, which could be dubbed the "international" or "transnational" phase. The wholesale importation of Western design methods and building technologies, and in many instances the modernization of Chinese portions of the city, would characterize this era, which would last until the Japanese occupation.

Although the favored language of many treaty port patrons was a range of expressions of Classical architecture, the 1890s and 1900s was perhaps the most stylistically eclectic. Since the boom in the numbers of foreign architectural firms coincided with the height of European nationalism leading up to the First World War, it is not surprising to find an assortment of very specific, ethnically affiliated styles, particularly in the newer, more northerly treaty ports. Becker & Baedeker of Shanghai specialized in a whole range of styles for the German community, including Romanesque revival, a half-timbered and clipped gabled medieval vernacular, and, in the instance of the Club Concordia (circa 1904–1907), "German Renaissance" (see Figure 8.6) (Cartwright and Wright, 1908; Warner, 1994). Various Teutonic revival styles too diverse to catalogue also played a prominent role in Qingdao's rapid development. Tianjin hosted a veritable "petting zoo" of national architectural styles, including everything from Tuscan villas in the Italian concession, to mansard-roof topped French bank buildings, to the crenellated Gothic of the British concession's Gordon Hall (see Figure 8.7). Land development companies in both Tianjin and Shanghai, such as the Crédit Foncier d'Extrême Orient and the China Land and Building Company, constructed suburbs of houses sporting faux half-timbering for the cities' well-to-do (Feldwick, 1917).

From the mid-1910s, firms began most frequently to employ the architectural language of Beaux-Arts classicism. Besides avoiding the references to nationalistic fervor that had brought about the "Great War," this style was more in touch with the increasingly restrained tastes of the era, particularly in

Figure 8.6 German Club "Concordia," Shanghai (source: Perkins, 1909: 176).

Note
One of the grandest works of the architecture firm of Becker & Baedeker, this was the center of German social life in Shanghai before the First World War. The arrival of professionally trained architects in China in the late nineteenth century brought a host of eclectic stylistic modes. This building, labeled "German Renaissance" style in its time, featured a mix of medieval and classical motifs resonant with that country's architectural history.

Figure 8.7 Gordon Hall, the Tientsin Club, and Russian Monument, Tianjin (source: Feldwick, 1917: 254).

Note
No treaty port hosted a more eclectic mix of architecture than Tianjin, as demonstrated by the turret flanked and battlemented Gordon Hall (perhaps the architectural grandchild of Windsor Castle), the Baroque Revival club building, and this onion-domed Russian monument. Because of its status as the closest port to Beijing and its development at the height of pre-First World War European nationalism, stylistic expression became synonymous with political identity here.

Britain and the increasingly important United States. This style definitely supplied the sort of monumentality that many of the banks, trading firms, and insurance companies (the engines of the treaty port economies) desired. The two most pervasive British firms of the era, Atkinson & Dallas of Shanghai, and Palmer & Turner of Hong Kong, would make the use of monumental classicism their forté, and establish branch offices in other ports to meet the demand for their firms' work. Few more monumental architectural statements were made in the treaty ports than Atkinson & Dallas's Kalian Mining Administration building (see Figure 8.8) at Tianjin (finished c. 1922) or Palmer & Turner's Shanghai headquarters of Hong Kong and Shanghai Banking Corporation (finished 1923) (Rea, 1922). The American firm of Murphy & Dana of Shanghai and New York would implement a perhaps thriftier and more succinct version of Beaux-Arts design in a whole series of branches for the International Banking Corporation (Cody, 2001). The ascendancy of Beaux-Arts classicism would only be challenged by an "adaptive Chinese style" that firms favored for institutional buildings and that was increasingly popular with the first generation of (largely foreign- and particularly American-trained) Chinese architects, which itself was based on Beaux-Arts principles (Cody, 2001; Kuan and Rowe, 2002; Lai, 2007). The 1930s would also see designers introducing Art Deco and, in a very limited way, International Style Modernism, but these movements were only beginning to get under way when Japanese aggression ended most construction in the ports (aside from collective housing), until the revival of trade with the West in the 1980s.

Not just Western styles but Western technologies were necessary to the building boom of the 1900s to the 1930s in China's treaty ports. First and foremost were systems of reinforced concrete construction necessary for the increasingly towering skylines of Shanghai, Canton, Tianjin, and Hankow (Cody, 2003). This became important not only to Western buildings, but also to the rebuilding of Chinese quarters of cities, and in particular the southern

Figure 8.8 The Kailan head office in Tientsin (source: from *The Far Eastern Review*, June 1931: 360).

Note
The head office of the giant Sino-English Kailan Mining Administration exemplifies a primary architectural movement in China's treaty ports of the 1910s and 1920s: Beaux-Arts classicism. Adopted by commercial institutions in the wake of the First World War, the academic, monumental, and formal style came to symbolize economic solidity. This building was designed by B.C.G. Burnett, the Tianjin representative of the Shanghai firm of Atkinson & Dallas.

treaty ports, where a modernized version of the Chinese shop-house that incorporated continuous arcaded sidewalks within its footprint became the pervasive building form with which to line newly widened streets. Western-style sanitation, including plumbing and sewage systems, was also important to the well being of the treaty ports, though it was not without problematic cross-cultural misunderstandings (Rogaski, 1999). Electricity was also an increasingly important imported technology that made the buildings of the early twentieth century possible. Many of the rooms of large hotel and office buildings would have been unbearable in China's summer without the particular aid of the electric fan, and electric lighting was also an obvious benefit in larger buildings with interior rooms. Of course, elevator technology was also very important as buildings of more than four or five stories became more common.

Building types supply the final realm in which China's treaty ports became increasingly parts of global networks. In fact, they introduced the Chinese populace to new socio-economic institutions and, in some cases, completely different spatial experiences. Western (often religious) philanthropic institutions often sponsored educational buildings on the periphery of treaty ports. The architecture of these institutions represented a stylistic convergence between Western and Chinese architecture, frequently as an intentional bridge between Western staff and Chinese students. Atkinson & Dallas's 1890s buildings for St. John's University were among the first to adopt a Chinese/Western hybrid language, although the buildings of the Episcopal institution were essentially just "compradoric" style with broad, spreading, upturned Chinese tile roofs (Cartwright and Wright, 1908; Feldwick, 1917; Smalley, 1998). Canton's Canton Christian College (begun 1905) of the American Board of Foreign Missions was probably the next to emerge, with a Beaux-Arts campus plan by the New York firm of Stoughton & Stoughton (Farris, 2004). The buildings (by Stoughton & Stoughton and others) were generally more decorative, an interesting synthesis of local materials and Chinese motifs in a fashion influenced by the Arts and Crafts movement. The trend reached its greatest extent under Henry Murphy, who designed campuses in the "adaptive Chinese" style based on Beaux-Arts principles for Fujian Christian University in Fuzhou and even more nationally prominent universities in Beijing and Nanjing (Cody, 2001). This "adaptive Chinese" architectural language would be used for primary and secondary schools, and by the later 1920s and 1930s, with the ascendance of the first generation of Chinese architects, public buildings more generally.

While educational buildings usually nestled into urban fabric or took up suburban locations, buildings for Western banks were among the most prominent and common landmarks of the business districts of the ports. British HSBC, the French Banque de L'Indo-Chine, the Japanese-run Bank of Taiwan and Yokohama Specie Bank, and America's International Banking Corporation (IBC; later Citibank) had presences in all major treaty ports. While other sorts of company offices, including great trading companies such as Jardine & Matheson, adopted different architectural forms and languages to suit local circumstances, banks by the 1920s displayed the language of Beaux-Arts classicism and contained monumental first-floor lobbies with offices above. The recognizable nature of the bank buildings was taken even a step further by IBC, which commissioned Murphy & Dana to design all of its Chinese branches on a model derived from the bank's Wall Street headquarters (Cody, 2001). It should also be noted that banks produced "tall buildings," such as the 1937 Bank of China by Palmer & Turner with Lu Qianshou (graduate of the AA in London), but that this and other (predominantly Hong Kong) examples are late arrivals on the treaty port skyline (Kuan and Rowe, 2002).

Tall buildings, while sometimes dedicated to a single purpose, equally could house multiple functions. The hotel (both standard and residential), the department store, and to a lesser extent the office building often combined functions to be the most prominent landmarks within the most developed treaty ports (Sanjuan, 2003). It is difficult to know where precisely to begin the story of the tall building in China's treaty ports. While massive galleried buildings in late nineteenth century Hong Kong, such as the Hong Kong Hotel, topped out at perhaps six stories, these seem to have been a reaction to unique circumstances (the scarcity of flat land, for one), and did not necessarily encapsulate a particular "idea" of the tall building. In Shanghai, the Palace Hotel, designed by the firm of Scott & Carter with Wong Fan Ki as general contractor, was hailed during its construction in 1905 as both "the largest building in that Settlement" and "the highest in Shanghai, having six stories, 90 feet from pavement to eaves, with a cellar under, and a roof-garden over the southwest portion" (Rea, 1905: 13, 15). Described then as being in "the Victorian Renaissance style of architecture," it was (and still is) situated on a prominent site, on the corner of the Bund and Nanjing Road. With a dining room on the top floor, and the roof garden above that, it was clear from the beginning that a chief attraction of tall buildings in China's treaty ports was going to be the view from the top. Following the Palace's lead, Shanghai's Astor House Hotel rebuilt its premises, which were completed around 1911 under the direction of Davies & Thomas (Rea, 1912). Though only five stories in height, the hotel did introduce the novel convenience of electric passenger elevators, and, in keeping with its exclusive reputation, the views from the upper floors were from private rooms, the best being from corner suites.

Canton entered the quest for a more impressive skyline shortly after the completion of its floodwall and bund in the mid-1910s. The Cai brothers, entrepreneurs from the Guangdong city of Zhongshan, built their over nine-story tall, reinforced concrete, cupola capped, freely neo-classical Daxin (or Dah Sun) Department Store to house the Hotel Asia, complete with roof garden and catering to both Chinese and Western patrons (Chan, 1999; Farris, 2004; MacPherson, 1998). Nearly simultaneously, other Cantonese businessmen were opening equally impressive department stores (in buildings which also included Western-style hotels) on Nanjing Road in Shanghai. The Sincere Company (c. 1916–1917), founded by Ma Yingbiao, occupied an entire city block at the intersection of Zhejiang and Nanjing Roads (Chan, 1999). The architectural firm of Lester, Johnson and Morris gave the building (which was actually more of a conjoined complex of five buildings) classical elevations thought to be "a free treatment of English Renaissance" (apparently meaning Christopher Wren-inspired monumental classicism), wide store-front windows, and a corner tower 150 feet (45.72 meters) high, "from which a magnificent view may be obtained and which ought to prove popular to the Chinese" (Rea, 1916: 254–256). The Wing On Department Store (1916–1918), founded by brothers Guo Luo and Guo Chuan, occupied an equally prominent site, taking up another solid block of Nanjing Road. Palmer & Turner (with Lam Woo & Company as contractor) designed its six stories also in a more or less Beaux-Arts mode, though this time the hotel took up a greater number of the upper floors, with a fifth-floor dining room and tea garden on the roof (see Figure 8.9) (Rea, 1918). The exact origin of the idea of placing hotels, dining rooms, and entertainment gardens on the Chinese department store roof is unclear, but it was clearly a strategy for entrepreneurs to diversify their sources of income (Chan, 1998). While neither Wing On nor Sincere was as tall as Daxin in Canton, they had a much larger imprint, and prospered to the extent that Daxin added its own Nanjing Road branch in the 1930s.

Buildings that housed offices also began to appear on treaty ports' skylines. Hankow received a mixed-occupancy five-story building in the form of the "local" architectural firm of Hemmings and Berkeley's Union Building by 1917 (Feldwick, 1917). The race for height returned to the Shanghai Bund in the 1920s, however. Palmer & Turner's design for the Chinese Maritime Customs House (1925–1928) on the Bund featured a restrained Greek-inspired

Figure 8.9 The Wing On store and Great Eastern Hotel, Shanghai (source: *The Far Eastern Review*, October 1918: 424).

Note
This was one of several Chinese-owned establishments that in tandem with Western establishments introduced the tall building to China. Palmer & Turner of Shanghai and Hong Kong were the architects.

classicism spanning ten stories and including a prominent clock tower (Wilkins, 1928). Palmer & Turner would, however, surpass its height with the Sassoon House/Cathay Hotel (1926–1929), a building which combined offices and banks on the first three floors with a hotel on the upper nine floors (Binder, 1929: 213–214). This building, 240 feet (73.15 meters) high, now loomed over its neighbor the Palace Hotel, which had started the upward trend in building. The Sassoon Houses's mixture of a "stripped classicism" with Art Deco ornament would predict trends in the 1930s in Shanghai. While the fourteen-story residential hotel dubbed Cathay Mansions (c. 1929–1930) sported an English Gothic façade that in the end seemed oddly blocky, the general trend was for architects' designs to enhance the upward thrust of the tall building.

Palmer & Turner's Metropole Hotel (1932–1934), a fully Art Deco fourteen-story tall building, was conceived of as a businessman's hotel (Rea, 1932). It sported an "Old English" grill and bar in its basement, telephone and radio plugs in every room, and some roof suites that opened onto roof gardens. Its walls and partitions were constructed of "aerocrete," a then state-of-the-art type of concrete formulated to lighten the load on the structure, installed by the contractor Sin Jin Kee, illustrating yet again the ability of Chinese builders to readily adapt to and adopt the technologies their patrons desired. The Metropole sat opposite the nearly identical Hamilton House apartments, also by Palmer & Turner. The grandest essay in modern architecture, sitting well inland from the river on Bubbling Well Road on Park Road, was the Park Hotel (1934) by Slovak émigré architect Laszlo Hudec (Hietkamp, 2007). This building, at twenty-two stories and 300 feet (91.44 meters) in height, was the tallest in Asia (Rea, 1935). The Park's Chinese investors, the Joint Savings Society, had offices on the ground floor adjacent the lobby, and the nineteenth floor was cordoned off for the executive committee and board of directors (and the stories above given over to mechanical functions), but a grill room on the fourteenth floor and a roof garden quickly became great attractions for the Shanghai public. While the other treaty ports were slower to develop quite as grand a skyline, they may well have been headed in Shanghai's direction. China's last great commercial skyscraper to be built for over forty years was Canton's much-beloved (as its Chinese name implies) Aiqun Hotel. The Deco-Gothic fourteen-story building occupies a flatiron-shaped lot on Canton's bund and was completed in 1937 to the designs of University of Michigan trained Chen Rongzhi (Lai, 2006).

Why was the tall building so important to the identity of China's treaty ports in the early twentieth century? The building type certainly represents the foreign inhabitants' intent to compete with their imperial centers in the modernity and grandeur of their skylines. More than this, however, the tall building represents a revolution in the Chinese way of seeing architecture, bringing it, in fact, more in line with Western ways of seeing. While some of the towers that punctuated treaty port skylines were no doubt exclusive, Canton's Daxin Building and Aiqun Hotel, and Shanghai's Sincere and Wing On Department stores, and to some extent the Park Hotel, were open to the populace at large, and played an important role in the cosmopolitan Chinese imagination.

The new experience definitive of the modern person was the ascent to the roof terrace of the Sincere, Wing On, or Daxin stores (see Figure 8.10).[6] The traditional architecture of southern Chinese port cities, particularly with regards to their commercial suburbs, had been landscapes of gradual disclosure. Chinese shops, which also could and did serve as makeshift dwellings, unfolded gradually for the consumer (Liang, 2007). From bags of goods displayed on street or sidewalk, to shop interior, to store room (but rarely to back room), traditional southern Chinese commercial space lured the visitor in. The disclosure of consumer goods by the ground-floor windows of Western-style department stores was, thus, immediately intelligible to a Chinese audience. Now the tall buildings of the treaty ports offered another perspective. Here, from a significant elevation, the city disclosed itself to the viewer, in a way that it had not before (with the possible exception of a religious ascent of a pagoda – an activity actually intended to draw the mind inward rather than engage it with an active cityscape). In the same way that the view from the top of New York's skyscrapers was inspiring contemporary Americans, this new perspective from tall buildings offered cosmopolitan Chinese in the treaty ports a position of privilege.

The third quarter of the twentieth century often saw a restriction of the view from above to the elites – for instance, only Mao and his officials were on top of Tiananmen gazing out at parading crowds. The popular view from above would be reintroduced, however, during the era of economic reform by the construction of spaces like the viewing platforms of the Pearl of the Orient TV Tower (flagship of Shanghai's new development on the Pudong) or even the much more modest rotating restaurant atop the new addition to Guangzhou's Aiqun Hotel.

Figure 8.10 View of Canton from the roof terrace of the Daxin Building, Japanese occupation era postcard (source: from the author's collection).

Note
This image is indicative of the new popular perception of the Chinese city made possible by the introduction of tall buildings by way of the treaty ports.

CONCLUSION

Looking broadly at China's treaty ports over their 100-year phase of initial development, several things become apparent about the influence networks of talent, design, and commerce – between them and with the imperial centers of the West – had on their architecture and urban form. The first is that, lacking absolute dominion, Western powers rarely had the desire, impetus, or control to introduce city planning to their Chinese settlements on a grand scale. It is only in instances of great single-state control (like Qingdao especially) that comprehensive city planning was employed. Therefore, the layout of streets and neighborhoods was largely contingent on local topography, economy, and power dynamics. The exception to this was the notion of the bund, which, while it could take rather different forms, was a notable common feature of the ports. It exemplified a prime factor in the treaty ports' success: Western merchants' economic and therefore physical position between a productive Chinese interior and water-borne multinational trade.

The treaty ports shared economic and social institutions such as colleges and universities, banks, hotels, and department stores, which brought with them their own structures and spaces from the West and adapted to their new environment successfully, taking on new meanings in the hands of Chinese consumers and often patrons. These ports, particularly the oldest, went through several phases of building practice, architectural technology, stylistic language, and architectural typology – and it is significant that they shared these trends in common. These phases did not lag much behind contemporary developments in architecture in many parts of the West (the United States included), and they parallel and demonstrate the initial phases of China's emergence as a modern power.

So what do the plans and elevations of a Chinese builder of a plain two-story dwelling for Western clients and the grand hotels of Shanghai and Guangzhou's bunds have in common? One answer might be that they demonstrate the reach of Western-style capitalism. Moreover, they both bear witness to the capacity of some Chinese people to acquire new ways of thinking and incorporate them into pre-existing fabrics of everyday life. In the post-Mao era of economic reform, China's historic treaty ports frequently became special economic zones, and they are today in the forefront of the country's current economic resurgence. What remains to be seen is what the modernized, consumerist Chinese way of seeing – a legacy of the treaty port era, revived over the last twenty years – will produce for the future.

NOTES

1 Precluded from discussion here are the Japanese treaty ports in Manchuria, which have their own separate set of historical concerns and processes of formation.
2 The chief difference between the colonies and the treaty ports was that these specialists were in China often recruited by consuls and/or concession councils (in the case of Britain, particularly from the ranks of those involved in building and administering the more fully colonial project of Hong Kong through the Surveyor General's Office).

3 There was a third Shandong treaty port, Weihaiwei, but it consisted more of a British military installation than an urban entrepot.
4 LMS Archives, Incoming Correspondence Box 7, Folder 1, Jacket B; Perkins Russell Papers, Folder 26b-13.
5 Perkins–Russell Papers, Folder 26b-7.
6 I owe this idea to Delin Lai, and we currently collaborate on its development in the context of research and writing on the hotel in twentieth century China.

9 STARING AT THE SEA, STARING AT THE LAND

Waterfront modernisation in nineteenth century Ottoman cities as a site of cultural change

MALTE FUHRMANN

Leon Sciaky grew up in Salonica during the final decades of Ottoman rule. His recollections, entitled 'Farewell to Salonica', are one of the most vivid accounts of everyday life in the port city before World War I. Based on a childhood memory of his father, he described how the first steamship entered the city's harbour:

> The news of a burning clipper had spread rapidly through the city and throngs had ascended the stone steps leading to the parapet. There was no mistake. A great cloud of smoke hung close to the water, not far from Küchük Karaburun, the Small Black Cape. As the excited crowd watched, the smoke came nearer and nearer, until they could distinguish a black hull surmounted by a black smokestack. They stood aghast as the first ship without sails, the first vessel mysteriously propelled by fire, dropped anchor before our shores.
>
> (Sciaky, 2000 (reprint): 30)[1]

The steamer and the Salonican public's reaction to it set a pattern that pre-configured much of public behaviour in that city and Ottoman port cities in general for the next three-quarters of a century. Roughly from the advent of regular commercial steamer traffic in the Mediterranean in the late 1830s until World War I, port city residents would turn their heads to the sea to find the new, the innovative, the modern. They expected it to originate overseas, to come from what was termed Europe at the time.

The gaze of the Saloniquenos staring at the sea, at what miracles or threats the revered overseas culture might bring them, was complimented by the gaze of those aboard the steamers, scrutinising the city they were approaching. The travellers arriving from the metropolis saw themselves at the centre of con-temporary aesthetics and believed the Ottoman realm to be subordinated to the same set of aesthetics (Pratt, 1992; Saïd, 1978; Todorova, 1997). Foreign travelogues almost invariably began their impressions of a given city with the favourable impression the Ottoman conglomeration gave from the sea, then contrasting this first impression with negative remarks about the city from up close. For example, travellers arriving in Smyrna would write hymns about the view from deck ('Coming from Europe, the Orient presents itself in front of one's eyes here for the first time in all its originality and the encounter from a distance is one that enchants the senses', wrote one observer (Scherer, 1866: 93–94)), but after hurriedly passing by boat to the piers and the narrow wharfs, they would find themselves cut off from the sea and abruptly hurled into street scenes they found hard to cope with.

> Those well versed in promenades would find rich bounty for their desire to see in Smyrna. There is no mention of elegant shops, galleries, and passages à la parisienne of course, there are no interesting little ladies to be followed, with tiny feet and flirtatiously high dresses, there are no carriages rolling through the street and if one tires, there are no omnibuses or coaches to lend a hand.... There is no chance of a sidewalk during the excursion, the pavement has holes the police would not allow and in some places resembles ours back home after the barricade fights of 1848. No peace for dreamy thoughts! Two fiery eyes glow brightly through a loose window grid towards you, you raise your head to see better, but a camel, approaching silently from behind with its soft steps, pushes your hat onto the nose. Having escaped this Charybdis, you fall into the Scylla of a Turkish hamal [porter] who is carrying on his broad, flatly bent back weights of up to ten hundredweights and pushes you with it onto the wall, leaving you to thank the heavens for the thin waist it has granted you.
>
> (Scherer, 1866: 91–94)

If the city where they went ashore did not reveal itself to the travellers, they did not conclude that they themselves had not made a sufficient effort to understand the Other; instead, they assumed that the city had failed to meet supposedly universal aesthetical criteria, such as easy access, regularity, cleanliness and easily discoverable visual highlights.

The major Ottoman port cities, and especially their waterfront districts, became the prime site of the symbolic engagement of these opposing gazes, for the sea was the Empire's primary link to Europe, bringing its merchandise, money, travellers, repatriates and also its cannons to the Ottoman shores.

THE WATERFRONT AS GATEWAY TO EUROPE

In the age of imperialism, the Ottoman Empire in many respects shared the fate of the nominally independent kingdoms of East Asia: Siam, China and Japan. It enjoyed most aspects of state sovereignty and even increased its control over affairs on its soil. However, this control was severely hampered by the Great Powers, especially Great Britain, France, Germany, Austria-Hungary and Italy, which through a series of treaties exercised considerable influence on the Empire's economics and politics. Ottoman state policy was geared towards avoiding the Chinese predicament of suffering direct territorial control by the Great Powers and instead following the Japanese example of revoking disadvantageous international treaties (Esenbel and Chiharu, 2003; Quataert, 2002; Schmidtpott, 2007; Worringer, 2001). What made the Ottoman Empire different from the East Asian monarchies was its proximity to 'Europe', that loose community of states that in the nineteenth century considered itself the centre of the world. This proximity stopped any Great Power from unilaterally imposing its rule on the Ottoman lands, as this would jeopardise the balance of power within Europe.

But did proximity render the Ottoman lands 'European'? Both foreign observers and local communities gave a variety of responses to this question; and for much of the nineteenth century, the Ottoman Empire was ruled by sultans who emphatically sought to position their country within Europe, if need be at the expense of time-honoured traditions. Far from innocently debating geographical correctness, they all perceived this issue as decisive in the struggle to come out on top in the 'Eastern Question', i.e. the struggle for control over the Eastern Mediterranean region following the apex of Ottoman power (1774–1922).

The Ottoman turn to the sea, at least from the late 1830s onwards, was intimately related to a repositioning of individuals, groups and public affairs in relation to 'Europe', an omnipresent other in late Ottoman society. (Western Europe, in a slow but thorough cultural revolution that lasted from the middle of the eighteenth to the middle of the nineteenth century, had itself discovered a new delight in orienting itself to the seaside, and particularly the urban waterfront (Corbin, 1988).) The Ottoman port cities were interconnected with this Europe through several networks, and the waterfront served as the focus of an exchange between the Western and Eastern parts of Europe and the Mediterranean. The waterfront catered to the two opposing gazes – to the sea and from the sea.

Networks between infrastructure developers based in Marseilles, London banks, Munich beer exporters (and other entrepreneurs) and their local partners played a major role in creating the waterfront interface between Europe and the Eastern Mediterranean. Other literal networks important here included the communications infrastructure of steamer, postal, telegraph and even railway services, and professional associations of merchants, construction companies, insurance businesses and educational associations (Gekas, 2009a; Kasaba *et al.*, 1986; Keyder *et al.*, 1993; Sifneos, 2005). But to a large degree, local agents took an active part in imagining and realising their own Europeanised vision of their city. Many of the port city inhabitants had never seen this overseas Europe, but they believed that they knew it through their education and their interactions with people of European origin in their cities. The names of elite clubs, hotels, restaurants and pharmacies are just one indicator of their strong urge to identify with the supposedly superior civilisation, among other internal references, repetitions and common imagination. These common references – inside Smyrna, Salonica and Constantinople, as well as between those cities – constituted symbolic networks through which locals imagined Europe in the Eastern Mediterranean. These symbolic networks were at least as important in shaping the Eurocentric waterfront façades of late Ottoman port cities as the practical ones. In other words, the Europeanisation of the waterfront was not simply the result of a simple transmission of Western know-how, technology and financing, but a process in which locals of the Eastern Mediterranean attempted to restructure their surroundings according to the European paradigm.

THE OCCIDENTALISM OF THE SULTANS: IMPERIAL WATERFRONT GLAMOUR

In the northern half of the Ottoman Empire, the three major ports were Salonica, Smyrna and Constantinople. Salonica (Salonico/Selânik/Thessaloniki/Solun) ideally combined a safe natural harbour in the Thermaic Gulf, with land routes allowing for fairly easy transfer from and to the Balkan hinterland by caravan or, later, railway. Smyrna (Izmir) occupies a similar position at the intersection of the Aegean and Anatolia. Constantinople (Istanbul/Carigrad), on the other hand, is located at the strategic entrance to the Black Sea, but was also the largest city in the region as well as the seat of a government and a military high command eagerly trying to adapt to the modern world in order to save the empire.

The initial step to shift Constantinople's centre of gravity away from the high hills of the old city and towards the seas that connected it to Europe was taken by the sovereign himself. In February 1856, Abdülmecid I declared the *Hâtt-ı Hümâyûn*, promising equality to all subjects regardless of creed, access to education and public office, and justice, as well as increased autonomy for the religious communities and the right for foreigners to buy property. In March 1856, he succeeded in having the Ottoman Empire recognised as a full-fledged member of the European Concert of Powers (the loose association of the Great Powers that sanctioned major political changes in Europe and arbitrated diplomatic conflicts) at the Treaty of Paris, settling the Crimean War. In May 1856, he officially moved the seat of power from the old palace, located on the hill and which had been the residence for sultans and emperors for one and a half millennia, to the newly built Dolmabahçe Palace. This gargantuan structure stretched along the Bosporus waterfront for 600 metres (656.16 yards), taking up 4.5 hectares (11.1 acres) in total. In designing its seaside façade, the sultan avoided traditional Ottoman or neo-Orientalist styles, opting for neoclassicism instead, to symbolically claim the country's place in Europe. While contemporary observers increasingly saw the historic city as hopelessly entrenched in Oriental ways, they deemed the new location in the vicinity of the European embassies dynamic and prosperous (Mansel, 1996).

But despite such interrelated significant changes, and the continued practice of erecting imperial seaside palaces, Abdülmecid's vision of a Europeanised Ottoman state lacked social breadth. Dolmabahçe Palace was mostly the domain of an elite of bureaucrats and military officers, whose influence on society was overestimated at court. However, the palace succeeded in giving a clear signal that the state not only tolerated but actively encouraged an orientation to and emulation of European culture.

State officials increasingly accepted the importance of satisfying both seaward and landward gazes. The interests of society at large revolved more strongly around the commercially used part of the waterfront than the restricted area of the seaside palace. Official urban planning aimed to create a transit zone here, where the sceptical gaze of the arriving foreigner was appeased by finding forms that seemed not too alien to the aesthetics he was accustomed to in Europe, and where a local could feel that the city was in tune with European tastes and did not have to fear the comparison. In his 1869 progress report on the transformation of Constantinople, Server Efendi recommended widening the street leading up the hill from Tophane towards the Austrian embassy, because this was often the first street arriving Europeans would see, as it connected the port facilities of Galata with the hotel area around Grand Rue de Pera. Later, in 1901, a travelogue in a European newspaper criticising the pollution and neglect of the waterfront squares personally disturbed Abdülhamid II to such an extent that he called for his ambassador to France and ordered him to win the best French urban planners and engineers for a grand-scale reordering of the city (Çelik, 1986).

SMYRNA: FROM PERIPHERAL SEMI-COLONIAL OUTPOST TO A MODEL OF THE WEST

But it would be a civic initiative that drove the redesign of the waterfront. In the Reform Era, the state called for the active involvement of Europeans in reshaping the state, its economy and its important cities. Smyrna's long-established commercial exchange with European ports, which was thriving, now seemed like a model that the rest of the Empire should follow, and the rise in turnover in the city's bazaars and the harbour seemed to justify investments to facilitate growth (Frangakis-Syrett, 1992; Goffman, 1999). Although the Gulf of Smyrna had in previous times been considered a good natural harbour, the new standards of the steamship era made it appear inadequate for ships eager to load and unload (Oberling, 1986). Also the old narrow and winding Street of the Franks that had been the main artery of the coastal quarter (inhabited predominantly by foreign subjects) did not represent the new notion of European supremacy in technology and culture, nor did the ramshackle quays. The Street of the Franks ran parallel to the waterfront, accommodating foreign consulates, warehouses, residential houses, churches, taverns and even theatres. The backs of the houses made up the waterfront. This was not a singular but a chaotic and uneven structure. All owners of a plot here had individually adapted it to their needs. Many warehouses on the Street of the Franks had back doors with private piers, which were convenient for the evasion of customs duties. Apart from the private piers, the sea was only accessible through a number of short alleyways and only at two points did the built waterfront expand into a publicly accessible wharf. Because of the lack of space at these spots, cafés had been erected on haphazard platforms on wooden poles stuck in the sea (Atay, 1998; Fröbel, 1891; Zandi-Sayek, 2000) (see Figure 9.1).

Debates about reshaping this waterfront had started around 1850, focusing on different aspects, such as spatial control, fiscal benefits, commercial growth, easing of traffic or creating leisure and entertainment possibilities (Zandi-Sayek, 2000). Through these debates, the new quays evolved into a panacea to cure all the city's economic, fiscal, social, recreational and image deficits. It is not surprising that, accordingly, the proposed construction plans increased in scale as the debate continued. In 1867, three holders of British passports residing in Smyrna acquired a concession to construct new port facilities. Their plans reflected the high hopes in the city: the new quays were

Figure 9.1 Smyrna, the Quais Anglais before the construction of the new quays, c. 1860 (source: Ahmet Piristina Municipal Archives and Museum, Izmir).

to stretch from Punta (now Alsancak) past the Frank Quarter, the bazaar area and the Konak (governor's office) up to the Imperial Barracks, taking up practically all the seafront of the city proper. Three and a half kilometres long (2.17 miles) and 19 metres (20.78 yards) wide, the new quays were to dominate Smyrna. They were designed to allow up to 300 ships to dock immediately on the waterfront and thus to unload their cargo without the use of tenders. A rail line along the quays was to serve for transporting both goods to and from the city's railways and people (by tram). Later a 900 metre (984.24 mile) long jetty would be added to protect part of the quays from stormy weather. The growing construction project was not only meant to make transport easier. The Société des Quais also intended to fill 14.6 hectares (36 acres) of sea, creating a whole new part of town. In order to do this, they constructed one broad road along the quays and another one between them and the old waterfront, both of them running the full length of 3.5 km (2.2 miles) (Oberling, 1986).

Not surprisingly, this building endeavour, hitherto the largest in the city, did not win the unmitigated support of the Smyrniotes. Those who had owned precious seaside territory faced the prospect of finding themselves stranded two blocks away from the water. The planned port fees did not appeal to the sea companies. The project encountered other problems. The gradual process of filling in the seawater covered the city with stagnant pools. The original stockholders could not manage the 6 million franc project, so that eventually the Marseilles-based construction-company Frères Dussaud took over from the bankrupt Société des Quais. Following the takeover, the British consul joined the opposition in order to prevent the French business endeavour succeeding where a nominally British one had failed. (On the opposition to the quays, see Frangakis-Syrett, 2001; Oberling, 1986; Zandi-Sayek, 2000.)

Despite civic opposition, financial difficulties and the interference of the British, the city completed the project after only eight years (1868–1875). Towards the end of this time, opposition to the project weakened decidedly, as it became obvious that the newly erected quarters would actually soon become the centre of Smyrna. Investors scrambled at the last minute to buy property on the Quays or at least on the second new street, Rue Parallèle, so that upon completion of the works there was no sizable free lot to be found (see Figure 9.2).[2]

This monument to progress and the European way of life was soon to be copied elsewhere. In 1870 the municipality of Salonica, similarly located at an intersection of land and sea routes and experiencing an increase in Mediterranean trade, began constructing a new, 1,650 metre (1 mile) long waterfront, which was to serve simultaneously as port and fancy new centre of town (Berov, 1985). Unlike Smyrna, modern port facilities were not part of the Quays' construction. A new port adjacent to the Quays was constructed only in 1896–1902 by concession to the French citizen Edmond Bartissol (Anastassiadou, 1997a; Dumont, 1992; Yerolympos, 1996). Here the symbolism of the act is interesting: to begin construction, the city ceremoniously tore down the seaside part of the Byzantine city walls and used the debris to fill and make new ground for new quays, streets and buildings. This was meant to illustrate that the city, having remained closed off and locked in its 'mediaeval' ways, was now opening itself to the fresh sea breeze, the influences blowing in from across the sea, i.e. Europe, intending to take in without hesitation its philosophies, fashions and commodities. The municipality undertook the construction directly, without giving concessions or hiring foreign firms, to avoid complications like those that Smyrna faced. But it encountered problems of its own, including embezzlement and lack of funding, which resulted in several delays and the selling of all new land intended for public buildings to finance the remaining works.

Interestingly, Constantinople reconstructed its quays much later than did the two Aegean port cities, in 1890–1895/1899 (Çelik, 1986). This delay can be partly explained by the size and multi-centred character of the city. While the wharf area in Galata and Eminönü, located on both sides of the mouth of

Figure 9.2 Smyrna, the Italian Post Office near Hotel Kraemer, c. 1900 (source: Ahmet Piristina Municipal Archives and Museum, Izmir).

the Golden Horn (Haliç), was the commercial heart of the city, the adjacent lower-class residential areas (predominantly Muslim around Eminönü and mostly non-Muslim around Galata, including a large number of foreign origin) prevented the transformation of the area into a zone for upper-class leisure and shopping. The stage for such social activities was set in the streets around the Great Powers' embassies in Pera (Beyoğlu), a 15-minute steep uphill walk from Galata. Thus, while the new Constantinople quays would change working practices, they did not affect leisure and free-time activities to the same extent. Like their counterparts, though, they would become a site for extended controversies.

THE NEW WATERFRONT ORDER AND WAYS OF WORKING

Citizens turning their gaze to the sea now stood on evenly paved quays that stretched for a considerable distance to either side; there were no more cafés on poles extending into the sea, no more private piers, or sheds or warehouses extending across the wharf. The new quays would now increasingly bring changes to everyday life in the port cities. They changed the rhythm of the working day. Arrivals and departures of steamers dictated the movements of many white-collar employees of companies involved in trade, as they depended on the postal service. The German E. Kauder recounts his impressions from a business trip to Smyrna just before the turn of the century:

> The Austrian Post is the institution that has the liveliest traffic. One has to see the shoving, yelling, and pushing in front of the pickup counter after the arrival of a postal steamer to have an understanding of the enormous business life that vibrates in Smyrna. All the day's activities are regulated according to postal matters. In the morning, one first takes a walk to the blackboard to see if and when a ship to Europe departs and at what time the deadline is for postal deliveries for this shipment (usually one hour before the steamer's departure).
>
> (Kauder, 1900: 319 (translation by author))[3]

What impressed the German visitor was seen as a cause of stress by locals. Ernest Giraud, entrepreneur and later president of the French Chamber of Commerce in Constantinople, satirically reflected on the change at the time of the completion of the Galata quays (see Figure 9.3). Life in the old days had been a pleasant equilibrium of work and relaxation. There would be one steamer for France on Wednesdays, so the correspondence would have to be done on Tuesdays and finished and sent Wednesdays before departure. Thursdays and Fridays would be spent on recovering in the countryside. Saturdays the arrival of the next steamship from Marseille with mail would bring new work, which in turn would be followed by another two days of recreation. But now eight steamers departed Constantinople weekly for Marseilles, not counting the passenger service of the Messageries Maritimes. The correspondents' eyes were used up from all the writing, country trips had become a matter of the past and the employees developed bellies (*Revue commerciale du Levant* 102 (September 1895: 93).

Figure 9.3 Constantinople, Galata district, view of Karaköy Square, Galata Bridge to the left, port to the right, c. 1913 (source: DAI Istanbul, German Archaeological Institute, Istanbul).

While the white-collar workers suffered from burnout and the messengers had to race to the post offices on the Street of the Franks, Rue Parallèle or the Quays several times daily, the consequences were more drastic for the manual labourers in the port. The new facilities made direct unloading from ship to the quays possible, thus threatening the livelihood of boatmen operating the tenders. The railways on the quays, designed to transport goods between ships and train stations, were serious competition for the porters. As these workers' interests coincided with those of many businessmen, who opposed the stiff new tariffs imposed by the new port authorities, and as porters and lighter boatmen were organised in tightly controlled guilds, they were in a position to take collective action against the reorganisation of port activities. In Constantinople, such resistance delayed the full imposition of modern port technology for several years. When the port facilities in Galata started operations in 1894, lightermen prevented a steamer from docking directly on the quays. In 1895, when a further section of the quays was opened, they set adrift the floating docks that were to replace their lighters. The French company operating the port had to submit to the guilds' Luddite resistance, and for several months Constantinople saw the spectacle of lighters unloading ships in front of an unused port infrastructure built to more quickly and efficiently complete the process. The port company succeeded in gradually suppressing the guilds' monopoly, but the conflict violently resurfaced in the short summer of Ottoman labour radicalism following the Young Turk Revolution of 1908 (Frangakis-Syrett, 2001; Quataert, 1983, 2002).

THE NEW WATERFRONT ORDER AND WAYS OF LIVING

The quays were not simply a means to transform economic processes. Soon after their inauguration in 1875, the city's residents used the Smyrna Quays, just like their Salonica counterpart, as a stage where they could reinvent their city according to the newly revered culture from across the sea. Here they could embrace and enact all attributes of modern Europe with vigour. The large shipping companies had their offices here, the Smyrna main offices of the important banks erected impressive buildings, and the consulates of most major European countries moved to the Quays. Fashion and consumer article stores tried to keep up with their overseas idols. Local entrepreneurs established large, representative and, by the standard of the times, comfortable hotels with adjacent luxurious cafés. The cafés served Pilsner beer, which was first imported from Austria-Hungary, then brewed in Smyrna by an Austrian immigrant (Atay, 1997; Barth, 1893) (see Figure 9.4).

These edifices and their users did not only intend to impose their interpretation of European-style modernity upon the Smyrna populace, but also to placate the critical gaze of arriving visitors, demonstrating that this version of modernity had already been successfully adapted and subsequently that Smyrna was under full European cultural hegemony. In the latter scheme, they mostly succeeded. Travellers' comments, especially about Smyrna, now came to much friendlier conclusions, especially when comparing the towns to other Ottoman coastal regions. The German traveller Paul Lindenberg, arriving from Palestine, commented:

> The next morning led us back into the world of modern life, when we anchored before Smyrna at the seventh hour.... In some streets the Orient has been almost totally forced to retreat. One European shop is followed by the next, and the thousand-fold choice of all European articles possible (and impossible) at comparatively cheap prices are on offer, next to Japanese and Chinese products. Even the big Parisian department stores have opened outlets here and find much interest.
>
> (Lindenberg, 1902: 113) (on Levantine department stores, see also Köse, 2006)

Hôtel "Olympos Palace".

Figure 9.4 Salonica, Hotel Olympos Palace with a restaurant serving Munich Spatenbräu beer, 1911 (source: Malte Fuhrmann).

Less impressionable travellers at least remarked upon the better state of streets and sidewalks in Smyrna compared to Constantinople, seeing herein a greater proximity to a Western idea of an orderly city (Schulz-Labischin, 1908), but the more critical noticed that this regularity ended at the point where one entered the older streets (Barth, 1893). Now the older parts of the city seemed like a reminder of times gone by, and its very presence seemed like a lingering resistance to the application of Western paradigms of order. But for European travellers seeking the exotic, they could prove to be the last haven for experiencing the Orient amidst an otherwise uniform urban modernity. In numerous travelogues and also photo series, foreigners often sought to avoid the Europeanised port area, stumbling around the more traditional Salonican upper town or the lively Smyrniote bazaar district instead (Kerr, 1920).

The Smyrniote and Salonican waterside building development did not end with the completion of the quays in the 1870s, but continued throughout the following decades of the Belle Epoque. A look around the Smyrniote Quays after the turn of the century finds ample illustration of the European presence there. Offices of the German, Austrian, Russian, French and British post clustered around. Shopping passages by the name of Kraemer, Hönischer and Bon Marché ran from the Quays to the Rue Parallèle, from there to the Quais Anglais (which had retained its name despite the construction of the new quays leaving it landlocked) and finally to the Street of the Franks. To eat out, one could choose between the restaurants République Française and Grand Bretagne; for a Western-style coffee or a pint of beer, there was the choice between Café Parisien, Brasserie Strasbourg or Brasserie Puntingam. If one fell sick, one could find remedies at such trustworthy institutions as the Royal English Pharmacy or Perini's Great Britain Pharmacy (Meyers, 1901).

The Kraemer brothers, Smyrniotes of Trieste origin, were leading entrepreneurs in the field of European-style amenities. Besides having introduced the first major beer garden on the Quays, they had also set up a bank bearing their name, a theatre and the first cinema in the city (Atay, 1997; Makal, 1992). Opened in 1908, the Grand Hotel Kraemer Palace, with its lifts and permanent electric light, made the first generation Grand Hotel Huck look third-rate (Meyers, 1914).

Some visitors remarked upon the mediocrity of the fine arts in Smyrna, particularly the theatres, limiting themselves to popular French and Italian operettas (Lindau, 1900; Philippson, 1910–1915).[4] But the locale which the men and women of the Europeanised élites of Smyrna flocked to was not the theatre, but the luxurious clubs. Entrance to or membership of transnational clubs like the Club des Chasseurs, the Cercle de Smyrne or the Cercle des Européens was deemed the pinnacle of social success – indeed, of Europeanness (Pınar, 2000). The most prestigious of them was the Sporting Club, with an extensive garden, salons with high roofs, its own theatre and a terrace overlooking the Quays (Lindau, 1900). Admission to one of the nationally exclusive institutions, such as the Greek Casino, also located on the quay, also conferred Europeanness. All this was possible because being European in the Ottoman port cities was not limited to a community clearly demarcating their difference to others by an exclusive myth of origin. Although origin mattered, the Eurocentric elite formed a society with its strict rules and etiquette, and those who succeeded in mastering these rules could be admitted into its locales (Anastassiadou, 1997a; Georgelin, 2003).

CORSO, REBETIKO AND NUDE BATHING: LOWER-CLASS APPROPRIATION OF THE QUAYS

These statements on the emulation of supposedly European mores can, however, only be supported wholeheartedly for the upper classes. Looking at the broader strata of society, the ambivalence between mimicry and appropriation, as well as the element of persistency or self-will, becomes more evident.[5] Here what one aims to adapt is clearly intermingled with what one is accustomed to and sees no need to relinquish. For example, despite their resistance to the modern port operations, the Christian port workers in Constantinople are reported to have been the first locals to adopt the working-class flat cap, which was worn by workers the world over in the first half of the twentieth century, presumably directly from their colleagues on the incoming ships.[6]

Like the port workers, the cities' wider public found ways to profit from the quays as the new interface with the overseas culture without abandoning all local particularities. The quays became a stage for some Ottomans to perform how European they were. Even before construction was completed, the Smyrna Quays were a great attraction for hordes of Smyrniotes. The common practice was to get dressed up as well as one could, and then as a couple or as a family go for an evening stroll along the waterfront, enjoying the fresh breeze coming from the sea and happily intermingling with the neighbours, relatives and friends one would inevitably run into every few metres. Sitting down in one of the expensive beer houses along the Quays was financially out of the question for most, but this did not seem to discourage the strollers participating in the 'corso' of Smyrna or the 'volta' of Salonica (Gavrilova, 2003; Vučinić-Nešković and Miloradović, 2006).[7] Indeed, for most European observers, the Smyrniote practice of walking up and down the promenade was in principle an adherence to 'civilised' Western behaviour.

Some of the occurrences accompanying it, however, were not, and the quays became a site of class and cultural collision, if not conflict. The German consul to Smyrna during the completion of the Quays, Julius Fröbel, particularly deplored the practice of many male youths who used the promenade for diving into the sea and would then climb back out and stand naked and soaking wet among the Smyrniote ladies in their Sunday best. Other underclass practices that spoiled the elegant atmosphere of the waterfront appeared more like curiosities to him, such as fishing or, especially, the gathering of clams from the quay walls.

On one point, though, the German consul preferred the Oriental to the European. He felt touched by the Greek songs he heard along the promenade:

> Coming from little orchestras in front of improvised coffee houses,[8] the wonderful sounds of Greek music boomed in the mild air.... In these sounds produced by the singing of an improviser, and the free accompaniment of a few string instruments and a dulcimer, sentimentality and a

burning passion combine to produce an effect which wakes in us, the children of a conventional culture, dormant feelings not experienced before, while reason poses to the thinking listener the question as to who and what these people are, whose innermost emotionality shows itself in such a way? – The singer, his head sideways inclined in hands, staring at the sky, sitting amidst the instrumental musicians, emits long, wailing sounds. The accompanying string instruments give these sounds, depending on the words' contents, sometimes a soft, sometimes a harsh, even screaming color, while the dulcimer most effectively decorates, varies, and interprets the simple theme.

(Fröbel, 1891: 617–618)

This romantic music, he assumed, would soon have to make way for waltz music and operetta songs, which could increasingly be heard in the simpler coffeehouses of Smyrna. But fortunately Fröbel underestimated the resilience of Anatolian popular music. Although so-called Bohemian orchestras composed of German and Austrian musicians as well as French and Italian singers now toured Eastern Mediterranean cities, this did not cause local music to disappear (Anastassiadou, 1997a; Barth, 1893).[9] Instead, local musicians adopted elements of waltz and operetta into their songs (Giannatou, 2000). Even after the Anatolian Greeks had been expelled to the Hellenic Kingdom in 1922, they continued to play this music, known as Rebetiko. The Hellenic authorities first banned this music because of its Asiaticness, but in the end gave up because of its immense popularity (Zelepos, 2001).

Not only Fröbel noted 'non-European' elements in the happenings around the waterfront evening stroll. In Salonica, the Greek-language newspaper *Hermes* polemically deplored the fact that some citizens came to the Quays dressed in 'pyjamas' (Yerolympos, 1997). This attack was aimed at those who declined to get dressed up in suit and tie to come to the Quays and preferred more comfortable or traditional dress. This comment demonstrates a social rift that had a cultural, social, but also spatial dimension (see Figure 9.5).

In Smyrna as well as in Salonica, local authorities, newpaper columnists and travelogue writers interpreted the reordering of the seaside as a fight of the new against the outdated, the old. They saw the presence of traditional dress, street grids and uses of the street per se as a resistance against the Europeanising paradigm. Especially the old Turkish Quarter on the hill, with its winding, haphazard streets, closed off courtyards and 'simple' coffeehouses, appeared to be a bastion of defiance against the clear ordered lines, big windows and flashy lights along the Quays. In their zeal for modernisation and modernity, the governors and municipal administrations now began a process of extending the quayside urban forms into the old city, building wide and even boulevards into areas they had cleared by demolition (or arson, as some rumours charged). It is at this point that the symbolic violence of newspapers such as *Hermes* and foreign commentators such as Fröbel, who felt entitled to pronounce verdicts on who was welcome on the quays and who was not, turned to physical violence against those wearing the wrong dress, inhabiting run-down houses and loitering around streets that did not fit into the new urban public image. But demolition was not the only form of violence connected to the quays (see Figure 9.6).

Figure 9.5 Smyrna, pedestrians wearing fez, turban and bowler hat, c. 1900 (source: Ahmet Piristina Municipal Archives and Museum, Izmir).

Figure 9.6 Salonica, uptown, date unclear (before 1922) (source: Historical Center Thessaloniki, Collection Roger Viollet, F2, E60).

THE WATERFRONT AS SITE OF VIOLENCE

The Europeanisation of Ottoman urban space has been lauded, both by contemporary commentators and in recent years as a process of intercultural harmony and peaceful modernisation to the benefit of all. However, this naïve perspective blacks out an important reason why Ottoman seaside residents had to turn their heads towards the water. Europeanisation was not only an act of 'symbolic violence'; it included very real violence, or at least the serious threat thereof. The steamship brought the mail, but it also increased the ability of naval powers to intervene or retaliate all over the world at fairly short notice.

It was a common opinion that whoever ruled the waves ruled the world (until World War I and its trench warfare, and for the Aegean region most importantly until the failed Allied landing at Gallipoli (Gelibolu)). Great Power intervention by means of naval vessels, sometimes on the side of the Ottoman government, sometimes against it, had been a common feature of most nineteenth century wars in the Eastern Mediterranean. During the Belle Epoque, it had become a common element of gunboat diplomacy for warships to parade around Ottoman ports to remind the locals of their place. One description of such a casual display of power was as follows:

> To maintain existing interests and as a threat to the Turkish government, the Great Powers sent numerous warships to Smyrna, which anchored in the outer harbour. Upon my arrival, one German, Italian, and Austrian ships had already anchored, and one fine day around noon, four more Italians came in. I watched their arrival from the quay. These colossuses seemed like mighty fortresses, they came closer at great speed, producing great masses of smoke. After anchoring, the salutes of the present flags of war began, which were greeted with varying amounts of cannon shots, depending on the rank of their commander. Since the greeted flags on the various ships reciprocated, the effect was a non-ending cannon thunder that attracted great human masses to the quay. Two days later, three Frenchmen arrived, then one Frenchman and one Russian, and each time the shooting was repeated. All in all, twelve warships lay in the harbour.
>
> (Kauder, 1900: 317, 318 (translation by author))

The prolonged stay of warships brought complications. French and German marines in particular could not resist bashing in each other's heads when meeting in the seafront bars. In 1876, a German died in a Smyrniote café in such an incident; in 1913, a fight in the prestigious Café Kraemer resulted in several serious injuries.[10] But city residents often treated the ships' shows of force lightly. The visit of a navy ship was the occasion to hold opulent balls for its country's more prestigious local citizens. The officers were often more interested in their dance partners, the young girls of Smyrna or Salonica, than in laying the city to waste. Also, the inspection of the engines of destruction by the local populace, a routine part of such visits, failed to strike the locals with awe. As one commander complained, the locals were accustomed to being treated to cigars and drinks when visiting the warships, and his neglecting to provide such hospitality threatened to result in unfavourable local press for the warship.[11]

While some warship demonstrations served simply to exact political pressure, such as in the description by Kauder above, at other times they were immediate reactions to violent events within the cities, and aimed at protecting the security of resident Europeans. The most drastic anti-European event took place at the beginning of the Belle Epoque in 1876. At the outbreak of riots between Christians and Muslims in Salonica, a group of Muslim militants who had gathered in the Saatli Cami (Clock Tower Mosque) lynched the consuls of Germany and France. A parade of warships threatened to lay waste to the Muslim upper town with their cannons, until the local authorities had hanged a selection of supposed ringleaders, deposed the governor and chief of police, and the consuls had received an honorary funeral, flanked by thousands of foreign marines (Mazower, 2006).

During massacres against Armenians in Constantinople in 1896, warships arrived but failed to intervene. In this case, the port played an important role in the events, as Armenian migrants from Eastern Anatolia figured prominently among the port workers, and Kurdish and other Muslim labourers from the East were involved in the violence, apparently hoping to take over their victims' jobs (Quataert, 1983; Riedler, 2011).

One case of collective violence in particular sticks out, as it especially targeted symbols of European-style modernity. In 1903, a radical faction of the Inner Macedonian Revolutionary Organisation, an organisation claiming to represent the suppressed Slavic (or Bulgarian) population of the Central Balkan provinces, targeted Salonica. This splinter faction took on the interesting name of Gemici (the Boatmen). It began by detonating a bomb aboard a French passenger steamship as it left the port (but in a manner that allowed the passengers to escape). The following night, it tried but failed to blow up the incoming train from Constantinople; blew up the supply line from the local gas factory, thus extinguishing all street lights; blew up the Ottoman Bank and the adjacent German Club; threw several hand-made bombs at other targets, such as the German school, the Ottoman Post Office, the Hotels Colombo and d'Angleterre, and the Brasserie Noubo on or near the quays. While some of these targets were of practical advantage, it seems the overall strategy of the Boatmen was to show to the Saloniquenos how quickly their city could be stripped of its modernity (Georgiev and Trifonov, 1995).[12]

CONCLUSION: END OF AN ERA

For roughly three-quarters of a century, the quays dominated urban life in the three cities discussed here. We can only speak of outright opposition against this new dominant site of urban space during the construction phase, when citizens deplored annoyances including building activities, embezzlement, higher port tariffs and the potential loss of jobs. Once finished, the quays found wide acceptance by the local public. The particular usages of the waterfront for nude bathing, clam fishing and performing local music can be seen as a rather original form of appropriation, but it would be an overstatement to label them a form of resistance. The violent incidences, such as the Gemici Uprising, obviously take waterfront modernity as centre stage, but their nominal political demands do not mention it. While Ottoman revivalism and separatist nationalisms deplored the West's political and economic dominance of the region, they for a long time did not criticise the cities' locale for enacting European culture. Only with the reorganisation of the region into nation-states between 1911 and 1923 did it become obvious that the new administrations sought to rewrite the urban fabric completely.

The deathblow to the quays as a site for enacting modernity came with the submission of the respective cities to nation-state rule. This happened most dramatically in Smyrna, where in 1922, after a three-year occupation by Greek troops, the Greek army retreated, leaving the city population at the mercy of the Turkish National Army under Mustafa Kemal. Three days after the Turkish Army had regained control of the city, a fire devoured most of the Christian quarters, including much of the quays, where refugees had been camping. Cut off from other paths of escape, many refugees leapt into the sea, hoping to be saved by the European and American warships. However, the foreign ships refrained from intervening and only saved very few lives (Georgelin, 2005).

Both the Greek state in Salonica and the Turkish Republic in Smyrna (and to a lesser degree in Constantinople) felt uneasy about the quays and their aura. They were a reminder of an epoch when the rulers, the administration and wide parts of the public had given priority to an overseas culture over the nation. This aura had to be expunged. Both in Salonica and Smyrna, the municipalities tore down most surviving Belle Epoque buildings on the waterfront, and commissioned urban planners rearranged the street grid according to modern urbanist paradigms. And the central government, local authorities and citizens' initiatives scattered statues of national heroes, such as President Mustafa Kemal (Atatürk), President Eleftherios Venizelos or even Alexander the Great throughout the former quays, as if to exorcise the distinctly European spirit of the waterfront.

NOTES

1 It seems unlikely that Leon Sciaky's (born 1893) father was old enough to witness the first steamer in Salonica, as the first such vessel reached Constantinople on 20 May 1828 and by 1836 the Austrian Lloyd was offering regular passenger and freight services from Trieste to all major ports of the Levant. The Marseilles-based Messageries Maritimes followed soon after. Probably Leon Sciaky is recounting the testimony of his grandfather.

2 Federal Archives Berlin Branch, (BA Berlin) R 901/39576, 107: Griesebach (Consulate) to German Foreign Office (AA) Smyrna, 25 June 1875 (confidential).

3 Under the capitulations system, the Great Powers maintained their own national post offices in the Ottoman Empire, which attracted the lion's share of international mail. The 1900 delivery time for letters was far superior to today's air mail delivery. A letter from Smyrna would reach Central Germany in four to six days.

4 Also: BA Berlin R 901/72865, Holthoff, Memorandum, no date.

5 I am referring to the category of '*Eigen-Sinn*', as employed in the works of Lüdtke (1993). The term, which has the double meaning of 'sense of self' and 'stubbornness', is used to describe a strategy in between submission and defiance, that is, reshaping the behaviour that the outside demands of one to accommodate one's own desires and interests.

6 *Revue commerciale du Levant* 212 (1904).

7 While the evening stroll along the quays existed in Constantinople, it was not the single most important site of leisure activities (*Revue commerciale du Levant* 109 (April 1896: 123).

8 The lower-class improvised coffeehouses had to make way once the Quay construction was finished.

9 See also: Political Archives of the German Foreign Office, Berlin (PA-AA) Saloniki 22 (Auskunftsgesuche), 55: H. Müller to Consulate, Friedenau 17 Aug 1904; 253, P. Stark to Consulate, 16 Apr 1904; Saloniki 32 (Nachlass Lüttgens).

10 PA-AA R 12788, unnumbered: Tettenborn to Foreign Office, Smyrna 20 Jan, 4 Apr 1877; Evangelisches Zentralarchiv (Evangelical Central Archives), Berlin (ezab) 5/1959, 140: Zschimmer to Supreme Church Council, 2 March 1877; Federal Archives–Military Archives, Freiburg im Breisgau, (BA-MA) RM 3/3036, 167: Breslau, Military Political Report. Smyrna 4 March 1913.

11 BA-MA RM 3/3037 (Military Political Reports) 1/14: Trummler to Mediterranean Division, at sea 10 May 1913.

12 Šopov (commercial agent) to Gešov (envoy), Salonica 17 Apr 1903 (Julian calendar). As one eyewitness put it, 'Concessions, industrial enterprises, gold: that was the fabric of that much vaunted civilisation of the West, and at that very core they would hit savagely' (Sciaky, 2000: 74).

10 TOWN PLANNING, ARCHITECTURE AND MIGRATIONS IN SUEZ CANAL PORT CITIES
Exchanges and resistances

CÉLINE FRÉMAUX

The Suez Canal opened in 1869, built in Egypt by Ferdinand de Lesseps and the *Compagnie Universelle du Canal Maritime de Suez* (hereafter the Suez Canal Company or 'the Company'). Dreamt of for centuries, this passage between the West and the East accelerated international trade and migration, and was a new place in itself. The Company created or developed three port cities on the land granted by the Viceroy of Egypt for infrastructure and worker housing: Port Said, on the Mediterranean Sea; Suez and its outer harbour at Port Tewfik; and Ismailia, administrative centre of the Suez Canal region, situated at the middle of the isthmus, with its shipyards (see Figure 10.1). The cities grew rapidly, reaching population levels in the thousands. Their architecture and urban form reveal the diversity of planning interests and populations who shaped them.

The complexity of Canal lands' status meant that many different participants had to negotiate town planning and building. Although the Suez Canal Company managed the territory conceded to it by the viceroy of Egypt, it still faced national town planning rules and national authorities' control, and despite the rules the Company imposed on its private builders, local customs still prevailed (see Figure 10.2). Yet because the cities were relatively new, the Company could sometimes secure exceptions or privileges. Migrants from a

Figure 10.1 Map of the Suez Isthmus, 1869 (source: Fontane and Riou, 1869: 4).

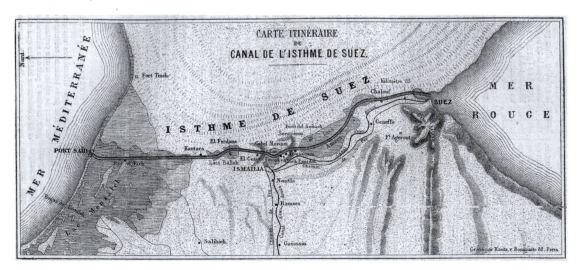

Figure 10.2 Arabic district in Port Said, c. 1920 (source: Archives Nationales du Monde du Travail (ANMT) 2000036 484).

Note
The Arabic district, built on common ground (i.e. it was under the control of both the Company and the Egyptian Government), was reorganised after the fire of 1888. Roads then became straight but were narrower than the roads of the European district. It was a commercial district with many entertainment spots.

variety of countries, attracted by work and opportunities to get wealthy, also shaped the three cities. Along with distinct Arabic and European quarters, they settled in Greek districts, remnants of Hellenic colonisation. Several places of worship testify to the national and religious variety of the communities (Lebanese, Greek, English, Italian). This variety helped these cities become centres of technology and knowledge transfer.

But cosmopolitanism had its limits. Their international identities, geographical location, and economic and geographic value in a strategic zone made the port cities of the Suez Canal witnesses to world and regional conflicts. Tensions between European countries resonated in local debates, for example between French and Italians for the takeover of the Suez Canal vicariate and over the design and construction of rival Catholic places of worship. And Europeans did not live easily among the locals. French architects and planners tried to import their own norms and forms (Rabinow, 1989) in these urban creations. But they faced different building and living habits. With hygiene as a key point of modern planning, the Company's engineers imagined a clear spatial discrimination between Europeans and natives.

This chapter analyses the parts different actors took in the construction of the three port cities, their urban and architectural design, and the exchanges between them and Europe from 1869 to 1956, the year the canal was nationalised by Nasser.

CONSTRUCTION: EUROPEAN DIVERSITY AND ITS LIMITS

The period from 1850 to 1950 was a high point of the European art of construction in Egypt (Volait, 2001). Cairo and Alexandria are already known as places where European construction professionals were highly active; we can now read the Suez isthmus towns as another important place where Europeans built many notable buildings.

From the beginning of the work on the Canal in 1869, the Company set a policy for employee housing, rapidly replacing the tents and huts of the first camps with more durable structures. Then an architectural firm, in conjunction with the medical service of the Company, designed houses responding to modern criteria of hygiene, comfort and aesthetics. The chief medic himself, Aubert-Roche, established house construction rules for the Company's engineers and architects in his 1869 report: 'The European who will live in the isthmus will then have to be careful. His house will face north...; walls will have a minimum thickness of 50 cms; the house will be surrounded by a gallery and big trees to avoid the sun from warming either the floors or the walls; bedrooms will be very high, well ventilated, with opposing shuttered windows, to control and direct light and draughts.'[1] His concern with hygiene was not separate, as we will see, from anxieties about local workers. The Company's architectural office conceived employee housing as villas 'à la française', and together these structures gave the canal towns a distinct identity (see Figure 10.3). Many visitors raved about the French touch or the seaside resort look given to Port Said or Ismailia by this use of imported forms or materials. Others, like the painter Narcisse Berchère, were disappointed by the journey: 'Nothing is less curious than these houses with roofs like ours, these cottages recalling our suburbs and, because they do in some way clash with local features, they make us long for the plain roofs of Arabian houses' (Berchère, 1863: 11).

The towns were heterogeneously European, however. Even though the Company employed mostly French architects, it signed a great number of building contracts with Italian builders. The Alberti Company, from Port Said, was charged with many works, among them the prestigious Port Said cathedral, and the Company regularly worked with Ladone and Costa Company, Ugo Rocchegiani or Scarpa & Co. And many Italian architects were very active in the isthmus towns. In 1888, one of the French newspapers

Figure 10.3 Residential area in Ismailia with villas set in extensive greenery designed for the Company's employees by the French architect Paul Albert, then head of the architecture department of the Company, 1920s (source: Archives Nationales du Monde du Travail (ANMT) 2000036 479).

Note
It differed a lot from the Arabic area, from the buildings to the activities that took place in them and the plantations.

of the isthmus praised the construction, by the architect L. Scarpa and the Antonio Ponelli Company, of one of the most beautiful buildings along the François-Joseph Quay in Port Said.[2] In 1936, the construction in Port Said of the Casa d'Italia by Clemente Busiri Vici was another occasion for Italian architecture to shine in Egypt (Godoli and Giacomelli, 2005). Italians were also very active in the real estate field, as can be read in the names embossed on the buildings façades or mentions in archives and documents. For example, the Coroni building in Port Said was well known for its innovative and 'European' character: 'Take the beautiful monument located at the corner of Commerce Street and Monge Street, belonging to Coroni Brothers: it has four floors, looks like a big house of any European big city and offers all conveniences. Iron has replaced wood in almost the entire building.... Large marble slabs make the building look like a palace.'[3] Silvio Simonini owned the three most important hotels in Port Said, the Casino Palace, the Continental Hotel and the Eastern Palace Hotel. One of the greatest buildings of the 1930s in Port Said bore on its gate the name 'Verivo'. Built by the engineer Louis Kolovitch, it housed a consulate, police stations and shipping companies' offices. Another notable building in town was named for the Italian Aquilina family.

The use of a specific style as expression of the patrons' origins was frequent: thus the Shaftesbury Building was erected at the corner of Al-Gomorya Street and Mohamed Mahmud Street in an authentic English style in 1910, while the Italian consulate and Villa Fernande were built in the 1920s in neo-Venetian style (see Figure 10.4). Many of the European buildings that did or still exist in Suez isthmus port cities were built for import and export trading companies, banks or real estate investors. In Port Said, one of the first concrete buildings was the Eastern Exchange Hotel, built by English investors in 1884 as an economic and trade centre and soon transformed into a hotel.

Figure 10.4 Italian consulate in Port Said, taken in 2004 (source: © Arnaud Duboistesselin, Cairo).

Note
This building assumes an Italian Renaissance style reminiscent of the country represented there.

With the creation of the Suez Canal ports, the Company borrowed technology and knowledge from European companies. The need for excavation machines led to great technical progress (Montel, 1998). Hardon Company and Borel Lavalley & Co., successively in charge of digging the waterway, recruited mostly French engineers trained at the Ecole Polytechnique or at the Ecole des ponts et chaussées, and bought machines from European firms. Hardon Company took on important projects all along the Suez Canal, especially bridge construction.[4]

Firms even imported construction materials from Europe, most of them shipped from Marseilles. For example, Trieste, Croatia and Hungary supplied wood, Great Britain coal (Montel, 1998). Materials for the construction of Suez dry dock were also imported: 'It has been necessary to import from Europe, despite the distance of 800 leagues, not only the workers and everything needed for everyday use, but all materials too, iron, wood, bricks, lime and even ashlars' (Stoecklin, 1867: 6). The volcanic ash used for the waterproof coating of the Canal's bed was imported from the Greek island of Kasos (Colonas, 2008).

But the only sand that European engineers would use in Canal works was thin local Egyptian sand, very similar to the marine sand from Fontainebleau, Montmorency or the Landes region in France. In 1868, François Coignet made this sand a central selling point in his bid to build lighthouses on the Mediterranean coast (see Figure 10.5): conglomerate concrete made from it was better than iron. Despite the local material, the Port Said lighthouse is an exemplary case of technological transfer across cultures, a kind of cosmopolitanism. The Company was in charge of the construction, but the Egyptian government chose, among the eighteen projects submitted, to assign the building of the Port Said lighthouse to the Coignet concrete company: 'Those [lighthouses] built in conglomerate concrete would look like those in stone and would present the same guarantee. These buildings would thus demonstrate that the sand of the Suez Isthmus is an inexhaustible construction material.'[5] Was this choice motivated by the company's argument for the use of Egyptian sand or by the successful use of this process in making artificial blocks of Port Said piers?

Roof tiles still visible on the most ancient buildings of Ismailia are stamped 'Martin frères, Marseille'. A Company engineer described in detail how builders came to use material from so far away:

> When the Ismailia buildings were erected, it was impossible to think of roof tiling. Transportation was still too defective; for example, window panes suffered major losses during shipping. Moreover, shipped tiles would have been subjected to damage, causing lack of the necessary supply. Since these materials can now reach the middle of the desert in good condition and because the enormous quantity of water poured into the isthmus made rain more frequent and the current roofs inadequate, we need to think about substituting tiled roofs for the former roofs made of palms and mortar.[6]

Figure 10.5 Port Said lighthouse, Coignet Cie, 1869, taken in 2008 (source: Céline Frémaux).

Note
It was the first building in conglomerate concrete of this height built in the world. The construction was achieved in a few months, one metre of concrete being conglomerated each day.

COSMOPOLITAN TOWNS: ORIGINS, MIGRATIONS

The adjective 'Lessepssian' is used by oceanographers to describe the ongoing migration of marine species across the Suez Canal.[7] But the most visible migrations induced by the enterprise of Ferdinand de Lesseps were human ones, most of them from the northern Mediterranean to Egypt. The lack of a term for the phenomenon doesn't mean that it was less important than that of aquatic vertebrates. The migration of workers gave the Canal towns their identity. The huge literature on Suez Canal towns is rich in precise descriptions or allusions to the cosmopolitan character of these towns. Paul Morand, in *La Route des Indes*, made the inventory of European migrants: 'The Canal is a true power: its army is English, workers are Greek, railway stationmasters are Italian and administration French' (Morand, 1936: 89). Early inhabitants' recollections are full of evocations of the juxtaposition of communities', of a 'savoir-vivre' and disparate populations. Jean-Marie Le Clézio remembered Port Said: 'the old city with wooden balconies, the shaded street with Greek merchants, the Turkish, the Maltese, the steam baths, the *ful* sellers and fishmongers' stalls' (Le Clézio, 2003). The architect-engineer Naguib Amin also recalled the times when Port Said was multilingual and multicultural: 'Here was the Canal culture: multiple and harmoniously heterogeneous' (Amin, 2006: 305).

Drill works and building management staff were mostly French – the engineers having been trained at the Ecole des ponts et chaussées (Montel, 1998) – but the composition of the worker class varied widely between the beginning of the works in 1859 and the inauguration of the canal in 1869 because of technological and political challenges. Among objections the Suez Canal project's opponents had raised was the job loss the Canal building would induce by attracting European workers to Egypt (Desplaces, 1859). Ferdinand de Lesseps assured critics there was no real risk because only *fellahin* – Egyptian farmers – would be employed. Indeed, the second concession act had stipulated that four-fifths of the workers employed in digging the canal would be Egyptians.[8] But Great Britain, the main agent of trade with the Orient, objected to the Egyptian *corvée* labour force. After the subsequent suppression of *corvée* labour in 1863, the Company turned to machines imported from France, such as bucket excavators, to get the work done; these did the work of a large number of workers but proved to be insufficient. The Company launched recruitment campaigns in Southern European countries, where workers were supposedly more adaptable to dry climates and hard work.

During the Suez dry dock construction, for example, Ponts et chaussées engineer Stoecklin sent Calabrians back to the south of Italy to hire more workers, and within a few weeks had signed contracts with some two hundred Italians (Stoecklin, 1867). Similarly, the Dussaud Company, put in charge of the works, organised the hiring of unskilled navvies and masons in Marseilles. The ones who accepted the offer were not French workers but mainly Greeks and Dalmatians (Stoecklin, 1867). Arabs too, from Upper Egypt, were employed on the site. Based on his experience, Stoecklin listed in his report the workers he employed according to their nationality and commented on the skills developed according to their origins (Stoecklin, 1867). The Company chief medic's report, written a year after the arrival of European labour force, described the value of the Company's hiring policy in racial terms: 'Since June 1st of 1864, Arab contingents don't exist any more.... The fears we might have had previously about acclimatisation, health and work efficiency of the white race were not warranted. The Arab and *fellahin* unskilled workforce can be replaced from the Mediterranean population, above all by Greeks, Maltese and Italians.'[9] Company employees were far from constituting the entire migrant population of the isthmus. The prosperity of ports like Port Said or Suez attracted people seeking prosperity, many merchants among them. In Port Said, the opening of stores and the building of private houses began around 1865, due to a new population of merchants and agents of ship-owners and manufacturers (see Figure 10.6).[10] And of course in addition to jobs offered by the Company and ship-owners, port activities, such as trade or coal transshipment, attracted a lot of European and Levantine migrants.

Although many workers left the site in 1869 when the work ended, many remained and either still worked for the Company or were hired by the numerous companies active in or around the ports. Greek workers constituted the core of the Company's employees at the beginning of the twentieth century, followed by Egyptians, Italians, Austrians and the French. During the next decades, the Company hired more and more Egyptians, but Italians and Greeks still remained numerous, followed, to a lesser extent, by the French and English (Funck-Brentano, 1947).

These towns remained melting pots as the cities became active ports. The Baedeker Guide listed about twelve European consulates in 1885 (Crosnier-Leconte, 2006: 21). Merchants and bankers accepted most currencies in these international ports: French francs, English pounds, Austrian crowns and Turkish pounds. Censuses of population, even in their probable lack of accuracy, reveal the coexistence of Arab and European communities. In Port Said or Ismailia, the Greeks constituted the most important of all the communities, occupying the largest space (see Figure 10.7). Less than twenty years after the opening of the canal to international navigation, Port Said already showed a

Figure 10.6 View of the port activities in front of the numerous trade building of the main riverside road in Port Said, postcard, c. 1920.

Greek stamp. A member of the Greek community wrote, with pride, in *Le Journal de Port Said* in 1888:

> There are 25,000 inhabitants in Port Said, of which 12,000 are Europeans, among them 6,000 Greeks or Rayas. So to speak, it's a Franco-Greek colony. Commerce Street looks like Hermes Street in Athens. The foundation stone of a magnificent church has just been laid. It will be built thanks to our pious colony's generous endowment. At Eldorado, the largest and most luxurious place in Port Said belonging to a Greek born in Cephalonia, there is a theatre performing operettas.[11]

Here the Greek community was characterised by its commercial activity. Greek grocers and bakers were located in Bazaar Street and Commerce Street. Au Mikado and Athanassoulis were among the most famous stores (Crosnier-Leconte, 2006: 51). Plots were bought and private stores were owned by Greeks. So the Company sold a plot in 1884 to Georges Coronis, a butcher.[12] In 1918, Dame E. Caloyeropoulo opened a brewery in Port Said.

Figure 10.7 Greek Orthodox church Sant-Menas in Ismailia, built in 1921–1935, taken in 2008 (source: Céline Frémaux).

Note
The second European community by number of inhabitants, the Greek community had its first chapel at the very beginning of the city. This larger one was built in the 1920s.

In Ismailia in 1867, the French writer Henri Baillère (1840–1905) discerned a very lively Arab village, a French town with a concentration of stores, administrative buildings and houses, and a Greek village huddled around the church: 'It was part of the desert: now, with 4,000 inhabitants, it's more than a town, there are three towns, gathered under the same name, and separated by the same space as before: the desert' (Baillère, 1867: 127). The smallest town of the isthmus, Ismailia had, according to the 1907 census, 11,448 inhabitants (Port Said: 49,884; and Suez/Port Tewfik: 18,347), of more than ten different nationalities, among them Egyptians, Greeks, Italians and Levantines[13] (see Table 10.1).

School statistics also illustrate the diversity. In Ismailia, the Brothers of Ploërmel school welcomed, between the two world wars, around sixty pupils aged 14–17: Greeks, Syrians and Italians.[14] In Port Tewfik, the seventy pupils of the Brothers were French, Italians, Greeks, Egyptians, Turkish, Armenians, Maltese and Syrians. They formed a religious mosaic as well: Catholics, Schismatics, Protestants, Muslims and Jews. A 1939 brochure offered by the shipping company Messageries Maritimes, and probably intended to relieve the apprehensions of passengers who had to stop over in the two maritime ports of the canal, specified that Port Said was 'a very cosmopolitan town of 120,000 inhabitants, among them 16,000 Europeans (French, Italians, Greeks, Yugoslavians)'.[15] Advertisements included in the brochure invited them to enjoy French and Italian cooking by 'Francesco', praised the famous French food at Bel-Air Hotel, recommended that they convert their currency at the exchange office of Ulysse Vafiadis or have their watches, jewels and eyeglasses repaired by N. Helpman.

At the inauguration of the canal, Port Said had two chapels, one Catholic and the other Greek, and a mosque (Crosnier-Leconte, 2006). Places of

Table 10.1 Census of the inhabitants of the towns of the isthmus, 1907.

Nationality	Number
Sedentary Egyptians	8,296
Greeks	1,078
Italians	469
French	343
Bedouin Egyptians	307
Syrians	238
Sudanese	227
Turkish	184
Austro-Hungarians	136
Other Europeans	75
English	29
Diverse	19
Algerians, Tunisians	12
Maltese and English settlers	11
Armenians	9
Arabs	6
Germans	5
Russians	4

worship, as well as cemeteries, give a quite precise idea of religious affiliation of the communities settled in the Suez isthmus. Cemeteries are the first evidence of the cosmopolitanism of the Suez Canal towns. The first cemeteries of Port Said were built in the very first years of workers' settlements, and were divided by religion, with Catholic, Orthodox and Muslim sections (Crosnier-Leconte, 2006). Family names and styles of funerary monuments reflect the national origins of the isthmus communities. Names embossed on the tombs in Catholic and Orthodox cemeteries of Port Said attest to the predominance of Italian and Greek families.[16]

Key points of community life, religious buildings – places of worship and schools – also manifested the religious diversity of the Suez Canal towns. The Company considered it its duty to support both communities, so long it was useful for its employees and the building's aesthetics were approved by the Company's architecture service. Thus, in 1923, the Protestant congregation's vice-president presented to the Company's superior agent a project for a church for eighty persons, among them sixty-five Company employees. The plan was realised by Auguste Pussot, himself a Company employee.[17] Another example is the contribution to the restoration of the Suez Protestant church, St Saviour, in 1952–1954, justified by the fact that around twenty Company employees' families were attending. Similarly, when the Greek-Orthodox archbishop petitioned the Company to build a chapel in Port Tewfik, the management committee claimed that the congregation was exclusively composed of Company workers with limited income and that the new chapel would be closer to their houses than the Suez one.[18] The Company supported Muslim employees in the same way as Christian and Jewish employees: it financed their places of worship on concession land, and controlled in the same way the quality of the architecture. The aid grant for a place of worship requested in 1951 by the trade union of Port Tewfik Company workers was included in the next year's budget. The pre-project plan, signed Ayar, was submitted to the direction committee, which didn't comment on this modest building with pillars and reinforced concrete flat roof.[19]

But cosmopolitanism had distinct limits. Europeans brought national tensions to the Suez zone along with building materials and design ideas. The most explicit story of European countries' competition in the Suez Canal area undoubtedly was the fight between French and Italian Franciscans for the Suez vicariate (Frémaux, forthcoming). In the historical context of the awakening of European nationalisms and in such international towns as those of the Suez Canal area, religious institutions necessarily played a political role. In Italy, an anti-British polemic had taken the form of writings claiming a 'Latin' Mediterranean ever since the Canal opening; this only strengthened after Mussolini proclaimed the Mediterranean Italian in November 1937. One goal was undoubtedly to obtain lower rates in the use of the Canal and to join the Company administration council, but another was to establish new Italian colonial authority (Bono, 2006). Now Italy declared that the Canal project itself had been conceived by the engineer Negrelli, called 'il vero creatore del canale di Suez' ('the true creator of Suez') (Sammarco, 1943). In debates over the possibility of the Catholic Church establishing an apostolic vicariate in concession lands, Italians argued that such a vicariate should also be Italian.

The Italian foreign affairs ministry viewed the case with great interest, conscious of the impact it could have on Italian prestige outside the country and, later, on national prosperity; ministers even pressured Italian Franciscans to intervene. Italy was aiming to create more colonies in this period, so an Italian vicar apostolic in Egypt would play an important diplomatic role. And Italy had an interest in having a presence alongside the canal, as did every country using the waterway for trade. In turn, the French government intervened through the French ambassador to the Holy See. The Canal vicariate was created on 12 July 1926 by a pontifical act of Pius XI and at last the Propaganda Fide Congregation, exercising remarkable diplomacy, chose as apostolic vicar apostolic Mgr Colomban Dreyer, an Italian-speaking Frenchman, who could promise to take into account the Catholic interests of each nationality.[20] The Company's general director announced this nomination to the management committee with satisfaction: 'The nomination of a French bishop to take care of the Suez isthmus religious establishments fulfils the Company's expectations.' The president added that he already knew Dreyer and thought highly of him: 'His nomination in the Canal is particularly satisfying.'[21] Viceroy Fouad I appreciated that the Holy See had entrusted the vicariate to the French, whom he considered to be the party most able to maintain good relations with the Company.[22] French architect Jean Hulot now built Port Said cathedral, financed by the Company (see Figure 10.8). It is dedicated to

Figure 10.8 Port Said Cathedral, Jean-Louis Hulot, French architect, 1937, taken in 2006 (source: Céline Frémaux).

Note
This church, symbol of the French domination of the Suez Canal area, assumed a neo-romanic style.

166

Mary Queen of the World; from the beach, she welcomes the ships. But instead of calming the waters of international competition, these decisions stirred them: Italians took it as the symbol of the gallicisation of the Canal and fights between the Italians and the French continued through petitions and demonstrations – and even thefts of the host and tearing down of pilgrimage posters. The struggle reached its peak in 1931 with a dispute over the language to be used in May religious ceremonies.[23]

The process of the creation of the Suez Canal cities has been quite different from that of other cities of the colonial world. Indeed, they look like company towns. And despite their cosmopolitanism and because the Company's leaders were French, the cities assumed a French character. Finally, while engineers and administrators came from diverse European schools, European workers were chosen by the Company for their supposed physical qualities, considered an extension of their nationalities. That means that among the European communities a clear hierarchy existed. The dominant classes of the urban societies of Port Said, Ismailia and Suez/Port Tewfik wrote this hierarchy on urban space. They occupied the central areas, and they imposed themselves as leaders in the main domains of urban life, such as religion.

PLANNING AND THE LIMITS OF COSMOPOLITANISM: IMPORTING EUROPEAN TENSIONS AND TRYING TO CONTAIN NON-EUROPEAN POPULATIONS

Cosmopolitanism had other limits. Migration and Company policy brought not only European equipment, personnel and conflicts, but European anxieties about non-Europeans. Even if they looked like towns 'à l'européenne' or 'à la française' where Italian, Greek or French architects worked, the Suez Canal towns, which rapidly became the first towns of Egypt, didn't only have foreign inhabitants. Many Egyptians settled there too, like their European counterparts migrating for work. And Egyptian investors lived in the port cities; they often built on public lands. When the Port Said governor decided in 1924 to create a seaside resort with sixty-three villas and a casino, the Egyptian newspaper *Al-Makattam* made a plea to these potential investors: 'It is unnecessary to underline the importance of this grandiose project. So we beg our co-nationals not to lose this opportunity since they could show their financial power and their capabilities in undertaking and realising such projects.'[24] Europeans were anxious about and looked down on such locals; engineers were anxious about and looked down on workers; and their anxieties found expression in anxieties about pollution. To address these, Company urban engineers imported doctrines of urban planning and principles of hygiene, the corollary of urban planning at the end of the nineteenth and the beginning of the twentieth century, to shape and reshape these port cities.

Ironically, the builders were almost as diverse as the populations they tried to control. Of the three types of land in the Suez Canal towns, each had its own management: the concession land, the public domain, and the common domain. The concession land, or the territory given to the Suez Canal Company for canal management, had been obtained from Egypt by Ferdinand de Lesseps, thanks to his diplomatic talents and to the good relationships he established with the royal khedivial family. The towns created or developed on the concession land nevertheless remained subject to governmental jurisdiction and to the Tanzim, which set planning rules.[25] For example, in 1888, the Tanzim promulgated a new building rule encouraging investors to build arcades, with three objectives: town beautification, traffic flow and public cleanliness.[26] The supporters of this type of construction evoked the elegance of the arcaded Tuileries quarter in Paris, while opponents argued that the required street-narrowing would ruin the beneficial effects of the air. They struggled until the Tanzim annulled the decree in July 1888 – an annulment that the Company appealed, winning the case on the grounds of aesthetics and homogeneity. The new judgement allowed companies to continue to build arcades in streets already under construction, and they became a distinctive feature of the towns (see Figure 10.9).[27] The public domain, outside the Company's concession land (that is, outside the area reserved for the Company's buildings), was managed by the Egyptian State, which directly interfered in the isthmus towns' development. Some parts of the

Figure 10.9 Building with arcades in Port Said, c. 1900, taken in 2009 (source: Céline Frémaux).

Note
Arcades, evoking the elegant Tuileries quarter in Paris, were introduced in Port Said at the end of the nineteenth century, to enhance towns' beautification, traffic facilities and public cleanliness.

same towns remained public. For example, in 1923, the governor, the representative of the Egyptian government in the area, presented to the king his projects for Port Said, including two public markets, one theatre, summer villas and public gardens. The king himself proposed the creation of an aquarium.[28]

Lastly, the common domain was under the joint responsibility of the Egyptian government and the Company. In 1869, the progress of the Canal work made it obvious that the Company would not use a large part of the concession land, especially the zones located in the area of the future towns. Then a new concession act was signed which allowed these empty zones to be sold. They formed the 'common ground' of both government and Company. The streets that were planned on the land built over the embankments (on the seashore in Port Said) were administrated by the Egyptian government and the Company. Road planning became a site of negotiation between the two parties. The plan was first conceived in 1887 by the ministry of public works.[29] It aligned new streets with the beach, and created many crossroads, squares and wide streets to improve traffic and to contribute 'to the settlement and the beauty of the town'.[30] Then the Company proposed a new plan with smaller plots, the selling of which would bring capital gains.[31] The government finally offered a compromise plan, maintaining the general ideas of the Company's plan, 'in order to get lands which could be divided into small plots to be sold more easily and with higher profits'[32] while also creating public roads and places in an aesthetic way. Indeed, government and Company interests sometimes tended toward the same objectives: financial, of course, but also planning and control. For example, in 1908, the Port Said common domain commission imposed strict rules on builders in order to create a certain style for the area. Buyers could only build one house on the plot and 'neither store, hotel, theatre, "café", bazaar, nor any other industry' was allowed.[33]

If Suez Canal towns were characterised, as every cosmopolitan town was, by the juxtaposition of areas corresponding to communities of different origins, they were similar, in segregating people along class and racial lines, to other colonial towns. Along with zoning types of land use, the Company partitioned the towns between the Arab and the European quarters. This spatial segregation was aiming at controlling real and imagined dangers of pollution.

Specifically, the Company settled the majority Egyptian population in distinct areas of the Suez Canal cities, separated from the European population. The Company's offices and houses were generally in mid-town, while the Arabic houses were as far as possible from it. André Guiter, a civil engineer, pointed out this spatial segregation in 1868:

> The population is divided in two parts: Arab and European. The latter is composed of French, Italians, Germans and Greeks. Each has its own area. The business part surrounds Leibnitz Square, also called the industrial area. The Arab population, the more numerous, is settled on and around Ibrahim Square, where the Company built a mosque and a bazaar. Houses made of boards, palm roofs and masonry are all around the square.
>
> (Guiter 1868: 44, my translation)

In others words, repeating the same planning module in the plan of Ismailia, designed in 1862, made it impossible to identify the European and Arab districts. Only the mode of building gradually distinguished the two areas, and in the Arab district informal urban development soon led the Company to transform the former star-shaped plan into a grid pattern with narrow streets. Jules Charles-Roux, Company administrator, described Ismailia in 1901 as a quiet town, with pretty villas surrounded by gardens. But he still found the Arab village exotic: 'Here you can't look for building regularity, neither for order or quietness' (Charles-Roux, 1901: 183).

In Port Said, the first inhabitants installed the first buildings in haste, parallel to the shore. The Company designed a regular plan only a few years after the works began, moving the native town to the west and clearly separating it from the European one. In 1865, 110 brick houses for the main employees faced the shacks, covered with palm roofs, of the Arab area.[34] The Company sought to impose an urban plan on the Arab area, specifically to divide it into regular plots to make it 'cleaner' (Frémaux, 2008: 75–101):

> Every nook and cranny in this irregular area is a source of infection that hygiene demands is made to disappear as soon as possible.... The three metre [10 foot] wide crossing lanes I propose to create will make it possible to require that the Arabs drop their waste, which could be picked by the street cleaning services.[35]

Here the French could only see Arab habits as dirty, and modernisation required the imposition of controlling measures. In Port Fouad, the Company built the separation of Arabs and Europeans into its original settlement.

Port Said had no more room by the beginning of the twentieth century. The Company therefore decided to relieve the African bank by transferring the main workshops and the main store to the Asian bank as early as 1914 and by building a new town on that side of the canal. Designed in 1910–1911, the town plan took shape after World War I. The Company conceived of Port Fouad, named after the Viceroy of Egypt, as a garden city with slightly curved streets to prevent the monotony of straight lines. The new city would have very wide avenues, in part to offer citizens perspectives on prominent buildings such as the lighthouse and the Port Said offices, or the statue of Ferdinand de Lesseps at the end of the eastern pier. Moreover they designed it to be a model of company housing and to compete with the most famous creations of this type (see Figure 10.10).[36] The general secretary of the Company laid out 'ideas which presided over the planning', including: 'build an airy town; make the circulation between the different areas easy; prevent native workers, on their way to the general workshops, from scattering all around the European quarters; create pleasant perspective views'.[37] The hierarchies are inextricable here: the houses' hierarchy matched that of the company and of workers' origins, so that employees and workers were housed separately, as were Europeans and natives, and the lower the population was on the hierarchy, the more polluting and the more Europeans wanted to avoid it.

Figure 10.10 European workers houses in Port Fouad, taken in 2009 (source: Céline Frémaux).

Note
The model is imported from France. They look like workers' houses built by the Mines Company in the north of France, as well as workers' houses built in the suburbs of Paris in the 1920s.

CONCLUSION

The built heritage and the numerous accessible archives give a precise idea of the process of planning the Suez Canal port cities. The construction zones and the cities themselves were places of technology and material transfers. The urban planning and architecture of the three cities of the Suez Canal manifested the domination of the French power over this part of Egypt, and also over other European countries. The Company, while cosmopolitan and international, always remembered its origin as the idea and realisation of the French hero Ferdinand de Lesseps.

Each of these cities was constituted in two parts. The first, central one, gathered European migrants. Far from being a real melting pot, these areas were divided by communities. Each of these communities imposed its identity in part with religious buildings. The planning and building there were a mirror of the struggles between European countries, especially strong in the context of the development of nationalism during the 1920s.

The second part gathered Arab people. Like other colonial cities, the Suez Canal cities were designed following a strict spatial discrimination based on contemporary scientific research discerning 'races' in part by construction abilities. This research considered hygiene a major point of urban and architectural modernity. Thus, urban planning clearly separated Europeans from natives on the grounds of cleanliness and order. In the beginning, European architects and engineers tried to impose their norms on the Egyptian people; hygiene, and modernity itself, was a colonial strategy. But they faced strong resistance. Locals adapted European models in the colonial world in different ways (Coquery-Vidrovitch and Georg, 1996: 290). Even if Europeans – and, in the present case, French elites – wanted these cities to reflect only themselves, they couldn't prevent residents from making a kind of *métissage*, weaving together local and outside cultures and cultural forms.

ACKNOWLEDGEMENT

I am grateful to Maryse Bideault, Michael Rinehart, Carola Hein and Lisa Williams for help with English translations.

NOTES

1 ANMT [Archives Nationales du Monde du Travail] 1995060 1416: Printed report of head doctor Aubert-Roche, 1869.
2 *Le Journal de Port Said*, 1 June 1888.
3 *Le Journal de Port Said*, 1 June 1888.
4 Archives kept by the Ecomusée du Bois-du-Luc, La Louvière, Belgium.
5 ANMT 1995060 4472: Letter from the administrator-director de Loynes to Company's vice-president, 8 December 1868.
6 ANMT 1995060 3138: Report of the Superior agency of the Company in Egypt about the repair of tiled roofs in Ismaïlia, 12 September 1867.
7 ANMT 1995060 3139: Report on Suez Canal Company's social policies for its employees' housing, December 1944.
8 2nd Concession Act signed by Muhammad Said Pacha, Viceroy of Egypt, 5 January 1856.
9 ANMT 1995060 1416: Report of head doctor Aubert-Roche, 1865.
10 ANMT 1995060 3139: Report on the Company's social policies for its employees' housing, December 1944.
11 *Le Journal de Port Said*, 2 June 1888.
12 ANMT 1995060 3138: Letter from the general secretary to the superior agent, August 1919.
13 *Statistical Yearbook of Egypt*, 1909.
14 Archives of the Brothers of Ploërmel 404/1.1.001: Mission of Egypt, typescript, sn, s.d. [ca 1936].
15 *Messageries Maritimes. Renseignements à l'usage des passagers, Port Said-Suez*, 1939.
16 Among the names found in the Catholic cemetery there are a lot of Italian patronymics such as: Sacco, Fabiano, Bonnici, Carli.
17 ANMT 1995060 1001: Letter from Prouteaux and Saint-Pierre to Serionne, 20 April 1923.
18 ANMT 1995060 1002: Report on management committee meeting, 1 September 1927.
19 ANMT 1995060 100: Pre-project for a place of worship in Port Tewfik, Ayar architect, 21 August 1951.
20 Vatican Archives AES; Africa Egitto 1925–1947; Pos. 18 Fas. 6: Letter from the Propaganda Fide congregation Cardinal prefect to the Secretary of the Governatorate of Vatican City State, 23 November 1926.
21 ANMT 1995060 1004: Report of Company's directive committee meeting, 3 January 1927.
22 Vatican Archives AES; Africa Egitto 1925–1947; Pos. 18 Fas. 6: Letter from Apostolic Delegate to the Secretary of the Governatorate of Vatican City State, 24 August 1926.
23 Vatican Archives AES; Africa Egitto 1925–1947; Pos. 18 Fas. 6: Secretary of the Governatorate of Vatican City State: pro-memoria, s.d. [1931].
24 *Al-Makattam*, 1 April 1924.
25 Tanzim: routes planning organisation.
26 Decree of July 1888 that authorised the building of arcades along the 15 to 30 metre (16.4–32.8 yard) wide streets in Port Said.
27 *Le Phare de Port Saïd*, 27 April 1889.
28 ANMT 1995060 1197: Report of Port Said municipal committee, 7 July 1923.

29 ANMT 1995060 3563: Plan of Port Said's new streets, established by the public works ministry, April 1887.

30 ANMT 1995060 3563: Letter of the under-secretary of state, public works ministry, to the Company's superior agent, 7 April 1887.

31 ANMT 1995060 3563: Company's plan, May 1887.

32 ANMT 1995060 3563: Letter from the Public Works minister to the Company's superior agent, 13 December 1887.

33 ANMT 1995060 3563: Schedule of conditions established by Port Said common domain commission, 1908.

34 ANMT 1955060 3139: Report on the Company's social policies for its employees' housing, December 1944.

35 ANMT 1995060 3563: Letter from Poilpré, chief of the domain service, to the president director, 15 April 1880.

36 ANMT 1995060 3138: Letter from the director of the mines of Drocourt, 27 July 1914: it detailed the price of the workers' houses of Drocourt and the type of concrete houses in the garden-cities of Drocourt.

37 ANMT 1995060 3138: Letter from general secretary to superior agent, August 1919.

Part III

DYNAMIC LANDSCAPES

Global change and local transformation

11 HAMBURG'S PORT CITYSCAPE
Large-scale urban transformation and the exchange of planning ideas

CAROLA HEIN

Designed to look like a ship's prow, the Chilehaus office building makes Hamburg's international maritime connections visible in form and name (see Figure 11.1). It showcases some of the elements typical of Hamburg's history, rooted as it is in the local elite's dedication to the port function, their creation of urban form for (maritime) business purposes, and their use of architectural imagery to express and even celebrate the global connections of the Hanseatic city. Funded during the early post-First World War years by Henry Barens Sloman, who made his fortune trading saltpetre from Chile, it was designed by the Hamburg

Figure 11.1 The Chilehaus Hamburg (source: Schulze, 1941).

Note
The Chilehaus Hamburg, an architectural icon of Hamburg's maritime trade, designed by the architect Fritz Höger, has inspired many other buildings since its completion in 1924.

architect Fritz Höger between 1921 and 1924, during a period of terrifying inflation. The result was an urban icon, an outstanding work of expressionism, celebrated in scholarly texts, tourist brochures, on stamps, and in later architectural works that refer to it (for example Busch and Sloman, 1974; Frank, 2003). Marrying local materials and imagery with the maritime tradition, Hamburg's trading history, and the name of another country, the building exemplifies global/local interactions in the built environment. After the loss of almost the entire German fleet in the First World War, the Chilehaus stood as the flagship of Hamburg's recovering shipping business. The building, erected on a triangular and sharply pointed lot between narrow streets near the waterfront, was part of a large-scale urban project in which Hamburg – once again – demolished old and poor areas next to the harbor and raised the land to build an office district that would match the earlier creation of a monofunctional warehouse district, the Speicherstadt (warehouse city). The Chilehaus and Hamburg itself are useful sites in which to discern interactions distinctive to port cities: between the global and the local, and between shifting social and economic flows and the changing built and urban environment.

This chapter concentrates on one set of social actors affecting these interactions historically and today: professionals closely studying foreign port developments, architectural design, and city transformation, whether architects, planners, engineers, or traders. They have made international networks visible by including foreign design concepts, architectural styles, or building materials, as well as by naming structures. Sometimes they have hidden or rejected foreign principles. Many have been from other countries. This chapter shows how and where they made foreign ideas local in the city's major urban transformations – specifically how they responded to global shipping and transportation patterns in those large-scale transformations, as well as in planning ideas and architectural design. It asks: How have global changes made an impact on the port and on the redesign of large areas throughout the city, and how have local forces, events, and requirements (including disasters and wars) lead to specific built and urban forms? Large-scale transformations are particularly appropriate for this examination as they require strong leadership, long-term planning, and big investments; they affect a large part of the population directly or indirectly, and can be subject to strongly voiced opposition. They are also particularly well suited to fuel changes in urban imagery.

For the purpose of this chapter, I have selected major exemplary urban changes that can be tied to the port function, without trying to cover the entire urban history of Hamburg or all the activities it houses. Building on a brief historic introduction to the ways in which the port activity has shaped the city of Hamburg, the examples in this chapter will be primarily post-nineteenth century. The changes in this period historically affected the different zones of the port: the port itself, the port area/waterfront, and through them the city as a larger entity (see also Chapter 1). But as the port detached from the city in the nineteenth and early twentieth centuries, specific changes there stopped affecting the larger city directly, while continuing indirectly to shape urban and architectural decisions. As port and city changed, they left behind built and urban structures that established a framework for future development. Even after the Second World War, as containerization required fewer and fewer workers and as the port separated almost completely from the city, the presence of the port continued to affect the city less directly as a place of labor, but indirectly as an economic force and a shaper of urban identity and new port cityscapes of leisure and tourism. I therefore also examine symbolic evidence, considering how shifts in iconic views of the city registered shifts in the built environment and the changing visibility of the waterfront and the working port. The analysis of major actors, policy and planning decisions promoted by the Hamburg government thus provides a lens to examine architectural design and urban transformations as part of the port cityscape and as expressions of a larger port-related global network.

HAMBURG AS A CASE STUDY OF PORT CITY TRANSFORMATION IN THE INTERNATIONAL CONTEXT

Founded in the ninth century as a fortification, the Hammaburg, Hamburg has for most of its history been a port (on the history of the port and the city, see, for example, Ellermeyer and Postel, 1986). For centuries, the city's long-distance waterway and major shipping lane was the Elbe River. The city was ideally located as a node between agrarian products from the east (copper, iron, herring, wood, wheat, etc.) and the main markets in the west (linen, spices, almonds, wine), with beer one of its main locally exported articles in the medieval period. Historical views of Hamburg, such as those by Georg Braun and Franz Hogenberg (1572) or that by E. Galli (1680), show the city from the south. Ships occupy the foreground of a fortified city dominated by churches and houses (see Figure 11.2). Hamburg's history is also intimately tied to other local waterways, notably the Alster River, dammed in the twelfth century to power a water mill to grind grain from the surrounding areas – thereby creating the Alster Lake. The city became a member of the Hanse, or Hanseatic league, a group of allied port cities in the North and Baltic Seas that dominated trade in the Middle Ages, and flourished as an important harbor city and trading nexus (Bracker, 1989). In its period as a free city-state, the city expanded on the north side of the Elbe. Harbor activity here was physically associated and intertwined with the city for many centuries. The Braun and Hogenberg map of 1588 shows how port functions effectively integrated the city's different urban landscapes (see Figure 11.3): Ships and barges would transport goods by canal to warehouses connected to the offices and houses of traders.

Merchants with global connections have traditionally held the main political positions in Hamburg. While urban form largely developed in response to local needs, Hamburg's leaders have always taken into account international technological and design concepts and borrowed or modified them if necessary to supplement innovative local developments. While the port and its traders historically shaped the city, a range of international actors connected with them made large-scale changes in the urban fabric. Local leaders adjusted the timeline of their projects in response to natural (or man-made) disasters such as fire and disease whenever it helped to promote their long-standing interests. Local particularities and events contributed to the shaping of a new city that continued to be determined by trade and by integration into international networks.

The harbor constituted a large portion of the entire city and influenced built form throughout the urban space. By the mid-seventeenth century, it was surrounded by a strong fortification, which included an inner harbor as well as the so-called Binnenalster (Inner Alster). Both the fortification and the harbor made visible the power and wealth of the city; accordingly, they appeared in representations of the city (see Figure 11.4). Over time, the urban imagery used to characterize the city changed. Views of the entire city over the Elbe had dominated representations of the city for centuries. But in 1796 the city built the Jungfernstieg – a fashionable tree-shaded promenade bordered on one side by offices and the houses of the local leading classes and on the other by the Binnenalster. The Jungfernstieg became the city's iconic and representative face, as the German architectural historian Hermann Hipp has called it (Hipp, 2003). The Alster water frontage, separate from the real waterfront, and disconnected from the working port, has come to feature water-related leisure activities (see Figure 11.5). A section of the city replaced the comprehensive views of old, the first in a series of functional separations that would take place over the next century. As Hipp pointed out, photography – introduced around 1842 to Hamburg – would further separate the city into visual motifs (Hipp, 2003).

THE GREAT FIRE OF 1842: DESIGNING THE MODERN CITY AND CREATING NEW URBAN IMAGERY

The Hamburg fire of 1842 was so big that it destroyed large parts of the inner city and the city burned for several days (Faulwasser, 1978 (reprint, original 1892)). Nevertheless, the port continued to function. The German poet and

Figure 11.2 View of Hamburg from the south with the Elbe River in the foreground, 1572 (source: Braun and Hogenberg, Hamburga, Florentissimum inferioris Saxoniae emporium, Anglorum frequentatione hoc tempore celeberrimum A[nn]o D[omi]ni: M.D.LXXII = Hambvrch Ein Vorne[m]liche Hansestat. Civitates Orbis Terrarvm, Liber Primvs. – Coloniae Agrippinae: Kempen, 1588. Courtesy: Staats- und Universitätsbibliothek Hamburg, KS 189/962).

Figure 11.3 Map of Hamburg showing the integration of trade into the core of the city, c. 1588 (source: [Hamburgum] Hambvrgvm. – [Agrippina Ubiorum Colonia], [c. 1588]. Braun, Georg/Hogenberg, Franz: Civitates Orbis Terrarum. Courtesy Staats- und Universitätsbibliothek Hamburg, KS Kt H 202).

part-time Hamburg citizen Heinrich Heine described the fire and the reaction of Hamburg's traders, who had saved the new stock exchange, pointedly noting that the city's financial books had been preserved (Heine, 2005). Many professionals took the catastrophic fire of 1842 as an opportunity to make changes. The crisis brought together the city's elite citizens to make the inner city a better place for business, and effectively to shape the emerging new maritime face of the Alster.

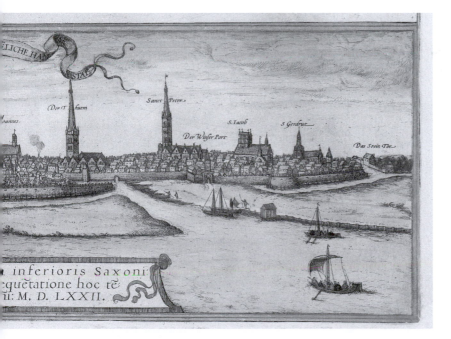

Figure 11.4 View of Hamburg from the north over the Alster, c.1855 (source: Panorama von Hamburg aus der Vogelschau-Hamburg, Berendson (c. 1855) Hamburg 1853–1856) Courtesy Staats- und Universitätsbibliothek Hamburg, AH C,54).

Figure 11.5 The arcades along the Kleine Alster designed by Alexis de Chateauneuf after the fire of 1842, taken in 2010 (source: Carola Hein).

The city invited the British-born and trained engineer William Lindley to plan the rebuilding of the city; it is not surprising that he responded by sending the copy of the plan that Christopher Wren developed for London after its catastrophic 1666 fire (Schumacher, 1920). In contrast to their British predecessors, who ignored the proposed transformation, the Hamburg elite came together to redesign the urban core, freeing the central land for business purposes and spending more time on their estates along the Elbe River slope between Altona and Blankenese or erecting new buildings (Borchard, 1992; Hoffmann, 1977). Faced with the fire's extensive destruction, Hamburg's elite redesigned the inner city, aware that they were creating the technical basis for a modern metropolis. To do so, they invited a small population of foreign-trained and educated practitioners who prepared urban design projects for the city, innovating in technology, urban organization, and architecture. Lindley's project provided the basis for large-scale change of land ownership; he also developed the city's sewage system (Pelc and Grötz, 2008).

Alexis de Chateauneuf, architect and Hamburg-born son of French immigrants, proposed several innovations for the built environment. Trained partly in France and partly under Friedrich Weinbrenner in Karlsruhe, he already had numerous projects to his credit that had changed the organization and structure as well as the form of the city. One was the innovative use of brick on the façades of major buildings. When designing the office building and warehouse for the iron-trading firm of Schulte and Schemmann (1843), he had separated its functions physically and visually by contrasting brick with plaster – thereby anticipating the future functional transformation of the city, in which storage would be separate from the office building. Chateauneuf, a well-traveled and truly European architect, was well aware of international architectural developments of his time, regularly referring to foreign competitions, such as the one for the London Parliament, in his writings on Hamburg (Klemm and Frank, 2000). He introduced aesthetic changes and innovations to the post-fire Alster, creating the Kleine Alster (Small Alster) basin to allow for better visual connection between the water and the city's new town hall, designing what Fritz Schumacher later called "Kunstwerk Hamburg," or Hamburg as a work of art (Schädel, 2006; Schumacher, 1920).

These changes in the mid-nineteenth century only confirmed the importance of the adjoining Jungfernstieg as the public core and the maritime business card of the city. They illustrated the wealth of Hamburg's traders and became key elements in the Alster-focused presentation of the city. For the new buildings around the Kleine Alster, Chateauneuf proposed and Hamburg's elite adopted an urban imagery featuring the forms of powerful Italian free cities. With Venetian-inspired Italianate arcades and urban design, they created a new urban ensemble of open spaces and public buildings that spoke of city-states, of powerful traders, and of wealth (Fischer, 1983; Lange, 1965; Schumacher, 1920). Many writers and other commentators have celebrated the combination of Jungfernstieg and Alster, of a Lindenallee and a water body known for leisure rather than work, in the center of a major city. Other urban representations reflect the shifting gaze of the citizens as well. Instead of views on the city from the south, the perspective of the southern river edge as perceived from the white villas along the Elbchaussee had already been the focus of artists since the late eighteenth century; they painted the Elbe view with ships on their way to the harbor moving past a pastoral landscape, the paradigm of the Hanseatic self-understanding and worldview, as Matthias Seeberg of the Altonaer Museum explains (Seeberg, 2007). (A more than 8 meter (26.2 foot)-long scroll from 1835 showing the entire panorama of the northern Elbe slope from Blankenese to Hamburg appears to be the exception (Meyer-Friese, 2007).) The shifting maritime gaze – from Elbe to Alster, and from urban background to landscape – accompanies the separation of urban functions and identities that characterized urban development in the nineteenth and early twentieth centuries.

Perhaps the city would have transformed the center even without the destruction caused by the fire. As Schumacher pointed out in 1920, the old city, as picturesque as it had been with its narrow streets, would not have survived (Schumacher, 1920). In fact, the reconstruction after the fire allowed Hamburg to build the modern city of the nineteenth century. With industrialization at that time, port activity was changing quickly. Hoyle defines this as the second phase of the port–city interface as characterized by "[r]apid commercial/industrial growth that forces the port to develop beyond city confines" (Hoyle, 1989: 432; see also Chapters 1 and 4 in this volume). Changing port functions were only one part of the urban transformation that reflected multiple international, national, and local needs. Other responses included traders' adaptation of the port to modern steamships and the city's creation of specialized districts for warehouses, businesses, and housing (both for the elite and for workers), both of which were complete within a century. The modernization of the port – or at least discussions of its future form – was among the earliest urban projects; many of the large-scale projects that followed were connected in some way to the port, and involved international professionals.

Successful execution of these plans placed Hamburg at the forefront of European cities and gave the city a new maritime face that later inspired other cities, including Boston (Haglund, 2003). In part because of Chateauneuf's work, the inner-city artificial lake has since come to represent Hamburg's urban center (Klemm and Frank, 2000; Spallek, 1978). Here the city's major shipping line, Hamburg-Amerikanische Packetfahrt-Actien-Gesellschaft (Hapag), or for short the Hamburg–America Line, would situate its headquarters in 1903, after leaving its headquarters in the Dovenfleet area near the port. The original construction, with its Renaissance façade (designed by the architect Martin Haller), rapidly proved too small, and Fritz Höger gained the contract for the extension and transformation of the building. The company's motto inscribed in the entrance hall of the headquarters – "Mein Feld ist die Welt" (The world is our oyster) – underscores the company's global reach, against the maritime background of the Alster (Wiborg and Wiborg, 1997) (see Figure 11.6).

HAMBURG'S NINETEENTH AND EARLY TWENTIETH PORT CITYSCAPE: SEPARATING FUNCTIONS

Living and working conditions in the city of Hamburg also changed extensively through the nineteenth century. It was traditional for commercial building to include housing, storage, and offices all in the same district. The city

Figure 11.6 The office building of the Hapag-Lloyd on the Binnenalster, contemporary photo (source: Hapag-Lloyd AG, Hamburg).

began to separate these functions. Elites moved their residences out of the center and the city built both a monofunctional warehouse area and a business district featuring office buildings (Kontorhäuser) housing many businesses connected to shipping. The warehouse zone was populated by neo-Gothic structures of local red-bricks bordering canals on one side, carefully designed by a team of engineers and architects under the direction of the city's superintendent engineer, Franz-Andreas Meyer, a monument to the city's dedication to port activities and of its architects to their design. These innovations have become part of Hamburg's image: This is a city willing to demolish and rebuild if the economic context changes. The switch in representation goes hand in hand with this broader transformation of the city (with or without disasters). In particular, the functional separation shows how the port economy can shape the city beyond the port area itself.

One might have expected technological innovation in port and shipping activities to be the driving forces of port and city transformation in this phase, as the rapid introduction of steamships between the 1840s and 1880s restructured maritime trade, port facilities, and port cities in multiple ways. Had the 1842 fire not intervened, the city might have initiated the urban change with port transformation. Hamburg was a leader in the field; a Dutchman, Jan Boissevain, even went to Hamburg to study the modern steam-powered vessels of the shipping lines, inspecting the harbor and the quays as well (see Chapter 7). Harbor improvement had been a major theme in Hamburg since the storm and flood of 1825, and local officials had already called upon foreign opinions (Maass, 1986, 1990). But few projects actually came to fruition. Several proposals after 1836 promoted a dock harbor, which seemed to provide the best protection against floods for the Niederhafen area and which would allow for easier transhipment. Debate over this option culminated in 1845, when William Lindley, together with James Walker, an English harbor engineer who had built docks in London and Dover, and Heinrich Hübbe, a civil servant, who had traveled to England in 1844 to study the latest harbor technology, presented a plan for a dock harbor with six docks, that could accommodate large ships that could unload regardless of the level of the tide, reflecting the English model on the Großen Grasbrook (Harms, 2008; Maass, 1990). The project proved too expensive and unconvincing and the English technology too expansive for Hamburg's 2 meter (6.5 foot) high tide.

These proposals would also have allowed the city to regulate port water heights, but would have strangled harbor traffic. A new administration in 1860 ousted the formerly highly respected Lindley from his post. At the same time, Hamburg's administrators pursued harbor expansion projects and took research trips abroad, as Dieter Maass explained in detail (Maass, 1990). Johannes Dalmann, director of construction related to water (Wasserbaudirektor since 1858), attempted to increase the flow of the Elbe to deepen its bed, arguing that its normal tide difference of 2 meters (6.5 feet) did not allow for a dock harbor. His proposal for a tidal harbor for the Sandtor and Grassbrook harbors and the creation of the Sandtorkai (1866), a wharf adequate for larger ships, proposed cranes, quay walls high enough for unloading, and railway connections; these provisions allowed much faster transhipment than did transport from ships anchored in the river.

As this harbor debate came to fruition, two events brought further change to port and city. Once again these transformations occurred in light of foreign architectural and urban exchanges. The opening of the city gates at night in 1860–1861 allowed citizens to move permanently into residences beyond the old walls, and thus freed city-center land for other uses. This land was available for urban redevelopment, after 1871, when Hamburg joined the German Empire (Deutsches Reich) and the city obtained an important compensation packet from the Empire for giving up its free city status. The city used the money to construct a new, duty-free warehouse district, the Speicherstadt, which has since become an architectural and urban icon and a historical monument. The Speicherstadt was conceived under the direction of the well-traveled urban planner Carl Johann Christian Zimmermann and the engineer Franz-Andreas Meyer, who had seen New York and Chicago and admired them for the modernity of their technical equipment and for the generous parks. Outsiders had described their projects as forms of "Americanism" – not necessarily in praise (Hipp, 1995: 7). In order to set up a tax-free harbor (in what is today the HafenCity area), the city evicted some 24,000 people from the harbor zone of the Kehrwieder and Wandrahm islands and demolished both elite and workers' housing (Maak, 1985; Meyer-Veden, 1990; Schubert and Harms, 1993) (see Figure 11.7). Following the removal of the residents and demolition of the existing buildings, the city built red-brick warehouses with rich decoration, narrow windows, and towers for winches and lifts. The ensemble, where goods such as coffee, tea, spices, or carpets were stored, faced the old city across the demarcation line of the Zollkanal (see Figure 11.8).

The creation of the warehouse district as a new monofunctional unit signaled the creation of other single-function areas – an office district and new housing areas. A cholera epidemic in Hamburg in 1892 had killed 8,000 people while sparing neighboring Altona, which, significantly, had already

(a)

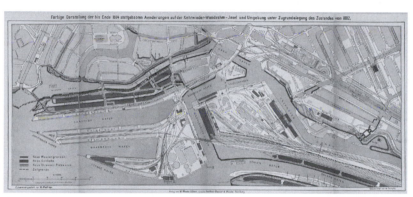

(b)

Figure 11.7 The area of the new warehouse district, the Speicherstadt.
(a) Before Hamburg's adhesion to the German tax zone in 1888.
(b) After 1894
(sources: Situationsplan des künftigen städtischen Freihafenquartiers zu Hamburg vor Beginn der Zollanschlussbauten 1883. Hamburg: Meissner, 1887, Staats- und Universitätsbibliothek Hamburg, KS 1018/14, and: Farbige Darstellung der bis Ende 1894 stattgehabten Aenderungen auf der Kehrwieder-Wandrahm-Insel und Umgebung unter Zugrundelegung des Zustandes von 1882/gez. von W. Schultz. Zsgestellt von W. Melhop. Kt. 6 aus der Beilagenmappe zu: Historische Topographie der Freien und Hansestadt Hamburg von 1880 bis 1895. – Hamburg: Mauke, 1895. Signatur: KS 1022/13: Kt).

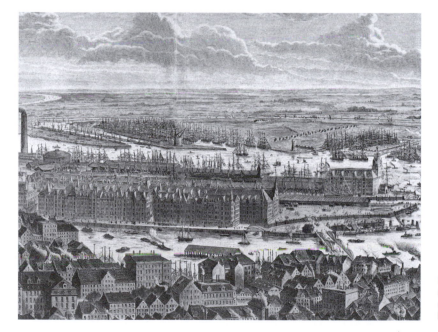

Figure 11.8 Drawing of the newly built Speicherstadt, late nineteenth century (source: bildarchiv-hamburg.de).

built a water filtration plant. Meyer built one in Hamburg in 1893, as Lindley had suggested much earlier but that only now became feasible (Schädel, 2006). Local business leaders and their internationally trained and well-traveled architects were again major agents of transformation. As Hamburg demolished old timber-framed buildings of the Gängeviertel that offered cheap but decayed homes to people who depended on proximity to the harbor, affluent citizens moved outside the city walls, raising the land and building the office district that would later host the Chilehaus. Leaving the former inhabitants to their own means, elites replaced old houses with innovative and distinctive office buildings, reflecting the international business of their owners. For example, Heinrich von Ohlendorff, who had earned his money through guano importation, funded the Dovenhof office building (1885–1886), designed by Beaux-Arts-trained Martin Haller. It was sited on the edge of the new free harbor and the Zollausland (the area beyond the local tax domain) and featured the newest building typology. Company headquarters had long existed in Hamburg, but office buildings for rent had earlier existed only in the United States and England (Hornbostel and Klemm, 1997). Haller designed it around an interior light court with the necessary stairs, elevators, and toilets so that renters would be able to adapt the building to diverse needs. Thus, he did not include load-bearing walls, instead putting in columns that allowed flexible internal arrangement. The building stood out also for its innovative technology, central heating system, complete electric installation, and use of an early elevator (the so-called paternoster) imported from England.

As the elite reorganized the city to respond to new technological, organizational, and political opportunities and demands, taking advantage of disasters as well, other urban change occurred largely unplanned, but also left its imprint on the city. For example, as a result of new international shipping and hiring practices, Chinese seamen and migrants set up (segregated) quarters in European seaports, including Hamburg, where they purchased shops and restaurants in the St. Pauli district. This was right on the waterfront and near the newly developed Landungsbrücken area (Amenda, 2006). Meanwhile Hamburg's shipping companies entered the business of migration. Starting in the mid-nineteenth century the city had become a node for migrants from other parts of Germany and Europe, who often reached the city by rail. At times, one-third of all migrants to America were in transit through Hamburg (Moltmann, 1986). As the ships carried staple goods such as tobacco, cotton, or rice from the United States, they transported linen, glass, and other manufactured goods from Germany that required little space. Early ships thus had spare transport space for migrants, until larger steamships built for migrants took over (see Figure 11.9). The Hapag, under Albert Ballin, who had become director in 1888, led the American migration business in Hamburg (Gerhardt, 2009; Ritter, 1997). Under Ballin's leadership the company set up barracks on the Veddel in 1900/1901 (also adorned with the company's motto "Mein Feld ist die Welt") to house the rapidly growing number of emigrants and to provide appropriately hygienic and sanitary conditions (Groppe and Wöst, 2007). It was not only the desire to protect its own citizens that drove the planners of the barracks; Hamburg was part of a larger network that included American administrators and laws about migrants and the ships that carried

Figure 11.9 The Kaispeicher and the Speicherstadt in 1930 with the Monte Rosa (source: hhla. de/hamburger-fotoarchiv.de).

them. Migrants with diseases, for example, would not be allowed to enter the United States and would require transport back to the port of origin.

The transformation/growth of the port and the embellishment and restructuring of the urban core for storage and administration had led the city to expel workers from the inner city at the end of the nineteenth century. To provide better transportation for them, notably the port workers, who now had to travel long distances to work, the city built the first public transportation railway lines to Barmbek and Rothenburgsort between 1912 and 1915, connecting the town hall and the central station to the new housing areas (Heinsohn, 2006; Pahl, 1980). The simultaneous move of port-related industry to these areas and the construction of canals that connected them to the port reinforced the importance of these working-class areas. But workers' housing was not a priority for the local elite. Workers themselves established housing cooperatives (such as the Schiffszimmerer Genossenschaft, the first one in Hamburg founded in 1875 by ships' carpenters (Schiffszimmerer Genossenschaft, n.d.)). It was only in the 1920s, after the First World War had increased the need for housing, that communal housing became a major policy concern. Even in that context, the city's international networks appeared. Fritz Schumacher, Hamburg's main urban planner from 1908 to 1933, had spent his childhood and youth in Bogotà and New York. Influenced by the Arts and Crafts and the American City Beautiful movements, he introduced American ideas – notably on urban parks (Stadtpark) – into city planning. His concept of the city as an entire work of art led him to apply his urban and architectural views to diverse structures from port-related structures (Lotsenhaus in 1913/1914; Heringskühlhaus in 1928/1929), to public buildings (Finanzbehörde in 1926; Museum für Hamburgische Geschichte in 1923; Hochschule für bildende Künste in1913), to large-scale housing districts, effectively tying the diverse parts of the city together through a unified design approach (Frank, 1994; Paschen, 1994).

The Nazis ousted Schumacher from his post in 1933, but the global character of the city withstood Nazi ideology nonetheless. They constructed most new buildings in major German cities according to neo-classical design, but partly exempted Hamburg, Germany's gateway to the world. The Hamburg-born architect Konstanty Gutschow, between 1939 and 1943 officially named architect of the Elbe slope and the rebuilding of Hamburg, projected skyscrapers along the Elbe River, as a new maritime sign specifically designed "to turn the face of Hamburg away from the Alster and towards the Elbe" (Dülffer, *et al.*, 1978: 191). The aligned buildings were often called "a string of pearls" (Bartels, 1991; Bose *et al.*, 1986; Düwel and Gutschow, 2008). He also envisioned an east–west street axis to facilitate cross-city transportation. The city's docks and wharves attracted Allied bombs and the harbor saw large-scale destruction. After the war, the Allied forces' desire for reparation and the wish to halt new German war activity stopped most port activity and temporarily suspended Hamburg's attempt at rebuilding. While the port opened again on June 1, 1945, the fate of the ship construction docks in particular was under question. The British occupying force even threatened to blow up the Howaldtswerke. The Hamburg senate appealed to British common sense, which had historically been much appreciated by Hamburg's citizens, to reject this idea (Anon., 1957). In the end, rebuilding of the harbor occurred rapidly despite the fact that its foreland and hinterland had radically changed due to the Second World War (Mühlradt, 1953). The rebuilt city referenced its harbor in its new office buildings. For example, the modernist architects Gottfried Schramm and Jürgen Elingius adorned a wall in an office building with a mosaic of Hamburg in 1730, centered on the harbor (Anon., 1957: n.p.).

During the nineteenth and early twentieth centuries, the international integration of the city was visible in Hamburg's urban transformation in multiple ways. Traders' adaptation of the port was only one part; others included the elite's creation of a new urban face that was focused on the office buildings and not on the working port; and the city's large-scale redevelopment, including the creation of a warehouse district, an office district, and elite and worker's housing. The newly defined city was ready to respond to new challenges.

SEPARATE BUT CONNECTED: THE CITYWIDE NET OF PORT CITYSCAPES – A NEW BUSINESS DISTRICT AND THE RETURN OF THE CITY TO THE WATERFRONT

In the post-Second World War period, Hamburg's port, like others worldwide, responded immediately to the ongoing transformations in the shipping world. As Hoyle has pointed out, industrialization, notably oil refining and containerization, led to the construction of port-specific industrial areas, a reduction of the workforce, and, in the longer run, to the abandonment of warehouses and other structures that no longer corresponded to the evolving needs of the port. Despite the withdrawal and separation of the physical activities from the waterfront and the city, large-scale redevelopment remained connected to the port in multiple ways, some hidden and some more evident. New infrastructure and new communication tools allowed quick travel across the city, and the size of some of these globally connected companies forced some out of the heart of the city, away from the Alster. As the city remodeled the harbor to accommodate containers and their ships, rapidly making it the largest German container harbor and a leader worldwide, it transformed some of the formerly rural areas south of the Elbe into harbor land (Grobecker, 2004). Meanwhile, the city developed a new monofunctional administrative business district and new housing districts on the outskirts.

To shore up its status as a leading European metropolis, Hamburg turned to other activities that were only partly linked to the port. Notably in the 1980s, the city established itself as Germany's leading media center, home to publishing houses, newspapers, and publicity firms (Kirsch and Schröder, 1994). The oil industry and its headquarters exemplify the decentralized placement of activities. Storage and refining are based within the harbor, but the administrative headquarters of the companies have changed their location. Hamburg has had its own petroleum harbor in the Veddel area since 1879 and the city has dominated Bremen in the petroleum trade since 1884/1885, when it also built its first storage tank (Maass, 1990). In 1890, the local leader in oil trade, the Riedemann company, established the Deutsch-Amerikanische Petroleumgesellschaft (DAPG) with a partner in Bremen and the American Standard Oil Company (Weber, 1952). Over time, it developed into Germany's top refinery center. Before the war, the country had imported petroleum from abroad, especially from Venezuela and Mexico; during the war, it tapped local oil reservoirs and further integrated the city into its hinterland. Oil was first transported in barrels, but by the 1930s companies had built large storage tanks in the Waltershof area. Refineries processed petroleum on the Grasbrook and in the Harburg areas of the port. In 1937–1938 the DAPG, predecessor of Esso/Exxon, erected its headquarters on the Binnenalster, diagonally opposite the Hapag building (1937/1938), emphasizing the primary position of the Alster as the first address of the city's business (Driesen, 2010; Weigend, 1956) (see Figure 11.10).

Figure 11.10 DAPG building on the Binnenalster, (built 1937–38) taken in 2010 (source: Carola Hein).

The advent of global headquarters (and thus new actors) in the place once dominated by local businesses signaled the beginning of a new globalized era in shipping with a less clearly identifiable local form. In Hamburg, this also meant the creation of a new business district, City Nord. It was first proposed by the city's head planner Werner Hebebrand in 1958 to host global companies that found the center of the city too confining and did not need the proximity to the working port or to the prestigious Alster. Hebebrand designed a green urban ensemble on the northern outskirts of the city; he populated it with individual large-scale buildings, each functioning almost as a single city (Hebebrand, 1957, 1967). At his instigation, it seems, the city administration persuaded major companies such as Esso and BP – partly connected to the city because of the oil infrastructure in the harbor – to move to the new district (Hein, 1991). Each company had to organize architectural competitions for its headquarters, and several of the City Nord buildings stand out as modernist icons of their time. Yet none of these buildings engages Hamburg's port city character. In fact, these port-related businesses were now largely disconnected from the water because of a new major technological change: containerization. Meanwhile, harbor related industries left the city and some of the remaining industrial relics came to host cultural institutions. It is thus not surprising that the city developed its infrastructure, including the Elbe Tunnel, opened in 1975.

BACK TO THE ELBE AND BEYOND: FROM CARPETS, COFFEE, AND SPICES TO LOFTS, GALLERIES, AND RESTAURANTS

Despite the overall detachment of port and city, the port remained symbolically connected to the identity of the city, through its economic power and financial importance, through harbor festivals and other events (including the fish market), and as an always-changing scene to be viewed during a promenade, while the Alster functioned as the leisure center for sailing sports, rowing, and paddling, with associated leisure facilities. As shipping companies abandoned their former warehouses and withdrew to the southern side of the Elbe in the 1990s, the city reclaimed the area along the waterfront for the creation of new multifunctional spaces for offices, housing, leisure, and urban icons. Waterfront regeneration was already a well-established tool for the revitalization of urban centers, and Hamburg – eager to defend its spot as a leader among European regions and as an innovative growth center – added its own version reflecting waterfront revitalization in Baltimore, London, Rotterdam, and Sydney, opting notably for a multifunctional redevelopment. The city's long history of large-scale urban transformation and international connections provides an additional opportunity to contrast current developments with historic changes, global ideas with local practices, and harbor area changes with city-wide transformations. These changes once more register with new iconic views of the city's maritime spaces.

As its harbor continues to expand (Freie und Hansestadt Hamburg *et al.*, 2007), so does the city. Under the slogan "Metropole Hamburg – wachsende Stadt" (Hamburg Metropolis – growing city) – chosen to defy the numerous cities battling the shrinkage of their population – the city government wants to expand the city itself into its southern industrial and harbor areas beyond the

Elbe River (Standortpolitik, n.d.). This was a district that it had largely abandoned during the container revolution. Parts of this larger strategy are the reuse of the city's landmark warehouse district, the Speicherstadt, and the transformation of a 157-hectare (388-acre) former harbor land area next to it into the HafenCity. Labeled Europe's largest urban renewal project, the project had its roots in the 1990s. Following the fall of the Berlin Wall and the reopening of Hamburg's traditional hinterland, the city leadership, through the city-owned Hamburger Hafen und Lagerhausgesellschaft mbH (today HHLA Hafen und Logistik AG), purchased firms and land in the area with the view of making it into a central European node. After an international competition, the winning design by the Dutch–German team Hamburgplan with Kees Christiaanse | ASTOC became the basis for the master plan of 2000. The plan presents Hafen-City as an extension of the inner city, almost doubling its size (see Figure 11.11). In contrast to other waterfront redevelopment projects and to Hamburg's history of separating urban functions into distinct zones, the new district is designed to be multifunctional and socially integrative. It will host office buildings, housing, educational, and cultural facilities, and is designed to include various income groups. Through extensive design competitions, city planners are carefully monitoring and controlling the area's architectural and urban design. Building on the examples of large-scale urban restructuring in the nineteenth and twentieth centuries, the construction of the HafenCity stands in context with other examples of urban transformation, including large-scale events such as world's fairs (Seville in 1992, Lisbon in 1998, Shanghai in 2010), the European capitals of culture (Thessaloniki in 1996, Marseilles in 2013), and the Olympics (Barcelona in 1992, London in 2012).

Figure 11.11 The general view of the HafenCity, 2010 (source: Michael Korol; Quelle: HafenCity Hamburg GmbH).

The HafenCity project is already taking shape, but much remains to be built. Officially initiated in 1997 and under construction since 2001, it has a tentative completion date of 2020–2025. The western areas of the zone, including the Sandtorkai neighborhood, are complete; some 1,500 people live in the HafenCity and about 6,000 people come there for work. Hamburg's firms and companies from across Germany have designed most of the office and housing projects. Meanwhile, the lighthouse projects in the harbor area, meant to promote Hamburg on the global scale, are the works of internationally known and celebrated architects. The Dutch Rem Koolhaas designed the new science center; the Italian Massimilio Fuksas, the cruise center; and American Richard Meier, the Hamburg–America Center. The Swiss architects Herzog & de Meuron designed a new concert hall for the Philharmonic Orchestra to put Hamburg on a par with other major metropolises, each of which features a venue for classical music. The new building, a glass structure that reminds the viewer of waves cresting, is currently under construction on top of a former red-brick warehouse building designed by local architect Werner Kallmorgen as part of modernist postwar reconstruction in 1966, the Kaispeicher A, which occupies a key location at the river's edge. It makes the statement that Hamburg is a port city and a cultural leader; and it presents itself as a contemporary Chilehaus, albeit in a more prominent location (see Figure 11.12). Critical comments on the rising price tag of the Philharmonie, paid for mainly by the

Figure 11.12a The new Elbphilharmonie under construction, 2010 (source: Carola Hein).

Figure 11.12b Herzog & de Meuron, the new Elbphilharmonie, Hamburg's new icon on the Elbe River, estimated completion 2012 (source: © Herzog & de Meuron).

city government, put into doubt the appropriateness of the project as a whole, but the HafenCity has already become an attraction for citizens and tourists alike, recently earning a review in the Travel Section of the *New York Times* (Williams, 2010).

Foreign architects similarly signed on to key landscaping projects: The architect Beth Galí (BB + GG) from Barcelona took on the design of the Überseequartier, the Magdeburger Harbor and the St. Annen Place. The landscaping of the Magellan-Terrassen, opened in 2005, is the work of the Spanish architects Benedetta Tagliabue and Enric Miralles (EMBT Arquitectes Associats from Barcelona). The carefully designed steps that lead to the basin of the Sandtorhafen already host cultural and artistic events, creating a space that reminds us of its function as a promenade of the Jungfernstieg, itself currently being revamped (Engel, 2003). Names of streets and places in the HafenCity are carefully selected to keep the memory of the former overseas trading spaces alive and to emphasize again the international connections. Contrasting with and sometimes replacing traditional local names, the HafenCity now features names such as Marco-Polo-Terrassen, and Vasco-da-Gama-Platz. The area around Magdeburger Hafen has been renamed to feature Asian city names such as Shanghaiallee, Korea-, Busan-, or Osakastraße. Names of famous local traders are another feature of the new map of the HafenCity (around Lohseplatz) (see Figure 11.13).

The quasi-governmental institution in charge of the HafenCity, the HafenCity GmbH (formerly GHS, Gesellschaft für Hafen- und Standortentwicklung mbH), is heavily promoting the project through various media channels building on a long marketing tradition (Amenda and Grünen, 2008; HafenCity, n.d.). Among its tools is a giant model of the HafenCity, a reflection of its predecessor from 1900 that the city used for promotional purposes and

Figure 11.13 Public Spaces on the Marco-Polo-Terrassen, taken in 2010 (source: Carola Hein).

exposed notably at the world's fair in Paris that year (Schürmann, 2008). Its marketing of central urban projects reaches beyond the city's administrative limits and contributes to the city government's promotion of the entire urban region (Metropolregion Hamburg, n.d.). It holds up HafenCity as a model of collaboration between private and public forces, a site for citizens from diverse social backgrounds, and as an exceptionally multifunctional and carefully designed new piece of the city. The new project reshapes Hamburg's imagery, turning the visitor's gaze (including that of cruise ship tourists) to the city's Elbe front.

The HafenCity has all the economic and cultural elements necessary for promoters to portray Hamburg as a leading maritime center, perpetuating the Chilehaus' evocation of a leading port cityscape, while the working port itself – where the multitude of goods transported are safely hidden in containers and out of sight – is located at a safe distance across the Elbe River. The official Hamburg website features the exact location of all ships in the harbor, promoting ship-spotting activities and inviting citizens and tourists alike to observe the constantly changing landscape featuring ships the size of skyscrapers (Hafenradar Hamburg, n.d.). The new citizens of the HafenCity can watch the port from their apartments or office windows, or from coffee shops on one of the generously designed public spaces. Houses and office spaces here and across the city refer to maritime traditions by using circular porthole windows, ship-style decks, or handrails shaped like railings. Meanwhile, the city government has rediscovered and transformed Wilhelmsburg (and the Veddel), traditional working-class areas connected to the port, as part of the project to cross the Elbe. There, where about 55,000 people from over 40 nations live, conversations at the International Building Exhibit (IBA) echo discussions of the HafenCity (IBA Hamburg, n.d.a). Scheduled to end in 2013, the IBA is the designated location for attempts to develop design solutions for the future of the metropolis (IBA Hamburg, n.d.b). The area has become a research laboratory for planners to explore co-existence, creative economies, and cohabitation between global and local needs and players. It will address diverse contemporary needs for social diversity, opportunities offered by international urban communities, the development of inner peripheries, and climate change (despite its own need to consume resources).

CONCLUSION

As the example of Hamburg shows, port and city are related in multiple ways, some obvious, some hidden. Some of these relations are physical; others are virtual or imaginary. From the early port city, where port functions were integrated into everyday life and into almost all locations, the city expanded and separated functions. Now, the harbor seems to live its own life and developments there do not have as much impact on the city as they did before. The harbor, withdrawn to the southern side of the Elbe, no longer provides large amounts of manual labor. Nonetheless, the relation between port and city development remains alive; the port needs the city and its citizens' support. As a scenic view from across the Elbe from offices, houses, and restaurants, and even from an old-age home in the former Union-Cooling storage building (Union-Kühlhaus) in Hamburg-Ottensen (Neumühlen), it is part of the local mental image or imaginary. For ongoing and possibly increased harbor transformation and expansion that might destroy environmentally sensitive areas, for the dredging of the Elbe, and for other port-related developments, the port authority will need the support of citizens and local institutions. The port's image is thus essential to the future of the port.

12 HOW MANHATTAN'S PORT SHAPED ITS STREETS AND BUILDING LOCATIONS

CAROL HERSELLE KRINSKY

New York City was established as part of a Dutch trading colony, rather than as an administrative city like Washington, D.C., a university center like Cambridge, England, or a religious refuge like Providence, Rhode Island. The relation to the waterfront and to port facilities has shaped land use in all boroughs, but it is especially noticeable in narrow, water-bounded Manhattan. It traces the port's functions through their impact on land uses, streets, and buildings. Scholars have addressed the history of the city and port (Albion and Pope, 1984 (1939); Federal Writers' Project, 1982; Condit, 1980; Jackson, 1995; Burrows, 1999) and have described the waterfront (recently Bone *et al.*, 1997; Rosen, 1998; Lopate, 2004), but the goal of this essay is to emphasize connections between the port and the land.

The original street layout facilitated access to the defensive fortifications and was devised to develop commerce; later private developments promoted farming and then land subdivision for building. The Commissioners' Plan of 1811 gridded the city for convenient real estate development, taking account of the maritime and industrial activities already in place and increasing. Developed primarily in the nineteenth century and later, New York City became for a time the world's busiest seaport. Recently, since the advent of containerized freight, it has yielded its position to facilities elsewhere along New York Harbor and to foreign rivals, as well as to air transportation of people and freight, although that is still largely accommodated within the city limits. Like other former industrial centers, New York City now must derive revenue from other sources, including tourism and culture. Neglected buildings and derelict neighborhoods that once accommodated port facilities have become art galleries, restaurants, and locations for computer-based innovation. Moreover, builders of high-priced apartment houses, hotels, and corporate offices that provide riverfront views have rediscovered a waterfront that they had shunned for several hundred years when it was the site of industry, overcrowding, and working-class activity. New York City therefore comes close to the phases charted by B.S. Hoyle (and discussed by Dirk Schubert in Chapter 4) in which city and port, once integral, become gradually separated, but in which the waterfront then attracts new uses (Hoyle, 1989).

The first known European to sail into New York Harbor was Giovanni da Verrazano (c. 1485–c. 1528), a Florentine who arrived in 1524, but nothing came of this expedition. Henry Hudson (died 1611) arrived in 1609 with the financial backing of the Dutch East India Company, superseded after 1621 by the Dutch West India Company. He sailed part way up the estuary now known as the North River below 30th Street and the Hudson River north of that. His report stimulated the creation of a Dutch trading colony in 1614. The traders took advantage of the harbor's multiple narrow entrances from the Atlantic Ocean that could be protected against invaders; its convenient bays and inlets; its temperate climate that predicted manageable winter ice; its deep water channels; the presence of shelter for ships along the island's lower east side; and its connection to the Hudson River on the west side, where ocean vessels could sail north for about 135 miles (217.3 km) to the present New York State capital at Albany. By 1626, the small settlement had prospered enough to prompt its governor, Peter Minuit, to seek to buy (as he saw it) Manhattan Island from the indigenous population. Native leaders did not think one could sell nature but they accepted objects in a ceremony of exchange – probably ironware and cloth – to the value of sixty guilders. The Europeans built a breastwork called Fort Amsterdam, later replaced by a sturdier fort with bastions near the former United States Custom House at the southern end of the island; an early nineteenth-century, improved fortification West Battery, now called Castle Clinton, still stands in the waterfront Battery Park. By the mid-1620s, the site was ambitiously named New Amsterdam, and it obtained municipal status in 1652–1653. In 1664, the British forced the surrender of the town to the Duke of York, whereupon the original New Amsterdam was re-named for him. Despite a year-long restoration of Dutch rule almost a decade later, the English prevailed under the Treaty of Westminster. Fortifications followed from 1796 onward to guard the waterways and the port installations (see Figure 12.1).

Figure 12.1 August R. Ohman's map of New York harbor, c. 1907 (source: Library of Congress, Prints & Photographs Division, pm 006071. Title: View of the city of New York and Vicinity, August, R. Ohman).

Note
Staten Island at bottom left, Brooklyn to its right, Queens above and right of Brooklyn, Manhattan in the centre, Bronx at top, New Jersey to left and above Staten Island.

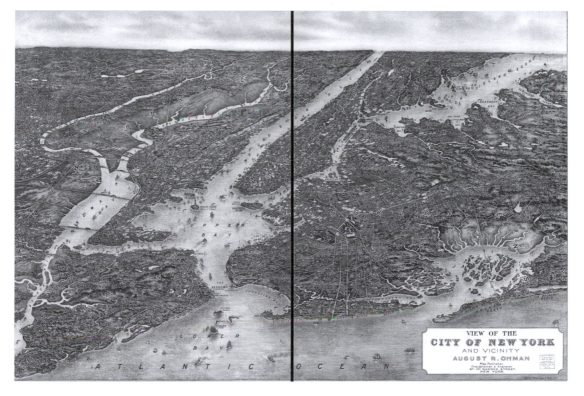

The opening of the United States Navy Yard in 1801 confirmed the status of New York as a major city and port. It occupied a protected location in Brooklyn along the East River in Wallabout Bay. But at this time, New York was just one of several important east coast seaports. It became pre-eminent at first after the war of 1812, when small, regularly scheduled packet shipping developed, and it flourished especially after the opening of the Erie Canal in 1825 (Albion and Pope, 1984: 38–51). Grain, other agricultural products, and mineral products could be shipped cheaply from the Midwest through the Great Lakes, then by canal to the Hudson River, and by water or rail south to New York Harbor. Investors also promoted other canals, including one between the port and important coalfields in Pennsylvania. Cotton, brokered and often shipped from New York to foreign manufacturers, brought the city's participants substantial revenue (Albion and Pope, 1984: 95–103; Woodman, 1968: 18–34). Ferry and highway connections, bridges, and tunnels later enhanced the centrality of the port.

New York City now encompasses five boroughs – Manhattan; Brooklyn and Queens, which are on Long Island; the Bronx, which is on the mainland; and Staten Island. Each borough has port facilities, but Manhattan's and Brooklyn's were initially the most important. The five boroughs were not unified into a single city until 1898, so Brooklyn was until then a separate municipality, with about 7 miles (11.3 km) of warehouses and docks between Red Hook, facing Upper New York Bay, and Newtown Creek, which divides Brooklyn from Queens along the East River. At present, Manhattan's maritime support installations are less significant than those of the more suburban Staten Island. The latter benefited from late nineteenth- to early twentieth-century industrial development, the opening of a bridge in 1931 to Bayonne in the neighboring state of New Jersey, which also borders New York's harbor, and the more recent installation of a container port. Staten Island's principal growth occurred after construction of the Verrazano-Narrows Bridge to Brooklyn in 1964, but by then the principal seaport activities had moved to New Jersey. Since the Bayonne Bridge is too low to guarantee passage of today's enormous container ships into Newark Bay, its present form threatens the economic viability of New York Harbor (Tirschwell, 2009; Todd, 2006).

The history of trade and industry created a legacy embodied in the city's physical form as well as in its buildings and their location. The port shaped the street pattern, influenced the distribution of buildings and the dynamics of land use, inflected zoning and new patterns of land use, and even affected the shape of waterfront rehabilitation long after containerization and other forces pushed port facilities elsewhere. Forces at play included urban policy, technological innovation, and globalization.

THE PORT AND THE STREET PATTERN

Manhattan's early street pattern was affected by the existence of the port. Settlers laid out roads to the fortification that protected the merchants and their ships to the north and east. The widest street, Broadway, runs along a slight north–south ridge, to prevent flooding. From it could be seen the port, which, in the city's early years, occupied the east side of the southern tip of Manhattan, which was largely sheltered from ice. The fort to the south and west therefore protected the port. The Dutch dug their customary canals to allow water-borne goods to be brought into the center; traces of these canals and streets parallel to them and to the harbor can be seen today in the irregular, dense, and narrow street pattern of lower (southern) Manhattan. Canal Street itself was built over a widened tidal channel through a salt marsh that ran from the site of the present courthouse square to the Hudson River.

Other institutions also shaped the street pattern. Under the Dutch in their later years, and then under the British until the American Revolution that began in 1776, the island settlement expanded to include farms to the north. To the south, across the East River (actually a strait), in the neighboring city of Brooklyn at the western end of Long Island, farming was a principal activity, although commerce developed opposite Manhattan. When these cities' population increased, especially after ferry service to Manhattan began in 1814, the farms became more profitable for development than for agriculture, and were divided internally by straight streets. If the farm boundaries did not cohere, neither did the resulting grids; that accounts for the irregular street patterns in parts of lower Manhattan and unexpected intersections in Brooklyn.

Under British rule, the established Church of England created Trinity Parish, which became one of Manhattan's major landowners, endowed with property by the crown and by donors. Developers divided the church's land, too, into gridded lots, although some of them later yielded to waterfront railroads, to the markets they served, and to port facilities.

In 1811, a municipal commission proposed a layout for Manhattan up to 155th Street, then considered to be the northernmost limit of future development, given the absence of mechanized transportation. The Commissioners' Plan provided for north–south avenues 100 feet (30.5 metres) wide and for 60 foot (18.3 metres) wide east–west streets; Broadway's course remained irregular, as it had long existed as a post road along a partly diagonal route. Another determinant was the existence of port facilities along the edges of Manhattan, especially on the emerging west riverfront, where a wide avenue could offer access to piers and accommodate the inevitable mixture of people, carts, vehicles, animals, and cargo. West-side docks largely supplanted the earlier ones on the east when nineteenth-century ships with deeper drafts required berthing on the North River rather than on the East River (Cohen and Augustyn, 1997). Consequently, it was unnecessary to replace the narrow streets of the Lower East Side waterfront with broad avenues; moreover, confiscating developed buildings there would have required large compensatory payments and new accommodation of the poor who walked to work from their tightly packed dwellings. Only north of this workers' district, and north of the earliest subdivided farms, do broader avenues open on the east side, starting at Houston Street (zero street under the new numbering system that was instituted north of the earliest farm subdivisions), and the avenues start at some distance from the waterfront, even though First Avenue approaches the river farther north where the island narrows. Some shipbuilding persisted until after the Civil War on the East Side up to 14th Street, but the work was done well east of First Avenue and did not affect the street layout. The east–west streets, less important for shipping, were made narrower so as to increase the land plotted for property development. Exceptionally wide east–west streets result from the intersection of Broadway with the avenues, creating irregular triangular spaces that encourage greater east–west street dimensions. The predominance of the avenues was determined in part by the hope for future traffic northward through an existing settlement in Harlem and to the mainland that starts in the Bronx (see Figure 12.2).

Industries tied to importing and exporting expanded in lower Manhattan. Merchants imported and sold clothing from England and then established local factories where American cotton could be made into the ready-made clothing that was increasing in importance. By 1850, New Yorkers produced between one-quarter and one-third of the garments made in the United States (Albion and Pope, 1984: 64). A tradition of small apparel manufacturing survives today in Chinatown.

Both the east and west side port facilities stimulated the development of markets. The 6 acre (2.4 hectare) Fulton (Street) fish market on the east side, inaugurated in 1821 and eventually the east coast's largest of its kind, has only recently moved from the southeastern waterfront. The Washington and Gansevoort food markets occupied several acres near the western riverfront, as did the West Washington live poultry market. The east and west side ports also stimulated the development of ferries and railroads that served them and the markets; the earliest railroad, a freight line originally called the Hudson River Railroad and later included in the New York Central Railroad system, reached northward to the state capital at Albany in 1851. In Manhattan, it ran at grade level on several streets, including Tenth and Eleventh Avenues, until its own right of way began north of 60th Street, about 4 miles (6.4 km) from its southern terminus. South of 60th Street, the waterfront was reserved for vehicular access to the piers, but the railroad ran close enough for convenient transportation of goods to and from the docks. A second railroad, along Eighth Avenue, opened a year later. The railroads confirmed the gradual shift of shipping from the east side to the west side, a move nearly completed by about 1870.

Along the North or Hudson River, immigrants at first arrived at random piers where they were subject to exploitation by rapacious countrymen (Albion and Pope, 1984: 348–351) but the City rationalized the immigration procedures. From 1855 to 1890, ever larger passenger ships deposited immigrants at the former Castle Clinton, which had become an entertainment center called Castle Garden in the 1820s but was reclaimed by the Federal Government as an immigrant station. The presence of newly arrived poor and confused people and their waiting relatives nevertheless reduced the social standing of the surrounding area until Ellis Island opened its facilities in 1892. The newcomers' removal to the island provided a socially more acceptable environment in nearby streets where new office buildings and even skyscrapers for newspapers, shipping lines, and insurance companies were rising by the turn of the century.

In the 1920s, the intense traffic to and from the west side waterfront at grade level made it urgent to elevate the railway from 34th Street southward

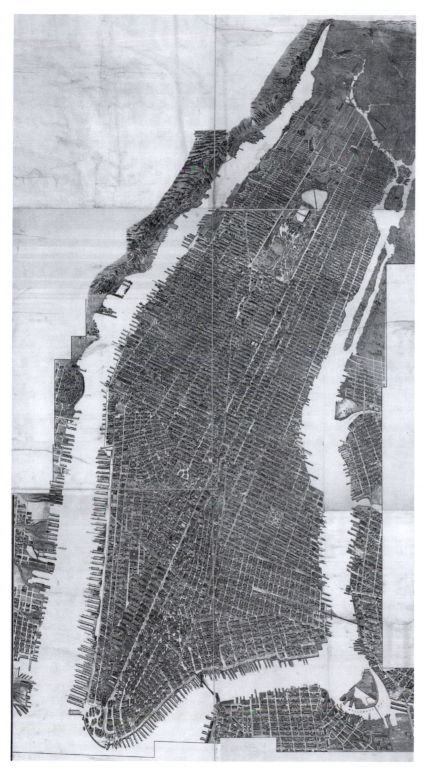

Figure 12.2 Bird's eye view map of Manhattan, c. 1900 (source: Library of Congress, Prints & Photographs Division, pm 005841 bx).

Note
The south end, showing piers, Broadway, organic street layout at south, gridded subdivisions farther north.

to Gansevoort Street; this construction is known as the High Line (see Figure 12.3). Begun in 1929, it was finished in 1941, designed to run in part through the middle of city blocks so as to avoid blighting an avenue. Near it, on pillars close to the waterfront, rose the Miller Elevated (alias West Side) Highway, an automobile road (1931–1948). During the 1930s, trucks that could pick up and deliver directly from one point to another reduced some of the traffic at the docks, especially after the opening of road connections to New Jersey on the mainland, including the Holland and Lincoln Tunnels (1927, 1937) and the George Washington Bridge (1931). Along the east side, the congestion caused by small streets, a dense population, markets, and the remnant of waterfront activity stimulated the construction of the Franklin D. Roosevelt Drive, elevated for much of its trajectory. Work started in 1934 and ended in 1954, following modified plans. The Drive passes close to surviving East River docks at South Street, which by the 1950s were no longer used for trans-Atlantic shipping and were largely derelict. When the Drive obscured the docks, their preservation inadvertently made possible their later incorporation into the South Street Seaport district.

Prosperity and suburbanization after 1945 led to the construction of other elevated roads past docks, particularly in Brooklyn (see Figure 12.4). Piers facing Manhattan in Brooklyn Heights are visible from the Brooklyn–Queens Expressway. Farther south, they are visible from the Gowanus Expressway. Shipping and related manufacturing and storage facilities in Upper New York Bay include the massive Bush Terminal (1890 ff.), in which were factories, warehouses, power plants, railways, highway entrances, and eighteen steamship piers on about 200 acres (80.9 hectares) of land. The Brooklyn Marine Terminal faces an uncertain future. Container facilities came to Red Hook in 1993, specializing in cocoa, coffee, and lumber, although they do not compensate for the predominance of containerized shipping in New Jersey. Red Hook itself, a neighborhood formerly home to stevedores and others connected to shipping, was severely damaged by the relocation of the port. Further injury came from highways that severed the housing from the port and, on the other side, from the rest of the borough. The predictable outcome was abandonment and population replacement by even poorer residents, who must live inconveniently distant from their places of work.

THE PORT AND THE BUILDINGS

In the earliest days, Manhattan's buildings were the modest one- and two-story structures common to any seventeenth- or eighteenth-century provincial town. The most prominent structure was the City Tavern, built of stone in 1641; it became the Dutch city hall in 1653. It faced the East River, where commerce and shipping then concentrated. A street from the waterfront that turned north at the east side of Battery Park remained the elegant residential street until the early nineteenth century; it occupied the center of the island, as far as possible from the waterfront with its inevitable noisy commerce, slime, and rats. Many early houses were made of wood, and were therefore subject to rot, collapse, and fire. The cold winters and the constant danger from domestic fires prompted construction in brick for those who could afford it;

Figure 12.3 High Line running through Bell Telephone Laboratories (later Westbeth Apartments), c. 1934 (source: Photographer unknown. Photo courtesy thehighline.org).

Figure 12.4 South Brooklyn Freight Terminal, 29th St Pier (source: Library of Congress, Prints & Photographs Division, HAER NY, 24-Brok, 55–1).

the port and the railroads of the nineteenth century eased the transportation of building materials to Manhattan Island and thereby reduced their cost. In addition, an enormous brickworks stood along the Brooklyn waterfront, receiving clay from New Jersey.

Port facilities clearly affected the distribution of buildings. By the early nineteenth century, commercial premises dotted the shoreline and continued to do so into the twentieth century. There were eventually ninety-nine piers on the west side up to 59th Street; there are now ten. Seventy-three piers survived to 1950 on the east side south of 24th Street, but fewer of them were then active.[1]

At South Street, the primary area for shipping before about 1860, brick and stone buildings housed commercial premises below storage areas. Some of these four-story buildings retained modest businesses until their restoration after 1966 as the South Street Seaport, featuring shops, restaurants, and a museum. From 1979 to 1985, the Rouse Corporation added other commercial buildings, forming a festival market (Bixby, 1972). Other waterfront buildings were warehouses, small factories, and repair shops tied to maritime industries. Hotels appeared by the 1820s if not earlier, along with taverns and restaurants, such as the rebuilt Fraunces Tavern. Beyond the Fulton Street fish market, northeast of Catherine Slip, lay the early nineteenth-century ship-yards, confirming the industrial nature of this stretch of waterfront. Small wonder that prosperous New Yorkers had already abandoned the area for quieter areas to the north, although some barge captains and their families lived on board, docked at the piers.

By the late nineteenth century, when most of the large-scale maritime activity had moved to the west side, the waterfront on the East River could attract only those who had work in the area, or those who were homeless.

Men without families congregated in this declining neighborhood. The Seamen's Church Institute, established in 1834 as the Episcopal Seafarers' Advocacy, saw the need for boarding houses and floating churches in the area to supplement its retirement home, the Sailors' Snug Harbor on Staten Island (which since 1976 has been a cultural center). The charity opened a larger building in 1913 with an annex for about 1,500 seamen, and established a merchant marine school in 1916. The city also responded to the need for a Municipal Lodging House, which, with its annex in a ferry shed at the foot of Whitehall Street, accommodated over a thousand unemployed and homeless men during the Depression of the 1930s. Another large facility that took advantage of proximity to the waterfront was the Hearst Publication Plant for the editorial and press rooms of several newspapers; heavy paper could be brought by water close to the site. Along the shores of Brooklyn, Queens, the Bronx, and Staten Island rose sugar refineries, bottling plants, warehouses, and other industries that benefited from ready access to vessels that carried products easily and cheaply to ships or railroads. The unsightly – albeit lively – waterfront buildings and activities also prompted the wealthy classes to live in the center of Manhattan Island where they could see each other or perhaps Central Park, rather than near industrial facilities.

Elegant commercial buildings also remained in the island's interior. During the nineteenth century, New York became the principal broker for southern agricultural products – especially cotton – that moved between the producers and foreign markets. After the Civil War, when exchanges for products either brokered or locally refined came into being, auxiliary services in law, banking, stock trading, and insurance developed. The former United States Custom House (1907) commands the view at Bowling Green, where Broadway begins; customs duties constituted the principal source of Federal revenue before the instigation of the permanent income tax in 1914. (It now houses a branch of the National Museum of the American Indian – like Sailors' Snug Harbor, an example of cultural re-use of port-related facilities.) On Wall Street stands the Stock Exchange, established in 1790 with its present four buildings that opened from 1903 to 1928. Diagonally opposite is the United States Subtreasury, built in 1842, with an exterior that resembles a Greek temple. The Produce Exchange stood nearby, and to the north lies City Hall; formerly on its square were the principal post office, as well as early skyscrapers built by newspapers and insurance companies, all of which had business connections to shipping. Offices for trans-Atlantic lines such as North German Lloyd and Cunard occupied prominent buildings on Broadway and streets immediately adjacent to it. The neo-Gothic Trinity Church, the original parish church of Manhattan, clad in brown sandstone in its third form of 1846, stands midway between the rivers, on Broadway at the end of Wall Street (King, 1980). The port, with its raucous noises, dirt, and working-class people, had obviously concentrated polite development elsewhere.

When the port shifted to the west side during the second quarter of the nineteenth century, the east riverfront attracted mainly industrial activity along a shore then becoming obsolete for major shipping. Swampy areas around the present 42nd Street were suitable only for noisome businesses such as stockyards and the glue factories that stood conveniently nearby. From the late nineteenth century, power plants occupied prominent locations on the waterfront, two of which, much enlarged, survived into the present century, although one was demolished in 2007. On the west side, the demands of commerce led to the sale of residential property to shipping companies and railroads. St. John's Park, a gated square surrounded by the homes of the wealthy from about 1825 to 1850, rapidly emptied as the freight railroad intruded and working people crowded the neighborhood, living in tenements that speculative builders erected for them nearby. Industrial activity reduced land value for housing and hence land prices, so that in 1869 the freight terminal of the Hudson River Railroad could move to the formerly elite neighborhood; the terminal closed only in 1936. Among other terminals and shipping facilities, docks existed for merchandise brought by ferry from the New Jersey shore of the Hudson River, where trains from the west terminated. In Manhattan, wooden float bridges carried rail cars to reach waiting ships; a few survive as curiosities.

Warehouses, brothels, saloons, cheap hotels, and shops catering to sailors lined the avenues near the western waterfront. The YMCA built a dormitory with recreational facilities for sailors, and in time the National Maritime Union located its headquarters on Eleventh Avenue; it moved in 1964 to a more distinctive building on Seventh Avenue and 12th Street in Greenwich Village, although the importance of the union had already been reduced by the decline in port activity. The railroads running parallel to the docks also made possible the creation of the aforementioned large produce and meat markets; another market distributed dairy products. The United Fruit Company owned extensive and imposing docks on the lower west side. In the twentieth century, farm products arrived at the markets by truck, although traffic congestion was by then a hindrance. The area bustled with taxis, carts, trucks, private cars, and grade-level trains before creation of the High Line and West Side Highway. The markets, too, made the area unsuitable for middle- and upper-class dwelling. Consequently, the people who lived near the west side docks were either temporary residents such as sailors, or they were working-class families of stevedores, market workers, warehousemen, and the like. Many were immigrants. Their presence impelled the wealthier classes to relocate ever farther to the north, a move facilitated by the introduction of elevated railways after the city authorized them in 1875 along Second, Third, Sixth, and Eighth Avenues, and by the subway system that opened between 1904 and 1940.

The same situation obtained in Brooklyn, where, except for Brooklyn Heights with its easy bridge and train connection to the Wall Street area, dockland was home to the working classes. Many of them held shipping-related jobs, and lived on nearby streets lined with four-story tenements interspersed with warehouses, brickworks, and small factories. One of the city's earliest and largest public housing projects, the Red Hook Houses (1936), was built for families whose breadwinners were employed at the docks. The handsome Sol Goldman and McCarren public swimming pools, opened in the same year in Red Hook and Greenpoint respectively, provided much-needed wholesome summer recreation for children of many industrial workers employed on the docks (Gutman, 2008).

The eastern waterfront, though little used for shipping by the early twentieth century, nevertheless retained some ferry and other docks, warehouses, and patches of lower social uses. The slums of the Lower East Side bordered the waterfront north of the former port area, the Gashouse District blighted the waterfront north of the slums from 14th Street northward, and on the present site of the United Nations headquarters north of 42nd Street stood the slaughterhouses that received animals brought by barge from rail terminals in New Jersey. Enormous laundries and breweries completed the industrial degradation of the waterfront. Later, the approaches to the Queens Midtown Tunnel, opened in 1936, cut a gash into the streetscape.

The use of the entire west side below 60th Street for docks, railroads, and highways made the western waterfront undesirable for high-rent office buildings and apartment houses. Warehouses were the logical building type for the area. Massive ones lined Twelfth Avenue and neighboring streets. Some survive, converted into personal storage units and arts- and computer-related premises. Train and shipping connections inspired a distinctive building type: the warehouse with internal rail spurs. The Central Stores (1891), a terminal for the Baltimore & Ohio freight lines, accommodated rail cars that entered from a float bridge. Ground-floor tracks as well as trucks entered its neighbor to the south, the enormous Starrett-Lehigh Building (1931), built on the Lehigh Valley Railroad freight terminal's site. The High Line passed through several other port-related buildings such as the Bell Telephone and present Chelsea Market buildings, in which secure delivery of merchandise via rail was a major attraction. Probably no other building type embodies as clearly as do these warehouses the connections among port facilities, railways, streets with trucking, and the buildings lining the portside avenues.

In the 1950s, containerization shifted port activity from Manhattan's west side to parts of New York Harbor closer to the deep waters of the Atlantic Ocean. Port Newark–Elizabeth Marine Terminal in New Jersey is now the major shipping location in New York Harbor. It has the principal container ship facilities in the northeastern United States. Twenty-five years ago, New York was still the world's principal port (*New York Times*, November 22, 2004), but it has yielded its primacy to international competitors. As containerization increased, removing port activity from New York City's five boroughs, there were also fewer trans-Atlantic passenger voyages, because air travel became faster and more affordable. After 1960, when jet airplanes came into wide use, they reduced demand for trans-Atlantic passenger ships that had berthed on the west side piers. Concomitantly, airports and air freight developed. In Queens, Idlewild (later John F. Kennedy Airport) opened in 1948 on Jamaica Bay, LaGuardia Airport having begun operation along Bowery Bay in 1931; Newark-Liberty airport, across the Hudson River in New Jersey, also serves the New York City area.

The airports, like the seaports, came under the jurisdiction of the Port Authority of New York and New Jersey, a bi-state agency created in 1921 and now in charge of bridges, tunnels, airports, and seaport installations, as well as buildings for bus transportation and at the World Trade Center (Doig, 2001). The Port Authority focused its building activities on airports, and on high-rise offices. Rail service was neglected, and the Port Authority, seemingly indifferent to the City, ignored the complaints of truckers who had to carry loads to and from the piers through Manhattan's dense traffic. By the later 1980s, many west side piers lay empty, their sheds having been demolished. Shipping by container had moved to new facilities in New Jersey, where trucks could approach the docks from the mainland.

THE PORT'S EFFECT ON ZONING AND THE RESULTING BUILDINGS

When New York City decided in 1916 to designate certain zones for commerce, for residence, and for unrestricted use in order to protect land values and thus the tax base, its zoning commissioners perhaps understandably slighted the waterfronts. By a resolution of the City Council that acquired the force of law, the city established that east of Third Avenue and west of Eighth Avenue landowners could build what they wished, subject to the requirements of the building safety and health codes. Between those avenues, more refined buildings were welcomed, such as office buildings, department stores, and apartment houses. These socially higher forms of architecture were already there, having clung to the center of the island, away from the port, the sailors' haunts, and the slaughterhouses. Following the introduction of zoning, hospitals grew rapidly in the unrestricted zone at the edges, where the land value was reduced by an owner's ability to build nearly anything next to anything else. Hospitals expanded as they continued to develop forms of treatment that suggested new internal planning. For Blackwell's (later Welfare, now Roosevelt) Island in the East River, the city designated a nineteenth-century penitentiary, a poorhouse, a tuberculosis hospital and one for chronic diseases, and an asylum for those with mental disorders; these did little to improve the view from Manhattan's east side that included industrial buildings in Long Island City and Astoria along the Queens waterfront. Before restrictions were put in place, these institutions had found proximity to the river convenient for dumping waste, just as early sewers and careless citizens did. As a result of having many hospitals along its trajectory, First Avenue has been facetiously nicknamed "Bedpan Alley"; a good many of Manhattan's most prominent hospitals still occupy the unrestricted zones on the east and west sides.

Fear of social contamination from sailors and warehousemen kept the most elegant office buildings and department stores within the boundaries of Third to Eighth Avenues and 34th to 59th Streets; the latter street marks the start of Central Park. Warehouses and factories were prohibited in this central district. They could not have afforded to relocate there anyway after 1916, when the zoning rules established the potential for higher land values where skyscrapers could rise dramatically and charge high rents per square foot. Zoning explains why the central area has major landmarks such as the Empire State Building, the Chrysler Building, Rockefeller Center, and later prominent office skyscrapers. It is also the department store district, from which new garment factories (with their immigrant workers) were excluded. It is often said that this district was zoned for high-rise building because it rests on bedrock, as does the Wall Street area, but tall buildings can be erected on piles. Other reasons include the framing of the district by the noisy elevated railways on Third and Eighth Avenues, the desire of wealthy landowners and tenants to be distant from the waterfront, the adjacency of Central Park to the district's northern boundary, and proximity to Grand Central Terminal and Pennsylvania Railroad Station, which gave commuting executives convenient access to midtown offices.

Zoning rules in force between 1916 and 1961 also required gradual setbacks until a tall building occupied only 25 percent of its site, after which a tower could rise as far as the owner wished. Setbacks provided some air and light in densely built areas. The need for air and light was particularly acute in lower Manhattan, where the Dutch-planned streets were in danger of becoming dark canyons. They had long been congested, even before skyscrapers were developed, since the higher classes of Dutch and British settlers had clustered there in earlier centuries, away from the port facilities. But the zoning regulations also prevented developers from overly competitive building, thereby preserving at least some amenity – and building value that supported the real estate tax base.

Despite the concentration of high-rise, high-value buildings in the center of the island, the United Nations headquarters (1947–1953), the World Trade Center (1972–1977), and Battery Park City (1979–) all lie along the present-day waterfront, as do the dramatic Waterside (1974) and Ruppert and Yorkville (1976) residential tower complexes. While most of them are enclaves with plazas rather than through streets, Battery Park City emphasizes the idea of streets for strolling and parks for residents and visitors – a postmodern urban model. The rebuilt World Trade Center will also reopen Greenwich Street, which had been closed by the original Center's platform. The first three did not have to obey zoning regulations because they occupy non-city land – international territory or land owned by a bi-state Port Authority of New York and New Jersey. These three projects were built, respectively, on the site of the earlier slaughterhouses or on landfill, and they all recognized the opportunity to erect large projects free from customary regulation. When the United Nations buildings were planned in the 1940s, other parts of the east side waterfront were being rehabilitated by slum-clearance measures such as the public low-income housing projects on the Lower East Side and privately sponsored middle-income projects north of 14th Street. In those less crowded premises, ordinary residents benefited from the riverfront's air and sunshine and park strips laid out for recreation, just as the wealthy, the diplomats, and the business executives did in their enclaves.

WATERFRONT REHABILITATION

New York City's original waterfront was not what it is today. Few original contours of southern Manhattan and northern Brooklyn survive. Landfill has enlarged most of the small islands in the harbor, and has increased the land of Manhattan substantially. At its southern tip, in Battery Park, engineers joined Fort (alias Castle) Clinton to the mainland after its defensive functions became obsolete; later uses included a concert hall, an aquarium, and a ferry ticket office. Pearl Street on the east side, now two blocks from the waterfront, used to lie near the water's edge, hence its name derived from abundant oyster shells. Nearby, Coenties Slip, formerly an inlet, was also filled in and paved, as Canal Street was. The Franklin D. Roosevelt Drive that runs overhead is built partly above landfill consisting of rubble from bombed British cities; it came after 1945 to New York as ballast for ships. Along its course lie strips of parkland and enormous public low-income and private moderate-income housing developments, the latter including Waterside (1974) and Stuyvesant Town/Peter Cooper Village (1947), built in part on filled land. On the Hudson shore, West Street did not originally exist, and the entire World Trade Center and Battery Park City were built on landfill, as were buildings north of them. Staten Island has also been modified.

The port facilities themselves have been transformed almost unrecognizably. The Navy Yard in Brooklyn, which had confirmed New York's status as a port, remained active for shipbuilding through the Second World War and even for some years after 1945. But after the 1950s, when Manhattan's shipping industry declined rapidly, the west side waterfront remained underused for over a generation. The area then was undervalued, as much of the shipping infrastructure lay nearby, increasingly decrepit. Some piers were quietly invaded for sunbathing or outdoor sports, or for less innocent activities. A pioneering new project there was the Westbeth housing for artists (1969) designed by Richard Meier, who installed apartments in a former telephone company laboratory building.

More recently, New York, like other cities, has reclaimed vacant port installations for new uses. Much of this is the result of private enterprise. The west side has seen the creation of a major 30 acre (12.1 hectare) sports complex (opened in 1994) at the nine surviving Chelsea Piers (1902–1907) from 17th to 23rd Streets, originally meant for passenger liners; the architects were Warren & Wetmore, co-designers of Grand Central Terminal. An esplanade with paths, playgrounds, and sitting areas now runs from the Battery northward along the Hudson riverfront; it is well used for bicycle riding, strolling, and skateboarding. Tenants in the adjacent buildings have changed as warehousemen and longshoremen yielded to art gallery and theater or nightclub owners. Between 34th and 38th Streets, commercial visitors flock to the Jacob K. Javits Convention Center (1986). North of that, at Pier 86, the *Intrepid*, an aircraft carrier from the Second World War, is now a museum of air, sea, and space. At the start of the present century, developers began to erect offices, hotels, and apartment houses, including several by prominent architects such as Meier, Jean Nouvel, Frank O. Gehry, and the Polshek Partnership. Their occupants can enjoy river views free of the grimy reality of industry and shipping. The Standard Hotel (2009), by the last-named firm, is built in part over the abandoned High Line, which has been made into an elevated linear park following the model of the Parisian Promenade Plantée that enhances a disused rail viaduct. Manhattan's old food markets moved north to the Bronx, replaced by restaurants and loft residences built into former industrial buildings. Remaining west side shipping piers accommodate the Circle Line sightseeing boats; the New York Waterway Ferries for commuters traveling across the river to Weehawken, New Jersey; and the Manhattan Cruise Terminal for ocean liners, built in the 1930s and modernized in 2007–2008. Most remarkably, the 28 acre (11.3 hectare) Riverbank State Park, begun in 1993, occupies a platform over the huge North River Wastewater Treatment Plant between 137th and 145th Streets, in operation since 1986.

The east side, too, has seen the construction of city-sponsored recreation spaces, along the East River. Starting in 1966, private developers teamed with historic preservationists to promote new uses for the former commercial buildings at South Street near Fulton Street. The project required city permits, eventual city investment, and compensatory zoning that produced massive office buildings nearby. Now business people at lunch and cocktail hours, and tourists at all times gather at the Seaport Museum and the adjacent restaurants, shops, historic ships, and harbor cruise piers. Some tenants maintain craft activities rarely preserved elsewhere. Opposite midtown Manhattan, in the industrial Long Island City section of Queens, the east riverfront has sprouted high-rise office and apartment houses and recreational facilities, including Gantry Plaza State Park (1998) that preserves railroad gantries left on the site. Parts of the industrial waterfront of Brooklyn, especially in districts facing Manhattan such as DUMBO (down under the Manhattan Bridge overpass), have become sites for new activities that cater to the affluent or to young adults with artistic or sophisticated tastes. This is a situation typical of many cities, in which obsolete and therefore low-rent buildings are adopted by the arts and entertainment industries. They gentrify the area and cause rents to rise later. But unlike some European cities with comprehensive government-sponsored master plans for the re-use of derelict areas, New York employs planning practices that often deal with discrete segments. Many projects are privately financed, and few are coordinated with each other. Whether public or private, the projects are subject to many reviews that delay and often prevent development, particularly if there is strong neighborhood opposition to the proposals or if demolition of historic property is part of the plan. Many developers, however, have become aware of the potential for enhancing new projects by incorporating aspects of significant older construction, or for adaptive re-use of existing buildings. To prevent high-rise, potentially congesting construction by less enlightened developers, public interest groups advocate for landmark designation of waterfront districts, especially on the west side near Greenwich Village, where residents hope also to preserve their views or their access to the waterfront. Farther north, community activists stalled massive high-rise construction over disused rail yards near the river, although dense residential development has occurred on the former freight yards since the mid-1990s at Riverside South (alias Trump Place) between 59th and 72nd Streets (see Figure 12.5). On the East Side, homeless sailors have long been gone from the South Street area, as the surviving historic buildings have been rehabilitated and turned into a museum, shops, restaurants, and other entertainment facilities, frequented by tourists and by young workers in the financial centers around Wall Street. A power plant south of the United Nations complex is gone, about to be replaced by tall apartment houses and some open park space. The city plans additional parks and bicycle paths along much of the waterfront, and part of this project has already been completed on both the east and west sides, supplementing amenities created earlier on the Lower East Side. The FDR Drive has gone underground along the Battery since 1951, enabling the preservation of the waterfront buildings and the park that originated in the Dutch defensive fort. Community organizations are less visible on the east than on the west side,

Figure 12.5 South Street Seaport, with Water Street in centre foreground, Franklin D. Roosevelt Drive in background, after 1954 (source: Library of Congress, Prints & Photographs Division, HABS NY,31-NEYO, 141–1).

but public pressure has been brought to bear on the reconstruction of sites in the East 30s along the water, formerly occupied by power plants. The dramatic expansion of hospital building along the East River has aroused little opposition, as these enclaves are beneficial, are usually not on land already containing housing, and are sources of jobs.

The port, then, whether active or nearly vanished, has been a determining factor in the design of Manhattan's street structure and in the types and location of buildings. The post-1811 grid skirted the existing organically developed street plan but facilitated transportation to and along the developing west side piers. The port facilities themselves helped to determine land use and zoning regulations by attracting complementary uses and repelling more elegant uses. The decline of Manhattan's port as an industrial center during the last generation has resulted in new, often recreational and residential uses for the waterfront and its former facilities and related industrial uses. This is the case in other cities, where disused ports are being converted to uses suited to education, technology, and leisure.

NOTE

1   Map of Manhattan from the Battery to 145th Street, 1901. New York Public Library, Stephen A. Schwarzman Building, Lionel Pincus and Princess Firyal Map Division, catalogue call number Map Division 09–1313, Digital ID psnypl_map_296.

13 HONG KONG'S GLOBAL IMAGE CAMPAIGN

Port city transformation from British colony to Special Administrative Region of China

MARISA YIU

From its conception as a British Colony to its current status as a Special Administrative Region of China, Hong Kong has been a tactical frontier with a geographical advantage, serving as a mediator between China and the rest of the world. Its identity as a global trade port has been central to this role, in part because governmental and private organisations have made the powerful image of Hong Kong as a dynamic port city central to local and international marketing and rebuilding campaigns. Hong Kong's formation can be considered a global image project, in which British and local players, under a variety of historical, political, and social conditions, and influenced by shifting transnational cultural practices, have imagined and then created Hong Kong's built environment. A nongovernmental organisation called the Trade Development Council (TDC) has played a uniquely important role in this high-stakes marketing game.

The TDC, formed by the British and the Hong Kong local business community in 1966, set out to promote local products and create a 'favourable' image for Hong Kong as a trading partner and manufacturing centre in the world (*Kompass: A Register of Hong Kong Industry and Commerce*, 1973). Originally comprising fifteen regional offices, today it has forty offices; it has devised forums, trade delegations, trade fairs, and promotional films in order to entice local and global firms to invest in Hong Kong. The TDC's innovative image-making strategies also influenced the construction of key buildings and port terminals in Hong Kong itself, helping to shape the city's iconic waterfront – which it then made more iconic through further marketing.

MODERNISATION AND TRADE NETWORKS: A BRIEF HISTORY BEFORE THE TDC

Integral to the TDC's impact on industrial land policy, harbourfront development, and urban strategies, are 'guanxi' networks – a Chinese term describing the basic dynamic in personalised networks of influence – linking the British Government with elite local Chinese businessmen. Indeed, the colonial government, local Chinese business elites, and the hard-working immigrant and refugee workforce have engaged with each other since the 1839–1842 Opium War.

Hong Kong operated as the administrative and financial centre of the opium trade, which powered its early rise as the hub of Asian trade and finance (Meyer, 2000). It brought people and trading companies to the forefront as intermediary actors between Chinese and Western firms. As in early Portuguese treaty ports (see also Chapter 2 and Chapter 8), such an intermediary was known as a 'comprador', and operated simultaneously as a hired strategist and manager for the foreign firm and as an independent merchant. 'Fluency in Chinese and pidgin English, the lingua franca of the treaty ports, placed [compradors] in a powerful position to deal with both sides of the trade' (Meyer, 2000: 53). This unique relationship between 'colonialism and collaboration' is a continuing pattern in Hong Kong today (Carroll, 2007).

A range of historical factors and emergent, complex, transnational social networks connected the city with the rest of Asia after the Second Opium War of 1856. Hong Kong would later represent itself as a product of this period's 'human vision, endeavour and enterprise', built on the diasporic global circumstances and local traditions of Chinese elites, British administrators and businesspeople, and immigrant refugee workers (McDonogh and Wong, 2005). From 1870 to 1871, private companies laid telegraph cables across Siberia to Vladivostok, and in the Sea of Japan; and submarine cables from India to most major trading and financial centres of Asia, Penang, Singapore, Batavia, Saigon, Hong Kong, Shanghai, Nagasaki and Vladivostok (Meyer, 2000). The Hong Kong and Shanghai Banking Corporation (HSBC) opened in 1864, with Hong Kong as its headquarters, marking Asia's political and economic transformation (Meyer, 2000); the success of the HSBC was not built on its status as a colonial bank but on its strong hold on the local market and extensive network with Chinese merchants in China and Asia (Lee Pui-tak, 2007). In the late 1930s, when Shanghai and Guangzhou (previously called Canton) fell to the Japanese, 600,000 immigrant refugees arrived in Hong Kong and industrialists from other cities in China moved their factories to Hong Kong, boosting the economy. Not only low-skilled workers but a 'chain migration of an elite' from Shanghai ensued; for example, cotton spinners moved their operations along with flight capital to create some of the most modern spinning factories in Asia (Siu-Lun, 1988). Due to the nature of refugees from the 1949 revolution, and later the excesses of the Cultural Revolution and the Japanese military occupation between 1941 and 1945, Hong Kong in many ways stands as an 'anomaly' in Asia (Ingham, 2007). It was unique in its openness to Chinese refugees when other Asian countries shut their doors (Meyer, 2000). All of these changes resulted in astronomical growth: at the end of 1947, Hong Kong's population was 1.8 million, in April 1950 the population grew to 2.36 million. By 1956 it was 2.67 million, and by 1966 it grew to 3.7 million (Sit, 1981). In 2010, Hong Kong's population was 7 million.

The overwhelming influx of refugees into Hong Kong in the years after the 1949 communist victory (or liberation) produced two contrasting effects: the proliferation of squalid squatter camps and an increase in the pool of talent. The textile industry was the largest employer in the workforce. Homeless people poured into the colony, and many erected squalid settlements that grew to a density of 2,000–3,000 people to the acre. According to the 1953 Government Review, these were the homes of some 250,000 people, around one-eighth of the population (Chambers, 1989). A variety of 'cottage' industries thrived here. The notorious squatter fire in Christmas 1953 in Shep Kip Mei, in which 58,000 of these people lost their homes, provoked the government in 1954 to act quickly, command colonial order and create resettlement housing for the mass public. Later, the sites became much needed industrial zones for 'flatted factories', five-storey buildings that contained domestic industries with communal facilities for small manufacturing enterprises. Thus the manufacturing boom coincided with the building boom.

Then, in 1952, Hong Kong lost a huge share of its shipping when the United States government sanctioned a trade embargo on China, prohibiting importation of merchandise from China or North Korea during the Korean War (McDonogh and Wong, 2005). These products included 'cotton piece goods and yarn, singlets, enamelware, torch, batteries, aluminumware, and plastics'.[1] Hong Kong manufacturers seized this crisis as an opportunity, starting small to large-scale enterprises to produce and export these products themselves. That year, the annual report from the Director of Commerce and Industry noted:

> one of the most significant changes was the increased export of locally manufactured products. For the first time in history Indonesia became Hong Kong's best customer. Further efforts were made to promote the overseas sale of Hong Kong products, although there is still much to be done in this respect.[2]

Land was critical to accommodate the expansion of the manufacturing sector. Extensive land reclamation provided space for the developing industrial areas of Kwun Tong and the north-eastern end of the harbour (see Figure 13.1). Industrial policies of the Hong Kong Government – such as offering land at concessionary prices and export promotion across a wide range of industries – attracted manufacturers. 'Provision of public rental housing at subsidised rates remained the greatest investment of government in industry.

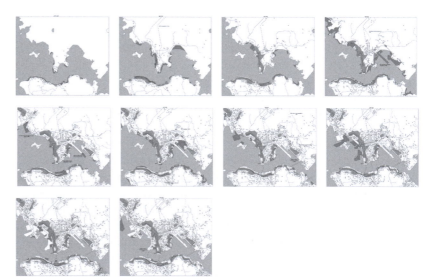

Figure 13.1 Land reclamation and development in Hong Kong (source: Illustration by Marisa Yiu and courtesy of author).

Note
Research from HKSAR Cartography by Survey Division; from up to 1887 to 2007.

It contributed substantial benefits to low-wage, labour intensive industries' (Meyer, 2000: 158). Such dynamic political and economic forces, in a notably chaotic environment, bolstered the continued power of social networks among manufacturers and between manufacturers, traders and financiers. 'The Chinese business sector extended global bridges to other social networks through Chinese and foreign firms. These networks provided information and assistance that supported the rapid adjustments of firms to global market conditions, and the absence of government subsidies and other guided interventions encouraged them to move quickly' (Meyer, 2000: 158). Thus, the flexibility of the economy and the workforce (both elite professionals and immigrant low-skilled labourers), government investment and enduring social networks were instrumental in the shaping of Hong Kong as a global port city.

THE BEGINNINGS OF THE TRADE DEVELOPMENT COUNCIL

In response to rapid industrialisation, the government formed a Trade Development Division in August 1953 within the Department of Commerce and Industry (which the government had set up in 1949) to promote the sale of Hong Kong products overseas, with an initial focus on trade and export clearance with the United States.[3] In December 1953, the Division published its first *Trade Bulletin*; by spring it was distributing over 6,000 copies monthly. The *Bulletin*, directed at overseas businessmen, was later supplemented by *Commerce, Industry, and Finance*, a pictorial commercial guide and business directory. The British Government produced its first trade publication, *Commercial Guide to Hong Kong*, touting Hong Kong's economic position and its harbour to overseas companies interested in doing business in the colony (see Figure 13.2). Between 1948 and 1956, Hong Kong participated in the annual British Industries Fair; sent government-sponsored Hong Kong displays to trade fairs in Toronto, Frankfurt, Seattle, New York, and Melbourne (Chambers, 1989); and 'displayed Hong Kong products on board the ship m.v. *Ruys* sailing between Hong Kong and South America via south Africa'.[4] Locally, individual commercial and trade organisations put on exhibitions in Hong Kong schools (St Paul's College and Wah Nam Middle School), naval dockyards and reclamation areas in Hung Hom from 1938 onwards (Chinese Manufacturers' Association of Hong Kong, 1994). Despite the unusual and sometimes ad hoc nature of these sites, some of these exhibitions were very big: for example, the Chinese Manufacturers' Association (CMA) started an annual six-week exhibition that attracted over one million visitors in 1953, including delegates from South East Asia, North America and Europe. Hong Kong's oldest trade and industrial association, the Hong Kong General Chamber of Commerce (founded in 1861), supported these individual firms by organising a wide range of other promotional activities within the region and further afield.

All of these groups, from the Department of Commerce to the Hong Kong Exporters Association (comprised of merchants and manufacturers), shared a 'common aim to protect the Colony's reputation for fair trading' (Chambers, 1989: 33–41). But the various overseas promotional missions competed and

Figure 13.2 Book cover of British Government's first trade publication, 1949.

217

overlapped, and suffered from poor organisation, limited capacity and inefficiency. In 1957, the subject of forming an organisation to unify the separate factions and represent the industry as a whole to coordinate overseas trade promotion activities was suggested by the Governor Sir Robert Black at a speech during the CMA's exhibition opening in 1958 (Chambers, 1989). Initially the government asked the CMA to amend its constitution and expand its membership beyond manufacturers, but the CMA declined. This prompted the government to form a Working Committee, in 1958, to assist industry and commerce. It would assume the role of the Commerce and Industry Department in promoting the image of Hong Kong overseas, and in protecting products and improving standards at home.

Len Dunning, who had worked in the Department of Commerce and Industry since 1955, was part of the Working Committee, along with various influential businessmen and governmental bodies. He described this phase of development of Hong Kong's trade as 'a massive evolution of free enterprise. It was the evolution of experience in trade and industry that enabled Hong Kong's traders to succeed' (Leong, 1999). Dunning was responsible for evaluating export promotion programmes in Switzerland, Italy, Britain and Austria (he was later the Executive Director of the TDC, from 1973 to 1985). Eventually he chose the Austrian model for Hong Kong. 'It was a small neutral country on the threshold of a great monolithic communist state', he pointed out. 'It was a crossroad of the western world, you might say. There were a lot of differences, of course, but the similarities were very strong and their experience was something to copy to a certain extent' (Chambers, 1989: 42–57). Hong Kong's economic success continued with larger infrastructural expansion: new airports, train networks and larger tourism networks supported improvement in communication and development. On 25 March 1965, the Working Committee on Export Promotion organisation was formed, which involved such important members as the colonial Governor Sir David Trench, Mr Wong Tok-Sau (President of the Chinese Manufacturers' Association), Mr Harold Lee (Chairman of the Hong Kong Tourist Association) and Sir Sik-nin Chau (Chairman of the Federation of Hong Kong industries). They saw an urgent need for an agency offering institutional frameworks to support trade.[5] The government gradually agreed. At the end of 1965, the Legislative Council voted in favour of a new Trade Development Council; on 1 October 1966, it passed the ordinance and officially established the TDC. The *Hong Kong Trade Bulletin* used the words 'dynamic' and 'galvanise' to describe the potential of the TDC, and emphasised the clout of the people who formed the organisation: 'Twenty experienced persons, two-thirds of them Chinese, made up the Council with internal coordinating committees that united various desks. Sir Sik-nin Chau was the first Chairman of the TDC and Mr. R.G.L. Oliphant was the Executive Director of the Council. Overseas representatives were: K.T. Woo in the United States, John Leckie in Western Europe, Irene Ward in London, Gerry Connington in East Africa and Bill Manson in Australia' (Trade Development Council, 1967: 84). The International Marketing Institute at Harvard was commissioned as the leading consultant to advise the council (Trade Development Council, 1967).

The TDC set up offices at the Ocean Terminal, a joint venture between the government and the Kowloon Wharf and Godown company; adjoining the star ferry concourse, it also included berthing facilities (four ocean-going liners), 7.5 acres (3 hectares) of wharf and transit shed space, cargo handling, banking, travel, telegraphic and typing services, nightclubs, car parks, exhibition areas and a self-contained shopping centre with more than one hundred shops (Chambers, 1989) (see Figure 13.3). The Council spent over HK$2 million on publicity activities ('Missions, Displays, and Festivals') over the world in its first two years to stimulate new opportunities and assist Hong Kong businessmen to make new contacts. This resulted in more than HK$18 million of new orders, or HK$7 million more than the HK$11.5 million annual cost of the TDC. Thus overseas promotion helped raise the profile of Hong Kong.

Through the design strategies and creative approaches outlined in the next sections, the TDC publicised and engendered Hong Kong's port development. Central to its efforts were themes of mobility and maritime activity.

DESIGN STRATEGIES: TRADE AND IMAGE PROMOTION FOR THE DEVELOPMENT OF HONG KONG AS A PORT CITY

Hong Kong's function as an innovative production and trade centre, as well as a port city, is reflected in the way in which the exhibitions excel. Furthermore, as the exhibitions attracted more trade, the TDC shaped Hong Kong's urban form.

Figure 13.3 Hong Kong Ocean Terminal in 1972 (source: courtesy of the HKSAR Government).

As soon as the TDC was set up in 1966, it launched an intensive programme of overseas promotions. It set up an 8,000 sq. foot (743 sq. metre)
pavilion at the International Samples fair in Barcelona in June 1966, winning
awards for its design and presentation. In autumn 1966, it held Hong Kong
promotions at Selfridges in London, New York City's Macy's and the Myer
Group Stores in Australia, which were selected and advised by their respective
TDC advisors.[6] It sent a major exhibit to the First Asian International Trade
Fair in 1966 in Bangkok: that, along with its 'striking design', had air-
conditioning to counter the 40 degree Celsius heat, so that, as one TDC
member said, 'We were literally an oasis in the desert' (Chambers, 1989: 61).
Their work could be political. During 1967, the turmoil of the Cultural
Revolution spilled over into Hong Kong, scaring the international community. In order to dispel their trepidation, the TDC organised a comprehensive
publicity and lecture tour across the US, continental Europe and the UK. In a
tone of concern in June that year, a TDC representative proposed to rebuild
confidence in Hong Kong among importers, retailers and manufacturers by
using subtle strategies to insert into their ads the theme of 'business as usual'.
The Brussels outpost concurred by recommending a low pressure campaign
'that carefully placed articles for at least two years'.[7]

In the few years after its inception, the TDC built regional offices in many
influential trade centres and port cities around the world: New York, Chicago,
Los Angeles, Toronto, London, Manchester, Stockholm, Brussels, Amsterdam, Frankfurt, Hamburg, Vienna, Milan, Sydney and Tokyo. By 1972, these
offices sponsored approximately thirty separate promotional projects each
year. The TDC's travel delegations triggered many conversations about
coping with rapid industrial growth. But promotion alone was not enough: in
correspondence and meeting minutes, TDC members now voiced concern
about a shortage of industrial land to attract overseas investors. The TDC
called on the colonial government to overcome the shortage and high land
costs that would inhibit future development, and to set up a 'central authority
to allocate efficiently industrial plots'.[8] Thus trade promotion motivated
urban development.

At the same time, in several trade missions in the 1960s and 1970s, the
TDC used design finesse and swift organisation to directly shape the image of
the port of Hong Kong as a site for economic and social exchange. Despite
TDC's quasi-governmental role, these missions were opportunity seeking ventures in forming creative new ground. The TDC thus acted as an ambassador
and spokesperson for Hong Kong's image overseas while being influential in
shaping its own urban form and city development.

THE 1967 SAFARI TRUCK, FROM EAST AFRICA TO THE NUREMBERG TOY FAIR

The TDC sent a trade exhibition to East Africa in 1967, touting it as an
'unusual' trade mission. G.J. Connington, the TDC's resident representative
for the Far East & Central Africa, announced: 'We are preparing a concerted
effort, not only to publicise Hong Kong products in East Africa but to ensure
that the selling delegation, which will accompany the caravan, will return to

Hong Kong with full order books'.[9] The exhibitors could not find suitable exhibition venues, so the TDC invented a self-contained mobile design unit made out of a truck and trailer, a miniature exhibition hall of approximately 1,000 sq. feet (92.9 sq. metres). A large colourful graphic reading 'Hong Kong safari' was displayed on both sides of the truck. 'It was a wonderful advertisement for the British colony as it travelled and attracted large crowds' (Chambers, 1989: 68). But the truck's mission didn't stop in Africa; and continued later in Germany (see Figures 13.4 and 13.5).

Figure 13.4 Safari Truck, East Africa trade mission, 1967 (source: image courtesy of Hong Kong Trade Development Council).

The Nuremburg Toy Fair in Germany, unlike Spain's Barcelona or Sweden's Stockholm, targeted specialised businessmen instead of the general public.[10] Hong Kong manufacturers of plastic flowers had discovered that their plastic extrusion machines could also make other toy products, so this was an exciting new field of manufacturing and marketing. In order to enter the new global toy market, Hong Kong had to attend this fair and make an impact. But as a newcomer to the exhibition and trade fair scene, Hong Kong had to fight hard for acceptance and recognition. Unfortunately, the organisers of the fair thought Hong Kong was a threat to European markets and refused to allocate TDC's 'requested 2000–3000sq ft space for the exhibition' (185.8–278.7 sq. metres) (Chambers, 1989: 68–69).[11] Instead of giving up, the TDC immediately requested permission for a parking space, and was granted one – the idea was to bring the safari truck and its portable exhibition space to Nuremburg and have a presence at the show despite the organisers' decision. Getting the parking space was just the beginning of the struggle to attend the fair, however. As Chambers explains, 'The safari truck was organised and taken out of storage … It was outfitted on a deck cargo ship bound for Marseilles, added with heaters to adapt to the cold Nuremberg weather' (Chambers, 1989: 68–69). But storms diverted the caravan to Livorno, Italy, where the truck was unloaded to be driven the rest of the way to Germany. Here the size of the caravan was one inch (2.54 cm) too large for

Figure 13.5 Safari Truck, East Africa trade mission, 1967 (source: image courtesy of Hong Kong Trade Development Council).

Italian roads, so it had to be driven to Marseilles instead, and from there finally to Nuremburg. There the TDC converted the truck into a toy house, with two German chimneys on the top for good luck and more than thirty-five products on display. But the German police challenged them on the grounds that the truck was now 'not a vehicle but a permanent building'. The delegation managed to convince them otherwise and they set up in their parking space. The project was successful: although for the next few years, Hong Kong's exhibit was still confined to the car park, it eventually made it into the main exhibition hall (Chambers, 1989: 42–57). Today, Hong Kong is the leading exporter of toys, suggesting that small efforts and creative perseverance can spark larger profitable returns later.

THE 1970 HONG KONG 'JUNK' AT THE JAPAN WORLD EXPOSITION IN OSAKA

Hong Kong accepted an invitation from the government of Japan to participate in the first world exposition staged in Asia, Expo '70, also known as the Japan World Expo; it's theme was 'progress and harmony for mankind'. It was held over a 183-day period in 1970 on a site of approximately 815.5 acres (330 hectares) in the Senrikyuryo area of Osaka. The event featured exhibitors from seventy-six countries, four international organisations, one foreign government (Hong Kong), three US states, three Canadian provinces, two US cities, one German city, two corporations, and thirty-two domestic organisations (Commemorative Organisation for the Japan World Exposition '70, n.d.). The TDC opened an office in Tokyo in 1971. The exposition attracted more than 64 million visitors, including Crown Prince Akihito of Japan, who was escorted through the industrial progress exhibition by the Cultural Heritage Department.[12] The Hong Kong Government Information Service predicted that 'the large majority will be Japanese nationals whose interest in Hong Kong will be either as actual or potential consumers of her products or as tourists, and will have the effect of enhancing the image of Hong Kong overseas and help show the Government's complete confidence in the future' (see Figure 13.6).[13]

The exhibit depicted many obstacles that Hong Kong had overcome, such as congested population and lack of housing, and emphasised manufacturing growth by showcasing products 'made in Hong Kong'. It showed achievements in land reclamation and mass housing, and showed the port's successful transition from trade entrepôt to leading manufacturing centre. Mr Graham S. Blundell, Exposition Administrator, was in charge of the Hong Kong Pavilion, and worked with architects and designers to build it. Mr B.J. Navetta, the Chief Designer of TDC, was involved with the various architects of the three firms Szeto W. & Partners; Spence Robinson & Co.; and Wong Ng Ouyang & Associates. The Hong Kong pavilion itself was an unusual part of the exhibition: it was a one-to-one scale installation of a Chinese boat, the type sometimes known as a 'junk', with lighting accents and a bronze coloured sail. Every morning, the delegation put on a sail raising ceremony and every evening a sail lowering ceremony, the sails powered by electric motors. The design team alerted the delegation to avoid using the word 'junk' when describing the

Figure 13.6 The Hong Kong Pavilion at the Japan Expo, 1970 (source: courtesy of the HKSAR Government).

boat or the sails, and to refer to them in press releases as 'batwing sails' or 'butterfly wing sails' instead. The boat themed pavilion was selected by Japan's government to appear in a reproduction of postcards that appeared in *Time* magazine.[14] Hong Kong's involvement in the first Asia Expo celebrated its adaptability, where its forward outreach via various built projects and media outreach began to generate Hong Kong's unique position and brand as an open liberal economy and as a dynamic port city of exchange.

1972 ONWARDS: PORT EXPANSION FROM KWAI CHUNG PORT TERMINAL TO KWAI TSING CONTAINER TERMINALS

Hong Kong's manufacturing expanded in the 1970s. The increased mobility of people and capital sparked discussions in the government and various enterprises; the TDC set out to promote Hong Kong's advancement in infrastructure. It made its first film, entitled *The Hand Shakes Like This*, showing foreigners doing business with ease, taking the viewer through crowds of Hong Kong factories, and dockland sites of cargo loading and unloading, the busy Kai Tak airport and harbour activity.[15] More practically, however, industrialists, shippers, members of the ship-owning community and the port authority all worried that the port of Hong Kong was not prepared for the 'container revolution'. The Governor of the Colony at that time, Sir David Trench (1964–1971), appointed a Container Committee 'to consider the implication for Hong Kong's trade and industry of the recent rapid world-wide development of transportation services' (Chambers, 1989: 49). It would bring together 'representatives of manufacturing, exporting, shipping organisations and of the relevant government departments' (Hong Kong Marine Department, 1966–1971: 18). In its first report, the Container Committee concluded: 'It could well be that unless we are prepared to receive and ship cargo by container and keep in step with world developments, we might find our Hong Kong economy severely damaged' (Container Committee, 1966: 7). The problem was dramatised in early 1967, when '613 large ships entered the port and caused harbour congestion' (Chambers, 1989: 64).

In response, the Committee designated an area at Kwai Chung to be developed as a container port. It met all the design criteria: it was available, located near a projected industrial zone with deep water, on a 95 acre (38.4 hectare) reclamation area, and cheap. On 5 September 1972, the third generation cellular container vessel *Tokyo Bay* (47,777 DWT) berthed at the new Kwai Chung container terminal in the port of Hong Kong, inaugurating the port's engagement with containerised shipping. Other technological innovations at the port included the world's first twelve-storey container warehouse freight station, constructed by Hong Kong & Kowloon Wharf Company and Godown Company (Hong Kong KWGC) for HK$32 million (its height was specially designed to address the site's limitations).

Indeed, the 1970s was a significant decade for Hong Kong, especially on the Kowloon side of the harbour. Governor Murray Maclehose (1971–1982) reversed the colonial policy of sending major revenues to London and instead used taxes to fund local construction projects. He also spearheaded a ten-year plan for public housing for the large number of Chinese immigrants. The first harbour tunnel was completed in 1972, connecting Hong Kong island and Kowloon peninsula (Lee, 2008). With infrastructural fervour inland, the port grew rapidly. In 1973, both the US Line and Sealand developed Hong Kong as a pivot for their US Trans Pacific shuttles (Robinson and Chu, 1981). The Kwai Chung terminal completed four berths in the 1970s and added two berths in 1987. With China's open door policy, Hong Kong rapidly expanded its trade from the late 1980s to the 1990s; and Hong Kong became an important trans-shipment centre for Chinese products (Ho, 2004). With two additional terminals later added in the 1990s, to connect the port to Stonecutters Island, the site was renamed Kwai Chung Container Terminals. In the 2000s, when Container Terminal 9 on the Tsing Yi Island was built, the entire area was renamed Kwai Tsing Container Terminals. Today, Hong Kong is ranked '2nd for World Port Rankings pertaining to Container traffic behind Singapore and 7th in total Cargo Volume', behind only Shanghai, Singapore, Rotterdam, Ningbo, Guangzhou and Tianjin (statistics from American Association of Port Authorities (AAPA), 2006). Since the first 1971 promotional film, TDC has continued to project the image of its ever-expanding and efficient port activity in Hong Kong in its various promotional packaging to attract investors and businesses. The deep waters of Victoria Harbour provide ideal conditions for berthing and handling all types of vessels, and Hong Kong is one of the busiest ports in the world in terms of shipping movements, cargo handled and passengers carried.

ICONIC ITERATIONS: THE TRANSFORMATION OF THE CONVENTION CENTRE

> Right at the height of the confidence crisis over Hong Kong's future, in the early 1980s, we announced that we'd build a Convention and Exhibition Centre. This announcement was an extraordinary positive step at a time when so many people wondered whether Hong Kong had a future at all.
>
> (Sarah Monks, TDC Director of Special Duties; quotation transcribed Trade Development Council, 2006)

As the Trade Development Council grew, the organisation outgrew its existing physical space. The pressures led to lobbying by various influential members from the business community in TDC for an increase in exhibitions and conference facilities. In 1964, the Hong Kong Tourist Association had commissioned a London firm to make recommendations on a special conference and exhibition trade fair facility. The Association pursued the concept, but financial resources and problems in site selection made implementation a challenge. During the period of 1970–1975, the chairman of the TDC, Sir Y.K. Kan, persuaded the government to consider that, 'with conventions, the exhibitions can enhance Hong Kong's image ... in trade not only do you have to be good, you have to show other people that we are good. That is really what trade promotion is all about' (Chambers, 1989: 92). Via various global networks and local 'guanxi' relations the private consortium Jardine, Matheson & Co., Ltd and the HSBC collaborated on a plan for a future Convention Centre. The result, the thirty-eight-storey building World Trade Centre adjacent to the Excelsior Hotel in Causeway Bay, was completed in 1975. The first three floors of the building's podium had meeting and reception areas that hosted more than 3,500 people, and banqueting space for 2,500 people.[16] It hosted numerous events, including the successful annual Ready-to-Wear Festival, which by 1976 was the highlight on TDC's calendar promotion and eventually led to a Hong Kong fashion showcase in Paris (Chambers, 1989: 79).[17] Such events elevated the status of the Convention Centre, but soon exceeded the available facilities (see Figure 13.7). People started to consider building another, even larger convention hall.

With the 1980 recession and the 1982 downturn in trade, the clamour for a new facility died down, but it picked up again with economic recovery in 1983. The campaign for a centre included many players, such as Hon. Lydia Dunn (appointed Chairman of the TDC in 1983), who 'represented the textbook example of a consensus politician: cool, calm, a powerful image of the territory's establishment'.[18] Talks and 'informal contacts', trade talks and key missions involving the Colony Governor, Sir Edward Youde, continued between Chinese and British parties in the midst of larger negotiations over Hong Kong's future.[19] In 1984, these Sino-British talks succeeded in establishing Hong Kong's independence. In accordance with the 'One country, two systems' principle agreed to and signed by Prime Ministers Zhao Ziyang and Margaret Thatcher, of the People's Republic of China (PRC) and the United Kingdom, respectively, Hong Kong's capitalist system would remain the same

Figure 13.7 Hong Kong Convention and Exhibition Centre showing its first phase, 1988 (source: courtesy of the HKCEC).

for fifty years, until 2047. This produced a renewed sense of commitment among businesspeople, and they continued to invest in the territory. In early 1985, the government granted the TDC a 7.7 acre (3.1 hectare) waterfront site in Wan Chai for its new convention and exhibition centre for a term of seventy-five years at a crown rent of HK$1,000 per year (Chambers, 1989: 104). The site's constraints produced a system of vertically stacked large conference rooms and meeting sections, equal to nine to twelve storeys off the street. The architectural massing, building structure and presence dominated the harbourfront (see Figure 13.8).

At the ground-breaking ceremony for the Hong Kong Convention and Exhibition Centre (HKCEC), Dunn said, 'I have no doubt when completed in 1988, the Centre will become another landmark representing Hong Kong's dynamism and ingenuity and its importance in the trading world' (Chambers, 1989: 104). In October 1986, Queen Elizabeth II laid the foundation stone of this new trade icon, and the TDC put up an exhibit called 'Showcase Hong Kong', displaying 3,000 high quality products (generally those typically presented to an overseas audience) from 472 companies. The construction was completed in thirteen months, with the selling point 'multi-functional flexibility'. Moreover, it would allow the local trading and manufacturing community to intermingle with international buyers. At its opening, multiple conferences and exhibitions were already booked for a few years in advance.

Here British colonial politics and private business enterprise showcase Hong Kong's marketing and manufacturing strength in a bold physical iconic

Figure 13.8 Hong Kong Convention and Exhibition Centre showing its full expansion, 2009 (source: courtesy of the HKCEC).

presence on the waterfront. The deal marked Hong Kong's unique strategic position, both financially and economically, during its time as a Special Administrative Region in its anticipated handover to China in 1997.

THE TRADE DEVELOPMENT COUNCIL TODAY

Ambitious architectural icons, container port terminals, waterway connections to Mainland China, and Hong Kong's status as the Special Administrative Region of China – in all of these domains we can see that the TDC played a central role in the rapid modernisation of Hong Kong. Through image building and exhibitions abroad, Hong Kong became a brand, utilising water and shipping themes to influence urban planning in general, and land reclamation. The TDC's global trade exhibitions and image campaigns can be understood as strategies that parallel the dynamic use of the waterways. Like the movement of goods, burgeoning maritime links, and ever-expanding shipping links between hinterland China and Europe, images and exhibitions manifest the power of collective intelligence and collaboration.

Hong Kong continues to act as a gateway and mediator between China and the rest of the world. From the ever-growing promotion networks of global capital, TDC's role now geographically extends further inland to mainland China because of the enlarging territory of trade manufacturing facilities in the greater Pearl River Delta and the consumption patterns within Hong Kong itself. These relationships demonstrate the power of economic and social interest that shift the identity of Hong Kong as a strategic site for exchange economically and creatively.

The port city of Hong Kong today is no longer centred on trade, but on financial power and creative industries. The new International Financial Centre (IFC) building in the Central District marks it as 'Asia's world city', a slogan adopted by the Hong Kong Special Administrative Region

Government under 'Brand Hong Kong'. (A project launched in 2001 by the Hong Kong Economic and Trade Offices, the Brand Hong Kong campaign is aimed at key business and government audiences overseas and on the Chinese mainland. It was coordinated by the Government's Information Services Department, and helps to create initiatives that communicate Hong Kong's competitive positioning.) With the new International Commercial Centre development (ICC) across the harbour in the future planned West Kowloon Cultural District, the IFC frames the new iconic skyline of the Hong Kong and Kowloon peninsula as one connected conceptual image at the harbourfront. Culture is on one side, and finance and trade on the other, both necessary to brand and build Hong Kong as a 'creative metropolis', a term that Bauhinia Foundation Research Centre (2007) (a local think tank) proposed for a policy submission paper on Hong Kong's creative positioning (*Hong Kong: A Creative Metropolis*). It notes that to maintain an advantage over other cities, 'Hong Kong is not just about the pursuit of economic growth or efficiency; but also about innovation, creativity and convergence of talents'. In contemporary Hong Kong, older industrial neighbourhoods such as Shep Kip Mei and Kwun Tong are becoming sites of new development for cultural and creative industries, while the urban waterfront of West Kowloon, on newly reclaimed land, anticipates future culture-led growth. Architecture and urbanism in the skyline are celebratory, as companies cultivate new identities and a global urban image.

Represented by the prominent Convention Centre on the Wan Chai waterfront, the port today is undergoing another new expansion. In 1988, HKCEC's original size was 193,750 sq. feet (18,000 sq. metres); in June 1997 at the handover from the British to the Chinese, its first expansion increased the space to 681,162 sq. feet (63,282 sq. metres); further expansion brought the Centre to 893,889 sq. feet (83,045 sq. metres) of exhibition space in 2009. The TDC not only promotes trade and services but now promotes Hong Kong at international art fairs and innovative technology conventions. On the recent updated website of BrandHK (BrandHK.gov.hk), the Convention Centre photograph dominates the website as an icon of 'enterprising', overlaid with keywords like 'efficient', 'resilient', 'can-do spirit', 'entrepreneurial' and 'industrious' as representations of Hong Kong's dominating culture. City marketing and branding have a concrete influence on urban design and architecture; and these campaigns help to propel Hong Kong into the future as a global creative metropolis.

NOTES

1 Annual Reports by the Director of Commerce and Industry, Archives of HK Public Records Office, 1951–1954.
2 Annual Reports by the Director of Commerce and Industry, Archives of Hong Kong Public Records Office, 1951–54.
3 Annual Reports by the Director of Commerce and Industry, Archives of Hong Kong Public Records Office, 1953–54.
4 Correspondence memo from the Director of Commerce and Industry, 14 January 1956, Archives of Hong Kong Public Records Office.
5 Report of the Working Committee on Export Promotion, 1 January 1966.

6 Hong Kong TDC Meetings, Council Papers, Archives of Hong Kong Public Records Office, 12 October 1966–16 June 1967.

7 Hong Kong TDC Meeting minutes, Archives of Hong Kong Public Records Office, 12 October 1966–16 June 1967.

8 Hong Kong TDC Meeting minutes, Archives of Hong Kong Public Records Office, 21 June 1973: letter from T.D. Sorby, Executive Director of TDC to Colonial Secretariat on the subject of *Land for Industry*.

9 Hong Kong TDC Nairobi Office – monthly reports, Archives of Hong Kong Public Records Office: 2.

10 Hong Kong TDC papers, 15 March 1967, Archives of Hong Kong Public Records Office.

11 Hong Kong TDC papers, 17 May 1967.

12 Hong Kong Government Annual reports, 1970: n.p.

13 Hong Kong Government Information Service Daily Bulletin, 8 June 1967: 3, Archives of Hong Kong Public Records Office.

14 Hong Kong TDC papers, minutes of the 4th meeting, 17 February 1968, Archives of Hong Kong Public Records Office.

15 12 August 1971 SCMP; Archives of Hong Kong Public Records Office.

16 *South China Morning Post*, 'The Hong Kong Convention Centre opening', Hong Kong, 4 September 1975: 9.

17 Hong Kong TDC papers on Hong Kong Ready-to-wear Festival, Archives of Hong Kong Public Records Office.

18 Green, Shane, 'A tear shed for Hong Kong', *South China Morning Post*, 14 February 1989.

19 Chung, Daniel, 'Informal contacts will continue', *South China Morning Post*, 10 December 1983.

14 DUBAI'S JEBEL ALI PORT
Trade, territory and infrastructure

STEPHEN J. RAMOS

> The decision to develop a modern port facility in Dubai proved to be one of the most enlightened taken during Sheikh Rashid's reign, for Dubai's exceptional port facilities and the subsequent foundation of the Free Zone at Jebel Ali have contributed more, perhaps, than any other innovation to the present success which Dubai enjoys.
>
> (Al-Gurg, 1998: 80)

Oil has historically been a mixed blessing for many countries in the developing world (Hayami, 1997).[1] But for the emirate of Dubai, oil profits funded a quick path to industrialisation (see Figure 14.1). When oil was discovered in Dubai in 1966, it was clear from the beginning that it would be a limited source of capital, and that complementary and diversified strategies would have to be developed in order to secure future wealth accumulation. In the 1970s, Dubai's economic diversification strategy would emphasise large-scale industrial infrastructure investment to help absorb liquidity from oil revenues and stave off the inflation that often accompanied oil profits (Morgan, 1979).

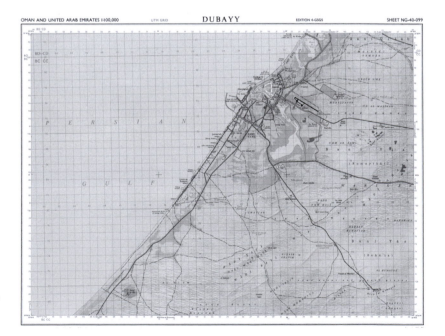

Figure 14.1 Map of Dubai, 1970; Mount Jebel Ali is located in the lower left corner near Abu Dhabi border (source: Motivate Publishing (Copyright C Motivate Publishing 2002)).

230

Dubai was a latecomer to both oil discovery and industrialisation (not discovering oil offshore until 1966), but was a clear beneficiary of those events in the first part of the century. It is located in the lower Gulf region, and before 1971 was a sheikhdom that was part of a larger British protectorate system known as the 'Trucial States'. Throughout the nineteenth and early twentieth centuries, British interests were mainly focused on the peaceful passage of their trade routes through the region. Oil discovery in Persia and Saudi Arabia at the beginning of the twentieth century, and shortly thereafter in Kuwait and Bahrain, brought a greater British involvement. Tumultuous political and economic events during the 1960s provoked the British government to withdraw all interests east of the Suez Canal by the end of 1971. With six other emirates, Dubai formed the federation of the United Arab Emirates (UAE) that year.[2] Nevertheless, a clear developmental blueprint had been established under the British protectorate throughout the Gulf based on oil and oil-based industrialisation: imported labour employed from the Asian Subcontinent for the construction industries, an emphasis on trade infrastructure to facilitate the boost in imports that oil profits precipitated, the export of the region's oil, and, later, those products that were oil derivatives.

The primary oil-based infrastructure that Dubai constructed was a port complex, the Jebel Ali Port, Industrial Area and Free Zone. Here, global trade networks made imprints on local territorial imperatives. Jebel Ali projects included the participation of British consultants for engineering, planning and architecture; incorporated free zone policies established throughout the British Empire; were influenced by US company towns and British Garden Cities; and imported Korean and Japanese equipment and technical expertise (Broeze, 1999: 181–185; Walker, 1984). Outward-looking, large-scale trade infrastructural facilities characterised Dubai's development over the past half-century, including the Dubai International Airport, Port Rashid, the World Trade Centre, Jebel Ali and the future Al-Maktoum International Airport. These large-scale, capital-intensive projects were managed by international joint ventures that brought international, skilled labour and industrial technology to the projects, which the emirate lacked, for potential knowledge and technology transfer (Al-Shamsi, 1999). This interface between global networks and local geography is the core dynamic of port cities, whose urban 'patterns ... are derived from and recondition economic, social, and political activities and values' (Konvitz, 1978: 6). Indeed, the emirate is best understood as a port geography, whose ancillary sectors and investments grew out of its central trade ambitions.

SITING JEBEL ALI PORT

Dubai has always been a city of merchants. The city's cosmopolitan vitality has its origins in the bustling trade activity in and out of its central creek. Dubai's first deep-water port – Port Rashid – was commissioned before the discovery of oil in 1965. By this time, increased trade along the creek continued to serve the construction and oil exploration boom of the 1960s, but an expanded deep-water port was needed to alleviate the month-long queues of ships waiting to unload cargo. Sheikh Rashid summoned the British Sir

William Halcrow and Partners engineering group to begin surveys for the new port just south of the Creek's entrance. Port Rashid opened in 1972, and by 1973 it had thirteen fully operational berths. With increased oil revenues and imports precipitated by 1973's international events, the offshore queue of ships waiting to dock at the new port spiked again. From 1972 to 1976, dead-weight tonnage offloaded at Port Rashid jumped from 600,000 to 3.4 million, and the number of days required for a ship to offload cargo went from six in 1974 to sixty in 1976 (Walker, 1984). By May 1976, Sheikh Rashid commissioned another expansion of Port Rashid, which was to increase its capacity to thirty-seven berths by 1980.

With imports increasing dramatically, by 1972 Dubai's leadership was already thinking of another larger port complex. As the story goes, consultants from Halcrow accompanied Sheikh Rashid bin Saeed Al-Maktoum – then ruler of Dubai – on his walks as he looked over the landscape for the right spot for the new port. The consultants suggested a location then known as Chicago Beach, named after the industrial company from Chicago that built the floating oil storage structures known as 'khazzans' (now called 'Jumeirah Beach'). This was closer to the city centre than Jebel Ali, and coastal currents would allow the new port to have a shorter approach channel (Davidson, 2008; Fleming, 2005). But Sheikh Rashid had other plans, and he decided to locate the new port at Jebel Ali (see Figure 14.2).

Jebel Ali is located close to the border with neighbouring emirate, Abu Dhabi. Members of the British navy mention the area of Jebel Ali variously as 'Gebil Ali', 'Jebel 'Alí', 'Jabal-al 'Ali' and 'Jabail' in their journal entries, and in 1864 one of these writers described it as 'the only hill on this coast ... in Dibai [sic] territory: it is 220 feet high, flat-topped, and lies 19 miles south-west of Dibai town and 4 miles inland, being separated from the sea by a strip of low desert' (Trench, 1994: 304). 'Jebel' means 'hill' or 'mount' in Arabic, and the Jebel Ali mount is one of the few examples of exposed rock made of sediment salt deposits near the UAE coast (Gabriel, 1987). In the early 1950s, it was one of Dubai's first onshore oil-drilling test sites, known as 'Bab One' (Davidson, 2008: 100), but after proving fruitless, exploration moved off-shore.

In late 1966, the government constructed a radio station here, although the location was still a contested territory with Abu Dhabi. In February 1968, however, Sheikh Rashid met with his Abu Dhabi counterpart Sheikh Zayed bin Sultan Al Nahyan at the border town of Al-Sameeh, where it was agreed that Abu Dhabi would cede the Jebel Ali territory to Dubai as a largely symbolic gesture to help facilitate their 1971 federation as the United Arab Emirates (Wilson, 2006; al Abed, 2001). The rulers also agreed that Abu Dhabi would be the temporary capital of the UAE until a new capital city could be built at the mutual border with Dubai (al Abed, 2001).

The announcement to build Jebel Ali came in August 1976, only months after the announcement to expand Port Rashid in May. The Port Rashid expansion was to make it the largest in the Gulf region, with thirty-seven berths, but shortly afterward Jebel Ali was to become the largest man-made port in the world, with 15 km (9.3 miles) of waterfront and sixty-seven

Figure 14.2 Jebel Ali Port construction, 1977 (source: Halcrow).

berths. The Jebel Ali Port, Industrial Area and Free Zone marks a definitive historical moment when Dubai's global aspirations were first realised through port engineering and construction.

PLANNING MINA JEBEL ALI PORT: TECHNOLOGICAL INNOVATION

When Sheikh Rashid announced the construction of the Jebel Ali project in 1976 he hired the Halcrow International Partnership as chief consultant for a joint venture that included the Gulf Colba group for land dredging, and the newly formed Mina Jebel Ali Construction Company, as the organisation in charge of managing, designing and building the port and industrial area (Halcrow International Partnership, 1979). Construction began soon after. Along with the rise in international oil prices and increased regional revenues, other incentives for port expansion throughout the Gulf, and in Dubai in particular, were technological innovation, specifically the container revolution in shipping, and wave study science.

The plans for Port Rashid's extension project included two berths that would be equipped with cranes to handle containers, roll-on/roll-off facilities (ro-ro) and lighter aboard-ship systems (LASH), located on a larger internal breakwater that Halcrow built on top of a large swath of reclaimed land. Mina Jebel Ali was to amplify the emirate's gamble on new port technology with many more ambitious container berths, using port equipment imported from Japan and South Korea, who by this time were important trading partners for Dubai oil (Broeze, 1999; Walker, 1984). Sheikh Rashid also signed an agreement with the US Sea-Land Company, the pioneer of containerisation, to manage the new port (Owen, 1978). By the early 1970s, containerisation was spreading throughout the world, and Malcolm McLean's Sea-Land was the premiere company for shippers interested in container transport and for port managers looking to expand trade routes. After signing the agreement to manage the new Jebel Ali Port, which was to open its initial container berths and services in 1979, Sea-Land initiated its first container routes to India in 1980. Sea-Land viewed the management of the Jebel Ali Port as an important stronghold for the region, and a strategic point for throughput for the new container route to India (see Figure 14.3).[3]

Technological innovation also helped to shape the port's site. The port design for Mina Jebel Ali was informed by research conducted on a 1:120 hydraulic model constructed at the Hydraulic Research Station at Wallingford in the United Kingdom. The model generated data on channel alignment and breakwater positioning so as to minimise wave activity for both the approach channel and the areas below and above the port's entrance (Halcrow International Partnership, n.d.: 2). Waves came predominantly from the northwest, and after running tests using both hydraulic and mathematical models, researchers found that a bend was required in the entrance channel, preferably as close to the entrance as possible, to maximise the energy of wave generation off the channel entrance. Construction of the inland berth areas involved massive dredging and excavation, and the sand and earth brought up were mainly compacted on the adjacent site to elevate it appropriately for industrial use (see Figure 14.4).

Figure 14.3 Image of original container cranes and transit sheds at Jebel Ali Port, 1980 (source: Halcrow).

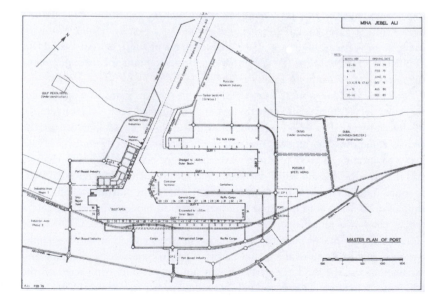

Figure 14.4 Jebel Ali Port and Industrial Area in plan, 1978 (source: Halcrow).

PLANNING THE PORT: INDUSTRIALISATION

The Jebel Ali port complex closely resembled the marine industrial development area (MIDA) projects launched in post-war Europe and Japan. MIDAs located industrial production and processing facilities next to ports for export- and re-export-oriented economic activity (Vigarié, 1981). Of these projects, Mina Jebel Ali most closely resembles the Japanese model, incorporating what is known as the *horikomi* method of heavy land reclamation and excavation in previously 'sandy or swampy zones' that was central in achieving the Japanese economic miracle of post-war recovery from 1960 to 1975 (Vigarié, 1981; Rimmer and Taniuchi, 1989). This resemblance is not a coincidence, for, as mentioned, Dubai maintained a close trading relationship with Japan through oil exportation, and in return received Japan's expertise and technology transfer in port management and machinery (see Figure 14.5).

The Jebel Ali agglomeration was strategically comprised of the Dubai Aluminium Company (DUBAL), an aluminium smelter and extrusion plant; Dubai Gas Company (DUGAS), a liquefied petroleum and natural gas works to process gas from the offshore oilfields that also produced the energy to run DUBAL; the Dubai Cable Company (DUCAB) for the production of electric cables; and a desalination and steam power station run by the heat energy output produced by DUBAL. Oilfield services and other related activities,

Figure 14.5 Map of Dubai, 2006, predicting a future of more major projects (source: Dubai GIS Center).

Note
The map shows infill development between creek and Jebel Ali along Sheikh Zayed Road, the main corridor closest to the coast and running parallel.

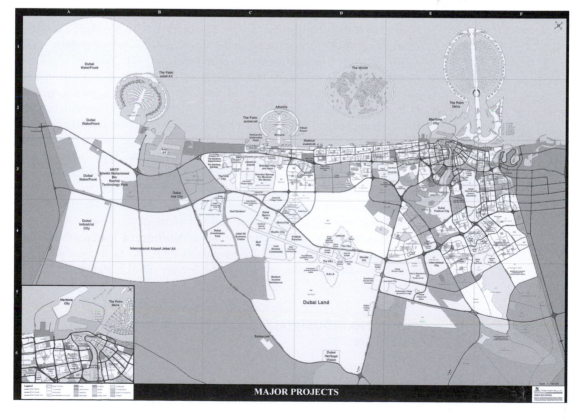

MAJOR PROJECTS

particularly those of the Shell Oil Company, previously located along the creek, would also be relocated to the new industrial site. The natural gas for DUGAS was generated from offshore oil extraction. While the industrial elements were perhaps not as important as the trade platform created here, the resources at the site would be useful for some degree of import-substitution industry for autonomous production, and these elements would help pave the path for the future light manufacturing activity in the area. In addition, while other industrial areas had been established along the creek, near Port Rashid and close to the airport, the scale of Jebel Ali's industrial component attracted much of the emirate's industrial activity, thus freeing up land closer to the creek and what was still considered 'downtown' Dubai in the original settlement around the creek at the northeast of the emirate.

PLANNING THE PORT AS A REGIONAL GROWTH POLE/GROWTH CORRIDOR

The regional planning and development literature (Friedmann and Weaver, 1979; Hoyle and Pinder, 1981) of this period proposed that cities respond to the increased spatial demands of port and cargo technology by expanding or relocating ports, particularly in France, England and the Netherlands. Moreover, planners often deployed 'growth-pole' theory as a way to both understand and plan for regional dynamics, specifically infill development along the corridors connecting new or expanded port facilities to the city centre (Dawson, 1996; Hoyle, 1996; Richardson, 1978). The British architect John Harris, who authored Dubai's first master plan in 1960, developed a second master plan in 1970 as a response to the accelerated urban growth of the 1960s. When Harris published the second plan in 1971, Mina Jebel Ali had not yet been commissioned. Harris proposed a ring-radial structure for the emirate, centred on the creek. In the first part of the 1970s, new large-scale projects, Port Rashid and the Dry Docks in Al-Shindigah, counterbalanced the Deira Corniche land reclamation project on the northeast side of the creek; the creek thus remained the central element and the urban growth axis for Harris's ring-radial structure. The tipping of this balance began with the construction of the World Trade Centre facility, followed by the National Cement Company locating further to the southwest in the first Al-Quoz industrial area. These moves can be understood as incremental changes from the 1971 Plan, but it was the Jebel Ali Port and Industrial Zone, with its superlative scale, that truly broke with Harris's ring-radial structure. It established a new growth pole and growth corridor perpendicular to the Gulf coast along the Abu Dhabi–Dubai Road (which would become Sheikh Zayed Road) (see Figure 14.6).

PLANNING INDUSTRIAL/CAPITAL NEW TOWN: SOBERED AMBITION

In September 1976, Sheikh Rashid commissioned the British architectural consultants Peddle, Thorpe, Chapman and Taylor (PTCT) to develop a master plan for the Jebel Ali New Town (port and airport facilities were to

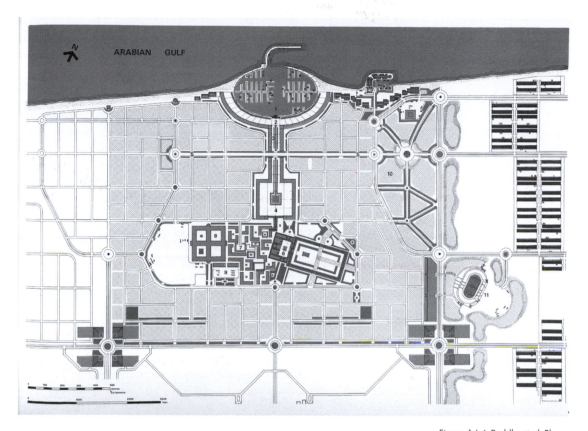

ARABIAN GULF

Figure 14.6 Peddle *et al.* Plan for Jebel Ali New Town, 1977 (source: by permission of Rodney Carran of Chapman Taylor).

be designed and overseen by Halcrow separately). Although the Dubai population at this time was little over 250,000 (Emirate of Dubai, 2003), Sheikh Rashid proposed an entire new town appendage as a part of the new industrial port complex. Some suggested that the Jebel Ali new city could become the capital of Dubai, and it was originally planned as the capital of the entire UAE.

A new town would give the emirate a dual urban system – the original walled settlement plus the new industrial/capital city of Jebel Ali – and change Dubai's regional shape. It would split complementary functions, 'Jebel Ali becoming the main industrial location with its port and airport providing for full international needs, and Dubai continuing to develop as the social, commerce and administrative centre' (Peddle *et al.*, 1977: 4). The guidelines Sheikh Rashid provided PTCT with for the commission offer an insight into the ruler's priorities for an infrastructure-led urbanism:

> Provide the conceptual framework for future development and examine and suggest the layout of the infrastructure of the area … Examine the provision of basic services, i.e. water, drainage and power supplies, and suggest how they might be accommodated and provide information on the basic road and transportation network … Liaise closely throughout with Halcrow Middle East Limited the consultants retained for the new

port and airport project ... Restricted timetable dictated by the fact that construction work on the harbour and some of the basic industries had commenced and it was essential to establish an overall framework for the town and the basic infrastructure provision.

(Peddle *et al.*, 1977: 1)

PCTC's plan suggested four phases, to be completed by 2007, with high, medium and low population and employment projections for the new town, along with programmatic square-metre projections for economic developments, and the corollary number of schools, health clinics and hospitals required for growth projections. Heavy industry is located just north of the port, there is a band that connects the port to the airport via a free zone, and another band of light industry is located to the southwest of the port. The new town centre is located further to the southwest, divided from the light industrial area by a thin strip of parkland, and circular residential areas are located both to the southwest of the town centre and just north of the heavy industrial area, where they meet with the existing residential areas of Jumeirah. The town centre includes a waterfront corniche around a small recreational port, with a monumental axis moving inland toward a main square. Finally, the PTCT plan also included an elevated mini tram for public transportation throughout the new town, and northward to the new residential areas projected just south of the Jumeirah district.

Whether because of inside political agreements, the fall in oil prices or the belief that the UAE, and Dubai in particular, had overextended its large-scale investments, or a combination of these factors, with political economic sobriety the Jebel Ali New Town project was scaled back significantly, and very little of the PTCT plan was built. By 1977, plans for the airport at the Jebel Ali New Town had already been dropped, and Dubai and Abu Dhabi had agreed to allow the latter to retain capital status for the UAE. The Jebel Ali projects that remained also indicated Dubai's overall urbanisation priorities: along with the port and industrial projects, the only remnants of the new town plan were an expatriate residential enclave described in the first phase of the PTCT plan, and a luxurious hotel with a small recreation port. Each project was structured as a joint venture to be managed, again, by Halcrow, who would also serve as architects for each project. The Jebel Ali Hotel and its marina was a 'luxury class' facility to properly receive and accommodate international industrialists at the Jebel Ali location, without them having to travel to Dubai. The hotel complex was completed in 1981 (see Figure 14.7).

Halcrow also designed the residential Jebel Ali Village, three hundred two- and four-bedroom detached units, plus a community centre, a primary school, and a small clinic and supermarket. They modelled it essentially on both the US company town and the British Garden City, with 30 metre × 30 metre (98.4 × 98.4 feet) residential plots (Sir William Halcrow and Partners, n.d.). The Village was initially built to house the professional team working on the Jebel Ali project, but was projected to eventually be passed over to those who would work at the functioning port complex. The isolated and autonomous residential area of Jebel Ali Village would serve as a model typology for future

Figure 14.7 Jebel Ali Hotel, 1983 (source: Halcrow).

semi-autonomous residential areas throughout Dubai (i.e. the Gardens, Emirates Hills, Jumeirah Lakes, etc.), along with the shopping malls in the southwestern end of the emirate that were aimed at serving these residential community districts (see Figure 14.8).

THE FREE ZONE: PLANNING FOR TRADE

Finally, continuing Dubai's tradition of free port policy inherited from the British, and a strong history of preferential merchant policies to attract regional trade routes, project plans from the late 1970s forward proposed that Jebel Ali should be an economic free zone. The Free Zone is an important example of how spatial organisation and political and economic policy mutually informed one another throughout Dubai's development. In 1984, Abu Dhabi passed the Commercial Companies Law, based on the *kafil* system, which stipulated that the only way for international firms to set up offices or factories throughout the UAE was through complex sponsorship agreements with local entities, wherein the local firms would assume 51 per cent ownership (Davidson, 2008: 114). Restrictive land laws prevented foreign companies from owning land.[4] In this unusual context, the Jebel Ali Free Zone opened in 1985, adjacent to the port. It began as a 10,000 hectare (24,711 acre) facility (with 42,000 sq. metres (452,084 sq. feet) dedicated to cold storage) for transhipment and re-export, particularly for goods passing

Figure 14.8 Jebel Ali Village, 1985 (source: Halcrow).

along the East Asia–Europe corridor (Broeze, 1999: 178). As the percentage of import/export for Dubai and the Gulf region hinterland grew, there was an increasing need for processing and assembly functions in the Free Zone. Sheikh Rashid was able to sidestep the federal law by allowing international firms to rent warehouse and small processing facilities in Dubai without having to find sponsorship. As Michael Pacione describes:

> Jebel Ali free zone [opened] in 1985 as an enclave where businesses could operate outside Dubai's customs and legislative barriers and benefit from a ready supply of low wage non-unionised labour. By 1995, Jebel Ali accommodated ... 800 firms from 72 countries, and included many major multinational corporations such as Nokia, Daewoo and Reebok seeking to penetrate the markets of the Arabian Gulf-Arab World ... The shift to higher value added manufacturing is evident in the Jebel Ali free zone where, as the economy has matured, attempts have been made to attract more high technology industries (such as assembly of computers and electronic equipment), and to phase out labour intensive industries (such as textile processing), dependent on expatriate labour.
>
> (Pacione, 2005: 257)

Thus the character of logistics and manufacturing activities has changed over time, just as the profile of the port and Dubai's economic aspirations have changed (see Figure 14.9).

Figure 14.9 Contemporary satellite image of Jebel Ali Port, Industrial Area and Free Zone, 2007 (source: Halcrow).

COMPETING INFRASTRUCTURE IN THE 1980S

Sheikh Rashid's cluster of trade and industrial projects grew throughout the 1970s, superseding first the scale of regional projects, and then outdoing the scale of any comparable global project. At the time, however, industry experts worried that these projects were overambitious and would become 'white elephants'. Concerns over local operating capacity were matched with the potential of Gulf port oversupply as a result of the construction boom, due to a general lack of regional project coordination. Indeed, the Dubai Aluminium Company (DUBAL) at Jebel Ali was modelled on Aluminium Bahrain (ALBA), which predated it, and the Jebel Ali Port itself was very similar to the ambitious Saudi port projects of Jubail and Yanbu (Korea Development

241

Institute, 1980). Concerns regarding oversupply were well founded: 'By the early 1980s laid up tonnage, especially tanker and dry-bulk, reached record levels (internationally) and was reflected in low levels of activity at many ports which only a few years earlier had been frantic in their efforts to expand facilities to accommodate rapidly increasing trade' (Hoyle and Hilling, 1984: 6). Firms engaged in rate-cutting competition throughout the region in the early 1980s when oil prices fell (Walker, 1984).

What could not have been predicted, however, was the Iranian revolution in February 1979, along with the subsequent conflict between Iran and Iraq throughout the 1980s that, once again, solidified Dubai's geographic position in the lower Gulf as a transhipment centre for the entire Gulf Cooperation Council (GCC) – the larger regional council formed in 1981 specifically to confront the regional economic downturn of the period. Attacks on commercial ships in the Gulf during the Iran–Iraq War opened an opportunity for Dubai to receive international cargo flows and re-route them for local and regional distribution (Pacione, 2005; Walker, 1984). This increased transhipment throughput was redirected to Dubai's two ports, away not only from Iran and Iraq, but also from Kuwait in the northern Gulf. The United States Navy began to use Jebel Ali as a regional port for its ships (today it is the most frequented non-US port in the world),[5] thus adding an element of military protection that is more traditionally provided by a port's country.

While falling oil prices would still greatly affect Dubai's growth rate (particularly compared with the vertiginous numbers of the 1970s), regional conflict, in its own way, provided a degree of economic stability for Dubai by spurring increased regional trade through its ports. Dubai was able to take advantage of events within the region, identify them as opportunities for its own benefit, and provide both facilities and policies to capitalise on these trade-related opportunities.

THE LEGACY

In 1988, the office of the Greek architect and planner Constantinos A. Doxiadis published the Dubai Urban Area Plan in a series of reports that detailed an exhaustive inventory of the land usage and resources of the metropolitan area. The Urban Area Plan made this insightful observation:

> Development of spatial growth in the urban area will essentially conform with past practices. That is, the majority of the growth will occur on an East–West axis extending from the Central Business District (CBD) to the airport, with the majority of infill development occurring in a North–South axis extending from the CBD to Jebel Ali.
>
> (Dubai Municipality, 1988: xiii)

Doxiadis's team understood that Dubai's urbanism historically followed the growth corridors established by large-scale infrastructure projects, and projected that future circumstances would follow the same pattern. Meanwhile, the new town and most of its residential surroundings would not be revisited until 2005, when Rem Koolhaas would be commissioned to design a new

'Waterfront City' in its place. With present international financial circumstances, it is likely that these projects will also return to a kind of hibernation until forecasts improve.

Jebel Ali succeeded in spite of recessionary downturns and the fall in oil prices in the region during the 1980s, and the various components that made up the Jebel Ali mega-project mark a 'before and after' moment for Dubai. The force and impact of Jebel Ali on Dubai's territorial organisation and growth coordinates were definitive. Jebel Ali served as a growth pole, and established a growth corridor that would guide infill development through today, as the corridor between Jumeirah and Jebel Ali was subdivided into a mosaic of superblocks for residential, commercial and limited industrial use. These regional dynamics were codified in the plans for the port and its components. They were also emphasised in Sheikh Rashid's development priorities for the new town project, which was eventually scaled back. In this regard, Jebel Ali was all the more indicative of Sheikh Rashid's understanding of urbanism and urbanisation as a series of clustered, strategic infrastructures-within-infrastructure. He reduced urbanism to clear, modern, discrete interworking parts, organised toward the objectives of trade, production and economic gain.

The scale of the Jebel Ali project gives one the impression that all the previous infrastructural endeavours of Sheikh Rashid – land dredging and reclamation, industrial areas, trade facilities, residential development, hotel infrastructure for tourism, free port policies and the airport – were all smaller sketches for the master work that was to be Jebel Ali Port, Industrial Area and Free Zone. If infrastructure is traditionally understood in urbanism as a blanket element to guide development through systems located underground (water), at ground level (roads) or above ground (electricity), within a modernisation process, Jebel Ali is a clear example of infrastructure as epic; infrastructure as monument; infrastructure as growth corridor (including the systems of roads, water, electricity) and growth axes (the creek and then Sheikh Zayed highway); and infrastructure as growth pole, as Doxiadis's plan wisely observed. Jebel Ali also marks the abandonment of master planning in Dubai for mega-projects with autonomous spatial logics.

NOTES

1   Hayami refers to this 'mixed blessing' as the 'Dutch disease', describing potential developmental retardation because of a country's oil assets.
2   The UAE is comprised of seven emirates, which include Abu Dhabi, Dubai, Sharjah, Ras al-Khaima, Fujairah, Umm al-Qaiwain and Ajman.
3   Sea-Land online archive, www.mgar.net/sealand2.htm. Morgen Henning, Records Management, A.P. Moller-Maersk.
4   The land law of 1960 established that non-nationals could not own land in Dubai, similar to the Kuwaiti land law which had already been passed. The 2002 land law in Dubai established freehold areas where non-Emiratis could own land, but this was primarily for residential development.
5   See Global Security, www.globalsecurity.org/military/facility/jebel-ali.htm. A laundry and swimming pool facility is located at the Jebel Ali for the US Navy, called the Kasbah Liberty Center, run by the United Services Organisation (USO).

15 CONCLUSION AND OUTLOOK
Mapping global networked urban form (in port cities)

CAROLA HEIN

Figure 15.1 The Chinese port of Canton, probably painted by a Chinese artist for European customers, shown with European merchant houses and Chinese boats that brought the goods from the large European sailing ships discharged 20 km (12 miles) away, around 1860 (source: Museum für Hamburgische Geschichte).

This volume sketches the reach and power of networked analysis using the example of port cities, aiming to showcase a new approach for sustained research that provides a basis for an interconnected analysis of built and urban form. Acknowledging that networks of trade help to form the built environment of port cities, as this volume does, allows us to trace the shifting importance of various centers around the globe and to read their built environment through multiple influences. It gives us a tool to study physical impact on urban form that results from real and virtual geographies, from shifts (and crashes) in financial flows, from migration, or from environmental transformation. By proposing to follow the ship, the trader, the container, or other aspects of networks into its urban locations and to investigate what happens in the built environment, it allows us to include symbolic architecture as well as the vernacular (see Figure 15.1).

New mapping techniques and capacities need to be explored to allow various disciplines to connect, for architectural historians, planners, economists, or sociologists to interact and converse. A global and multi-layered map of port design through history, of the construction of finger-piers, or container ports, overlaid with a map of concrete flows of goods and people, or the evolution of railway stations in ports and their connection to the hinterland could advance the proposed networked analysis. New kinds of data collection and research, based on diverse data series coming from historians, economists, or sociologists, could be integrated to find new and innovative ways of understanding evolutionary processes through a networked analysis of the built environment. For example, the opening of the Panama Canal and the consequent reshaping of shipping lanes are well documented by geographers and could provide a basis for a networked analysis of the cities affected by this change, allowing for a truly global appreciation of the transformation (Philip, 1922) (see Figure 15.2).

Conversations with the various professionals, decision-makers, and citizens involved in specific projects, such as waterfront revitalization, would be another story to pursue in this search for a networked analysis of port cityscapes. These extensive exchanges between professionals promise to be a gold mine for researchers. For example, consider planning historian David Gordon's account of his time with the Toronto waterfront redevelopment agency in the 1980s in a letter to the author in September 2010:

Figure 15.2 George Philip, reshaping of shipping lanes after the opening of the Panama Canal, 1922 (source: David Rumsey Map Collection, www. davidrumsey.com).

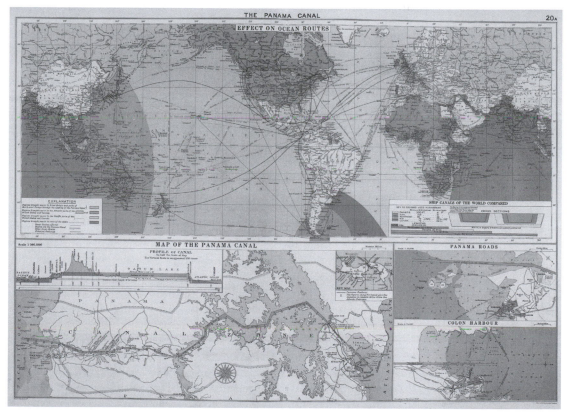

It slowly dawned upon us that our city was not the only one struggling to re-purpose and re-image its abandoned waterfront. There was no text-book on how to redevelop a waterfront – we were all making it up as we went along. It was amazing to watch as a new network of knowledge emerged after designers and politicians toured the various projects that had achieved early success, especially Baltimore and Boston. It seemed like we were receiving visitors from different cities almost every week in 1985 and we were soon comparing ideas in conferences and exchanges of staff, developers, and consultants. We then watched in astonishment as the local developer Olympia & York quickly moved from the Queen's Quay Terminal project on the Toronto harbourfront to develop mixed use projects in Boston, San Francisco and New York. It appeared that their run had come to an end with the spectacular 1992 bankruptcy at Canary Wharf, only to see the firm re-emerge with a network of interna-tional capital to buy back the project and complete it during the next decade.

(Gordon, personal communication)

Besides drawing on such personal accounts (in interviews and memoirs), researchers could seek records of travel itineraries of leaders of other redevel-opment agencies, or of professional tourist groups visiting exhibitions on these waterfront redevelopments. Furthermore, as Gordon's career history indicates, practice and academia were closely connected. Another example is that of Benjamin Thompson, designer of Quincy Market and Harborplace, who was also Chairman of the Department of Architecture at the Harvard Graduate School of Design, another institution with global reach (Frieden and Sagalyn, 1989).

Advertisements of major shipping companies, the linkages they establish between distant locations through advertisements for maritime travel, and the buildings the companies showcase provide another theme for research. In a different field, the study of the machinery used in the construction of land rec-lamation projects, or of the big cranes that serve global ports, would allow us to identify other networks. More generally, as this volume shows, if networks of trade and transport shaped port cities at a certain time, they also comprise personal, physical, and other relationships that persist beyond the reasons for which they were initially created. It is worth investigating how they continue to allow cities to address new themes of common interest, such as the trans-formation of former harbor areas or the redefinition of identity after port functions move. A consideration of networked ecologies, of fauna and flora arriving via shipping lanes, or of food systems, and their networked expres-sion in the built environment would lead to a better understanding of various networks and their local impact; port cities can be appropriate catalysts for that research.

Why these studies matter is further illustrated by an example from my research on the global architecture of oil. The switch from coal to oil as a fuel for ships as well as a cargo was another major technological change that we have not examined extensively in this book, but it has extensively reshaped maritime networks. It merits further investigation (and is part of my separate book project). The discovery of petroleum, its extraction, refinement, and intense use as fuel for machines have created and transformed shipping realms and port cities around the world. As production and consumption sites have been located in different parts of the world, major American and European oil companies created port installations in Indonesia, Russia, the Middle East, or South America. Their interests helped create and shape new ships (tankers, first), new shipping passages such as the Suez Canal, new harbor installations, and new port cities. A map established by BP showing the global flow of oil gives an idea of the enormous amount of just one product being mostly shipped (only at times pumped by pipelines) between continents (see Figure 15.3).[1] An analysis of financial movements that correspond to these flows of petroleum can reveal the concrete number of dollars that correlate with the new buildings and enormous urban transformation that have emerged in the Persian Gulf area. While new construction there has been studied by writers on architecture, making visible the connections between these buildings and their multiple networks of research, design, materials, funding, etc. would allow us to understand the hidden identities and specific agendas of these linked places.

But although it focuses on port cities, this volume more largely calls for multiple disciplines to come together to create a networked analysis of the built environment as a whole, to read historical and contemporary cities and buildings and their connections in dynamic, interdisciplinary, and exciting ways. This conclusion looks beyond port cities to suggest that there are many more case studies to be developed, whether deploying the categories outlined

Figure 15.3 Oil trade movements in 2009 (source: copyright BP).

Major trade movements 2009
Trade flows worldwide (million tonnes)

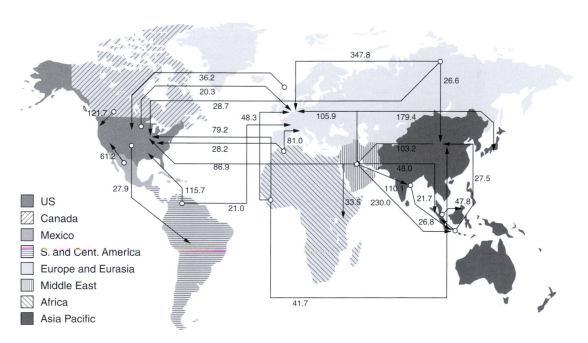

US
Canada
Mexico
S. and Cent. America
Europe and Eurasia
Middle East
Africa
Asia Pacific

in the introduction (global networks, regional processes, dynamic landscapes) or using other terms. A networked analysis, as highlighted through the chapters of this book, offers a new viewpoint, providing a tool to study old and new dynamics in the world, and not just in research. Using maps for studies of architectural and urban form offers fruitful possibilities. Some architectural history books have started to use maps to demonstrate the simultaneous spatial presence of similar architectural styles as well as diverse approaches to the built environment in the West and around the world (Ching *et al.*, 2006; Steer and White, 1994). These scholars concentrate on architectural monuments, placing them in their context of time and space. The present book takes this approach further.

Whether historical or explicitly current, networked analysis of the built environment can illuminate multiple topics. Consider an investigation of Versailles that would explore the provenance of its building materials, workers, and design concept; featuring, for example, the copper mine and associated town of Falun in Sweden that provided the copper used for its roofs in the seventeenth century. Placing the analysis of the Palace next to that of the mining town, studying the export flows and income of the mine in relation to the construction of the town and palace (even though they are spatially separate) opens up new perspectives in the study of global architectural and urban form. Or consider geographical maps that feature the trading ranges of merchants in Tallinn, or the map room of the Doge of Venice that was painted in the sixteenth century, or that of Francesco II Gonzaga of Mantua in the 1490s, who had a room decorated with wall paintings that featured eight cities, arranged to alternate maritime cities with inland ones – "Constantinople, Rome, Naples, Florence, Venice, Cairo, Genoa and, as the eighth city, possibly Paris or Jerusalem" (Bourne, 1999: 52). These maps raise a range of new questions: Beyond the practical use of geographical maps, why did powerful people feature trading routes and destinations in private and public buildings, visible every day? Did it shape the development of architecture and urban form in the cities of Tallinn, Venice, or Mantua?

Mapping and analyzing the impact of global connections on the built environment can help us trace simultaneous developments that respond dynamically to outside incentives. As networks change in extent, duration, stability, or type of participants, they influence the design and transformation of new buildings and landscapes. Industrialization and globalization in the nineteenth and twentieth century exponentially increased networks, as the chapters in this book show. Many other sites beyond port cities still await research, even as huge changes continue to unfold. They should yield new insight into the importance of networks through time, the long-term impact of globalization on built form, and on ways in which networks of elites and their buildings for administration, housing, leisure, and other purposes differ from earlier ones. Now, in a time of increased globalization, a networked analysis will allow us to explore beyond the borders of a single city, region, or country, to learn how specific economic activities influence the built environment and social conditions in distant locations. One can thus imagine a study of working-class housing and industrial design in India or China linked to administrative headquarters and residences in American suburbs, replacing research that would have mapped the social impact of economic activities in a single city. This approach would reveal hidden identities as well as city branding achievements and opportunities (Donald *et al.*, 2009; Greenberg, 2008), and foster a resonant understanding of any given city as part of networks across time, space, or social boundaries. It will also allow us to investigate the growing virtual character of trade (via the networks of the internet) and its peculiar relationship with the ongoing exchange of actual goods among still-real places and people around the world.

NOTES

1 BP, "Oil trade movements," www.bp.com/sectiongenericarticle.do?categor yId=9023778&contentId=7044199 (accessed 09/14/2010).

BIBLIOGRAPHY

Aerts, Remieg and De Rooij, Piet (2006) *Geschiedenis van Amsterdam*. Amsterdam: Sun.

Aggarwala, Rohit (2002) *Seat of Empire*. New York: Columbia University Press.

Akveld, Leo M. and Bruijn, Jaap R. (eds.) (1989) *Shipping Companies and Authorities in the 19th and 20th Centuries*. The Hague: Nederlandse Vereniging voor Zeegeschiedenis.

al Abed, Ibrahim (2001) Formation and evolution of the federation and its institutions. In: al Abed, Ibrahim and Peter Hellyer (eds.) *United Arab Emirates*. London: Trident Press.

Al-Gurg, Easah Saleh (1998) *The Wells of Memory*. London: John Murray.

Al-Shamsi, Fatima (1999) Industrial strategies and change in the UAE during the 1980s. In: Abdelkarim, Abbas (ed.) *Change and Development in the Gulf*. New York: St. Martin's Press.

Albion, Robert Greenhalgh and Pope, Jennie Barnes (1984) *The Rise of New York Port, 1815–1860*. Boston: Northeastern University Press; reprint of 1939.

Amenda, Lars (2006) *Fremde–Hafen–Stadt*. Hamburg: Dölling und Galitz.

Amenda, Lars (2008) Gateway to the world. In: *Journeys of Expression VII: Celebrating the Edges of the World. Conference Proceedings*, February 29–March 1, Reykjavik, Iceland, compiled and designed by Daniela Carl, Leeds (CD Rom).

Amenda, Lars and Grünen, Sonja (2008) *Tor zur Welt*. Munich: Dölling und Galitz.

American Association of Port Authorities (AAPA) (n.d.) World port ranking, http://aapa.files.cms-plus.com/Statistics/WORLD%20PORT%20 RANKINGS%2020081.pdf (accessed 09/14/2010).

American Association of Port Authorities (AAPA) (2006) statistics from www.aapa-ports.org.

Amin, Naguib (2006) Vers un Lendemain lumineux. In: *Port Saïd, Architectures XIXe–XXe siècles*. Le Caire: IFAO.

Anastassiadou, Méropi (1997a) *Salonique 1830–1912*. Leiden: Brill.

Anastassiadou, Méropi (1997b) Sports d'élite et élites sportives à Salonique au tournant du siècle. In: Georgeon, François and Dumont, Paul (eds.) *Vivre dans l'Empire ottoman*. Paris: L'Harmattan.

Ander, Hans and Ekman, Johan (2001) *Norra Älvstranden: The Process*. Gothenburg: City Planning Authority and Norra Älvstranden Utveckling AB.

Anon. (1957) *Dokumente vorbildlichen Wiederaufbaues der Hansestadt Hamburg*. Hamburg: van Yperen Verlag.

Anon. (2005) V&A exporting expertise. *Cape Business News*, 29 June, at www.cbn.co.za/dailynews/787.html (accessed 28/10/2008; this item has subsequently been removed from the website).

Antunes, Catia (2005) *Globalisation in the Early Modern Period*. Leiden/Amsterdam: Aksant.

Armytage, Frances (1953) *The Free Port System in the British West Indies*. London: Longmans.

Arvind Palat, Ravi (1991) Symbiotic sisters. In: Kasaba, Reşat (ed.) *Cities in the World System*. London: Greenwood Press.

Association Internationale Villes et Ports (n.d.) www.aivp.org/spip.php?sommaireandlang=en (accessed 06/01/2010).

Atay, Çınar (1997) *19. Yüzyıl İzmir Fotoğrafları*. Istanbul: Akdeniz Medeniyetleri Araştırm.

Atay, Çınar (1998) *Osmanlı'dan Cumhuriyet'e İzmir Planları*. İzmir: Yaşar Eğitim ve Kültür Vakfı.

Autoridad Portuaria de Santander (ed.) (1998) *La memoria del territorio*. Santander: Autoridad Portuaria de Santander.

Baggerman, W. (1994) *700. De zevenhonderd van Rotterdam*. Rotterdam: Gemeente Rotterdam.

Baillère, Henri (1867) *En Egypte, 1867*. Paris: J.B. Baillère et fils.

BallinStadt(n.d.)www.ballinstadt.net/BallinStadt_emigration_museum_Hamburg/english_BallinStadt_das_Auswanderermuseum_Hamburg_besonderes_Ausflugsziel_Ausflugsort_Erlebnisort_Freizeit_leisureworkgroup_Geschaeftsfuehrer_Jens_Nitschke_Berater_Museen_Fachmann_Entwicklung_Konzeption_Design_Erlebniswelt_Erlebnismuseum.html (last accessed 09/15/2010).

Baltic Sail (2010) www.balticsail.info/2010/start.htm (accessed 09/15/2010).

Barnekov, Timothy, Boyle, Robin, and Rich, Daniel (1989) *Privatism and Urban Policy in Britain and the United States*. Oxford: Oxford University Press.

Bartels, Olaf (1991) Hamburgs Elb-Gesichter. In: Höhns, Ulrich (ed.) *Das ungebaute Hamburg*. Hamburg: Junius.

Barth, Hans (1893) *Unter südlichem Himmel*. Leipzig: Renger.

The Bauhinia Foundation Research Centre (2007) *Hong Kong: A Creative Metropolis*, www.bauhinia.org/publications/CreativeSubmissionPaper_ENG.pdf.

Bayly, Christopher A. (2004) *The Birth of the Modern World, 1780–1914*. Oxford: Oxford University Press.

Beaverstock, Jonathan. V. (2002) Transnational elite communities in global cities. In: Mayr, Alois, Meurer, Manfred, and Vogt, Joachim (eds.) *Stadt und Region*. Leipzig: Deutsche Gesellschaft für Geographie.

Bense, Max (1949) *Technische Existenz*. Stuttgart: Deutsche Verlags-Anstalt.

Bentley, Jerry H., Bridenthal, Renate, and Wigen, Kären (eds.) (2007) *Seascapes*. Honolulu: University of Hawai'i Press.

Benton, Gregor and Gomez, Edmund Terence (2008) *The Chinese in Britain*. Basingstoke/New York: Palgrave Macmillan.

Berchère, Narcisse (1863) *Le Désert de Suez*. Paris: Hetzel.

Bergère, Marie-Claire (1998) *Sun Yat-sen*. Stanford, CA: Stanford University Press.

Bernard, Henri (1934) *Le Frère Bento de Goes chez les musulmans de la Haute-Asie*. Tientsin: Hautes Etudes.

Berov, Ljuben (1985) The course of commodity turnover at the Thessalonica port and the West European economic cycle in 19 C. up to 1912. *Etudes balkaniques* 4: 72–88.

Bethencourt, Francisco and Curto, Diogo Ramada (2007) *Portuguese Oceanic Expansion, 1400–1800*. Cambridge: Cambridge University Press.

Bianchini, Franco (2006) European urban mindscapes. In: Weiss-Sussex, Godela and Bianchini, Franco (eds.) *European Studies: Urban Mindscapes of Europe*. New York: Rodopi.

Bilbao Acedos, Amaya (2003) *The Irish Community in the Basque Country*. Dublin: Geography Publications.

Binder, Gertrude (1929) New buildings in Shanghai. In: Rea, George B. (ed.) *The Far Eastern Review*. Manila/Shanghai: G.B. Rea.

Bixby, William (1972) *South Street: New York's Seaport Museum*. New York: David McKay.

Bläsing, Joachim (1973) *Das goldene Delta und sein eisernes Hinterland 1815–1851*. Leiden: Stenfert Kroese.

Bloom, Nicholas D. (2004) *Merchant of Illusion*. Columbus: Ohio State University Press.

Blussé, Leonard (1981) *Companies and Trade*. Leiden: Leiden University Press.

Bone, Kevin, Bone, Eugenia, and Betts, Mary Beth (1997) *The New York Waterfront*. New York: Monacelli.

Bono, Salvatore (2006) Il Canale di Suez. *Mediterranea. Ricerche storiche* 8: 411–422.

Bonz, Gunther (2006) *Die wirtschaftspolitische Bedeutung des Hafens für Hamburg*. Hamburg: Jahrbuch der hafenbautechnischen Gesellschaft.

Borchard, Rolf Reiner Maria (1992) *Die Hamburger Elbchausseee*. Berlin: Ernst und Sohn.

Borscheid, Peter (2004) *Das Tempo-Virus*. Frankfurt am Main: Campus.

Bortolotti, Landro (1970) *Livorno dal 1748 al 1958*. Florence: Olschki.

Bose, Michael, Holtmann, Michael, Machule, Dittmar, Pahl-Weber, Elke, and Schubert, Dirk (eds.) (1986) *"...ein neues Hamburg entsteht... ": Planen und Bauen von 1933–1945*. Hamburg: VSA-Verlag.

Boswell, Terry, Misra, Joya, and Brueggeman, John (1991) The rise and fall of Dutch hegemony. In: Kasaba, Reşat (ed.) *Cities in the World System*. London: Greenwood Press.

Bourne, Molly (1999) Francesco II Gonzaga and maps as palace decoration in Renaissance Mantua. *Imago Mundi* 51: 51–82.

Boxer, Charles R. (1969) *The Portuguese Seaborne Empire*. London: A.A. Knopf.

Boyce (R. H.) (n.d.) Mr. Boyce's reports to Secretary of Works on Legations and Consulates, Public Records Office, Kew, WORKS 10–56/6: 77.

Bracker, Jörgen (1981) Am Endpunkt des Gezeitenstroms. In: Bracker, Jörgen and Prange, Carsten (eds.) *Alster, Elbe und die See: Hamburgs Schiffahrt und Hafen in Gemälden, Zeichnungen und Aquarellen des Museums für Hamburgische Geschichte*. Hamburg: Das Topographikon.

Bracker, Jörgen (1989) *Die Hanse*. Hamburg: Schmidt-Römhild.

Braudel, Fernand (1979) *Civilisation matérielle, économie et capitalisme XVe–XVIIIe siècle*. Paris: Colin.

Braudel, Fernand (1998) *Das Mittelmeer und die mediterrane Welt in der Epoche Philipps II.* Frankfurt am Main: Suhrkamp.

Braudel, Fernand (2001) *Les Mémoires de la Méditerranée.* Paris: Editions de Fallois.

Breen, Ann and Rigby, Dick (1994) *Waterfronts.* New York: McGraw-Hill.

Breen, Ann and Rigby, Dick (1996) *The New Waterfront.* London: Thames and Hudson.

Brockey, Liam Matthew (ed.) (2008) *Portuguese Colonial Cities in the Early Modern World.* Farnham, UK/Burlington: Ashgate.

Broeze, Frank (ed.) (1989) *Brides of the Sea.* Honolulu/Kensington, NSW: University of Hawai'i Press/New South Wales University Press.

Broeze, Frank (1991) Albert Ballin: the Hamburg–Bremen rivalry and the dynamics of the conference system. *International Journal of Maritime History* 3: 1–32.

Broeze, Frank (1995) *Maritime History at the Crossroads.* St. Johns, Canada: International Maritime Economic History Association.

Broeze, Frank (ed.) (1997) *Gateways of Asia.* London: Kegan Paul International.

Broeze, Frank (1999) Dubai. In: Fisher, L.R. and Jarvis, A. (eds.) *Harbours and Havens.* St. Johns, Canada: International Maritime Economic History Association.

Broeze, Frank (2002) *The Globalisation of the Oceans.* St. John's, Canada: International Maritime Economic History Association.

Broodbank, J. (1921) *The History of the Port of London.* London: Daniel O'Connor.

Brown, Peter H. (2009) *America's Waterfront Revival.* Philadelphia: University of Philadelphia Press.

Brownill, Sue (1993) *Developing London's Docklands.* London: Paul Chapman Publishing.

Brownill, Sue (1994) Selling the inner city. In: Gold, John R. and Ward, Stephen V. (eds.) *Place Promotion.* Chichester: John Wiley and Sons.

Bruttomesso, Rinio (1983) *Waterfront – A New Urban Frontier.* Venice: International Centre Cities on Water.

Bruttomesso, Rinio (1993) *Waterfronts: A New Frontier for Cities on Water.* Venice: International Centre Cities on Water.

BTA Architects Inc. (n.d.) www.bta-architects.com/c/portfolio_.html (accessed 05/01/2010).

Burrows, Edwin G. (1999) *Gotham.* New York: Oxford University Press.

Burton, Valerie (2001) Boundaries and identities in the nineteenth-century English port. In: Gunn, Simon and Morris, Robert J. (eds.) *Identities in Space.* Aldershot/Burlington: Ashgate.

Busch, Harald and Sloman, Ricardo Federico (1974) *Das Chilehaus in Hamburg.* Hamburg: Christians Verlag.

Buse, Dieter K. (2008) Encountering and overcoming small-city problems. *Journal of Urban History* 35: 39–52.

Cadell, Christopher, Falk, Nicholas, and King, Francesca (2008) *Regeneration in European Cities.* York: Joseph Rowntree Foundation.

Callahan, Maureen (1981) *The Harbor Barons.* Ann Arbor, MI: University Microfilms International.

Cambridge Seven Associates Inc. (n.d.) www.c7a.com/Portfolio/aquariums/index.asp (accessed 06/01/2010).

Carmichael, Ann G. (2003) Bubonic plague. In: *The Cambridge Historical Dictionary of Disease.* Cambridge: Cambridge University Press.

Carroll, John M. (2007) *Edge of Empire*. Hong Kong: Hong Kong University Press.

Cartwright, H.A. and Wright, Arnold (1908) *Twentieth Century Impressions of Hong Kong, Shanghai, and other Treaty Ports of China*. London: Lloyd's Greater Britain Publishing Company.

Cassis, Youssef (1994) *City Bankers 1890–1914*. Cambridge: Cambridge University Press.

Çelik, Zeynep (1986) *The Remaking of Istanbul*. Seattle: University of Washington Press.

Cesarani, David and Romain, Gemma (eds.) (2006) *Jews and Port Cities 1590–1990*. London/Portland, OR: Valentine Mitchell.

Chambers, Gillian (1989) *Supertrader*. Hong Kong: Hong Kong Trade Development Council.

Chan Wai Kwan (1991) *The Making of Hong Kong Society*. Oxford: Clarendon Press.

Chan, Wellington K.K. (1998) Personal styles, cultural values, and management. In: MacPherson, Kerrie (ed.) *Asian Department Stores*. Honolulu: University of Hawai'i Press.

Chan, Wellington K.K. (1999) Selling goods and promoting a new commercial culture. In: Cochran, Sherman (ed.) *Inventing Nanjing Road*. Ithaca, NY: Cornell University Press.

Charles-Roux, Jules (1901) *L'Isthme et le canal de Suez*. Paris: Hachette.

Chatziioannou, Maria Cristina (2005) Greek merchant networks in the age of empires (1770–1780). In: McCabe, Ina B., Halfatis, Gelina and Minoglou, Iōanna Pepelasis (eds.) *Diaspora Entrepreneurial Networks*. Oxford: Berg.

Checkland, Sydney and Checkland, Olive (1984) *Industry and Ethos: Scotland, 1832–1914*. Oxford: Wallingford.

Chesneaux, Jean (1968) *The Chinese Labour Movement, 1919–1927*. Stanford, CA: Stanford University Press.

China Correspondence, British Foreign Office. Public Records Office, Kew, FO 17/373, dispatch no. 101 April 1862.

Chinese Manufacturers' Association of Hong Kong (1973) *Kompass: A Register of HK Industry and Commerce*. Summary of Trade Development Council from Chinese Manufacturers' Association of Hong Kong. 3rd ed. Hong Kong: Kompass.

Chinese Manufacturers' Association of Hong Kong (1994) *The Chinese Manufacturers' Association of Hong Kong*. Hong Kong: The Association.

Ching, Francis D.K., Jarzombek, Mark M., and Prakash, Vikramaditya (2006) *A Global History of Architecture*. Chichester: John Wiley and Sons.

Christaller, Walter (1969 (1933)) *Die zentralen Orte in Süddeutschland*. Darmstadt (Jena): Gustav Fischer.

Christiansen, Flemming (2003) *Chinatown Europe*. London: Routledge.

Christopoulos, Marianna D. (2007) Greek communities abroad. In: Pan-Montojo, Juan (ed.) *Communities in European History*. Pisa: Pisa University Press.

Church, Robert F. (1968) *Case Studies: Containerization*. Evanston, IL: The Transportation Center at Northwestern University.

Cini, Umberto (2007) La Trajectoire de deux communautés marchandes à Livourne entre le XVIe et le XXe siècle. In: Bruneau, Michel, Hassiotis, Ioannis, Hovanessian, Martine, and Mouradian, Claire (eds.) *Arméniens et Grecs en diaspora*. Athens: Ecole Française d'Athènes.

Cody, Jeffrey W. (2001) *Building in China*. Seattle: University of Washington Press.

Cody, Jeffrey W. (2003) *Exporting American Architecture, 1870–2000*. London: Routledge.

Cohen, Jean-Louis (1995) *Scenes of the World to Come*. Paris/Montreal: Flammarion/Canadian Centre for Architecture.

Cohen, Jean-Louis and Damisch, Hubert (eds.) (1993) *Américanisme et modernité*. Paris: Flammarion.

Cohen, Jeffrey (2008) The fabric of a maritime city: streetscapes and building patterns of mid-19th century Philadelphia as a port. Presentation at the Port Cities conference at Bryn Mawr College, November 16, 2008. Bryn Mawr, Bryn Mawr College.

Cohen, Paul and Augustyn, Robert (1997) *Manhattan in Maps, 1527–1995*. New York: Rizzoli.

Colonas, Vassilis (2008) L'Apport des archives privées grecques. Communication on the occasion of the presentation of the research project "L'Isthme de Suez," Agence Nationale de la Recherche, Paris, April 18.

Commemorative Organisation for the Japan World Exposition '70 (n.d.) www.expo70.or.jp/e/index.html.

Condit, Carl (1980) *The Port of New York*. Chicago: University of Chicago Press.

Connolly, James (2008) Decentering urban history. *Journal of Urban History* 35: 3–14.

Container Committee (1966) *Report of the Container Committee*, December: 7, Hong Kong: Government Printer.

Containerisation International Yearbook (1971–1980) London: Informa.

Cook, Ian (2004) *Waterfront Regeneration*. School of Geography, University of Manchester Spatial Policy Analysis Working Paper no. 51. Manchester: University of Manchester.

Coquery-Vidrovitch, Catherine and Georg, Odile (eds.) (1996) *La Ville européenne outre mers: un modèle conquérant?* Paris/Montreal: L'Harmattan.

Corbin, Alain (1988) *Le Territoire du vide*. Paris: Aubier.

Corbin, Alain (1994) *The Lure of the Sea*. Cambridge: Polity.

Corbin, Alain (1999) *Meereslust*. Frankfurt am Main: Fischer.

Crosnier Leconte, Marie-Laure (2006) Histoires, architectures. In: *Port Saïd: architectures XIXe–XXe siècles*. Le Caire: IFAO.

Crow, Carl (1933, reprinted 1984) *Handbook for China*. Oxford: Oxford University Press.

Davidson, Christopher (2008) *Dubai*. New York: Columbia University Press.

Davis, Colin J. (2003) *Waterfront Revolts*. Urbana/Chicago: University of Illinois Press.

Davis, Ralph (1973) *The Rise of the Atlantic Economies*. Ithaca, NY: Cornell University Press.

Dawson, Andrew H. (1996) Cityport development and regional change. In: Hoyle, Brian (ed.) *Cityports, Coastal Zones, and Regional Change*. Chichester: John Wiley and Sons.

De Antonellis Martini, Liana (1968) *Portofranco e Communità etnico-religiose nella Trieste Settecentesca*. Milano: A Giuffrè.

De Goey, Ferry and Van de Laar, Paul (1995) Scheepsfinanciering. *Tijdschrift voor Zeegeschiedenis* 14, special issue: 23–61.

De Klerk, Leo, Van de Laar, Paul, and Moscovier, Herman (2008) *G.J. de Jongh*. Bussum: Uitgeverij Toth.

De Nijs, Thimo (2001) *In veilige haven*. Nijmegen: Sun.

Delaforce, J. (1990) *The Factory House at Oporto*. London: Christopher Helm Publishers.

Delaney, Enda and MacRaild, Donald W. (eds.) (2007) *Irish Migration Networks and Ethnic Identities since 1750*. London: Routledge.

Denison, Edward and Ren, Guang Yu (2006) *Building Shanghai*. Chichester: Wiley-Academy.

Dennys, Nicholas B., King, Charles, and Mayers, William (1867) *The Treaty Ports of China and Japan*. London: Trubner and Company.

Desplaces, Ernest (1859) *Le Canal de Suez*. Paris: Librairie Hachette et Cie.

Dogo, Marco (1996–1997) Merchants between two empires. *Etudes balkaniques* 32–33: 85–96.

Doig, Jamieson W. (2001) *Empire on the Hudson*. New York: Columbia University Press.

Dolowitz, David P. and Marsh, David (1996) Who learns what from whom?, *Political Studies* 44: 343–357.

Dolowitz, David P. and Marsh, David (2000) Learning from abroad. *Governance* 13: 5–24.

Donald, Stephanie Hemelryk, Kofman, Eleonore, and Kevin, Catherine (eds.) (2009) *Branding Cities*. New York: Routledge.

Downs, Jacques (1997) *The Golden Ghetto*. Bethlehem, PA: Lehigh University Press.

Driesen, Oliver (2010) *Welt im Fluss*. Hamburg: Hoffmann und Campe.

Driessen, Henk (2005) Mediterranean Port Cities: Cosmopolitanism Reconsidered. *History and Anthropology* 16(1): 129–141.

Du-Plat-Taylor, Francis Maurice (1949) *The Design, Construction and Maintenance of Docks, Wharves and Piers*, 3rd edn, London: Eyre and Spottiswode.

Dubai Municipality (1988) *Dubai Urban Area Plan*. Report No. 5, May: xiii.

Dubin, Lois (1999) *The Port Jews of Habsburg Trieste*. Stanford, CA: Stanford University Press.

Dubin, Lois (2004) "Wings on their feet … and wings on their head": reflections on the study of port Jews. In: Cesarani, David and Romain, Gemma (eds.) *Jewish Culture and History* 7: 1–2.

Ducher, Daniel (1989) Docks de Londres. *Urbanisme* 229: 22–25.

Dülffer, Jost, Thies, Jochen, and Henke, Josef (1978) *Hitlers Städte. Baupolitik im Dritten Reich*. Cologne/Vienna: Böhlau.

Dumont, Paul (1992) Le Français d'abord. In: Veinstein, G. (ed.) *Salonique, 1850–1918: la "ville des juifs" et le réveil des Balkans*. Paris: Editions Autrement.

Düwel, Jörn and Gutschow, Niels (2008) *Fortgewischt sind alle überflüssigen Zutaten: Hamburg 1943*. Berlin: Lukas-Verlag.

Echenberg, Myron (2007) *Plague Ports*. New York: New York University Press.

Echenberg, Myron (2008) Port cities and public health: control measures against bubonic plague, 1900–1950. Presentation at the Port Cities conference at Bryn Mawr College, November 16, 2008. Bryn Mawr, Bryn Mawr College.

Echinard, Pierre (1973) *Grecs et philhellènes à Marseille*. Marseille: Institut Historique de Provence.

Editorial (1982) Londres: Contrastes et mutations. *Urbanisme* 190/191: 74–75.

Edwards, Brian (1992) *London Docklands*. Oxford: Butterworth Architecture.

Eilers, Reimer (2009) *Das neue Tor zur Welt*. Hamburg: Mareverlag.

Ellermeyer, Jürgen and Postel, Rainer (eds.) (1986) Stadt und Hafen. Hamburg: Christians Verlag.

Elliott, John H. (2007) *Empires of the Atlantic World*, London: Yale University Press.

Emirate of Dubai (2003) *Dubai Population Census*. Dubai: Dubai Statistics Centre.

Engel, Dorothée (2003) *Der Jungfernstieg*. Hamburg: Die Hanse in der europäischen Verlagsanstalt.

Enterprise Real Estate Services [formerly Enterprise Development Company] (n.d.) www.ereserve.com/spec.html (accessed 07/06/2005; note that this site has subsequently been removed from the web).

Esenbel, Selçuk and Chiharu, Inaba (2003) *The Rising Sun and the Turkish Crescent*. Istanbul: Boğaziçi University Press.

Esherick, Joseph (ed.) (1999) *Remaking the Chinese City*. Honolulu: University of Hawai'i Press.

Evans, Richard J. (1987) *Death in Hamburg*. Oxford: Clarendon Press.

Fainstein, Susan (2001) *The City Builders: Property Development in New York and London, 1980–2000*. Lawrence: University Press of Kansas.

Fainstein, Susan (2008) Mega-projects in New York, London and Amsterdam. *International Journal of Urban and Regional Research* 32: 768–785.

Farris, Johnathan (2004) Dwelling on the edge of empires: China. Ph.D. dissertation, Cornell University.

Farris, Johnathan (2007) Thirteen factories of Canton. *Buildings and Landscapes* 14: 66–82.

Faulwasser, Julius (1978 (reprint of 1892)) *Der große Brand und der Wiederaufbau von Hamburg*. Hamburg: Ernst Kabel.

Federal Writers' Project (1982 (reprint of 1939)) *The WPA Guide to New York City*. New York: Pantheon Books/Random House.

Feist Hirst, Elisabeth (1967) *Damião de Góes*. Mouton: The Hague.

Feldman, Gerald D. (1993) *The Great Disorder*. Oxford/New York: Oxford University Press.

Feldwick, W. (ed.) (1917) *Present Day Impressions of the Far East and Prominent and Progressive Chinese at Home and Abroad*. London: Globe Encyclopedia Company.

Fennema, Meindert and Heemskerk, Eelke (2008) *Nieuwe netwerken*. Amsterdam: Uitgeverij Bert Bakker.

Ferrara degli Uberti, Carlotta (2004) The "Jewish nation" of Livorno. *Jewish Culture and History* 7: 157–170.

Fischer, Manfred F. (1983) Der Rathausmarkt in Hamburg und die Piazza San Marco in Venedig: zur Chronik eines Mißverständnisses. *Römisches Jahrbuch für Kunstgeschichte* 20: 83–105.

Fleming, Chris (2005) *The Dubai Coastline: The Formative Years*. Swindon: Halcrow Group Ltd.

Floor, Willem (2006) *The Persian Gulf*. Washington, DC: Mage Publishers.

Fontane, Marius and Riou, E. (1869) *Le Canal maritime de Suez illustré*. Paris: Auguste Marc et Cie.

Forbonnais, François Véron Duverger de (1755) *Questions sur le commerce des Français au Levant*. Marseille: Carapatria.

Foster, Janet (1999) *Docklands*. London: UCL.

Frangakis-Syrett, Elena (1992) *The Commerce of Smyrna in the Eighteenth Century, 1700–1820*. Athens: Centre for Asia Minor Studies.

Frangakis-Syrett, Elena (2001) The making of an Ottoman port. *Journal of Transport History* 22: 23–46.

Frank, Hartmut (ed.) (1994) *Fritz Schumacher.* Stuttgart: Hatje.

Frank, Hartmut (2003) Gestus und Gestalt. In: Turtenwald, Claudia (ed.) *Fritz Höger (1877–1949).* Munich/Hamburg: Dölling und Galitz.

Frattarelli-Fischer, Lucia and Villani, Stefano (2007) People of every mixture: immigration, tolerance and religious conflicts in early modern Livorno. In: Issacs, Ann Katherine (ed.) *Immigration and Emigration in Historical Perspective.* Pisa: Edizioni Plus.

Freie und Hansestadt Hamburg, Behörde für Wirtschaft und Arbeit, Hamburg Port Authority, and Gotthardt, Christian (2007) *Im Focus dynamischer Wachstumsmärkte.* Hamburg: Freie und Hansestadt Hamburg.

Freire Costa, Leonor (2004) Merchant groups in the 17th century sugar trade. *Journal of Portuguese Studies* 2(1): 1–11.

Frémaux, Céline (2008) Santé et hygiénisme dans les villes du canal de Suez. *Egypte/Monde arabe* 3(4): 75–101.

Frémaux, Céline (forthcoming) The missionaries in the cosmopolitan towns of the Suez isthmus (Egypt). In: de Meulder, Bruno and de Maeyer, Jan (eds.) *Spatializing the Missionary Encounter.*

Frieden, Bernard and Sagalyn, Lynne (1989) *Downtown Inc.* Cambridge, MA: MIT Press.

Friedmann, John and Weaver, Clyde (1979) *Territory and Function.* Berkeley: University of California Press.

Fröbel, Julius (1891) *Ein Lebenslauf.* Stuttgart: Cotta.

Fuhrmann, Malte (2007) Meeresanrainer – Weltenbürger?, 2, 17, 2007. *Comparativ* 2: 12–26.

Funaro, Liana Elda (2006) Massoneria e minoranze religiose nel secolo XIX. In: Conti, Fulvio (ed.) *La Massoneria a Livorno.* Bologna: Mulino.

Funck-Brentano, Christian (1947) *Compagnie universelle du canal de Suez.* Paris: de Clermont.

Gabriel, E.F. (ed.) (1987) *The Dubai Handbook.* Ahrensburg: Institute for Applied Economic Geography.

Gavin, Angus (1996) *Beirut Reborn.* London: Academy Editions.

Gavrilova, Rayna (2003) Historische Anthropologie der Stadt. In: Kaser, Karl (ed.) *Historische Anthropologie im südöstlichen Europa.* Vienna: Böhlau.

Gekas, Athanasios (Sakis) (2004) The port Jews of Corfu and the 'Blood Libel' of 1891. *Jewish Culture and History* 7: 171–196.

Gekas, Athanasios (Sakis) (2009a) Class and cosmopolitanism: the historiographical fortunes of merchants in Eastern Mediterranean ports. In: Fuhrmann, Malte and Kechriotis, Vangelis (eds.) *The Late Ottoman Port-cities and Their Inhabitants: Subjectivity, Urbanity, and Conflicting Orders*, special issue of the *Mediterranean Historical Review* 24(2): 95–114.

Gekas, Athanasios (Sakis) (2009b) Class and national identities in the Ionian Islands under British rule. In: Beaton, Roderick and Ricks, David (eds.) *The Making of Modern Greece: Nationalism, Romanticism, and the Uses of the Past (1797–1896).* Aldershot: Ashgate.

Georgelin, Hervé (2003) Smyrne à la fin de l'empire ottoman. *Cahiers de la Méditerranée* 67: 125–147.

Georgelin, Hervé (2005) *La fin de Smyrne.* Paris: CNRS Editions.

Georgeon, François and Dumont, Paul (eds.) (1997) *Vivre dans l'Empire ottoman.* Paris: L'Harmattan.

Georgiev, Veličko and Trifonov, Stajko (eds.) (1995) *Makedonija i Trakija v borba za svoboda: Krajât na XIX – načaloto na XX vek*. Sofia: Prosveta.

Gerhardt, Johannes (2009) *Albert Ballin*. Hamburg: Hamburg University Press.

Giannatou [Yannatou], Savina (2000) *Songs of the Mediterranean* (CD), sleeve notes.

Gilbert, David and Driver, Felix (2000) Capital and empire. *GeoJournal* 51: 23–32.

Glaser, R., Haberzettl, P., and Walsh, R.P.D (1991) Land reclamation in Singapore, Hong Kong and Macao. *GeoJournal* 24: 365–373.

Global Harbors: A Waterfront Renaissance Documentary (n.d.) www.global-harbors.org/index.html (accessed 05/01/2010).

Godeaux, Jean and Toulemont, Anne (eds.) (1990) *A Propos des Migrations lessepsiennes*. Monaco: Musée océanographique.

Godoli, Ezio and Giacomelli, Milva (eds.) (2005) *Architetti e Ingegneri dal Levante al Maghreb 1848–1945*. Firenze: Maschietto.

Goffman, Daniel (1999) Izmir. In: Eldem, Edhem, Goffman, Daniel, and Masters, Bruce (eds.) *The Ottoman City between East and West*. Cambridge: Cambridge University Press.

Gonçalves Horta, Jose (2008) Image and Representations of Ireland in Portugal (1830–1925). Unpublished Ph.D. ms., University College Cork, Ireland.

Goodman, David (1997) *Spanish Naval Power, 1589–1665*. Cambridge: Cambridge University Press.

Goor, Jurien Van (1986) *Trading Companies in Asia: 1600–1830*. Utrecht: HES Uitg.

Gordon, David L.A. (1997) *Battery Park City*. Amsterdam: Gordon and Breach.

Goss, Jon (1988) The built environment and social theory: towards an architectural geography. *Professional Geographer* 40: 392–403.

Gottdiener, Mark (1994) *The Social Production of Urban Space*. Austin: University of Texas Press.

Grabher, Gernot (2006) Trading routes, bypasses, and risky intersections. *Progress in Human Geography* 30: 163–189.

Greefs, Hilde (2008) De terugkeer van Mercurius. *Tijdschrift voor Sociale en Economische Geschiedenis* 5(2): 55–86.

Greenberg, Miriam (2008) *Branding New York*. New York: Routledge.

Grenet, Mathieu (2006) La Loge et l'étranger. *Cahiers de la Méditerranée* 72: 225–243.

Grenet, Mathieu (2010) Culte orthodoxe et stratégies communautaires. In: Dumons, Bruno and Hours, Bernard (eds.) *Villes et religions dans l'Europe moderne et contemporaine*. Grenoble: Presses Universitaire de Grenoble.

Grobecker, Kurt (2004) Abschied von einer Idylle. In: Grobecker, Kurt (ed.) *Hafen Hamburg*. Hamburg: Koehlers Verlagsgesellschaft mbH.

Groppe, Hans-Hermann and Wöst, Ursula (2007) *Über Hamburg in die Welt*. Hamburg: Ellert and Richter Verlag.

Guimerá Ravina, Agustín (1985) *Burguesía extranjera y comercio atlántico*. CSIC: Santa Cruz de Tenerife.

Guiter, André (1868) *Lettres et notices sur l'isthme de Suez*. Alexandria: Imprimerie nouvelle.

Gutman, Marta (2008) Race, place, and play. *Journal of the Society of Architectural Historians* 67: 532–561.

HafenCity publications (n.d.) www.hafencity.com/de/presseportal-der-hafencity.html (last accessed 09/29/2010).

Hafenradar Hamburg (n.d.) http://hafenradar.hamburg.de/ (accessed 11/08/2010).

Haglund, Karl (2003) *Inventing the Charles River*. Cambridge, MA: MIT Press.

Hajer, Maarten A. (1993) Rotterdam. In: Bianchini, Franco and Parkinson, Michael (eds.) *Cultural Policy and Urban Regeneration*. Manchester: Manchester University Press.

Halcrow International Partnership (1979) Mina Jebel Ali: Brochure for the Inauguration, on 26th of February, of Mina Jebel Ali. Produced by John Cordery Associates Limited.

Halcrow International Partnership (n.d.) Mina Jebel Ali: Project Information Packet for internal use.

Halcrow, Sir William and Partners (n.d) *Jebel Ali Village City*. Promotional publication.

Hall, Kenneth (ed.) (2008) *Secondary Cities and Urban Networking in the Indian Ocean Realm, c. 1400–1800*. Lanham, MD: Lexington Books.

Hall, Peter (1998) *Cities and Civilization*. New York: Pantheon.

Hall, Thomas (1991) Urban planning in Sweden. In: Hall, Thomas (ed.) *Planning and Urban Growth in the Nordic Countries*. London: Spon.

Halpern, Paul G. (1994) *A Naval History of World War I*. Annapolis, MD: Naval Institute Press.

Harms, Hans (2003) Restructuring of central areas in port cities. In: TU Delft, Alfa-Ibis Network (ed.) *Globalization, Urban Form and Governance*. Delft: TU Delft.

Harms, Hans (2008) Changes in seaport cities, large-scale infrastructure projects to 'modernise' traditional ports in the 19th century: London, Hamburg, Rio de Janeiro. Presentation at the Port Cities conference at Bryn Mawr College, November 16, 2008. Bryn Mawr, Bryn Mawr College.

Harvey, David (1990) *The Condition of Postmodernity*. Oxford: Blackwell.

Harvey, David (2001) *Spaces of Capital*. Edinburgh: Edinburgh University Press.

Hasegawa, Junichi (2003) The rebuilding of Osaka. In: Hein, Carola, Diefendorf, Jeffry, and Ishida, Yorifusa (eds.) *Rebuilding Urban Japan after 1945*. London: Palgrave Macmillan.

Haupt, Adolf (1934) *Guide to Tsingtao and Its Environs*. Qingdao: George G. Talberg's International Bookstore.

Hayami, Yujiro (1997) *Development Economics*. Oxford: Clarendon Press.

Hebebrand, Werner (1957) *Contemporary Architecture and City Planning in West Germany*. New York: Cooper Union for the Advancement of Science and Art.

Hebebrand, Werner (1967) *Städtebau, gestern und heute*. Nuremberg: Städtebauinstitut.

Heimerdinger, Timo (2005) *Der Seemann*. Cologne/Weimar/Vienna: Böhlau.

Hein, Carola (1991) City Nord – die Geschäftsstadt im Grünen. In: Höhns, Ulrich (ed.) *Das ungebaute Hamburg*. Hamburg: Junius.

Heine, Heinrich (2005) *Deutschland. Ein Wintermärchen*. Stuttgart: Reclam.

Heinsohn, Ralf (2006) *Schnellbahnen in Hamburg*. Norderstedt: Books on Demand GmbH.

Hertslet, Godfrey (1908) *Treaties etc. between Great Britain and China and Foreign Powers*. London: Harrison and Sons.

Heseltine, Michael (1987) *Where There's a Will*. London: Hutchinson.

Hietkamp, Lenore (2007) The Park Hotel in Shanghai. In: Kuo, J. (ed.) *Visual

Culture in Shanghai, 1850s–1930s. Washington, DC: New Academia Publishing.

Himer, Kurt (1927) *Geschichte der Hamburg-Amerika Linie, Vol. 2: Albert Ballin*. Hamburg: Gustav Petermann.

Hipp, Hermann (1995) Ein neues Hamburg. In: Meyer-Veden, Hans (ed.) *Hamburg. Historische Photographien 1842–1914*. Berlin: Ernst und Sohn.

Hipp, Hermann (2003) Die Geschichte des Jungfernstiegs. In: Engel, Dorothée (ed.) *Der Jungfernstieg*. Hamburg: Die Hanse in der europäischen Verlagsgemeinschaft.

HKTDC Council Papers (n.d.) HKSAR Government Public Records.

Ho, Pui-Yin (2004) *Challenges for an Evolving City*. Hong Kong: Commercial Press.

Hoffmann, Paul Th. (1977) *Die Elbchaussee*. Hamburg: Broschek Verlag.

Hofland, Peter (1998) *Leden van de Raad*. Amsterdam: Gemeentearchief Amsterdam.

Hohenberg, Paul and Lees, Lynn (1996) *The Making of Urban Europe, 1000–1994*. Cambridge, MA: Harvard University Press.

Hohn, Uta (2008) Von Teleport zu Rainbow Town. In Schubert, Dirk (ed.) *Hafen- und Uferzonen im Wandel*. Berlin: Leue.

Hollamby, Ted and Da Luz, Paul (1988) Londres ouvre ses docklands à l'investissement privé. *Urbanisme* 225: 12–17.

Holme, Thomas (1774) Thomas Holme's description of the city of Philadelphia. In: Reed, John (ed.) *An Explanation of the Map of the City and Liberties of Philadelphia*. Philadelphia: Brooks.

Home, Robert Keith (1997) *Planting and Planning*. London: Spon.

Hong Kong Daily Press (1914) *The Directory & Chronicle for China, Japan, Korea, Indo-china, Straits Settlements, Malay States, Siam, India, etc*. Hong Kong: Hong Kong Daily Press Ltd.

Hong Kong Department of Commerce and Industry (1949) *A Commercial Guide to Hong Kong*. Hong Kong: Ye Olde Printerie.

Hong Kong Government (1970) *Annual Reports*. Hong Kong: Hong Kong Government.

Hong Kong Marine Department (1966–1971) *The Port of Hong Kong*. Hong Kong: Government Printer.

Hopkins, Anthony G. (ed.) (2002) *Globalisation in World History*. London: Pimlico.

Hornbostel, Wilhelm and Klemm, David (eds.) (1997) *Martin Haller*. Hamburg: Dölling und Galitz.

Hoyle, Brian S. (1970) *Seaports and Development in Tropical Africa*. London: Macmillan.

Hoyle, Brian S. (1988) Development dynamics at the port-city interface. In: Hoyle, Brian S., Pinder, David A., and Husain, M. Sohail (eds.) *Revitalising the Waterfront*. London: Belhaven Press.

Hoyle, Brian S. (1989) The port-city interface. *Geoforum* 4: 429–435.

Hoyle, Brian (ed.) (1996) *Cityports, Coastal Zones, and Regional Change*. Chichester: John Wiley and Sons.

Hoyle, Brian Stewart and Hilling, David (1970) *Seaports and Development in Tropical Africa*. London: Macmillan.

Hoyle, Brian S. and Hilling, David (eds.) (1984) *Seaport Systems and Spatial Change*. Chichester/New York: John Wiley and Sons.

Hoyle, Brian S. and Pinder, D.A. (eds.) (1981) *Cityport Industrialisation and Regional Development*. Oxford: Pergamon.

Hoyle, Brian S., Pinder, David A., and Husain, M. Sohail (eds.) (1988) *Revitalising the Waterfront*. London: Belhaven Press.

Huetz de Lemps, Christian (1975) *Géographie du commerce de Bordeaux à la fin du règne de Louis XIV*. Mouton: Paris.

Hugill, Stan (1967) *Sailortown*. London/New York: Frank Cass.

Hyde, Francis E. (1957) *Blue Funnel*. Liverpool: Liverpool University Press.

IBA Hamburg (n.d.a) Mission to Show the Future, www.iba-hamburg.de/en/01_entwuerfe/3_mission/mission_zukunftzeigen.php. (accessed 03/28/2011)

IBA Hamburg (n.d.b) www.iba-hamburg.de/en/00_start/start.php (accessed 10/13/2010).

Imrie, Robert and Thomas, Huw (eds.) (1999) *British Urban Policy*. London: Sage.

In de Rotterdamsche China-Town (1922) *Het Leven*, March 27.

India Office Records (c. 1822) Canton Agency Consultations. British Library, G/12/229.

Ingham, Michael (2007) *Hong Kong*. Oxford/Hong Kong: Signal Books/Hong Kong University Press.

Israel, Jonathan I. (1989) *Dutch Primacy in World Trade 1585–1740*. Oxford: Clarendon Press.

Jackson, Kenneth T. (ed.) (1995) *The Encyclopedia of New York City*. New Haven, CT/New York: Yale University Press/The New York Historical Society.

Jacobs, Wouter, Ducruet, Cesar, and De Langen, Peter W. (2010) Integrating world cities into production networks: the case of port cities. *Global Networks* 10: 92–11.

Jones, Geoffrey G. (2000) *Merchants to Multinationals*. Oxford: Oxford University Press.

Kamen, Henry (2003) *Spain's Road to Empire*. London: Penguin Books.

Karstedt, C. and Worm, T. (1999) Container. *Mare* 12: 58–65.

Kasaba, Reşat, Keyder, Cağlar, and Tabak, Faruk (1986) Eastern Mediterranean port cities and their bourgeoisies. *Review* 10: 121–135.

Katsiardi-Hering, Olga (1986) *I elleniki paroikia tis Tergestis (1751–1830)* [The Greek parish of Trieste (1751–1830)]. Athens: National Capodistrian University Press.

Katsiardi-Hering, Olga (2001) La presenza dei Greci a Trieste. In: Finzi, Roberto and Panjek, Giovanni (eds.) *Storia economica e sociale di Trieste, vol. I*. Trieste: LINT.

Kauder, E. (1900) *Reisebilder aus Persien, Turkestan und der Türkei*. Breslau: S. Schottlaender.

Keeling, David J. (2005) Waterfront redevelopment and the Puerto Madero Project in Buenos Aires, Argentina. In: Chabrera, Vicent Ortells, Kent, Robert B. and Martí, Javier Soriano (eds.) *Cities and Urban Geography in Latin America*. Serie Colección Américas. Castellon de la Plana: Publicaciones Universitat Jaume I.

Kennedy, Charles Stuart (1990) *The American Consul*. New York: Greenwood Press.

Kennedy, Christopher (2011) *The Evolution of Great World Cities*. Toronto: University of Toronto Press.

Kerr, Alfred (1920) *Die Welt im Licht, vol. II: Du bist so schön!* Berlin: Fischer.

Keyder, Cağlar, Özveren, Y. Eyüp, and Quataert, Donald (1993) Preface: port-cities of the Eastern Mediterranean, 1800–1914. *Review* 16(4): v–vii.

Kieserling, Manfred (2000) *Singapur*. Frankfurt am Main: Suhrkamp.

King Abdullah Economic City (n.d.) Phase 1 Projects, www.kingabdullahcity.com/en/CityInProgress/Phase1Projects.html (accessed 09/14/2010).

King, Anthony D. (1997) *Culture, Globalization and the World-System*. Minneapolis: University of Minnesota Press.

King, Anthony D. (2007) Boundaries, networks, and cities. In: Çinar, Alev and Bender, Thomas (eds.) *Urban Imaginaries*. Minneapolis/Bristol: University of Minnesota Press/University Presses Marketing.

King, Moses (1980) *King's Views of New York 1896–1915 and Brooklyn 1905*. New York: Arno Press.

Kirsch, Thomas and Schröder, Hermmann-Dieter (1994) *Medienplatz Hamburg*. Hamburg: Verlag Kammerer und Unverzagt.

Klemm, David and Frank, Hartmut (2000) *Alexis de Chateauneuf 1799–1853. Architekt in Hamburg, London und Oslo*. Hamburg: Dölling und Galitz.

Knight, Franklin W. and Liss, Peggy K. (eds.) (1991) *Atlantic Port Cities*. Knoxville: University of Tennessee Press.

Konvitz, Josef W. (1978) *Cities and the Sea*. Baltimore, MD: Johns Hopkins University Press.

Konvitz, Josef W. (1993) Port cities and urban history. *Journal of Urban History* 19: 115–120.

Korea Development Institute (1980) *Manpower Development Master Plan for Jubail and Yanbu*. Seoul: Royal Commission for Jubail and Yanbu, Kingdom of Saudi Arabia.

Korthals Altes, Theo E. and Galesloot, Hansje (2008) Stichter van graanburcht aan het IJ. *Ons Amsterdam* 60(6): 258–261.

Köse, Yavus (2006) Basare der Moderne von Pera bis Stamboul und ihre Angestellten. In: Köse, Yavus (ed.) *Istanbul vom imperialen Herrschersitz zur Megapolis*. Munich: Meidenbauer.

Kraas, K. (2004) "Model city" Singapur. In: Altrock, Uwe and Schubert, Dirk (eds.) *Wachsende Stadt*. Wiesbaden: VS Verlag für Sozialwissenschaften.

Kuan, Seng (2004) Image of the metropolis. In: Seng, Kuan and Rowe, Peter G. (eds.) *Shanghai*. New York: Prestel.

Kuan, Seng and Rowe, Peter G. (2002) *Architectural Encounters with Essence and Form in Modern China*. Cambridge, MA: MIT Press.

Kuitenbrouwer, Maarten and Schijf, Huibert (1998) The Dutch colonial business elite at the turn of the century. *Itinerario* 22(1): 61–87.

Küttner, Sibylle (2000) *Farbige Seeleute im Kaiserreich*. Erfurt: Sutton.

Lai, Delin (2006) *Jindai Zhejiang Lu*. Beijing: Zhongguo shuili shuidian chubanshe.

Lai, Delin (2007) *Zhongguo jindai jianzhushi yanjiu: Studies in Modern Chinese Architectural History*. Beijing: Qinghua Daxue chubanshe.

Landry, C. (2008) *The Creative City*. London: Earthscan.

Lane, Tony (1990) *The Merchant Seamen's War*. Manchester/New York: Manchester University Press.

Lange, Günther (1965) *Alexis de Chateauneuf: ein Hamburger Baumeister; 1799–1853*. Hamburg: Verlag Weltarchiv.

Läpple, Dieter (1994) *Hafenwirtschaft, Handwörterbuch der Raumordnung*. Hanover: ARL.

Le Clézio, Jean-Marie Gustave (2003) La Port saïdienne. *Le Figaro*, January 8.

Lee, Leo Ou-fan (2008) *City Between Worlds*. Cambridge, MA: Belknap Press of Harvard University Press.

Lee, Pui-tak (2007) A brief discussion of British banks in Hong Kong and Shanghai from the 1830s to the 1930s. In: *The Development of Banks in Shanghai and Hong Kong*. Hong Kong: Hong Kong by Museum of History and the Shanghai Bank Museum.

Lefèbvre, Henri (1974) *The Production of Space*. Paris: Editions Anthropos.

Leong, Cindy (1999) *Lessons from the Past*. In: *Super Trader Hong Kong*, product magazine published by the Trade Development Council, www.hongkongtdc.com/prodmag/sptrader/spt199901ed.htm. (accessed 28/10/2008; this item has subsequently been removed from the website).

Lesger, Clé (2006) *The Rise of the Amsterdam Market and Information Exchange, c. 1550–1630*. Aldershot: Ashgate.

Levinson, Marc (2006) *The Box*. Princeton: Princeton University Press.

Lew, Bryan and Cater, Bruce (2006) The telegraph, co-ordination of tramp shipping, and the growth in world trade, 1870–1910. *European Review of Economic History* 10(2): 147–173.

Liang, Samuel Y. (2007) Ephemeral households, marvelous things: business, gender, and material culture in flowers of Shanghai. *Modern China* 33(3): 377–418.

Lindau, Paul (1900) *An der Westküste Klein-Asiens*. Berlin: Allgemeiner Verein für deutsche Literatur.

Lindenberg, Paul (1902) *Auf deutschen Pfaden im Orient*. Berlin: F. Dümmler.

Liss, Peggy K. (1983) *Atlantic Empires*. Baltimore, MA: Johns Hopkins University Press.

Löbe, Karl (1979) *Metropolen der Meere*. Düsseldorf/Vienna: Econ.

London Docklands Development Corporation, LDDC people (n.d.) www.lddc-history.org.uk/veterans/index.html (accessed 06/01/2010).

London Missionary Society Archives (n.d.) Incoming Correspondence. University of London, SOAS Archives, Box 7, Folder 1, Jacket B.

Lopate, Phillip (2004) *Waterfront*. New York: Crown.

LoRomer, David (1987) *Merchants and Reform in Livorno, 1814–1868*. Berkeley: University of California Press.

Lu, Junhua, Rowe, Peter G., and Zhang, Jie (2001) *Modern Urban Housing in China, 1842–2000*. Munich: Prestel Verlag.

Lüdtke, Alf (1993) *Eigen-Sinn: Fabrikalltag, Arbeitserfahrungen und Politik vom Kaiserreich bis in den Faschismus*. Hamburg. Ergebnisse-Verlag.

Lyall, Katherine C. (1982) A bicycle built-for-two: public–private partnership in Baltimore. In: Fosler, R. Scott and Berger, Renee A. (eds.) *Public–Private Partnership in American Cities*. Lexington, MA: Lexington Books.

Maak, Karin (1985) *Die Speicherstadt im Hamburger Freihafen*. Arbeitshefte zur Denkmalpflege in Hamburg No. 7. Hamburg: Christians Verlag.

Maass, Dieter (1986) Die Rolle der Wasserbaudirektion beim Ausbau des Hamburger Hafens zwischen 1860 und 1910. In: Ellermeyer, Jürgen and Postel, Rainer (eds.) *Stadt und Hafen*. Hamburg: Christians Verlag.

Maass, Dieter (1990) *Der Ausbau des Hamburger Hafens 1840 bis 1910*. Hamburg: Schiffahrts-Verlag Hansa.

McCauley, Conor (2009) Interview with Sue Brownill, May 28.

McDonogh, Gary and Wong, Cindy (2005) *Global Hong Kong*. New York: Routledge.

McGovern, Stephen (2008) Evolving visions of waterfront development in postindustrial Philadelphia. *Journal of Planning History* 7: 295–326.

MacPherson, Kerrie L. (ed.) (1998) *Asian Department Stores*. Honolulu: University of Hawai'i Press.

Magee, Peter (2008) Ports without water and the ship of the desert. Presentation at the Port Cities conference at Bryn Mawr College, November 16, 2008. Bryn Mawr, Bryn Mawr College.

Mainichi Newspapers (1968) Here comes Expo '70. Tokyo: Mainichi Newspapers.

Makal, Oğuz (1992) İzmir Sinemaları. In: Beygu, Şahin (ed.) Üç İzmir. Istanbul: Yapı Kredi Yayınları.

Mandilara, Anna (1998) The Greek business community in Marseille, 1816–1900: individual and network strategies. Unpublished Ph.D. thesis, European University Institute, Florence.

Mansel, Phillip (1996) *Constantinople*. London: Murray.

Marseillese Chamber of Commerce (Chambre de Commerce de Marseille) (1862) *Compte-rendu de la situation industrielle et commerciale de la circonscription de Marseille*. Marseille: Barile.

Marshall, Richard (ed.) (2001) *Waterfronts in Post-industrial Cities*. London/New York: Spon.

Maruri Villanueva, Ramón (1985) *La burguesía mercantil santanderina, 1700–1850*. Santander: Universidad de Cantabria.

Mävers, Joachim (1968) Container-Terminal Hamburg (Burchardkai). *Das deutsche Magazin für Containerverkehr* 1: 39–45.

Mazower, Mark (2006) *Salonica*. New York: Knopf.

Metropolregion Hamburg (n.d.) www.metropolregion.hamburg.de/ (accessed 09/23/2010).

Metzger, John T. (2001) The failed promise of a festival marketplace. *Planning Perspectives* 16(1): 25–46.

Meyer, David Ralph (1991) The formation of a global financial centre. In: Kasaba, Reşat (ed.) *Cities in the World System*. London: Greenwood Press.

Meyer, David R. (2000) *Hong Kong as a Global Metropolis*. Cambridge/New York: Cambridge University Press.

Meyer, Han (1999) *City and Port*. Utrecht: International Books.

Meyer-Friese, Boye (2007) Mit zweierlei Maß. In: Altonaer Museum (ed.) *Alles im Fluss*. Hamburg: Altonaer Museum.

Meyer-Veden, Hans (1990) *Die Hamburger Speicherstadt*. Berlin: Ernst und Sohn.

Meyers (1901) *Meyers Reisebücher, Griechenland und Kleinasien*. Leipzig: Bibliographisches Institut.

Meyers (1914) *Meyers Reisebücher, Balkanstaaten und Konstantinopel*. Leipzig: Bibliographisches Institut.

Miller, Michael B. (2003) The business trip. *Business History Review* 77 (Spring): 1–32.

Miller, Raymond Charles (1969) The dockworker subculture and some problems in cross-cultural and cross-time generalizations. *Comparative Studies in Society and History* 11: 302–314.

Millspaugh, Martin (n.d.) The Sydney story: Darling Harbor. In: Global Harbors: A Waterfront Renaissance, www.globalharbors.org/sydney_darling_harbor.html (accessed 10/13/2010).

Mitchell, George H. (1917) *Sailortown*. London: Jarrolds.

Model for the world: examples of port cities influenced by Baltimore's waterfront renaissance (n.d.) In: Global Harbors: A Waterfront Renaissance, www.globalharbors.org/model_for_the_world.html (accessed 10/13/2010).

Moltmann, Günter (1986) Hamburg als Auswandererhafen. In: Ellermeyer,

Jürgen and Postel, Rainer (eds.) *Stadt und Hafen.* Hamburg: Christians Verlag.

Monclús, Francisco Javier (2003) The Barcelona model: an original formula? *Planning Perspectives* 18: 399–421.

Montel, Nathalie (1998) *Le Chantier du canal de Suez (1859–1869).* Paris: Informa/Presses de l'Ecole Nationale des Ponts et Chaussées.

Morand, Paul (1936) *La Route des Indes.* Paris: Plon.

Morgan, David (1979) Fiscal policy in oil exporting countries, 1972–1978. *Finance and Development* (December): 14–17.

Mousson, André (1995) *Kerkira ke Kefalonia. Mia periigisi to 1858* [Corfu and Cephalonia. A tour in 1858)]. Athens: Istoritis.

Mühlradt, Friedrich (1953) Hafenplanung und Hafenbau. *Hamburg und seine Bauten 1929–1953.* Hamburg: Architekten- und Ingenieur-Verein.

Müller, Leos (2004) *Consuls, Corsairs and Commerce.* Uppsala: Acta Universitatis Upsaliensis.

Murphey, Rhoads (1970) *The Treaty Ports and China's Modernization.* Ann Arbor: University of Michigan Center for Chinese Studies.

Newitt, Malyn (2008) Mozambique Island. In: Brockey, Liam Matthew (ed.) *Portuguese Colonial Cities in the Early Modern World.* Farnham/Burlington: Ashgate.

Newman, Peter and Thornley, Andy (1996) *Urban Planning in Europe.* London: Routledge.

Ngai, Mae M. (2005) *Impossible Subjects.* Princeton: Princeton University Press.

Ngalamulume, Kalala (2008) Yellow fever and plague epidemics and governance in Saint-Louis-du-Senegal, 1850–1920. Presentation at the Port Cities conference at Bryn Mawr College, November 16, 2008. Bryn Mawr, Bryn Mawr College.

Nicholls, Robert J., Susan Hanson, Celine Herweijer, Nicola Patmore, Stéphane Hallegatte, Jan Corfee-Morlot, Jean Chateau and Robert Muir-Wood (2007) *Rankings of the World's Cities Most Exposed to Coastal Flooding Today and in the Future. Executive Summary.* Paris: OECD.

Nugent, Walter (1992) *Crossings.* Bloomington: Indiana University Press.

O'Flanagan, Patrick (2005) Transformations. In: Crowley, J.S., Devoy, R.J.N., Lenihan, D., and O'Flanagan, P. (eds.) *Atlas of Cork City.* Cork: Cork University Press.

O'Flanagan, Patrick (2008) *Port Cities of Atlantic Iberia, c.1500–1900.* Aldershot: Ashgate.

O'Flanagan, Patrick and Walton, Julian (2004) The Irish community at Cadiz during the late eighteenth century. In: Clarke, H., Prunty, J., and Hennessy, M. (eds.) *Surveying Ireland's Past.* Dublin: Geography Publications.

Oberling, Pierre (1986) The quays of Izmir. In: Batu, Hâmit and Bacqué-Grammont, Jean-Louis (eds.) *L'Empire Ottoman, la République et la France.* Istanbul: Isis.

Olsen, Joshua (2003) *Better Places Better Lives.* Washington, DC: Urban Land Institute.

Oosterwijk, Bram (1979) *Vlucht na Victorie.* Rotterdam: Dona Pers Produkties.

Osterhammel, Jürgen (2009) *Die Verwandlung der Welt. Eine Geschichte des 19. Jahrhunderts.* Munich: C.H. Beck.

Osterhammel, Jürgen and Petersson, Niels P. (2003) *Geschichte der Globalisierung. Dimensionen, Prozesse, Epochen.* Munich: C.H. Beck.

Owen, G. (1978) Survey of Middle East Ports. *Dock and Harbour Authority* 59(695) (October): 164–168.

Pacione, Michael (2005) City profile: Dubai. *Cities* 22(3): 255–265.

Pahl, Elke (1980) Die Zerstörung des Gängeviertels. In: Redaktionskollektiv (ed.) *Autonomie*. Hamburg/Tübingen, Autonomie 3.

Panessa, Giangiacom (1991) *Le comunità greche a Livorno*. Livorno: Belforte.

Pappas, George (2005) How Melbourne became a city to be copied. *The Age*, October 6, reproduced at www.theage.com.au/news/business/how-melbourne-became-a-city-to-be-copied/2005/10/05/1128191785284.html (accessed 06/01/2010).

Paris, Erato (2001) Les grecs de Marseille dans la deuxième moitié du XIXe siècle: une perspective nationale et transnationale. *Revue européenne des migrations internationales* 17: 23–42.

Park, Katharine (2003) Black death. In: Kiple, Kenneth F. (ed.) *The Cambridge Historical Dictionary of Disease*. Cambridge: Cambridge University Press.

Parry, John H. (1966) *The Spanish Seaborne Empire*. London: Hutchinson.

Paschen, Joachim (ed.) (1994) *Fritz Schumacher*. Hamburg: Medien-Verlag Schubert.

Pearson, Michael N. (1998) *Port Cities and Intruders*. Baltimore, MD: Johns Hopkins University Press.

Peddle, Thorp, Chapman, and Taylor; in conjunction with Roger Tym and Associates (1977) *Jebel Ali New Town*. London: Photoprinters.

Pelc, Ortwin and Grötz, Susanne (eds.) (2008) *Konstrukteur der modernen Stadt*. Munich: Dölling und Galitz.

Penn, William (1774a) An abstract of the charter of the city of Philadelphia. In: Reed, John (ed.) *An Explanation of the Map of the City and Liberties of Philadelphia*. Philadelphia: Brooks.

Penn, William [and first purchasers] (1774b) An Abstract of the Concessions of Mr. Penn to the first adventurers and purchasers in Pennsylvania. In: Reed, John (ed.) *An Explanation of the Map of the City and Liberties of Philadelphia*. Philadelphia: Brooks.

Penn, William (1983) Letter to the Committee of the Free Society of Traders 1683. In: Soderlund, Jean R. (ed.) *William Penn and the Founding of Pennsylvania 1680–1684*. Philadelphia: University of Pennsylvania Press/ Historical Society of Pennsylvania.

Perkins, Charles B. (1909) *Travels from the Grandeurs of the West to the Mysteries of the East*. San Francisco: Charlton B. Perkins Co.

Perkins, Kevin (2001) *Dare to Dream*. Sydney: Golden Wattle.

Philip, George (1922) *The Panama Canal*. Liverpool: Philip, Son and Nephew, Ltd.

Philippson, Alfred (1910–1915) *Reisen und Forschungen im westlichen Kleinasien*. Gotha: Perthes.

Phillips, Carla Rahn (2007) The organization of oceanic empires. In: Bentley, Jerry H., Bridenthal, Renate, and Wigen, Kären (eds.) *Seascapes*. Honolulu: University of Hawai'i Press.

Phillips, Carla Rahn and Phillips, William (1997) *Spain's Golden Fleece*. Baltimore, MD: Johns Hopkins Press.

Phillips, Gordon and Whiteside, Noel (1985) *Casual Labour*. Oxford: Clarendon.

Phillips, Philip Lee (1926) Afteykenige van de Stadt Philadelphia in de Provincie van Penn-Sylvania in America no de copie London in intneder duys laeten synden door Jacob Claus G. Drogenham, FEC. In: *A Descriptive List of Maps and Views of Philadelphia in the Library of Congress, 1683–1865, in 1926*. Washington: Library of Congress.

Pınar, İlhan (2000) Yüzyıl sonunda yüzyıl başı retrospektif bir gezi denemesi. *İzmir Kent Kültürü Dergisi* 1: 158–161.

Piquet, Caroline (2005) Port Fouad: new-harmony in the Suez isthmus. In: Barjot, Dominique (ed.) *Le Travail à l'époque contemporaine*. Paris: Editions du CTHS.

Porfyriou, Heleni (2007) La diaspora greca fra cosmopolitismo e coscienza nazionale nell'impero asburgico del XVIII secolo. *Città and Storia* 2: 235–252.

The Portsmouth Society (1998) Cape Town lessons for Gunwharf. *Portsmouth Society News*, January.

Pratt, Mary L. (1991) Arts of the contact zone. *Profession* 91: 33–40.

Pratt, Mary L. (1992) *Imperial Eyes*. London: Routledge.

Price, Jacob (1974) Economic functions and the growth of American port towns in the eighteenth century. *Perspectives in American History* 8: 123–186.

Priebs, Axel (1998) Hafen und Stadt. *Geographische Zeitschrift* 1: 16–30.

Procter, Christopher (1997) Ashton Raggatt McDougall's masterplan for Melbourne's largest project – rejuvenation of the Docklands – is out in public. *Architecture Australia*, reproduced at www.archmedia.com.au/aa/aaprintissue.php?issueid=199703andarticle=1 (accessed 07/01/2010).

Puerto Madero (n.d.) www.puertomadero.com/i_planes11.cfm (accessed 06/01/2010).

Quataert, Donald (1983) *Social Disintegration and Popular Resistance in the Ottoman Empire, 1881–1908*. New York: New York University Press.

Quataert, Donald (2002) The industrial working class of Salonica, 1850–1912. In: Levy, Avigdor (ed.) *Jews, Turks, Ottomans*. Syracuse, NY: Syracuse University Press.

Rabinow, Paul (1989) *French Modern*. Cambridge, MA: MIT Press.

Radtke, Kurt Werner (1990) *China's Relations with Japan, 1945–83*. Manchester/New York: Studies on East Asia.

Rea, George Bronson (ed.) (1904–1941) *The Far Eastern Review*. Manila/Shanghai: G.B. Rea.

Reiss, Hans (ed.) (1984) *Emmanuel Kant: Kant's Political Writings*. Cambridge: Cambridge University Press.

Reps, John W. (1969) *Town Planning in Frontier America*. Princeton: Princeton University Press.

RETE (n.d.) Asociación para la collaboración entre Puertes y Ciudades, www.reteonline.org/ (accessed 09/15/2010).

Revue Commerciale du Levant. bulletin de la chambre de commerce française de Constantinople, 1800–1923, Constantinople.

Richardson, Harry W. (1978) *Regional and Urban Economics*. Harmondsworth: Penguin.

Ridings, Eugene (2001) Chambers of Commerce and business elites in Great Britain and Brazil in the nineteenth century. *Business History Review* 75: 739–773.

Riedler, Florian (2011) Armenian labour migration to Istanbul and the migration crisis of the 1890s. In: Freitag, Ulrike, Fuhrmann, Malte, Lafi, Nora, and Riedler, Florian (eds.) *The City in the Ottoman Empire: Migration and the Making of Urban Modernity*. London: Routledge.

Rimmer, Peter and Toru Taniuchi (1989) Japan's seaports and regional developments during the era of high-speed growth, 1960–75. In: Broeze, Frank (ed.). *Brides of the Sea*. Honolulu: University of Hawai'i Press.

Ritter, Gerhard A. (1997) Der Kaiser und sein Reeder. *Zeitschrift für Unternehmensgeschichte* 42: 137–162.

Robinson, Ross and Chu, David (1981) Containerization and the port of Hong Kong in the 1970s. In: Sit Fung-Shuen, Victor (ed.) *Urban Hong Kong*. Hong Kong: Summerson.

Rogaski, Ruth (1999) Hygienic modernity in Tianjin fits. In: Esherick, Joseph (ed.) *Remaking the Chinese City*. Honolulu: University of Hawai'i Press.

Rose, Richard (2005) *Learning from Comparative Public Policy*. London: Routledge.

Rosen, Laura (1998) *Manhattan Shores*. New York: Thames and Hudson.

Rotterdam: the Kop van Zuid (n.d.) In: Global Harbors: A Waterfront Renaissance, www.globalharbors.org/rotterdam_kop_van_zuid.html (accessed 10/13/2010).

RTKL Associates Inc. (n.d.) www.rtkl.com/Projects (accessed 06/01/2010).

Rudolph, Wolfgang (1979) *Die Hafenstadt*. Erfurt: Edition Leipzig.

Ruiz Nieto-Guerrero, María Pilar (1999) *Historia urbana de Cádiz*. Seville: Caja de San Fernando.

Rusk, Dean (1996) *Baltimore Unbound*. Baltimore, MD: Abell Foundation.

Russell-Wood, Anthony J.R. (1998) *The Portuguese Empire, 1415–1808*. Baltimore, MD: Johns Hopkins University Press.

Saïd, Edward (1978) *Orientalism*. New York: Random House.

Sammarco, Angelo (1943) *Suez*. Milan: Garzanti.

Sanjuan, Thierry (ed.) (2003) *Les Grands Hotels en Asie*. Paris: Publications de la Sorbonne.

Sassen, Saskia (1991) *The Global City*. Princeton: Princeton University Press.

Scammell, Geoffrey V. (1992) *The First Imperial Age*. Routledge: London.

Schädel, Dieter (2006) *Wie das Kunstwerk Hamburg entstand*. Hamburg: Fritz-Schumacher-Institut.

Scherer, Hermann (1866) *Reisen in der Levante 1859–1865*. Frankfurt am Main: Winter.

Schiffszimmerer Genossenschaft (n.d.) www.schiffszimmerer.de/ (accessed 09/19/2010).

Schijf, Huibert (1993) *Netwerken van een financieel-economische elite*. Amsterdam: Het Spinhuis.

Schmidtpott, Katja (2007) Offene Häfen, geschlossene Gesellschaft. *Comparativ* 17: 51–63.

Schubert, Dirk (2001) Mythos "europäische Stadt." *Die alte Stadt* 4: 270–290.

Schubert, Dirk (ed.) (2008a) *Hafen- und Uferzonen im Wandel*. Berlin: Leue.

Schubert, Dirk (2008b) Transformation processes on waterfronts in seaport cities. In: Kokot, Waltraud (ed.) *Port Cities as Areas of Transition*. Bielefeld/ New Brunswick, NJ: Transcript Verlag.

Schubert, Dirk (2009) Ever-changing waterfronts. In: Graf, Arndt and Huat, Chua Beng (eds.) *Port Cities in Asia and Europe*. London/New York: Routledge.

Schubert, Dirk (2010) Bibliography by the author including further references on the projects, www.tu-harburg.de/b/kuehn/themen/wfb.html (accessed 10/13/2010).

Schubert, Dirk and Harms, Hans (eds.) (1993) *Wohnen am Hafen*. Hamburg: VSA.

Schulz-Labischin, Gotthold (1908) *Die Sängerreise der Berliner Liedertafel nach dem Orient*. Berlin: Liedertafel.

Schulze, Adolf (1941) Hansestadt Hamburg (special issue). *Deutschland. Zeitschrift für Industrie, Handel und Schiffahrt* 9.

Schumacher, Fritz (1920) *Wie das Kunstwerk Hamburg nach dem großen Brande entstand*. Berlin: Verlag von Karl Curtius.

Schürmann, Sandra (2008) The Hamburg Harbor model from 1900 and its international impact and context. Presentation at the Port Cities conference at Bryn Mawr College, November 16, 2008. Bryn Mawr, Bryn Mawr College.

Sciaky, Leon (2000 (reprint)) *Farewell to Ottoman Salonica*. Istanbul: Isis.

Searle, Glen (2005) The Redfern-Waterloo Authority. Paper delivered at Second State of Australian Cities conference, Griffith University, Brisbane, November–December.

Seeberg, Matthias (2007) Der Blick auf den Fluss. In: Altonaer Museum (ed.) *Alles im Fluss*. Hamburg: Altonaer Museum.

Seed, John (2006) Limehouse Blues. *History Workshop Journal* 62: 58–85.

Sehepunkte (n.d.) http://hsozkult.geschichte.hu-berlin.de/zeitschriften/id=135andcount=386andrecno=3andausgabe=2861.

Selekou, Olympia (2004) *I Kathimerini Zoi ton Ellinon tis Diasporas. Dimosios ke idiotikos vios (19os-arches tou 20ou aiona)*. Athens: Ethniko Kentro Koinonikon Erevnon.

Shakespeare, Howard (1989) The Spanish royal trading companies. *Journal of the International Bond and Share Society* (Spring–Autumn): 1–4.

Short, John Rennie, Kim, Yeung, Kuus, Merje, and Wells, H. (1996) The dirty little secret of world cities research. *International Journal of Urban and Regional Research* 20: 697–717.

Shott, John G. (1961) *Progress in Piggyback and Containerization*. Washington, DC: Public Affairs Institute.

Sifneos, Evridiki (2005) Cosmopolitanism as a feature of the Greek commercial diaspora. *History and Anthropology* 16: 97–111.

Sit, Victor F.S. (1981) *Urban Hong Kong*. Hong Kong: Summerson.

Siu-Lun, Wong (1988) *Emigrant Entrepreneurs*. Hong Kong: Oxford University Press.

Skeldon, Ronald (ed.) (1994) *Reluctant Exiles?* Armonk, NY/London: M.E. Sharpe.

Skinner, G. William (1977) *The City in Late Imperial China*. Stanford, CA: Stanford University Press.

Smalley, Martha (1998) *Hallowed Halls*. Hong Kong: Old China Hand Press.

Society for the Diffusion of Useful Knowledge (1840) *Marseille. Ancient Massilia*. London: Chapman and Hall.

Spallek, Johannes (1978) Alexis de Chateauneuf und William Lindley. Dissertation, Hamburg University.

Spence, Jonathan D. (1990) *The Search for Modern China*. New York: W.W. Norton and Co.

Standortpolitik (n.d.) www.wachsende-stadt.hamburg.de/index-flash.html (accessed 09/23/2010).

Staples-Smith, H. (1938) *Diary of Events and the Progress on Shameen, 1859–1938*. Self-published.

Statistical Yearbook of Egypt (1909) Statistical Department of Cairo, Cairo.

Steer, John and White, Antony (1994) *Atlas of Western Art History*. New York: Parchment Books.

Stoecklin, A. (1867) *Notice sur la construction du bassin de radoub de Suez (Egypte)*. Bordeaux: Imprimerie A. Bord.

Subramanian, Lakshmi (ed.) (2008) *Ports, Towns, Cities*. Mumbai/New Delhi: Marg Publications/Variety Book Depot.

Syme, Duncan (2000) Born again: the resurrection of Cardiff Bay. *Locum Destination Review* 2, at www.locumconsulting.com/pdf/LDR2Born_again.pdf (accessed 06/01/2010).

Tabili, Laura (1994) *"We Ask for British Justice."* Ithaca, NY/London: Cornell University Press.

Tamse, Coen A. (1981) The Netherlands consular service and the Dutch consular reports of the nineteenth and twentieth centuries. *Business History* XXIII(3): 271–276.

Taselaar, Arjen (1998) *De Nederlandse koloniale lobby*. Leiden: Research School CNWS.

Taylor, Peter J. (2003) *World City Network*. London: Routledge Chapman and Hall.

TDC (n.d.) www.Hong Kongtdc.com/prodmag/sptrader/spt199901ed.htm. (accessed 28/10/2008; this item has subsequently been removed from the website).

The Far Eastern Review, June 1931

The Far Eastern Review, October 1918

Thomas, Hugh (2004) *Rivers of Gold*. Penguin: London.

Thornley, Andrew (1991) *Urban Planning under Thatcherism*. London: Routledge.

Thornton, Richard C. (1969) *The Comintern and the Chinese Communists 1928–1931*. Seattle/London: University of Washington Press.

Tirschwell, Peter (2009) Bayonne Bridge replacement gains favor. *Journal of Commerce Online*, April 23.

Titanic Quarter (n.d.) www.titanic-quarter.com/index.php (accessed 09/15/2010).

Todd, Susan (2006) Bayonne Bridge in need of replacement. *Newark Star-Ledger*, May 19.

Todorova, Marija (1997) *Imagining the Balkans*. New York: Oxford University Press.

Trade Development Council (1967) Hong Kong industry's formidable vanguard. *Hong Kong Trade Bulletin* 84–88.

Trade Development Council (2006) *Metamorphosis. Hong Kong – 40 years of Trade Exhibition* (DVD).

Trench, Richard (ed.) (1994) *Arab Gulf Cities*. Oxford: Archive Editions.

Trivellato, Francesca (2009) *The Familiarity of Strangers*. New Haven, CT/London: Yale University Press.

Tsin, Michael (1999) Canton remapped. In: Esherick, J. (ed.) *Remaking the Chinese City*. Honolulu: University of Hawai'i Press.

URBACT II (n.d.) http://urbact.eu/en/header-main/our-projects/ (accessed 06/01/2010).

Van de Laar, Paul (2000) *Stad van formaat*. Zwolle: Waanders.

Van de Laar, Paul (2003) Port traffic in Rotterdam. In: Loyen, Reginald, Buyst, Erik, and Devos, Greta (eds.) *Struggling for Leadership*. Heidelberg: Physica-Verlag.

Van Driel, Hugo and Schot, Johan (2005) Radical innovation as a multilevel process. *Technology and Culture* 46 (January): 51–76.

Van Dyke, Paul A. (2005) *The Canton Trade*. Hong Kong: Hong Kong University Press.

Van Lennep, F.J.E. (1962) *Late Regenten*. Haarlem: H.D. Tjeenk Willink and Zoon N.V.

Van Zanden, Jan Luiten (1987) *De industrialisatie in Amsterdam 1825–1914*. Bergen: Octavo.

Van Zyl, Pieter S. (2005) V&A Waterfront development, reproduced at http://capeinfo.com/component/content/article/115 (accessed 06/01/2010).

Vassilikou, Maria (2002) Greeks and Jews in Salonica and Odessa. In: Cesarani, David (ed.) *Port Jews*. London: Frank Cass.

Venturi, Scott Brown and Associates, Inc. (2003) *Penn's Landing Planning Study*. Philadelphia. Venturi, Scott Brown and Associates.

Verhetsel, Ann and Sel, Steve (2009) World maritime cities. *Transport Policy* 16: 240–250.

Vigarié, André (1981) Maritime industrial development areas. In Hoyle, Brian S. and Pinter, David A. (eds.) *Cityport Industrialisation and Regional Development*. Oxford: Pergamon.

Villeneuve, Sylvaine (1988) L'Envers de la Flambée du foncier. *Urbanisme* 225: 18–21.

Vlami, Despina (1996/2000) *Business, Community and Ethnic Identity*. Ph.D. thesis, European Universitary Institute, Florence, 1996; published in Greek as *To fiorini, to sitari kai he odos tou kypou. Ellenes emporoi sto Livorno, 1750–1868* [The fiorino, the wheat and garden street. Greek merchants in Livorno, 1750–1868]. Solonos: Themelio.

Volait, Mercedes (ed.) (2001) *Le Caire-Alexandrie*. Le Caire: Cedej-IFAO.

Vučinić-Nešković, Vesna and Miloradović, Jelena (2006) Corso as a total social phenomenon: the case of Smederevska Palanka, Serbia. In: Roth, Klaus and Brunnbauer, Ulf (eds.) *Urban Life and Culture in Southeastern Europe*. Ethnologia Balkanica 10 ed. Berlin: Hopf.

Wagenaar, Michiel (1990) *Amsterdam 1876–1914*. Amsterdam: Amsterdamse Historische Reeks.

Walker, Anthony R. (1984) Oil-dependent economies and port development. In: Hoyle, Brian S. and Hilling, David (eds.). *Seaport Systems and Spatial Change Technology, Industry, and Development Strategies*. Chichester: John Wiley and Sons.

Wallace, David (2004) *Urban Planning/My Way*. Washington, DC: American Association of Planners.

Wallerstein, Immanuel (1976) *The Modern World-System*. New York: Academic Press.

Wang, James, Olivier, Daniel, Notteboom, Theo, and Slack, Brian (eds.) (2007) *Ports, Cities, and Global Supply Chains*. Aldershot: Ashgate.

Ward, Stephen V. (2000) Re-examining the international diffusion of planning. In: Freestone, Robert (ed.) *Urban Planning in a Changing World*. London: E. and F.N. Spon.

Ward, Stephen V. (2002) *Planning the Twentieth-Century City*. Chichester: John Wiley and Sons.

Ward, Stephen V. (2006) Cities are fun! In: Monclús, Francisco J. and Guardia, Manuel (eds.) *Culture, Urbanism and Planning*. Aldershot: Ashgate.

Ward, Stephen V. (n.d.) The globalisation of the Baltimore model of waterfront development: a case study of developer as agent of transnational diffusion. Available from the author.

Warner, Torsten (1994) *German Architecture in China*. Berlin: Ernst und Sohn.

Warrender, Pamela Myer (2007) *Pamela: In Her Own Right*. Prahran, Victoria: Hardie Grant.

Warrender, Pamela Myer (2009) Interview with author (and follow-up personal communications), 5, 10, 12 August.

The Waterfront Center (n.d.) www.waterfrontcenter.org/ (accessed 06/01/2010).

Waterfront Communities Project (n.d.) www.waterfrontcommunitiesproject.org/ (accessed 06/01/2010).

Weber, Kurt (1952) Hamburg – Deutschlands größter Ölhafen. *Der Hamburger Hafen*. Hamburg: Ludwig Schultheis Verlag.

Weigend, Guido G. (1952) Ports: their hinterlands and forelands. *Geographical Review* 42: 660–672.

Weigend, Guido G. (1956) The problem of hinterland and foreland as illustrated by the port of Hamburg. *Economic Geography* 32: 1–16.

Weigend, Guido G. (1958) Some elements in the study of port geography. *Geographical Review* 48: 185–200.

Weiss-Sussex, Godela and Bianchini, Franco (eds.) (2006) *Urban Mindscapes of Europe*. Amsterdam/New York: Rodopi.

White, Norval and Willensky, Elliot (2000) *AIA Guide to New York City*. New York: Three Rivers Press.

Whittingham-Jones, Barbara (1944) *China Fights in Britain*. London: W.H. Allen and Co.

Wiborg, Susanne and Wiborg, Klaus (1997) *The World Is Our Oyster*. Hamburg: Hapag-Lloyd.

Wiedenfeld, Kurt (1903) *Die nordwesteuropäischen Welthäfen London, Liverpool, Hamburg, Bremen, Rotterdam, Amsterdam, Antwerpen, Havre in ihrer Verkehrs- und Handelsbedeutung*. Berlin: Mittler.

Wiese, Bernd (1981) New ports as nodes for industrial and urban development: the cases of Richards Bay and Saldanha in South Africa. *Geojournal* 2: 51–58.

Wijtvliet, Cornelis (1989) De Nederlandse Handel-Maatschappij. *Jaarboek voor Geschiedenis van Bedrijf en Techniek* 6: 96–118.

Wilbanks, James H. (ed.) (2006) *The Vietnam War*. Aldershot: Ashgate.

Wilkins, H.F. (1928) Shanghai's new Customs House. In: Rea, G. (ed.) *The Far Eastern Review*. Manila/Shanghai: G.B. Rea.

Williams, Gisela (2010) A new face for Hamburg's harborfront. *New York Times*, July 18.

Wilson, Graeme (2006) *Rashid's Legacy*. Dubai: Media Prima.

Witthöft, Hans J. (1977) *Container*. Herford: Koehlers.

Witthöft, Hans J. (2000) *Container*. Hamburg: Koehlers.

Wong, Bernard P. (1982) *Chinatown*. Fort Worth, TX: Holt, Rinehart and Winston.

Wood, Stephen (2009) Desiring Docklands. *Planning Theory* 8: 191–215.

Woodman, Harold D. (1968) *King Cotton and His Retainers*. Lexington: University of Kentucky Press.

Woods, James R. (1972) The container revolution. *Journal of World Trade Law* 6: 661–692.

Worringer, René (2001) *Comparing Perceptions*. Chicago: Chicago University Press.

Wrenn, Douglas M., with Casazza, John A. and Smart, J. Eric (1983) *Urban Waterfront Development*. Washington, DC: Urban Land Institute.

Wright, Jim (2008) Ports and maritime networks in the Mediterranean: an archaeological perspective. Presentation at the Port Cities conference at Bryn Mawr College, November 16, 2008. Bryn Mawr, Bryn Mawr College.

Yerasismos, Stéphane (1999) Cosmopolitanism. In: Meijer, Roel (ed.) *Cosmopolitanism, Identity and Authenticity in the Middle East*. Richmond: Curzon.

Yerolympos, Alexandra (1996) *Urban Transformations in the Balkans (1820–1920)*. Thessalonika: University Studio Press.

Yerolympos, Alexandra (1997) Conscience citadine et intérêt municipal à Salonique à la fin du XIXe siècle. In: Dumont, Paul and Georgeon, François (eds.) *Vivre dans l'Empire ottoman*. Paris: Editions L'Harmattan.

Young, Barry (1988) Darling Harbour. In: Webber, G. Peter (ed.) *The Design of Sydney*. Sydney: Law Book Co.

Zandi-Sayek, Sibel (2000) Struggles over the shore. *City and Society* 12: 55–78.

Zelepos, Ioannis (2001) *Rebetiko*. Cologne: Romiosini.

Zhuwei, Tie (1998) *Liao Chengzhi zhuan*. Beijing: People's Press.

INDEX